AF519324

Modernization, Globalization and Social Transformation

Modernization, Globalization and Social Transformation

Essays in Honour of Professor Yogendra Singh

Edited by
Ishwar Modi

RAWAT PUBLICATIONS
Jaipur • New Delhi • Bangalore • Hyderabad • Guwahati

ISBN 978-81-316-0507-3

Published by
Prem Rawat for Rawat Publications
Satyam Apts, Sector 3, Jawahar Nagar, Jaipur 302 004 (India)
Phone: 0141 265 1748 / 7006 Fax: 0141 265 1748
E-mail: info@rawatbooks.com
Website: www.rawatbooks.com

New Delhi Office
4858/24, Ansari Road, Daryaganj, New Delhi 110 002
Phone: 011 2326 3290

Also at Bangalore, Hyderabad *and* Guwahati

Typeset by Rawat Computers, Jaipur
Printed at Chaman Enterprises, New Delhi

Contents

Preface

Honouring one's teachers and eminent scholars in the discipline has been a long and established academic tradition. In pursuance of the same and to pay my obeisance to my Guru and one of the most eminent sociologists and social scientists of India, Professor Yogendra Singh, I decided to bring out a Festschrift more than two years ago. Professor Yogendra Singh is presently Emeritus Professor of Sociology at the Centre for the Study of Social Systems, Jawaharlal Nehru University, New Delhi. He is also its founder. He has occupied senior academic and administrative positions at various universities including University of Rajasthan and Jodhpur University. He has been the member of the Research Advisory Committee of the Planning Commission and the Indian Council of Social Science Research and also Convener of the National Panel on Sociology of the University Grants Commission. He has also been the President of the Indian Sociological Society. He has lectured at several universities abroad and has done fieldwork in South Asian countries. He is the recipient of several awards for his contributions to sociology and social anthropology. He is a teacher and scholar *par excellence* and his grip on theory has been acclaimed far and wide. Besides his scholarship, he is also a very fine human being. This combination makes him not only dear but respectable to one and all. His humane qualities, sympathetic attitude and understanding of men, matters and situations make him the most sought after guide and mentor. His seminal work *Modernization of Indian Tradition* (1973) has influenced and continues to influence generations. His multifarious and multifaceted contribution to the discipline of sociology and allied fields of knowledge is too well known to the students and teachers of sociology and social sciences in India and abroad. The prestigious Lifetime Achievement Award of the Indian Sociological Society was conferred on him in the year 2007. While Professor Singh has significantly contributed through his writings on social and cultural change, modernization, globalization, social stratification, Gandhi and non-violence, teaching of sociology, sociology for India, aspirations of the young, urban communities, religion, and on several other themes and social phenomena, the main thrust and the central theme of his writings centres around social change, modernization, globalization and social transformation. As such, it is in the fitness of things that the main theme of this

Festschrift, which is being brought out in honour of Prof. Singh, has been entitled as *Modernization, Globalization and Social Transformation.*

To begin with, I had thought that only the contributions from the students of Prof. Yogendra Singh would be included in this Festschrift. However, it soon became known to other scholars in the country and they started asking me why they are being excluded? As such, I let the project known to other colleagues, friends and admirers of Prof. Yogendra Singh. And then began the process of receiving the papers from all parts of the country and from abroad as well. I have by now received more than 80 contributions and there is hardly any region in the country from where these papers have not been sent. In fact, several colleagues asked me to wait for their contributions since they were equally keen to pay their respect and gratitude to Professor Yogendra Singh and his scholarship. Taking cognizance of the magnitude of the received papers it looked difficult to include all the papers in only one volume. Moreover, all the papers are focused not directly on the main theme of the Festschrift "Modernization, Globalization and Social Transformation" but related to it in their various ramifications and linkages in the context of the area specializations of the contributing authors. As such, it was thought proper that rather than bringing out an unwieldy volume it would be much better to divide it into some thematic schema and hence not one but four volumes. Some contributing friends and colleagues, who have always been very cooperative and kind to me, will probably feel disappointed by non-inclusion of their papers in the very first volume but I am sure they would realize that it was neither practical nor justified and feasible. Hope they would understand and appreciate.

While I am thankful to all the contributors for their all-out efforts in contributing original papers for this Festschrift, I am particularly thankful to those colleagues and scholars who were among the first to send their papers and had to wait for so long to see this Festschrift the light of day. A few of them are now no more with us. My special gratitude and remembrance to Professors M.S. Gore, Victor S. D'Souza and Indra Deva. I do hope it would definitely be possible to present the other three volumes of this Festschrift to Professor Yogendra Singh before he turns 80 in 2012 as has been assured and planned by Mr. Kailash Rawat and his sons Pranit and Sachin of Rawat Publications. Heartfelt thanks to them all for their constant encouragement and support.

I must also express my heartfelt gratitude and thanks to Professor Yogendra Singh for permitting me to undertake this endeavour and then for having agreed to grant me his interview, and to his wife Smt. Gujrati Devi Singh and their daughter Dr. Neerja Singh for providing me some of the biographical inputs about Prof. Singh. I am also thankful to my wife Shakuntala for her continued support and encouragement to complete this project. My special thanks to my elder son Rohit (formerly from the Indian Administrative Service) who so graciously and competently assisted me in interviewing Prof. Singh. I would also like to thank Mr. Uday Singh, Office Assistant, India International Institute of Social Sciences, for his assistance in preparing the manuscripts for publication.

Ishwar Modi
Director
India International Institute of Social Sciences
Jaipur

Introduction

Ishwar Modi

Prof. Yogendra Singh was born on November 1, 1932 in a small village Chowkhara in Uttar Pradesh, near Nepal border. Like most villages of that time, it was a typical zamindari village, with widely prevalent feudal system. He had most of his early education in the village primary school and thereafter in local schools. The village was strategically located and much in contact with British administration. Three thousand inhabitants lived in a traditional style with separate streets for trading communities, zamindars, etc. Thanks to the frequent and close contacts with the British, the village was experiencing modernization and westernization even as it practised feudalism. Young Yogendra's first lessons gave him an early repertoire of the zamindari system. He observed, at first hand, the misery and disenchantment with the system.

Yogendra Singh studied Literature (both English and Hindi) and Economics for his undergraduation. Being perceptive and sensitive to social reality, Singh's natural instinct was to become a writer and he joined the Department of English Literature at Lucknow University. However, he soon got disillusioned with the teaching methodology and contacted Professor D.P. Mukerji, an established writer and a novelist of some repute, in the Department of Economics. Yogendra Singh had excellent grades and was welcomed by the Department of Economics (having two streams of Economics and Sociology). He took courses in Theory of Economics, and Income but majored in Sociology, since he "wanted to draw from and learn the lessons contained in reality".

In 1955, Singh started his Ph.D. under the supervision of Prof. Baljit Singh, an economist, who took over as Professor and Head of the Department of Economics. It was about time when D.P. Mukerji retired. For his doctoral work, Yogendra Singh did not choose a theoretical topic, since Sociology for him was not an armchair discipline. Trained in Economics and armed with statistical tools, young Singh wanted to understand and explain 'group dynamics' and establish empirical basis of rural transformation. His own native village Chowkhara and five other villages spread over six districts provided the perfect 'laboratory for observation' for him to draw from. He obtained his Ph.D. in Sociology in 1958.

Yogendra Singh wanted to add realism to the romanticism of the world of knowledge, and the legitimacy of Sociology came from its ability to draw lessons from the real world. Oxford and Cambridge Universities established a separate Sociology Department in 1950s. Sociology at that time was trying to collate and interpret statistical hard data on issues not covered by government surveys and census.

During an hour long conversation, Professor Singh explained his belief that the Sociology of Marx, Weber and Durkheim was not necessarily relevant to India. In fact, he refers to Professor Sarkar's seminal work (of 1,000 pages) *Positive View of Hindu Sociology*, and argues that Indian Sociology is based on empirical observations and positivism. It is based on Shukraniti, a critique of what is happening around. The Indian sociologists of his generation did not subscribe to western refrain of studying reality as 'here and now'; it was not a complete and correct understanding of Indian traditions, deep rooted in the studies of Shrutis, Stutis, Sutras (including Kamasutra), Upanishads and the Vedas. If Professor Radhakamal Mukerjee surveyed the working classes, Professor D.P. Mukerji combined History and Sociology. Prof. Singh himself has written about the intellectual growth and studies of Sociology in his article in Sabyasachi Mukherjee's volume on 'Intellectuals'.

From 1958 to 1961, Professor Yogendra Singh taught Sociological Theories and Social Pathology to postgraduate students in the Department of Sociology and Social Work, Institute of Social Sciences, Agra. During the same period, he published his doctoral work in the form of papers (8/9 of them), finding his "monograph to be too empirical to constitute readable text". He joined the University of Rajasthan as Lecturer in 1961 and was promoted as Reader in the very next year where he remained until 1969. During 1966–67 he was invited to the McGill University, Montréal, Canada, as a Visiting Associate Professor where he completed most parts of his seminal work *Modernization of Indian Tradition*.

When asked about the major concern of a sociologist in his times, Professor Singh explained that the concerns were essentially twofold. The first challenge was to discover, expound and explain the 'Indian identity'. In the wake of independence, there was a new-found Indianness which found several expressions. Sociologists wanted to comprehend, discern and disseminate this 'identity' and 'self-consciousness' of a free Indian. The second focus was to help in the reconstruction and planning of the country. For this purpose, they focused on the study of social structure and social formations.

The concerns were pragmatic rather than theoretical. There, of course, was the third element with its various debates and discussions on caste versus tribe, macro versus micro, village or nation and so on and so forth.

Two principal debates focused on:

(i) Can India survive as a democracy, given its mass of illiterate population; and

(ii) Can India grow, given its religious propensity and preoccupation, with Gods, spiritualism, etc.

Professor Singh believes that American anthropologist, Milton Singer came closest to understanding Indian social reality when he says that "saving proclivity of Indians is very high". He goes further by saying that Indian middle class makes measured choices of consumption, unlike his western counterpart, who is a consumerist.

When queried about challenge facing the sociologist of his times, Professor Singh responded that 'operationalization' was the biggest challenge, of how to convert ideas into operational categories, as evidenced in his co-authored work with T.K.N. Unnithan: *Sociology of Non-violence and Peace* (published in two volumes) for which they both went to conduct interviews of elite to Sri Lanka and Nepal. There were challenges of converting Gandhian thought into utilitarian concepts. There were challenges of using past historical data in this new/changed social reality and ever changing present. The village studies posed their own operational challenges.

Then, there were challenges of articulation and presentation. How do you operationalize the views of intelligentsia into practical interpretations, especially when the process was essentially through dialogical interaction, rather than formal communication? The mindset of intellectuals was not prepared to accept the Gandhian system/value of non-violence. It wanted general embededness – compassionate and free from conflict. It wanted harmony. Reflecting his own personality and belief systems, Professor Singh argued that there was always the challenge of presenting differing viewpoints in a harmonious, non-conflicting and non-antagonistic manner.

Prof. Singh also talked about the challenges of using new statistical models (in an era with no access to modern computing power) to predict and advise on issues of social planning. He cited an example where they had taken up an ambitious study of estimating the needs of three cities (Jaipur, Ajmer and Kota) and how they will grow from mid-sixties to the end of the century. They had to convert their empirical survey observations into estimates of growth and planning consequences thereof.

What surprised us was when Prof. Singh talked about the challenges of acceptance. He pointed out that logistic difficulties led him to curtail on international projects. Equally daunting were the challenges of underlying anxieties and insecurities regarding our study of neighbouring countries. There were incessant questions on what we are studying and why. They attributed motives and viewed us with suspicion, just as we accused others of western bias. We were viewed with similar suspicion and "lack of acceptance" by smaller neighbouring countries (Sri Lanka and Nepal). To quote Prof. Singh, there were challenges "from text to context".

When asked to comment on challenges being faced by today's Sociologist, Prof. Singh observed that it is not fair for him to critique contemporary Sociology or sociologists. He pointed out that each generation evolves its own contemporary issues and objects of study. Every generation has its own consciousness, which evolves out of the new/changed environment it faces. He further said that there is too much fluidity in structure and formation of social realities. Old categories seem inadequate to capture or predict social behaviour. The old concepts have undergone a change as have their traditional meanings. He illustrated by citing the example of caste as 'biradari' and/or 'kinship location'. He observed that the zamindari system had almost disappeared as had traditional occupational affiliations. There are different dynamics of change – both internal and external. There is rise in prosperity levels leading to change in consumption pattern and household behaviour. All these need to be studied using empirical evidences.

Professor Singh felt that being a sociologist today is much more challenging. He observed that increase in education levels and general awareness implied that the writings have become visible and are subject to greater scrutiny and questioning. He emphasized the 'reflexive role' of modern-day sociologist, and advocated the need for more meaningful studies in the context of accelerating economic development, rapid urbanization and changing job profiles. There is need for cross-mirroring and of 'I versus my objects and subjects'. The social endeavours are much more challenging and take discourse away from mundane surveys and surface realities.

Professor Singh emphasized the 'accountability' and 'empathy' in sociological studies. He talked of 'identity solipsism' (everyone contained in identity). He argued that for better appreciation of social reality, one has to understand both the normative principles and the class character. He questioned the viewpoint that empathy and identification are essential to construct and appreciate social reality (should only females study females or should only dalits study dalits). He asked if non-female or non-dalits have no psyche and/or ability for objective assessment.

When questioned on globalization and its impact, Prof. Singh observed that social reality is no more national. Globalization of cultures is a fact of life. But equally true are under-currents of sub-nationalism or other identities. The diasporas have grown phenomenally both in number and diversity – religious, regional, caste – leading to emergence of new tensions and new perspectives. This also offers new opportunities and new sites for field work, like internationalization of Gurus, development of new cults, new meaning of religiosity, etc. He pointed out that internationalism has to be understood with no histories.

There is need to improvise and to innovate. He argued that we would have to comprehend and analyse changed reality, may be with fresh perspective and new concepts. There is need to undertake empirical studies to find out the hidden factors, and not just the manifest factors, behind the dynamic of changing reality. Before concluding, he reiterated that today there is 'hope' and this is an 'aspirational generation'. We need to understand, appreciate and further their 'hopes and aspirations' if we have to stay relevant.

II

The very first paper of this Festschrift "Yogendra Singh: An Apostle of Conceptualization and Theorization" by K.L. Sharma, the senior most student of Prof. Singh, as may be expected, is a review of the major contributions and singular academic achievements of Prof. Singh. Profiling Prof. Singh, Sharma observes that "Yogendra Singh is an enchanting teacher, speaker and scholar, and he is a fine human being, a thorough gentleman and a true democrat. As a scholar, Singh has successfully synthesized theory and fact, knowing the mutual bearing of both." Sharma delineates that Yogendra Singh seems to be a centrist. At JNU he was known as one of the best minds and an architect of the concept and theory of modernization. Sharma further observes that Yogendra Singh is an assimilationist, a liberal and open scholar. He is popularly known as a theorist par excellence. Borrowing John O' Neil's expression "sociology as a skin trade", Sharma observes that Yogendra Singh has been a champion of "reflexive sociology". He shaped sociology at JNU, by bringing together scholars of different orientations and preferences. Yogendra Singh has not stood simply for conceptualization and also not for description alone. He looks at both as interwoven. However, his conceptualization is of a much higher level than most Indian sociologists. And, for this reason, he is generally seen as an apostle of conceptualization and theorization.

Devorah Kalekin-Fishman of the University of Haifa, Israel, in her very comprehensive paper on "Transforming Sociology: A Modern Discipline Encounters Globalization", outlines how sociology is undergoing transformation in the wake of globalization. The point of departure of her paper is "the difficult problem of the relationship between globality (or globalities) and modernity (or modernities)" (Robertson and White, 2005: 345–46). But it is important, to her mind, to note that an even more difficult problem underlies this one. While, as Robertson and White insist, there are issues related to globalization that only sociology can deal with, sociologists' awareness of globalization as a phenomenon arises from patently modern evidence. 'Things' do not fit well into the grids that block out modern life. Because of a pervasive feeling that life is changing, 'the modern' is giving way to 'the global' and part of the process is the development of a kind of industry of description and explanation. Throughout her paper, she has taken seriously the assertion that globalization signals a transformation of the world we live in, and that as part of the rush of a globalizing world, sociology, too, is undergoing a transformation. What she has done in this article is to sketch the principles that she thinks have to underlie this kind of analysis. She begins by marshaling evidence that sociology is indeed a discipline of modernity and then points out contemporary developments in sociology which indicate how sociology is being transformed by globality. She concludes that in confronting the emergent sociology, there is no need to rely on philosophy for its legitimation. The point is to clarify and re-clarify what is happening in the world which is beginning at every moment. Sociologists equipped to amass particulars so as to lay out the designs of assemblages and to examine their inner facets, sociologists who can extrapolate to the threats of oppression from a host of virtual institutions are sighting the nature of the era and creating a veritable sociology of globality.

While Devorah Kalekin-Fishman outlined how sociology is undergoing transformation in the wake of globalization, Paramjit S. Judge, reflects on sociology in India again in the context of globalization in his paper "Sociology in India in the Context of Globalization: Issues and Challenges". He emphasizes that any exercise in mapping the current status of any social science discipline is a mammoth task, as it involves the normative concerns as well as the personal perceptions of the sociologist who treads this path. The paper is a self-critical reflection on the developments in sociology in terms of challenges it is facing due to globalization in India. The revolution in technology, particularly in the field of information technology, has changed the way the people understood the world and their relationships. What is called the age of globalization is nothing but the domination of communication technology which facilitated the simultaneity in the experience of individuals as consumers of market and information. The pragmatics of the contemporary world is moving towards the strong belief in the efficacy and adequacy of technology to deliver goods as well as solve the problems of humanity. It has been argued that the future of sociology depends upon not only the research priorities of the Indian state but also the ability of the institutional basis of Indian universities. The overall decline in the teaching and research in sociology is linked with the decline in the university system. As such, what is happening in India is that sociology is achieving excellence in the metropolitan centres, but the peripheries are getting pauperised. The most crucial element in the future of sociology is how does Indian state reorients its policy.

Volker H. Schmidt, in his paper "Late Modernization in the Age of Globalization: East Asia and Beyond", observes that the breakthrough to modernity marks a world historical turning point, giving rise to a new societal formation that differs fundamentally from its evolutionary precursor. The term 'modernization' refers to the dynamic aspect of modernity – the processes and products of change that accompany the transition from pre-modern to modern society and beyond. At the same time, it signifies conscious efforts on the part of influential societal actors to set in motion, by means of rational planning, developments that result in what is understood as modernity (or high or advanced modernity) at a particular point in time. He further observes that once modernity had broken through somewhere (according to conventional wisdom, the first world region to experience this was northwestern Europe), this fact alone altered the environment of all other societies, pressuring them to react and adapt. Both modern and pre-modern societies (continue to) modernize, but they start from different levels of development. 'Late modernization' is the process by which initially 'backward' societies try to catch up with the leaders in modernization. The earliest cases of successful late modernization were those of Germany and Japan. Initially drawing upon the experience and knowhow of various western countries that were ahead of them at the time, later become models for other latecomers themselves. He also holds that many of the phenomena associated with modernity reached the non-western world other than Japan only after the Second World War and the collapse of colonialism. While globally-oriented from the outset, the process of modernization was much accelerated in the post-war era, especially during the past three decades, and while no part of the world remained unaffected, East Asia experienced the most dramatic and thoroughgoing change. Schmidt's paper reconstructs the key features of East Asia's modernization process, compares it with those of/in other world regions and asks what lessons it might provide for (some of) these others.

Lech W. Zacher in his paper "Technological vs. Political Modernization: Interactions and Feedbacks", emphasizes that *modernization* is a de-facto everlasting process of making everything modern (i.e., counter-traditional). Modernization is the creation, introduction and diffusion of novelties or innovations of all types – scientific, technological, organizational, institutional, social, political, cultural, environmental, and so on. And yet, he laments that it is rather common in the social sciences to not properly consider the role of technology, in general, and technological innovation, in particular, in modernization processes, as well as in the sphere of politics. The main cause is probably the constant appeal of rather obsolete concepts and theories – seen often by many scientists as relevant forever in spite of the hard fact that they refer to totally different realities than the times we live in. Meanwhile, the development of technology generates many radical and profound changes in virtually all spheres of human and social life. Of course, technological impacts touch various social phenomena and change in differentiated ways, and are not necessarily total and unequivocal (sometimes they are not evident and difficult to identify). Zacher's thesis is not connected with any type of technological determinism; it points out only the empirically-evident fact that technology has been, throughout human history, a dominant driving force of development and its transformations. There was not a single period in history without technology, technological innovation, and their applications (of course, the scale, span and effects vary spatially and in time). Therefore, it seems quite justified to connect the stages of modernization with the subsequent stages of technological development – the great industrial revolution of the 18th century (which produced a new type of society called the industrial society), the scientific-technological revolution situated in the middle of the 20th century (characterized by crucial innovations and their applications, especially in the field of new materials, nuclear energy and automation), and subsequently information and communication technology (ICT), biotechnology and nano technology. The ongoing information revolution (also known as cybernetic, computer, telematic and digital) is an actual form of scientific and technological revolution. New technologies in addition to their vast applications and wide diffusion require strategies, policies, and some control, involving all actors and stakeholders of modernization. At the same time, the concept of technology assessment was potentially a great invention for ameliorating the effects of modernization. However, the effects of revolutionary changes in science and technology and their massive use are real challenges for politics and people's lives. These changes not only cause the general "acceleration of everything" (discussed by Gleick, Eriksen, and Virilio), but also impose adaptation. Those which are unable to adapt are excluded and, as a result, are alienated from modernization processes. Those countries, regions, societies, groups of people, and even individuals become a 'burden' to development, and at the same time constitute a potential power of resistance and even destruction (in the form of new Luddites). Paradoxically, emerging societies – informational, networked, digital, mediumistic and relational – aspire to be (or at least aspire to be called) *knowledge societies*. But, the question is whether postmodern societies are really becoming knowledge-based societies. Economies are surely increasing, but societies? Modernization, especially when successful, is not automatic (as we know some civilizations, empires, states, industries and professions declined and finally fell down). Differentiation of modernization processes is significant, throughout history and today, and probably in the future as well. There are pioneering countries (societies) and imitators, as well as countries lagging behind and countries already excluded. We deal with a great variety of models of modernization, including its ways, strategies, policies, and effects and impacts (including negative impacts). Comparative studies show a phenomenon which can be called *shallow modernization*. There are many countries, parts of countries, or whole regions (e.g., Eastern Europe, Latin America, Asia) in which modernization was (or sometimes still is) shallow. This situation can be called a *modernization divide*. Zacher further points out that in theories of modernization it is often presumed – implicitly or explicitly – that there is one common pattern for all. But it seems that our traditionally universalist mindset and world view are now changing, which is a benefit for the social sciences and political practice. However, the major thrust of Zacher is that all in all technology, technological innovations, and their massive, diverse applications play a great role in the stimulation of political modernization (not only in the leading countries). They transform societies as well as their structures, consciousness, attitudes, aspirations and visions, not to mention education, skills and behaviour.

Continuing the debate on modernization but shifting its focus on India, Anand Kumar in his paper "Modernization of Indian Tradition and the Gandhian Way: Towards a Sociological Invitation", posits that it may not be inappropriate to suggest that the challenge of understanding modern India cannot ignore the twin needs of explaining modernization of Indian tradition and contextualizing the Gandhian way as they are intertwined in so many ways. But most of the social scientists have adopted the path of avoidance about it by separating the processes of the making of Indian modernity and the rise of Mohandas to 'Mahatma Gandhi'. Often there is overemphasizing of the structural-functional aspect of modernization of India by separating the historical from the sociological in it. Given such a setting, it is very significant that this togetherness of Indian modernity and Gandhi has been recognized, analysed and critiqued by Professor Yogendra Singh by constantly visiting this theme in his analysis of modernization, stratification and social change in India since 1973. His analysis has been based upon historical facts as well as sociological theories. It has underlined the continuities and changes promoted by Gandhi through his unique ideological approach, political methodology and civilizational vision. The studies about the interrelations between modernization of Indian tradition and the Gandhian way by Yogendra Singh have acquired a new relevance in the 21st century India because of accurateness of some of his conclusions, reflections and evaluations of the strengths and weaknesses of the ideological, structural and institutional aspects of Indian modernity as well as the Gandhian way. They caution us to recognize that nationalism and democracy in India have come into being in a special historical context which separates the Indian trajectory of modernization from the western experience. Anand Kumar further maintains that Yogendra Singh is cognizant of the ideological plurality, with due significance of Gandhism, inherent in Indian modernity. According to Yogendra Singh, Marxism, democratic liberalism and Gandhism stand out as three ideological systems which inform the processes of political and cultural modernization in India. Of these three, only Gandhism offered a truly alterative model of modernization in conformity with the Indian ethos. However, according to Anand Kumar, any understanding about the role and impact of Gandhi in the context of Indian modernization project should include a clear analysis of the similarities and differences between the approaches of Gandhi and Nehru. He points out that according to Yogendra Singh, the shift of emphasis from the mass politics of

Gandhi to the elite politics of Nehru has been an important structural change in India's political modernization which took place following independence. Such a situation, according to Anand Kumar, will lead to the emergence of the forces of political radicalization which will be hard to counter. Like several eminent scholars, Anand Kumar also maintains that studying about modernization and its historical route in India has been a great contribution of Professor Yogendra Singh. He has educated three generations of Indian academicians and policy makers through his teaching, research and writings about its strengths, contradictions and challenges. It will be very meaningful for anyone who wants to understand the Indian journey from a colony to an independent nation-state, from tradition to modernization, from hierarchy conscious social formation to egalitarianism-oriented society to engage with his writings.

P.N. Pandey in his paper "Modernity, Postmodernity and Global Development", has focused on the history as well as the recent trends of modernity in the wake of global development. It encompasses a comprehensive theoretical perspective of modernity, postmodernity and global changes and highlights the emerging trends of modernity with the vision and perception of the contemporary theorists of modernity and postmodernity in social sciences. The author has analysed modernization as a movement for changes in the economy, polity and social structure in terms of its impact on the developed as well as the developing societies of the world. The manifest consequences of the said impression of modernization, development and sustainable development, as realized by the developing nations, have also been discussed in detail with the findings of the researches and investigations. The experience of industrially developed societies of the West, specially the USA, the UK, France, Germany, Italy and others, indicates that these societies have reached the zenith of the techno-industrial and economic development. Their economic, political and social systems operate through electronic machines and technological devices. Such societies are, in other words, computerized social systems. Zbigniew Brzezinski, a contemporary social scientist, observes that America is in the midst of transition that is both unique and baffling and is going to be the first 'technotronic society' of the world. Pandey further observes that most of the classical sociologists who were born before the so-called modern society have envisioned the arrival of modern era in their own way.

This is paradoxical to note that the outcome of the western developmental programmes has disheartened the developing nations. The ever-increasing social and economic disparities, discrepancy and differentiations and the gap between the rich and the poor indicate that the ideology of modernization through development based on egalitarianism and equality has proved elusive and dilemmatic to the societies of Asia and Africa. Pandey cites several studies to indicate the economic and cultural crisis of the West. He has also extensively reviewed the views of several scholars on modernity and postmodernity. He concludes by observing that postmodernity is being characterized with ephimerality/discontinuity and differentiation. It is timeless, depthless and ahistorical since it conceives the world as technological entity rather than a natural or ecological entity. To some, it is pastiche or what one can call a random cannibalization of the styles of the past. It is a chaotic-mass-mediated individual preference-based phenomenon and has decoupled the relation between the life world and the system.

Moving from the debate on modernization to the core issues of globalization, Partha Nath Mukherji, in his paper "Globalisation: Where Lies the Choice?" argues that one of the major fallacies in the fierce debate between the protagonists and antagonists of globalization lies in conflating the globalization of neo-liberal economy of market fundamentalism with globalization per se. It is argued that while globalization per se, premised on the IT revolution by its function of time and space compression, is irreversible, neo-liberal market fundamentalism is. Unlike the open-arm welcome to modernization, globalization has met with a turbulent reception. It is also argued that the nation-state far from withering away has acquired new significance under changed circumstances. The neo-liberal hegemony on globalization is not the end of history but only the beginning of a new era of struggles and transformations ahead.

The paper on "Globalization and Modernity: Indian Scenario" by Jaikant Tiwary and Manish Tiwari seeks to conceptualize globalization via consideration of modernity. Features of globalization and modernity are examined on their intended, manifest, positive as well as unintended, latent and negative consequences. The paper also examines the consequences of global economic integration for a national economy in the context of interdependence and competition between economies in the world market. It explores the problematic of globalization in the context of vital social concerns such as the digital divide, deepening of disparity, rising unemployment, growth of consumer culture, plight of farmers and the working class, future of nation-state, etc. Mercerization of social issues is the new concern characteristic of the globalized era. It deals with the structural content of problems facing the society which is delinked from everything except market opportunities.

Ishwar Modi, in his paper "Globalization, Marginalization and Social Transformation: The Context of Indian Rural Society", emphasizes the importance ofz rural society in understanding Indian society as a whole, in spite of the fact that Indian rural society has undergone considerable change in the recent past, particularly since independence. Now that the pace of change has become extremely rapid and critical due to globalization, there is an urgent need to understand as to how globalization is impacting Indian society, particularly the rural one. Agreeing with the view that there is an almost unanimous consensus about globalization being a complex and multidimensional process, Modi moves on to identify the causes of globalization as well as its effects and how these can be judged since there is a growing concern about the direction globalization is currently taking. Its advantages are too distant for too many, while its risks are all too real as benefits of globalization have been unequally distributed, both within and between countries. As elsewhere, the impact of globalization has been mixed in India too. There had been winners and losers both. On the whole, the life for the rural poor in particular and masses at large has become far more painful and insecure due to the panic and penury resulting from globalization. Modi further points out that the talk of globalization will be meaningless if it is not examined in the context of social development. Likewise, no meaningful sociology can be done in India and social development ensured without concern for the dalits, the Adivasis, and the indigenous and vulnerable marginalized people as poverty in case of these groups is not only an economic state but is basically a process of social exclusion and marginalization.

As such, social development and marginalization are directly related to social transformation. No social transformation more so a desired social transformation is possible unless social development of the marginalized and excluded groups, particularly that of rural India, is undertaken in an earnest spirit and sustained manner since these groups are still, and going to remain, at the lowest level of society for long. The spirit of social transformation must adhere the way it has been defined as a multidimensional process of accelerated social change, as also the radical change in the mindsets, lifestyles, ways of thinking and doing, and creating a desire to achieve an egalitarian social order with improved quality of life and happiness. Examined from this perspective, the condition of the marginalized and the excluded groups, more so in the rural India, is rather pathetic. These groups are often faced with double and triple discrimination. It is only through the empowerment of the large number of marginalized groups that India can be empowered. The process of globalization, only if rationally redesigned, can yield much better, positive and acceptable results.

Besides the political and the major consequences for the world economy, very often concerns have been raised with regard to the impact of globalization on culture. As such it is no surprise that several contributors to this Festschrift have examined the impact of globalization on culture in its various ramifications. Eminent social scientist Yogesh Atal, in his paper on "Globalization and the Future of Cultures", has examined the relationship between globalization and cultures in a very comprehensive and multifaceted manner. He begins his dialogue by observing that orientation to change has changed over time. Rather than focusing on the past, and reconstructing the journey from the past to the present, social scientists began investigating the changes in contemporary world. And, as we approached close to the 20th century, the focus of change shifted again – this time from the present to the future. Atal submits that the concept of Globalization is the product of this last phase. He emphasizes that we must admit that this is the period of understanding the process of globalization, and not of passing judgement on it. It is a new coinage passed on to us from the international political arena. As a concept, it is still being sculpted. Collapse of communism, leading to the liberalization of the economies and increasing democratization of polities, has created new conditions for international interactions in almost all the fields. But, depending on our subject specialization, we view this process as economic, political, cultural, or a total mix of all these aspects of our life. Like the previous concepts of westernization and modernization, globalization is also used in two distinct senses – as an ideology and as a process. Atal shares the view that globalization is a process, and not a deliberate ideology imposed by some agency as we continue to be one world with many voices, and with several cultures, and yet all the societies of the world are in the grip of this overwhelming process of globalization. Questions concerning culture, such as the following, are being raised in the context of rapidly enveloping process of globalization: Will economic and technological progress destroy the cultural diversity and bastardize our cultures? Will we witness a return of intolerant chauvinism that would make cultures retreat to their shells? Will there be a judicious fit between the old and the new? Where are we going? Where shall we reach? What will be the fate of our cultures? Atal attempts to answer these questions in a broader sociological perspective. He further observes that what appears striking is the fact that despite so much of give and take occurring between cultures – call it by whatever name such as westernization, modernization or even globalization – cultures have maintained their identities, and the globe is characterized by the heterogeneity of cultures. In the midst of sea-change experienced by non-western societies, one notices a reassertion of their respective cultural identities. The resurgence and revival of traditions are manifestations of this assertion. Such a situation leads us to ask the following questions: What is the function of cultural identity? Does it create solidarity among the people who belong to that culture? Or, does this process lead to the emergence of sub-regional loyalties which may become secessionist? What happens when a person is sandwiched between dual loyalties – for example, religious identity versus cultural identity? How does culture give identity to its people? Can newer identities be created by manipulating cultural symbols? Do identities really empower? Or, are they fictitious? Atal maintains that very little attention has been paid to these worrisome queries in the analyses of globalization. He also emphasizes that there is a need to establish a relationship between the concepts of 'change' and 'future'. In his view, both concepts are diachronic, but change is past-oriented and future is forward-looking. One is rooted in history; the other is dependent upon our powers of prediction. He concludes by observing that all cultures in future will look different from what they are today, with changes in the profiles of their demography and literacy, and with the continuing onslaught of technology and its attendant ramifications. But they will remain, and remain different with their own identities. Similarities in material culture – the externalia – will not obliterate differences in values and ways of life. Neither will there be a single future for the globe, nor a single global culture. Multiple cultures will have multiple futures. Heterogeneity will continue to prevail. As such, the challenge before us is to investigate the new phenomenon of change as it occurs in our society and brings about transformation of our cultures without erasing their identities.

Continuing the debate on the linkages between globalization and culture, Chandan Kumar Sharma, in his paper "Globalization, Culture and Change", observes that though the conventional understanding of culture projects it as an innocent, apolitical phenomenon, the recent cultural theories have forcefully brought out the political character of culture. It is through culture that the collective identity and the world view of a community finds its expression. Thus, appropriating the culture of a people has always been an important agenda for forces seeking to establish hegemonic dominance over a people. This appropriation has seen its most conquering form under the contemporary process of globalization. The paper explicates the inherent economic interests of the process of globalization and its exploitation of culture to further these interests. It argues that the much-celebrated propaganda of change globalization is said to have brought about needs to be accepted with circumspection.

B.K. Nagla, in his paper "Globalization and Its Impact on Culture", maintains that globalization is as fascinating a term these days as modernization, development and change have been during the last 20th century. To think of the world as a global village was once a day dreamer's delight. Not any more. Instead, the end of the 20th century will be remembered for bringing the dream of globalization to reality. On the one hand, several outcomes of this transformation are within the reach of a large number of human beings. Availability of fax machines and internet facility are its examples. Who could have thought of its widespread availability in India three decades ego? Globalization as a trend would create its impact on each area of human activity. On the other hand, the process of globalization has generated universal disenchantment. Those applaud its arrival are fewer. Disenchantment prevails not only in the developing but also in the developed world. It needs to be analysed as to what lies at the root of such disenchantment. It is in this context that the paper first examines the historical perspective of globalization and then the notions or concepts of globalization and localization and how this can be conceptualized as well as its relationships between the global and the local. It also looks at the theories of globalization. Finally, it examines the implications of the impact of globalization on culture.

Continuing the discussion on the interface between globalization and culture, S.M. Michael, in his paper on *"Globalization and Culture: Solidarity with Social Movements for a Humane Society"*, observes two major trends in the globalized world of today. On the one hand, some scholars believe that there is only one direction left for the world that is to imitate and incorporate the ideology of the triumphant global free market capitalism and its consequent economic, social, political and cultural path. This position is articulated by Fukuyama in his celebrated volume *End of History* (1992). Opposing this view some other scholars are of the opinion that today's world is a diversified world. We cannot trust any of the major ideologies. We need to recognize, and further multiculturalism and suspect and oppose the ideologies which try to homogenize cultures, peoples and religions. In today's world both these ideological trends co-exist with their variations. Thus, we see the dominance of the globalization of the consumerist market capitalistic culture, economy and politics on the one hand, and postmodernism, multiculturalism, nationalism and fundamentalism on the other. People of different countries and regions are sandwiched between these conflicting and contradicting trends of world history. All the same, the problems of poverty and injustice have also increased.

In the globalized world of today, we need to ask ourselves what globalization means for the poor, oppressed and the marginalized. Are they able to experience a sense of common humanity with the rich and the affluent? Or is globalization the luxury of the rich and the powerful? Michael further emphasizes that as citizens of the world, we need to be concerned about human dignity and social justice for all people. In the context of globalization, we need to give a direction to globalization in such a way that the poor and the downtrodden receive the attention and care that is due to them. As concerned citizens, we need to ask what globalization means for the poor, the dalits, tribals and other weaker sections. Within the dreams and aspirations of these marginalized groups there lingers the hope of fairness and justice that humanity could offer in the world of globalization.

Taking cognizance of the same concerns as outlined above, Maitreyee Bardhan Roy, in her paper "Global Society: A New Paradigm in Social Science Research", discusses the impact of dissatisfaction and disarray on socio-political and cultural strata. She begins by observing that the post-1990 policies on liberalization and globalization in India have brought about a new paradigm in social science research. The 'world society' concept has influenced the socio-economic-cultural fabric of the country. Top class multinational corporations (having their head offices in US) became the major decision-makers in the country's economic scenario. The impact of it has been distinctly observed in the state policies too. Considering the existence of the diversified socio-cultural and political groups in the country, her research intends to talk on the development of a convergent society in India instead of the existence of diversified traditional social customs preserved from the past. She further observes that the socio-economic-cultural scenario in India has been constantly pursuing for protection of its cultural heritage from foreign power ever since British colonialism, post-independent neo-colonial dominance, post-1990 globalization and liberalization either through post-Nehrubian socialistic paternalism and mutual respect or Indira Gandhi's policy on self-preservation and self-sufficiency. Constant political insight and indirect interference of foreign power threatened the unity and integrity of the country also. The cultural mixture and preaching for its dominance brought about a strong reaction on traditional ethos. Thus, India witnesses diversified socio-cultural and religious conflict nurtured by socio-political-religious conservatism with heterogeneous and multicultural ideologist preaching convergent culture and the strong believer of separatist perception working for separate entity. The research intends to look into the impact of this constant threat faced by the nation from the dawn of civilization. Globalization and liberalization are creating pressure on the national leadership to conform the diversified ideological upheaval threatening the nation-state. The methodology adopted for the purpose of the study includes both historical and the evaluative aspects. The historical part of the study concentrates on the cultural heritage of India while the evaluative part talks on the convergence of policies taken up by the state in the arena of globalization and liberalization.

Taking the debate on globalization further and to correlate it to the issues of social transformation, S.L. Sharma, in his paper "Globalization and Social Transformation in India", argues that an overarching trend of our times – globalization – signifies a transformative force of enormous significance. It represents a force of reorganization of global economic order based on advocacy of open door economic policy between nations, entailing significant socio-cultural fallouts. While its importance as a catalyst of economic transformation in the developing countries has been widely acknowledged, its role in their socio-cultural transformation has not yet received an intense scholarly attention. It is, therefore, time to undertake systematic studies of the socio-cultural impact of globalization in developing countries. A modest attempt in that direction is made in this paper with a focus on India, one of the major beneficiaries of globalization. Sharma further observes that a look at the sociological discourse on globalization in India reveals that it has been concerned more with the cultural consequences of globalization than with its social outcomes, which is also evident from the writings of Singh (2000) and Dhanagare (2003) among others. The social fallouts of globalization have received at best a cursory treatment. A question of seminal sociological significance to ask in this regard is: whether globalization has generated a trend of social transformation in India and, if so, what is its direction? This precisely is the question the author seeks to address in the present paper. In order to deal with this question in a systematic manner, he sets for himself the following specific tasks: (i) to clarify the concept of globalization; (ii) to problematize the term 'social transformation' and articulate it as a concept; (iii) to delineate the socio-cultural fallouts of globalization in India; and (iv) to apprise their transformational potential.

While Sharma analysed the interface between globalization and social transformation in India more from a conceptual perspective at a general level, Biswajit Ghosh, has examined this interface in the specific context of Yogendra Singh's contribution and thoughts on culture change in contemporary India in his paper "Globalization and Social Transformation: Yogendra Singh on Culture Change in Contemporary India". Ghosh holds that Singh's contribution to the exploration and analysis of social change in India in general and cultural changes in the context of globalization in particular is immense. Singh is one of the pioneering Indian sociologists to notice multiple changes in our economy, society, culture and politics since the introduction of economic reforms. This essay argues that there is enough sociological acumen to support Singh's view about cultural globalization in India today. He correctly argued that the quality of resilience and adaptability that Indian culture had shown during westernization is yet being maintained despite certain qualitative changes in recent times. Singh noticed that along with homogenization of certain aspects of Indian culture, globalization has also helped in accelerating the growth of self-consciousness and cultural identities. The growing disparities among different segments of Indian population and the resultant unevenness in the spread of a global culture also proliferates diversity. As a corollary, several aspects of our custom and tradition continue to exist side by side as there are both adoption and rejection. A reading of Singh's essays on globalization has made Ghosh realize that the process is much broader, complex and multifaceted. Hence, according to Singh, emphasis on plurality, identity and continuity is essential for a creative balance between continuity and change in Indian society.

Moving beyond the interface between globalization and social transformation, Binay Kumar Pattnaik, focuses his attention on globalization of science and technology in his paper "Globalization of Science and Technology in Developing Countries: A Sociological Perspective". His paper is a comprehensive attempt to capture the effects of the ongoing process of globalization in the domain of science and technology in a few leading developing countries. After having articulated the implications of globalization for the scientific and technological regimes in developed as well as developing countries, both being two ends of the same process, the paper articulates and formulates the effects of globalization under four headings, such as: (1) internationalization of higher education, (2) emergence of entrepreneurial universities, (3) internationalization and globalization of R&D, and (4) social impacts of the ICT revolution. The paper concludes that the relationship between countries at the centre and a few leading countries at the periphery has undergone a qualitative change and as a result the latter are making an entry into the domain of semi-periphery countries.

Like science and technology, globalization has also impacted the new emerging new middle class in India. This is what N. Rajaram has forcefully brought out in his paper "The Indian Middle Class in the Era of Globalization and

Liberalization: Continuity and Change". According to him, the Indian middle class today is a contrast in some ways to the middle class at the time of independence. At that time, the middle class was characterized by probity, secularism and concern for others. This world view existed till India opened up its economy in early nineties. Since 1991, the middle class expanded rapidly. This emerging middle class was termed as 'new' middle class in contrast to the 'old' middle class at the time of independence. This new middle class became more consumerist and self-centred, even while the work situation became more insecure. Its taste and lifestyle came under transnational influence. Along with this changing lifestyle, it exhibited increasing religiosity in spheres which were hitherto taboo like educational institutions. Women belonging to this emerging middle class became visible. They expanded their spheres of choices and thus changing the norms of family and at work places. But, along with these changes, there was also a negative development: sex-selective abortion increased especially in regions where there was economic development and where the middle class expanded. Thus, in the era of liberalization and globalization, Indian middle class is characterized by tension of contradictory pull of continuity of traditional normative structure in some areas while bringing changes in others.

Antony Palackal also takes up the issues of middle class in India in the wake of globalization and explores the manner consumer culture constructs the identity of the middle class people in India in his paper "Shifting Identities: Consumer Culture and the Middle Class in a Globalized World". Consumer culture, presumably, the pervasive by-product of globalization, forms the specific canvas of this article. It is argued that the cultural underpinnings of globalization spearheaded by the permeating consumer culture impinge on the formation of the self. The issue of identity is more pressing and contested than ever before in contemporary societies. The author submits that the field of consumer culture is more likely the privileged stage where the contestations and negotiations of identities of the middle class occur in contemporary society. Set on the wider canvas of contemporary phenomenon of globalization, it broadly seeks to deal with the sociological debate on the dialectics between the macro and the micro aspects of globalization. More specifically, the paper proposes to embark upon a sociological inquiry into the everyday practices of social life in the age of globalization that unravels the subjective orientations in building life trajectories.

It is in the broader context of the debates on modernity, advance modernity and modernization process that Sherry Sabbarwal, focuses her attention on the conceptualization and construction of 'risk society' at a theoretical level. In her paper on "Modern Society and Risk: Towards a Cultural Understanding of the Risk Society", she argues that risk society, a term coined by German sociologist Ulrich Beck after the Chernobyl disaster, has become an oft-used expression in the discourse on risk – a condition which is widely discernible in every aspect of modern-day society – be it economic, environmental, political or social. The phenomenon of risk and the role it plays in present-day social reality is a subject that has attracted a great deal of attention of social theorists in the past decade. Discussed first in 1986 by Ulrich Beck in his famous work *Risk Society: Towards a New Modernity*, it set into motion a lively debate on the various aspects relating to risk – its definition, perception, causes, coping mechanisms, etc. Another seminal work on this topic was *The Consequences of Modernity* by

Anthony Giddens, which came out in 1990. While Beck defines it mainly in terms of the dangers and uncertainties brought on by the modernization process, Giddens relates it to the concept of security and believes that the society in the phase of advanced modernity is increasingly preoccupied with the future and the hazards that it brings with it. A third variant of the theory appeared in 1992 with the publication of *Risk and Blame: Essays in Cultural Theory* authored by anthropologist Mary Douglas in collaboration with A. Wildavesky. Despite their different accounts, the three scholars provide us with a most detailed theoretical explanation of the culture and politics of risk. Although the risk theory has met with stringent criticism from different quarters, yet its significance in the modern-day world cannot be denied. The paper argues that although the conceptualization of risk by Beck and Giddens has its merits, there is need to take another serious look at the social constructivist and cultural approach to risk as propounded by Mary Douglas.

Overall, the present volume of the four-part Festschrift for Professor Yogendra Singh outlines not only his academic journey and the world view on the relevance of Western scholars but also the major concerns and challenges before the sociologists in India, then as well as now, more so in the context of globalization. Besides this, several contributors to this volume have also extensively and critically reflected on his academic contributions and his personality. Taking into cognizance the thrust of this volume entitled *Modernization, Globalization and Social Transformation* almost all the contributors have focused not only on the conceptual dimensions of the concerned phenomena and their interlinkages but have also examined in detail the relationship of these phenomena with other contemporary social/sociological concerns such as marginalization, social movements, middle class, consumer culture, ethnicity, and even global society and risk society.

1

Yogen

An Apo

K.L. Shar

It is not an
scholar w
teacher, co
'friend'. It
academic
particular
more than
therefore
tions to av
Jewo global
himself no
critics. Th
commitme
and semi
aging inte
including
K. Bose,
in his adm
own, invol
his studen
criticisms
counter in
112–17; 20
immensel
mentione
has taken
Louis Dum
and many
words/con

1

Yogendra Singh

An Apostle of Conceptualization and Theorization

K.L. Sharma

It is not an easy task to offer freely comments on writings and contributions of a scholar who has been personally known and associated with this author as a teacher, colleague and 'friend'. When a person has been a teacher, colleague and 'friend', it creates moral/scientific dilemma in assessing his/her writings and academic role. The task of writing on the contributions of Yogendra Singh in particular is certainly a perplexing task for me due to my association with him for more than half a century. Keeping in view my association with Singh, I would, therefore, take utmost caution in my observations and comments on his contributions to avoid even inadvertent and surreptitious likings/dislikings.

I would like to mention here that Yogendra Singh has rarely defended himself nor he has stimulated his colleagues and students to defend him from his critics. In fact, he has a very few critics mainly because of his genuine commitment and scholarly pursuits. Even in face-to-face situations, meetings and seminars, he would mildly respond, though knowing fully well the disparaging intentions of his critics. None of Yogendra Singh's senior students, including this author, and late N.K. Singhi, I.P. Modi, Dipankar Gupta, Pradeep K. Bose, J.S. Gandhi, Nirmal Singh, C.N. Venugopal, etc., have felt a need to speak in his admiration. Yogendra Singh has never believed in creation of a cult of his own, involving his admirers and students. Even when M.N. Srinivas was not alive, his student and a senior sociologist A.M. Shah would not tolerate his teacher's criticisms (Singh, 2006: 108–12; Oommen, 2008: 60–81), and would quickly counter in strongest possible way, in defence of Srinivas (2005: 238–49; 2006: 112–17; 2008: 388–402). The other quality of Yogendra Singh which adorns him immensely is that he hardly notices whether he is 'quoted', 'referred', 'cited' or 'mentioned' by the fellow colleagues in their writings or not. On the contrary, he has taken a due cognizance of the writings and contributions of M.N. Srinivas, Louis Dumont, T.N. Madan, A.M. Shah, André Béteille, A.R. Desai, M.S. Gore, and many others. Capacity to transform elaborate narrations into a few words/concepts and to explain huge piles of descriptions with words/concepts is unique characteristic quality of Yogendra Singh. Appropriating such a rare skill, he has absorbed a wide range of concepts and theories in his writings.

Yogendra Singh was born on November 1, 1932, at village Chaukhara in the then Basti district of Uttar Pradesh. Coming from a zamindar family, and sensing the wave of social change after India's independence and the abolition of the zamindari system, he realized the significance of modern higher education. Out of the three top ranking universities of Uttar Pradesh, namely, Allahabad, Lucknow and Benaras, he opted for Lucknow University for higher education. Singh obtained Master's degree in 1955, and had the privilege of being taught by eminent scholars, such as Radha Kamal Mukherjee, D.P. Mukerji, D.N. Majumdar, Baljit Singh, A.K. Saran, etc. In 1958, Singh did Ph.D under the supervision of Baljit Singh. He moved to the Institute of Social Sciences, Agra, in 1958, as a lecturer, where he spent three years. R.N. Saxena was Director of the Institute, and S.K. Srivastava, R.N. Srivastava and A.S. Mathur were other teachers. Not seeing much potential there for his academic growth, Yogendra Singh joined in 1961 the newly established Department of Sociology at the University of Rajasthan, where he was elevated to the position of Reader in 1962. The other two colleagues of Singh at Jaipur were T.K.N. Unnithan and Indra Deva. In 1962, the department expanded further with an addition of five more teachers.

In the 1960s, the Department of Sociology at Jaipur was known as one of the best in India, along with the departments at the Universities of Delhi, Chandigarh, Bombay, Pune, Baroda, etc. Despite efforts of the late Prof. M.V. Mathur, who was also Vice-Chancellor of Rajasthan University, and a member of the D.S. Kothari Commission, Yogendra Singh was not elevated to the position of Professor at the University of Rajasthan. In June 1970, Singh joined University of Jodhpur (later on renamed as Jai Narain Vyas University) as Professor. He stayed there for nearly one year, and in 1971, G. Parthasarthy, the founder Vice-Chancellor of the newly established prestigious Jawaharlal Nehru University (JNU), invited Yogendra Singh as Professor and Chairperson of the Centre for the Study of Social Systems (CSSS), School of Social Sciences. Singh remained at JNU till 1997, and after his superannuation, he has been Emeritus Professor. At JNU, besides, being Chairperson of the CSSS, he was also Dean of the School of Social Sciences and Rector (Pro-VC). The CSSS is popularly known as the Y. Singh's Centre.

The CSSS is one of the leading centres of sociology in India. The colleagues who were appointed in the first five years during the chairpersonship of Yogendra Singh included, besides this author, C.N. Venugopal, T.K. Oommen, Partha Nath Mukherjee, M.N. Panini, Ravindra K. Jain and Nirmal Singh. Later on, J.S. Gandhi, Nandu Ram, Ehsanul Haq and Dipankar Gupta were inducted. Except Ehsanul Haq, all of them have superannuated or taken retirement. At present, Anand Kumar, Maitrayee Chaudhuri, Susan Vishwanathan, Tiplut Nongbri, Surinder Jodhka, Avijit Pathak, Renuka Singh, Nilika Mehrotra and some recently recruited members are at the CSSS. C.N. Venugopal, Nirmal Singh, J.S. Gandhi and Dipankar Gupta were doctoral students of Yogendra Singh at the CSSS. This author was his first Ph.D student at the University of Rajasthan.

Ehsanul Haq, Maitrayee Chaudhuri, Avijit Pathak and Renuka Singh were doctoral students of T.K. Oommen, Nirmal Singh, J.S. Gandhi and K.L. Sharma, respectively.

After his superannuation, Yogendra Singh and Mrs Singh live in New Delhi, with their only daughter Neerja Singh and her husband Hulas Singh. Singh has been constantly writing even after 1997, when he formally superannuated from JNU. He completed a major project on Indian Civilization (2010) along with D.P. Chattopadhyay, and currently, is Coordinator of the ICSSR's project on Writing of Trend Reports in Sociology and Social Anthropology. Singh has written three Trend Reports for the ICSSR (1974a: 311–82; 1974b: 383–431; 1985: 37–79).

Yogendra is a soft-spoken person, with a sense of genuine humility and sociability. He has hardly annoyed others, not even to those who opposed him or did not like him for the reasons known to them alone. In general, he is a private person, likes good food and occasional drinks, in company of personal friends and family members. He is highly respected as a fine human being and a very unassuming, well-read, and sound scholar. In classroom, he has been liked by one and all as a great teacher, knowledgeable and articulate. His reading is not confined to disciplinary boundaries. As an awakened citizen and educated member of society, he knows about economic scenario, politics, literature, health and nutrition, sports, cinema, etc. Most of the members of his extended family have settled down in Delhi. He has maintained ties with his native village in eastern Uttar Pradesh. He has taken care of the members of his extended family even at the expense of his immediate nuclear family.

Yogendra Singh has never made conscious efforts to seek favours and positions of status and power. He has kept distance from politicians and bureaucrats. Thrice he was offered vice-chancellorship, which he politely declined. Though he would have accepted vice-chancellorship of JNU, which escaped him, even after he was told by a responsible person to accept it, not to decline. There are several other aspects of Yogendra Singh's personality, which need to be appropriately incorporated in his biography/autobiography. This is the third felicitation volume in honour of Professor Yogendra Singh. The first volume was edited by K.L. Sharma (1994) and the second one was brought out by the late N.K. Singhi (1996). Both the volumes, honouring Yogendra Singh, were published by Rawat Publications, Jaipur. I am happy that the third volume is being brought out by I.P. Modi, who was a Ph.D student of Professor Yogendra Singh, at the University of Rajasthan. This volume too is published by Rawat Publications.

II

Yogendra Singh deserved to be a Professor much earlier at the University of Rajasthan. Even after being Reader for nearly eight years (1962–70), when he was not elevated to professorship, V.V. John, Vice-Chancellor of Jodhpur University, offered him professorship in 1970. Alongwith the position of Head of the Department, Singh was also offered some other positions as well. Just after one year's stay at Jodhpur, in May 1971, Singh was invited by Jawaharlal Nehru University to lead the newly established Centre for the Study of Social Systems (CSSS), where he remained for his remaining academic life, nearly 27 years. After his superannuation, Singh is Professor Emeritus at the CSSS.

Yogendra Singh is abundantly rich by way of his two qualities: (1) an enchanting teacher, speaker and scholar, and (2) a fine human being, a thorough gentleman and a true democrat (citizen). Not only students of sociology were benefited by his scholarship, even several students of other disciplines used to attend his lectures. Some people have admiringly named Yogendra Singh as India's Talcott Parsons, "an incurable theorist". However, in my opinion, it is an exaggeration and not a true characterization. "Perception" is basic to Parsons' understanding of social reality or to his "abstracted empiricism" as C.W. Mills comments about Parsons in *Sociological Imagination* (1970). Because for Singh, the field studies, including Six Villages of Uttar Pradesh (1969), study of Chanukhera in Basti district (1970a), urban survey in Rajasthan (1966), teaching profession at the Rajasthan University (1972a), peace and non-violence in India, Sri Lanka and Nepal (1972b), etc., conducted by him, have been the source of conceptualization as well as validation of the existing concepts and theoretic constructs. Singh's real contribution lies in his ability to transform empirical realities into concepts and theoretical frameworks and in examination of theoretic constructs for understanding of social reality at the ground level.

Yogendra Singh seems to be a centrist, and this trait is reflected in his life-situations and in his writings. He has been admired by a cross-section of scholars, including Rama Krishna Mukherjee, K.M. Kapadia, A.R. Desai, M.S. Gore, K.S. Singh, J.P. Naik, M.S.A. Rao, I.P. Desai, V.S. D'Souza, and many more. He has/had personal friends drawn from different disciplines and places, such as J.C. Gupta, R.N. Srivastava, P.L. Rawat and K.B. Garg. He worked with T.K.N. Unnithan and Indra Deva at Jaipur. Some of the students of Singh, besides this author, are: late N.K. Singhi, I.P. Modi, Pushpendra Surana, late Nimi Baxi, Dipankar Gupta, Pradip Bose, Nirmal Singh, C.N. Venugopal, J.S. Gandhi, Jagbandhu Acharya, Madhu Nagla, Kameshwar Chaudhary and Biswajit Das.

Yogendra Singh has not been keen to take up administrative positions. This is also a fact that he has never indulged in a rat race for positions of power and authority. He does not belong to an extreme school of thought, such as Marxism or Functionalism. His 'middle path' approach is based on a pragmatic eclecticism. M.N. Srinivas was out and out for field studies on the pattern of British functionalism, particularly practised by A.R. Radcliffe-Brown. The other extreme approach, namely, Marxism, was advocated by A.R. Desai, in its orthodox form. Yogendra Singh has drawn from all major sociologies of the world, including American, British, French and German. Talcott Parsons, Ralph Dahrendorf, B. Malinowski, A.R. Radcliffe-Brown, T.B. Bottomore, C. Levi-Strauss, Alain Touraine, P. Bourdieu and Louis Dumont find reflections in Yogendra Singh's writings and lecturers, besides the classics of Karl Marx, Max Weber and Emile Durkheim.

III

In a recent article, Maitrayee Chaudhuri (2011: 158–87), while describing the practice of sociology at the CSSS, JNU, undermines the role played by Yogendra Singh in shaping sociology in India in general and at the CSSS in particular. However, the fact is that under the guidance of Singh, Talcott Parsons, Robert K.

Merton, George C. Homans, Marian J. Levy, and anthropologists, including A.L. Kroeber, Margret Mead, etc., were included in the programmes of study at the CSSS. So was the case of many European sociologists. Yogendra Singh emphasizes on a composite nature of sociology, with a right 'mix' of western and Indian concepts, frames of references, field studies, and historical data. Yogendra Singh is not for Marxist theory and method alone, and nor is he for structural-functionalism alone. He prefers a "fusion of the paradigms", and this requires a human rapport among the faculty, which is often difficult to achieve. He succeeded in this endeavour to a great extent in taking the CSSS to a considerable height.

Maitrayee Chaudhuri's description and interpretation of the studies and research at the CSSS are partial and half-truths. For example, for the first five years, Yogendra Singh was the unquestioned guide and philosopher at the CSSS. Everyone followed his line of thinking with regard to the development of the Centre and its programmes of study and research, including the researches on social movements and professions. Six of us, including Yogendra Singh, T.K. Oommen, P.N. Mukherjee, C.N. Venugopal, M.N. Panini and myself, were for a unified approach and action plan. In the next five years, in general, Yogendra Singh provided academic leadership to the Centre. The CSSS was perhaps the only Centre at JNU, where scholars and students of all shades and opinions were accommodated with ease and understanding. This was not true about some other Schools and Centres. Some worshipped Marxism, others hated Marxism. Chaudhuri is not right when she says: "Thus, while a Marxist perspective (dominant outside CSSS in JNU) was not evident in CSSS in the 1970s, those students who were influenced by Marxism were largely free to pursue their orientation." Marx, Weber and Durkheim were taught at length at the CSSS right from the day one.

Before joining JNU in 1971, Yogendra Singh had written an article on caste and class (1968a), which was highly acclaimed by many scholars. Class and ethnicity were realized equally important issues along with caste in the studies of social movements, conducted by T.K. Oommen, P.N. Mukherjee and K.L. Sharma, on agrarian, Naxalbari and Jharkhand movements, respectively. Based on the field studies, they published on three movements in journals and books. Dipankar Gupta, Pradeep Bose, Anjan Ghosh, Jogbandhu Acharya, Amrita Chhachi, Maitrayee Chaudhuri, and many other students pursued, generally speaking, variants of the Marxist approach in their doctoral studies.

Chaudhuri has mentioned (op. cit.: 177) that in early years, Yogendra Singh, T.K. Oommen, Ravindra Jain and C.N. Venugopal shaped the Centre. She has forgotten the fact that T.K. Oommen and C.N. Venugopal joined the CSSS in 1971 after Yogendra Singh. Along with this author, M.N. Panini and P.N. Mukherjee joined the CSSS in 1972 (July–August), and Ravindra K. Jain in 1975. Ignoring such facts leads to distortion and misrepresentation. Chaudhury's description of the CSSS is obviously biased as thirteen works of Oommen have been cited, whereas only four writings of Yogendra Singh are mentioned. She has not taken a note of the writings in early years on movements and professions by half a dozen faculty members. She has also overrated her own contribution to the making of sociology at the CSSS. I do not wish to say more about Chaudhuri's paper, except that it lacks a balanced and composite view of the development of sociology at the CSSS. A serious academic endeavour must be based on sound facts rather than casual corridor talks and cafeteria gossips.

IV

Yogendra Singh has persistently demonstrated a very sound understanding of the discipline of sociology in particular and social sciences in general, in both teaching and discussions and debates. Singh's lectures at JNU were attended by the students of other disciplines as well. His students and colleagues have often thought of him as the most knowledgeable scholar on sociological theory, philosophy and methodology. Yogendra Singh has a wide array of themes on which he has written with care and concern. The following topics have attracted him most:

- Theory and Method
- Social Stratification and Mobility
- Modernization
- Professions
- Social Change
- Indian Sociology
- Culture and Society

It may also be pertinent to mention here that Yogendra Singh is seen as a scholar par excellence in domains of sociological theory and modernization. His book *Modernization of Indian Tradition* (1973a) provides a pathbreaking paradigm shift in the understanding of social change and development. It is also an invigorating critique of the explanations of social change put forward by M.N. Srinivas, Louis Dumont, etc. Singh has analysed Indian society in terms of what he now says: *caste, class and community* (2009). Both Srinivas and Dumont have seen caste as an ideational system, based on the principle of pure and impure and the hierarchy emanating from this framework. Caste is also class and power, a resource, and a means for mundane activities as well. Singh has provided constructive criticisms of both Srinivas and Dumont with his integrated approach to the study of social change.

Initially, Yogendra Singh published a couple of papers in the *Journal of Social Sciences* (1958; 1959a; 1960a; 1960b; 1961) started by the Institute of Social Sciences, Agra University, Agra. These and some other papers (1959b; 1959c; 1960c; 1960d) were based on the data collected for his Ph.D thesis from six villages of Uttar Pradesh. The main issues in these papers were related to land reforms and social tensions, factions, crime, social problems and caste stratification. These papers were written by Singh between 1958–1961, the period of his stay at the Agra University. Articles published by Singh in *Sociological Bulletin* (1964; 1968a; 1973a), *Seminar* (1965; 1967a; 1968a; 1970a), *Economic and Political Weekly* (1970b), *Contributions to Indian Sociology* (1970c), and *International Social Science Journal* (1979) made him quite known in the discipline throughout India. The publication of his *Modernization of Indian Tradition* has made an everlasting impact on both students and teachers. The articles written between 1961–1970 were outcome of his teaching and research at the University of Rajasthan. The manuscript for *Modernization of Indian Tradition* was written when Singh was on a sabbatical at the McGill University, Canada, in 1966–67, on the invitation of Alien D. Ross, an eminent sociologist. It is during this decade, Yogendra Singh shaped himself as a scholar, well-versed in sociological theory. His lectures reflected a sound grounding in philosophical roots of sociological theory – functionalism, Marxism, structuralism, phenomenology, critical theory, etc. He was particularly enchanted by Talcott Parsons and Robert K. Merton. He was equally knowledgeable about Karl Marx, Max Weber, Emile Durkheim, and British, German and French sociologies (Singh, 1989).

While discussing the scope and method of sociology in India, Yogendra Singh (1967b: 21) refers to five major theoretical orientations in Indian sociology, namely, (1) the comparative historical approach, (2) philosophico-sociological approach, (3) logico-philosophical approach, (4) structural-functional approach, and (5) statistical-positivistic approach. A brief description of these orientations as perceived by Yogendra Singh may be presented here. G.S. Ghurye is considered by Singh as the main architect of the comparative historical approach as he contributed to the studies of caste system, kinship, Indian aborigines, dynamics of aesthetics and costumes, Indian cities, rural India, comparative analysis of civilizations, Hindu knowledge system and values, etc. Ghurye made use of history and epics temporal dimension, pan-indic and linguistic-civilizational context, conceptual and analytical terms and concepts, and synthesis of indology and sociology. K.M. Kapadia, a student of Ghurye, carried forward Ghurye's comparative historical approach. However, another student of Ghurye, namely, A.R. Desai, has followed "materialistic-dialectical" model of analysis.

Radha Kamal Mukherjee is considered by Yogendra Singh as the chief advocate of the philosophical-sociological orientation. Singh writes: "In his (Radha Kamal Mukherjee) approach a synthesis between the symbolic-social and the existential bases of society has been attempted. Nature of man has been conceived as bio-social-spiritual, an arrangement of levels and hierarchies which also reflects into the multidimensional nature of society and its basic categories, such as norms and values. This renders the whole scheme of analysis modern yet rooted into the tradition with all its uniqueness" (ibid.: 22). Mukherjee has made use of morals, values, art, symbols, regional cultures, etc., in his theorization of Indian society. He has synthesized the instrumental or functional explanation with symbolic and hierarchical constructs. Thus, Mukherjee has transformed sociology into philosophy. He has provided a general theory of man and society, by interrelating place-work-folk.

Another variant of the philosophico-sociological approach is provided by D.P. Mukerji. Initially, Mukerji talked of a Hindu theory of man and society, but later on considered *tradition* and *sangh* (community) as the main source of the development of personality. Subsequent to this, Mukerji took a more analytical and dialectical approach to the study of Indian society and culture. Mukerji combined the Marxist approach with the dialectical and adaptive nature of Indian tradition. Yogendra Singh observes that unlike Radha Kamal Mukerjee's thinking, the works of D.P. Mukerji have been less architectonic, more analytically rigorous, and definitive in nature. He writes: "Both of them, however, reject reductionism, in sociological analysis, emphasise the study of tradition and take a traditional point of view. Both of them reject Talcott Parsons' general theory of action. However, theoretical contributions of both Radhakamal Mukerjee and D.P. Mukerji have largely remained ignored in contemporary sociological writings and teaching" (ibid.).

A.K. Saran also falls in the philosophico-sociological approach, who takes an anti-positivistic and traditionalistic view. The case of logico-philosophical theory of A.K. Saran offers a systematic treatment of tradition in general. Singh writes: "It (Saran's theory) draws from those sources of philosophico-religious writings which emphasise the transcendental unity of world religion, posits a religious or symbolic point of view of social system and human nature, and treats all contemporary traditions as deviations from the given path" (ibid.: 25). According to Singh, Saran's view offers little possibility of integration with other sociological approaches.

The structural-functional approach has focused on the studies of village community, religion, rituals, class, caste, power, communication and change. A large number of studies can be found in this category, drawing clues from both the British and the American structural-functional orientations. Yogendra Singh lists four features of the structural-functional approach as reflected in Indian sociological studies and analyses. These are: (1) social phenomena as a timeless system or subsystem, having an internal functional integration and composite character; (2) systematic analysis of interlinkages and reciprocal interactions of different aspects of society and culture; (3) analysis of change on the diffusionist model, rather than historical-dialectical; and (4) a rich tradition of scientific observation and depth analysis of social phenomena based on field studies.

Lastly, the statistical-positivistic approach is based on surveys, particularly to know economic and demographic structures and change therein. Yogendra Singh observes: "The study of sociological phenomena with the help of statistical techniques implies commitment to nominalism and atomism in regard to the nature of social reality, which has a narrowing influence in the frame of reference of sociological analysis" (ibid.). There are also a couple of studies which have laid emphasis on *indology*, unbounded/limitless units, internal and external dimensions of social reality, rejection of 'abstracted empiricism', and unique nature of Indian society.

Yogendra Singh's understanding of theoretical underpinnings and implications in Indian sociology is also reflected in another article (1967b: 165–83), in which he delineates the *sangh* or collectivity approach of Radha Kamal Mukerjee, interpretive approach of D.P. Mukerji, and subjective–interpretive analysis of R.N. Saxena and logico-philosophical theorization by A.K. Saran. Based on the writings of Louis Dumont, D.F. Pocock, F.G. Bailey and discussions held at the Mt. Abu seminar in 1965 on Sociology in India, Yogendra Singh outlines the following points:

1. the methodological multiplicity in the theory and practice of Indian sociology;

2. the deeper intellectual and methodological dependence of sociology in India on models and concepts devised in the West; and
3. the growing emphasis in the orientation of sociology towards the study of change and development with positivistic methods (ibid.: 171).

V

The foregoing description indicates about Yogendra Singh's interest and understanding of sociological theory in general and his ability to evaluate sociological writings in the 1950s and 1960s. Though Yogendra Singh gained recognition as a young scholar at the University of Rajasthan (1961–1970), his pathbreaking book *Modernization of Indian Tradition* created a scholastic departure in his academic trajectory as it reflected his enormous intellectual calibre and canvas to assimilate theory and facts, with reference to change and modernization in Indian society. This was the time when M.N. Srinivas reigned supreme in sociology and social anthropology at Delhi School of Economics, University of Delhi. Before this *magnum opus* was out in 1973, Yogendra Singh was already at JNU, New Delhi. The book provides a lucid analysis of both structural and cultural approaches to social change, and suggests, keeping in view the relevance and limitations of the two approaches, a paradigm for an integrated approach.

Modernization of Indian Tradition is a comprehensive treatise on social change, providing a vivid description of the concepts and approaches of social change in India. Singh finds 'modernization' as an all-inclusive concept. His ability to transform facts into concepts and to evaluate concepts in empirical contexts and situations is more than evident in *Modernization of Indian Tradition*. Singh's integrated approach brings out a holistic view of social change, in terms of heterogenetic and orthogenetic sources, cultural structure (little and great traditions) and social structure (micro and macro structures). Modernization and traditionalization are on two sides of social change – both cultural and structural. Yogendra Singh is being acknowledged as an architect of the concept of modernization, which is a useful paradigm for the study of Indian society.

VI

The success of the formulation of an assimilative approach to social change motivated Yogendra Singh to envision themes, such as "ideology, theory and methods in Indian sociology", "functional metaphor in Indian sociology", "the relevance of social sciences in India" and "the role of social sciences in India: sociology of knowledge" (2004). The two essays, entitled, "Ideology, theory and methods in Indian sociology" and "Functional metaphor in Indian sociology", Yogendra Singh says, "are treatments of the ideological, theoretical and methodological elements in the growth of Indian sociology" (ibid.: V). "These two essays deal with the patterns of theoretic differentiation in Indian sociology, its 'metaphoric' rather than formal character, and its evolution in methodological and normative directions" (ibid.: V-VI). He further writes: "The distinguishing feature of Indian sociology here turned out to rest in its essential historicity, its colonial heritage and its cognitive hiatus. It leaves its imprint on the main theoretic and operational choices of Indian sociologists. The ideology in Indian sociology is broadly defined in terms of this dialectic between historical and cognitive forces" (ibid.: VI).

Yogendra Singh has attempted a periodization of Indian sociology, which includes (1) 1952–1960; (2) 1960–1965; (3) 1965–1970; and (4) 1970–1977 (ibid.). These periods characterize adaptive changes and innovations, shifts in theoretic priorities and beginning of some critical tensions in theory and ideology of Indian sociology, a marked sociological self-awareness and growth of new directions in theoretical and substantive contributions, and a move towards a new maturity exploring new horizons of knowledge, respectively. However, Singh also observes that such a periodization does not show succession of paradigms as one moves from one period to another. Despite overlapping of themes in the four periods, and co-existence of competing paradigms and theoretic orientations, Singh outlines four main theoretic orientations, which are: (1) philosophical, (2) culturological, (3) structural, and (4) dialectical-historical (ibid.: 81).

As I have pointed out earlier that besides drawing upon the masters of sociology, such as Karl Marx, Max Weber, Emile Durkheim, Singh has also drawn extensively from the Indian masters, namely, G.S. Ghurye, Radha Kamal Mukerjee and D.P. Mukerji in formulation of his integrated approach to theory and ideology in Indian sociology. He has referred to the writings of M.N. Srinivas, André Béteille, Louis Dumont, A.M. Shah, along with others, quite often in his interpretation and analysis. But Srinivas, Béteille, Dumont and Shah have hardly referred to either Singh's *Modernization of Indian Tradition* or his "Essays on Ideology and Theory in Indian Sociology". It may be noted that the book *Modernization of Indian Tradition* by Singh is the most sought after treatise on social change in the Indian universities and colleges. S.C. Dube often used to speak very high of Yogendra Singh as a mastermind in sociological theory and methodology.

Since 1970s, Indian sociology has witnessed a multiplicity of discourses, ranging from being 'consensual' to 'dialectical-historical' to 'critical' and 'symbolic-phenomenological' orientations. Yogendra Singh has discussed these developments in the post-1970 period, in "Worldview of Sociology and the Challenge of Post-Modernity", and "Challenges of Globalization, Identity and Economic Development: An Indian Experience" (2004, op. cit.: 21–40; 221–236). Based on the related literature in the 1960s and 1970s, Yogendra Singh (1974a; op. cit.: 333–431) classifies approaches to social change into three broad heuristic categories: (1) evolutionary approaches; (2) cultural approaches: Sanskritization–Westernization; Little and Great Traditions, and Multiple Traditions; and (3) structural approaches: Differentiation and Mobility Analyses and Dialectical-Historical Approaches. Besides these broad approaches, Singh also describes significance of Cognitive Historical Approach and Institutional Approach (ibid.: 416–19).

Singh writes: "The formulation of a theory of social change is one of the most involved issues in contemporary sociology" (ibid.: 421). Seeing the multiplicity of conceptual schemes about social change, Singh observes that there are no theories of social change, what we have today are 'ideal types' and 'continua'. He writes: "There is urgent need, therefore, to study social change from a systematic and dialectical-historical frame of reference so that a truly diachronic study may be possible" (ibid.: 421). Singh also says: "A truly viable theory of change needs to go beyond comparison to the level of formulating general propositions based on time-bound logical set of variations in social phenomena" (ibid.: 421). A theory of social change needs to incorporate the concept of time both 'reversible' (mechanical) and 'irreversible" (evolutionary). To some extent, dialectical approach answers this need, as it incorporates time into the explanation of social change.

Social change is a prime theme in Yogendra Singh's writings (1993; 2000). Social change can be viewed as a response to a set of key challenges to the evolution of Indian society into a democratic nation-state. With such a meaning of social change, Yogendra Singh discusses the principles relating to a quality of life for its citizens, levels of social justice, economic security, and peaceful relationships and harmony among religious, ethnic and caste groups. Singh raises questions regarding development, nation-state, uneven outcomes, disintegration, crises and impediments in Indian society (1988a; 1988b; 1988c). He also deals with the emerging patterns of social stratification and mobility, reservation outcomes, and the emergence of a substantial middle class. He observes that a mix of success and failure of the development initiatives is creating problems for both legitimation and delegitimation of the existing institutions.

In the post-globalization era, Yogendra Singh has focused more on the significance of culture in the wake of globalization. New culture changes have occurred through the emergence of the information society. There is a resurgence of the consciousness of identity among ethnic groups, minorities and weaker sections of society. Globalization, telecommunication revolution and the emergence of market economy have affected local cultures as well as the regional and national cultures. Besides affecting culture, globalization has also effected change in education in general. New problems of cultural and symbolic domination, assertion of religious and ethnic identities, migration and diaspora, and cultural contradictions and rivalries have surfaced in the past two decades.

VII

Yogendra Singh has significantly contributed to the study of social stratification (1974b, op. cit.: 311–82; 1985, op. cit.: 37–79). The sociology of social stratification relates to the nature of social order, social equality and inequality, social justice, power and the nature of man. Further, Singh argues that social stratification is related to the questions of theory, structure and process. "The theory of social stratification implies a set of concepts, propositions and assumptions that are verified and validated and constitute an explanatory system" (ibid.: 311). There is also a theoretic divergence about the explanation of social stratification, namely, (a) based on functional significance, and (2) access to institutionalized power. Approaches to the study of social stratification, structural units and processes provide a complete picture of social stratification in any given society. With such an analytical framework, Yogendra Singh authored the first trend report on social stratification for the ICSSR (ibid.).

The second trend report on social stratification (1985, op. cit.: 37–79) is also authored by Yogendra Singh. Singh argues in the second report that the studies of social stratification were no longer confined to functional and dialectical approaches in the 1970s. There was global disenchantment in general, and an urge for new paradigms was evident in tilt towards phenomenology, Marxism, ethnomethodology and indigenization of concepts and approaches. Decline of 'positivism' and 'structural-functionalism' could be seen in the resurgence of the above approaches. For example, caste was increasingly seen as a system of exploitation and superordination rather than a functional division of society. Yogendra Singh categorizes the theoretic concerns in the studies of social stratification in the seventies as follows:

1. structural-functional;
2. structuralist;
3. structural-historical; and
4. historical materialist or Marxist.

A comprehensive review of the studies of social stratification was done based on the above categorization of theoretical approaches. Singh observes that theoretically the seventies mark some new orientations in studies of stratification and some innovations in methodology. He points out a process of (i) concretization of class–caste contradictions as a result of the emergent economic and political forces, and (ii) polarization of caste–class identities through the crystallization of the middle class–caste dominance in the rural society. These forces have sharpened the schism in the ideological consensus about the system of stratification (ibid.: 68).

It is not that Yogendra Singh has undermined or undervalued the significance of empirical studies. He has pointed out that the use of historical sources of data, analysis of the origin or evaluation of social stratification and study of caste system as a macro-structural phenomenon have been lacking in the field of social stratification (1986a: 325–28). He also observes that most of the studies were descriptive and reported microcosmic view of social reality. The issues of concept, ideology or method were not raised. Class analysis as a frame of reference remained almost ignored during the first four decades since India's independence. While presenting a comparative picture of theoretical and methodological orientations in the 1960s, 1970s and 1980s, Singh highlights that in the 1980s, the new orientations in the studies of social stratification were: (1) debate on the role of ideology in the paradigms of the studies of social stratification; (2) revival of historical and evolutionary perspectives; (3) emergence of dialectical paradigm as a new theoretical orientation; and (4) increasing concern about issues of relevance both from social and conceptual points of view in the studies of social stratification. These are analytical illustrations of the emerging issues in the studies of social stratification.

VIII

The range of themes covered by Yogendra Singh is quite broad, but transformation of facts into concepts and of the concepts into theories (theoretic formulations) remains as a constant feature in his studies, interpretations and analyses. His own studies of six villages in Uttar Pradesh (1958, op. cit.; 2009, op. cit.), and particularly of Chanukhera (1970a: 241–70), traditions of non-violence and peace (1968b; 1972a), academic role-structure and modernization (1972b), etc., are an example of the bearing of facts on theory and that of theory on facts. Theoretical constructs guide exploration of facts. This is evident from his study of teachers of the University of Rajasthan, way back in 1969–70. Singh writes: "Our assumption is that, in an empirical formulation of modernization, the nature of roles and role-structures could be derived from an analysis of interdependent variables which may be related to elements in the motivational structure (e.g., aspiration and morale), and the system of values (e.g., commitment, universalism, authoritarianism) relevant to modernization" (1972b, op. cit.: 196). This study of university teachers centres around the concept of role where its chief components are: (a) activities, (b) operative norms, and (c) fundamental values. Role-structures have been deduced rather than directly observed. The variables in role-structures are, namely, modernization, aspiration, commitment, morale, and authoritarianism. Here, Yogendra Singh not only engages himself in conceptualization and theorization, but he also applies, with precision, a statistical model, though without undermining the significance of a mechanical model, to the understanding of modernization in a formal academic setup. Yogendra Singh has also written on "Legal System, Legitimation and Social Change" (1978: 135–57), explaining significance of law as an agent of social change.

Yogendra Singh wrote on Indian sociology (1967b; 1984a; 1984b; 1984c; 2004), keeping in view ideology, theory and method in Indian writings ranging from 1950s till 1990s. However, an overview of Indian sociology from 1970–85 provided by Yogendra Singh, on the request of the Editor of *Current Sociology* and the *XI World Congress of Sociology*, under the title "On the Social Conditioning of Indian Sociology: The Perspective" (1986b), is the finest analysis of Indian sociology. Singh writes: "This overview of Indian sociology from 1970–85 has been undertaken to examine the extent to which theoretical and cognitive systems of sociology are socially conditioned" (ibid.: 97). A comprehensive analysis of the historical and social conditions has impinged upon the major conceptual schemes, theoretical preferences and substantive concerns. The question of *relevance*, in relation to epistemology, theory and the ideological formulation of the substantive areas of research, is a key in Singh's analysis of the dynamics of Indian sociology in the 1970s and 1980s (1984a; 1984b; 1984c). It is argued that the social and historical concerns of Indian society have led to a change from a structural-functional paradigm to critical theory, Marxism, structural-historical analysis, structuralism and ethnosociology. Covering just a period of one and half decades (1970–85) of Indian sociology, Yogendra Singh cites 659 articles and books, which, in turn, speaks of his liberal thinking and an inclusive approach to the understanding of Indian society. Sociologists from Delhi University, with the exception of M.S.A. Rao, have hardly taken a serious note of the contributions of Yogendra Singh and some of his colleagues at JNU. Singh's *Modernization of Indian Tradition* has been mentioned casually as one of many writings on the theme of modernization and his critique of the concept of 'sanskritization' (Deshpande, 2003; 2008: 172–99). André Béteille has rarely referred to Yogendra Singh's contributions to Indian sociology. He refers once Yogendra Singh's *Modernization of Indian Tradition* along with Milton Singer's *When a Great Tradition Modernizes* (1972) as having concern with both tradition and modernity. Singh has brought a collection of articles – *Essays on Modernization* (1978a) as well, in addition to *Modernization of Indian Tradition* (op. cit.).

On the contrary, I.P. Desai was not only enchanted with Yogendra Singh's writings and human qualities, he also co-authored an article with Singh on "Caste and Politics" (1967) in *Economic and Political Weekly*. A.R. Desai published a comprehensive article based on his study of six villages in Uttar Pradesh (1969) in his edited volume *Rural Sociology in India*. Yogendra Singh has co-authored with Ralph Dahrendorf et al., a book on *Social Aspects of Scientific and Technological Revolution* (1978). He has also co-authored another book *Sociology of Culture* (1991) with Boris Erasov. Professors K.M. Kapadia, M.S. Gore, Y.B. Damle and Dhirendra Narain had immense appreciation for Yogendra Singh as a scholar. Look at any writing of Yogendra Singh, one can find references of a large number of writings by M.N. Srinivas, André Béteille, A.M. Shah, Veena Das, etc. However, contrary to this is not seen. Let me make it clear that Yogendra Singh has never thought of citations of his writings, nor has he ever spoken about it. At JNU, he was considered as a highly respected teacher and a thinking and reflecting scholar. Students from other Centres and Schools would often attend his lectures on classical thinkers, namely, Karl Marx, Max Weber, Emile Durkheim, etc. His lectures were heard with rapt attention. He generally mesmerized the students. Every lecture was taken as a good dose of wisdom and excellence.

IX

Yogendra Singh's persisting quest for conceptualization and theorization is reflected in a recent paper (2009, op. cit.: 178–95) based on the observations of the village which he has been studying for more than half a century. Singh writes: "Thinking of the conceptual categories leads us to the notion of their power of explanation of the social processes and realities that a researcher has under observation" (ibid.: 179). The nature of methods and conceptual formulations employed in a given study grants the power of generalization to the findings. While justifying M.N. Srinivas' study of a single village (1996: 656), Yogendra Singh writes: "My observations about issues of praxis and conceptual categories are drawn from a single village study based on observation form 1955 to 2007" (2009; ibid.: 181). Social praxis is the major factor in the formulation of the conceptual categories such as *community, caste* and *class*. Singh writes: "Social praxis includes all forces, endogenous and exogenous to the system, that energise and activate the historical forces, structural contradictions, and movements within the system, generating pressure for change, both adaptive and entrepreneurial or innovative. Social praxis also includes deliberate intervention to bring about desired changes in the system through introduction and implementation of policies of planned social change and development. Conceptual categories and the process of concept formation at each period of historical transition in the social system have to take into consideration the changing faces of social reality.

This is a primary task of a social researcher. Concepts being abstractions from given realities, the changes that reality itself undergoes through time should meaningfully impinge upon concept formation. Even if the conceptual terms remain unchanged, the substantive changes in composition of its elements may necessitate rethinking about the concepts" (op. cit.: 183–84).

Yogendra Singh comments that several studies of villages in India portray continuity and change (Chauhan, 2009) focusing on the substantive domains of communities, castes and classes. Singh writes: "The issue of concept formation is not raised or, whenever sensitivity about it exists, the treatment is anchored in established theoretical models such as Marxism, structuralism or functionalism, or other variants" (ibid.: 184). Singh argues for the need to rethink about the conceptual categories of community, caste and class, based on the changes observed by him during 1955–2007 in Chanukhera. The historical forces have transformed the village into a multi-caste, multi-religious one, with new group dynamics, roles and traditions, involving community and caste.

X

B.K. Nagla (2008) opines that Singh is the main advocate of cultural approach in Indian sociology. Study of culture has been a constant attraction for Yogendra Singh (1973a, op. cit.; 2000, op. cit.; 2010, op. cit.). Singh discusses both the textual traditions and the varying social contexts. Both matter a lot in culture discourse. The two imply the structure of culture and processes of culture change. Singh writes: "Culture is not merely a normative construct as formalized by the 'texts' or a scripted and prescribed style of expression of the values, beliefs and aesthetic standards to which members are expected to conform. As a living reality, culture is grounded in the existential, ecological, social and political settings of the society. These forces continually impinge upon the 'scripted text' of culture, accord it the capacity of creative innovation and improvization, reform or even repudiation" (2010, op. cit.: 451). The concept of culture has four attributes as outlined by Yogendra Singh. These are: (1) normative principles and value-orientations of the people in a society; (2) mental, normative and behavioural patterns; (3) cultural relativism; and (4) manifest and latent levels (ibid.: 451).

For quite some time, Yogendra Singh has been focusing on linking culture and development (2000, op. cit.; 2009, op. cit.). In a paper (2010, op. cit.), Yogendra Singh analyses identity and development in the context of cultural discourse in India. According to Singh, all the salient cultural discourses have had their respective ideology of exclusion and inclusion. For example, the colonial discourse promoted both inclusionary identities and also on the contrary adopted policies promoting the identities of caste, religion, language and ethnicity. The reform movements promoted both inclusion and exclusion. The orthodox Muslim movements promoted inclusionary ideology of Islam. Singh writes: "Today, cultural nationalism ideology is confronted with several competing inclusionary cultural discourses, such as the Hindutva ideology, democracy–civil culture ideology and the ideological forces sponsored by globalization of economy, new processes of communication and culture" (2009: 460). Exclusion–inclusion are not simply due to religious divides. Economy, education, inequalities, domination and exploitation within a given religion also create exclusion–inclusion (Singh, 2007: 195–218).

XI

Influence of a scholar on his/her discipline is a matter of perception of the students, colleagues and peer group. Sometimes ideological moorings also play a significant role in the image-making of a teacher, particularly among the followers of a particular ideology. At times, even apparent value neutrality is encashed for gaining credibility. A.W. Gouldner (1973: 3–26) blamed Max Weber that the latter appropriated value neutrality/objectivity, in fact, to propagate a given ideology, may be to counter Marxist approach. Dipankar Gupta (2011) praises André Béteille for being an *anti-utopian* because he discusses the basic institutional requirements of democracy, and addresses questions of equality and development. Béteille often explains that he understands Marxism and its relevance, but he does not accept its orthodoxy.

In fact, Yogendra Singh is far more liberal and open in his approach to the study of Indian society. He has written with an ease on rural society, factions, crime, youth, caste, class, social stratification, change and modernization, nature and relevance of sociology, law, academic profession, theory and method in Indian sociology, cities, peace and non-violence, culture, globalization, etc. In most of his writings, transformation of facts into concepts and analytical categories and examination of concepts and theories for exploration of facts are clearly visible. Quoting Stanlislav Andreski (1972), we can say that there is no "manipulation through description" and "the smoke screen of jargon" in Yogendra Singh's writings. Also, there is no 'camouflage' or hidden agenda in the name of objectivity and methodology. There are certain norms and ideals which cannot be ignored while undertaking the advancement of knowledge. Every generation of knowledge creators encounter enemies who would not be kind to new ideas and frameworks. Overcoming of the stumbling blocs is the true test of a scholar. Yogendra Singh has been successful in freeing himself from dogmas as he has ably crossed both the substantive and theoretical bottlenecks as reflected in his writings on social stratification, culture, change, modernization, globalization and theory and method in Indian sociology.

Singh has truly considered "sociology as a skin trade", "a reflexive sociology", as John O'Neill (1972) rightly discusses on the intellectual status of a whole range of the scholars who have contributed to the shaping of sociology as a human science. Peter L. Berger draws a distinction between 'thinking' and 'reflecting' as the latter implies far more concern and creativity for understanding of human society. It would not be an exaggeration if Yogendra Singh is rated as a 'reflecting' social scientist, writing on Indian society for more than half a century. As a person, he is a thorough gentleman, well-mannered, unassuming and unpretentious. He would express even his dissenting opinion in a very polite way, and would always accept the 'consensus' view/decision. In this way, he is a true democrat. Most of these attributes of Yogendra Singh are evident in his scholarship.

References

Andreski, Stanlislav (1972) *Social Sciences as Sorcery*. Harmondsworth: Penguin Books.

Chaudhuri, Maitrayee (2011) "Looking Back: The Practice of Sociology in CSSS/JNU", in Sujata Patel (ed.), *Doing Sociology in India: Genealogies, Locations and Practices*, New Delhi: Oxford University Press, pp. 158–87.

Chauhan, B.R. (2009) *Rural Life: Grass Roots Perspective*. New Delhi: Concept Publishing Company.

Desai, I.P. and Yogendra Singh (1967) "Caste and Politics", *Economic and Political Weekly*, Vol. II, No. 17.

Deshpande, Satish (2003) *Contemporary India: A Sociological View*. New Delhi: Penguin Books.

—— (2008) "Modernization", in Veena Das (ed.), *Handbook of Indian Sociology* (Oxford paperbacks, Third impression), New Delhi: Oxford University Press, pp. 172–99.

Gouldner, Alwin W. (1973) *For Sociology, Renewal and Critique in Sociology Today*. Harmondsworth: Pelican Books.

Gupta, Dipankar (ed.) (2011) *Anti-Utopia: Essential Writings of Andre Beteille* (Oxford Indian paperbacks), New Delhi: Oxford University Press.

Mills, C.W. (1970) *Sociological Imagination*. Harmondsworth: Penguin Books.

Nagla, B.K. (2008) *Indian Sociological Thought*. Jaipur and New Delhi: Rawat Publications, pp. 239–65.

O'Neill, John (1972) *Sociology as a Skin Trade: Essays towards a Reflexive Sociology*. London: Heinemann.

Oommen, T.K. (2008) "Disjunctions between Field, Method and Concept: An Appraisal of M.N. Srinivas", *Sociological Bulletin*, Vol. 57, No. 1, pp. 60–81.

Shah, A.M. (2005) "Sanskritisation Revisited", *Sociological Bulletin*, Vol. 54, No. 2, pp. 238–49.

—— (2006) "Some Further Thoughts on Sanskritisation: Response to Nirmal Singh's Rejoinder", *Sociological Bulletin*, Vol. 51, No. 1, pp. 112–17.

—— (2008) "Violation of the Norms of Academic Discourse", *Sociological Bulletin*, Vol. 57, No. 2, pp. 388–402.

Sharma, K.L. (ed.) (1994) *Social Inequality in India: Essays in Honour of Professor Yogendra Singh*. Jaipur and New Delhi: Rawat Publications.

Singer, Milton (1972) *When a Great Tradition Modernizes*. New York: Praeger.

Singh, Nirmal (2006) "Some Comments on Revisited Sanskritisation", *Sociological Bulletin*, Vol. 55, No. 1, pp. 108–12.

Singh, Yogendra (1958) "Land Reform and Social Tensions in Villages", *Journal of Social Sciences*, Vol. I, No. 2, Institute of Social Sciences, Agra University, Agra.

—— (1959a) "Group Status of Factions in Rural Community", *Journal of Social Sciences*, Vol. II, No. 1, Institute of Social Sciences, Agra University, Agra.

—— (1959b) 'Institutional Factors in Land Reform Policy', paper presented at 42nd Annual Conference of Indian Economic Association, and published in Conference Number of the *Journal of Indian Economic Association*.

—— (1959c) 'Role of Sociology in Planning', paper presented at the Social Planning Seminar, organized by the Institute of Social Sciences, Agra University, Agra, and published in *Journal of Social Sciences Supplement*, Institute of Social Sciences, Agra University, Agra.

— (1960a) "Social Change and Social Problems: A Study of Crime in Six Villages of UP", *Journal of Social Sciences*, Vol. II, No. 2, Institute of Social Sciences, Agra University, Agra.

— (1960b) "Youth Problem and Welfare: A Sociological Approach", *Economic and Political Weekly*, Vol. XII, No. 45.

— (1960c) "Development of Caste Consciousness in Indian Children from 4 to 10" (with S.D. Singh and K. Singh), *Journal of Research (Letters)*, Vol. VIII, Part 1, Agra University, Agra.

— (1960d) "Role of Sociology in Planning", *Journal of Social Sciences Supplement*, Institute of Social Sciences, Agra University, Agra.

— (1961) "Changing Caste Stratification and Problem of Integration of Indian Society", *Journal of Social Sciences Supplement*, Institute of Social Sciences, Agra University, Agra.

— (1964) "Cultural Integration and Changing Values", *Sociological Bulletin*, Vol. XIII, No. 2.

— (1965a) 'Disciplinary Growth of Sociology and its Teaching in India', Sociology in India, *Seminar*, Vol. 109.

— (1965b) "Traditional Culture Pattern of India and Industrial Change", in A.B. Shah and C.R.M. Rao (eds.), *Tradition and Modernity in India*, Bombay: P.C. Manaktala & Sons Pvt. Ltd.

— (1965c) *Towards a Sociology of Culture in India*. With T.K.N. Unnithan et al. (eds.), New Delhi: Prentice Hall of India.

— (1966) Jaipur City: A Study of Selected Sociological and Economic Aspects, Vol. I, Jaipur City, Vol. II, Ajmer City and Vol. III, Kota City (mimeographed), jointly with T.K.N. Unnithan.

— (1967a) "The Scope and Method of Sociology in India", in T.K.N. Unnithan et al. (eds.), *Sociology for India*, New Delhi: Prentice Hall of India.

— (1967b) *Sociology for India*. With T.K.N. Unnithan et al. (eds.), New Delhi: Prentice Hall of India.

— (1968a) "Caste and Class: Some Aspects of Continuity and Change", *Sociological Bulletin*, Vol. XVII, No. 2.

— (1968b) *Sociology of Non-violence and Peace*. Co-author with T.K.N. Unnithan, New Delhi: Council for Social Development.

— (1968c) 'Academic Colonialism: Sociological Issues', *Seminar*, 112.

— (1968d) "The Class Structure and Political Processes in Village India", in M.V. Mathur and Iqbal Narain (eds.), *Panchayati Raj, Planning and Democracy*, New Delhi: Asia Publishing House.

— (1969) "The Changing Power Structure of Village Community: A Case Study of Six Villages in Eastern U.P.", in A.R. Desai (ed.), *Rural Sociology in India* (4th revised edition), Bombay: Popular Prakashan, pp. 711–23.

— (1970a) 'Modernisation: Political Aspects', *Seminar*, April.

— (1970b) "Indian Council of Social Science Research: Its Promise and Dilemmas", *Economic and Political Weekly*, Vol. V, No. 16.

— (1970c) "For a Sociology of India", *Contributions to Indian Sociology*, Vol. 15, No. 4.

— (1970d) "Chanukhera: Cultural Change in Eastern Uttar Pradesh", in K. Ishwaran (ed.), *Change and Continuity in India's Villages*, New York: Columbia University Press, pp. 241–70.

—— (1972a) "Academic Role Structure and Modernisation", in Satish Saberwal (ed.), *Beyond Village*, Simla: Indian Institute of Advanced Study.

—— (1972b) *Traditions of Non-Violence*. Co-author with T.K.N. Unnithan, New Delhi: Heinemann.

—— (1973a) *Modernization of Indian Tradition*. New Delhi: Thompson Press.

—— (1973b) "The Role of Social Sciences in India: A Sociology of Knowledge", *Sociological Bulletin*, Vol. 22, No. 1.

—— (1974a) "Sociology of Social Stratification", in *A Survey of Research in Sociology and Social Anthropology*, Vol. I (ICSSR), Bombay: Popular Prakashan, pp. 311–82.

—— (1974b) "Concepts and Theories of Social Change", in *Research in Sociology and Social Anthropology*, Vol. I (ICSSR), Bombay: Popular Prakashan, pp. 383–431.

—— (1975) "Process of Socialisation and Education", in I.P. Desai and M.S. Gore (eds.), *Sociology of Education in India* (reprint), New Delhi: NCERT.

—— (1977) "Ideology, Theory and Method in Indian Sociology", in Stein Rokkan (ed.), *A Quarter Century of International Social Science: Papers and Reports on Developments, 1952–77*, New Delhi: Concept.

—— (1978a) *Essays on Modernization*. New Delhi: Manohar Publications.

—— (1978b) *Social Stratification and Social Change in India*. New Delhi: Manohar Publications.

—— (1978c) *Social Aspects of Scientific and Technological Revolution*. Co-author with Ralph Dahrendorf et al., London: Sage.

—— (1979) "Constraints, Contradictions and Interdisciplinary Orientations: The Indian Context", *International Social Science Journal*, Vol. XXXI, No. 1.

—— (1984a) "Relevant Sociology (I): Conceptual Issues", *Relevant Sociology*, Vol. 1, No. 1.

—— (1984b) "Relevant Sociology (II): Conceptual Issues", *Relevant Sociology*, Vol. 1, No. 2.

—— (1984c) *Image of Man: Ideology and Theory in Indian Sociology*. New Delhi: Chanakya Publications.

—— (1985) "Sociology of Social Stratification", in *Survey of Research in Sociology and Social Anthropology, 1969–1979 (ICSSR)*, New Delhi: Satvahan Publications, pp. 37–79.

—— (1986a) "Some Emerging Issues in the Indian Sociology of Social Stratification", in K.L. Sharma (ed.), *Social Stratification in India*, Delhi: Manohar Publications.

—— (1986b) *Indian Sociology: Social Conditioning and Emerging Concerns*. New Delhi: Vistaar Publications. Earlier this was published in *Current Sociology* as mentioned in the text.

—— (1986c) "Law and Social Change in India: A Sociological Perspective", *Relevant Sociology*, Vol. III, Nos. 1–2, April-October.

—— (1988a) "Quest for Relevance: Teaching and Research in Sociology", *Indian Journal of Social Sciences*, Vol. I, No. 1.

—— (1988b) "Literature and Social Change: A Sociological Perspective", *New Horizon (ICCR)*, New Delhi.

—— (1988c) 'Social Process and Dimensions of Indian Nationalism' (I.P. Desai Memorial Lecture), Surat: Centre for Social Studies.

—— (1989) "Relevance of Max Weber for the Understanding of Indian Reality", in Krishna Bhardwaj and Sudipto Kaviraj (eds.), *Perspectives on Capitalism: Marx, Keynes, Schumpeter and Weber*, New Delhi: Sage.

—— (1990) "Country-Town Nexus: Social Transformation in Contemporary Indian Society", in K.L. Sharma and Dipankar Gupta (eds.), *Country-Town Nexus*, Jaipur: Rawat Publications.

—— (1991) *The Sociology of Culture*. Co-author with Boris Erasov, Moscow: Progress Publishers.

—— (1993) *Social Change in India: Crisis and Resilience*. New Delhi: Har-Anand Publications.

—— (2000) *Culture Change in India: Identity and Globalization*. Jaipur and New Delhi: Rawat Publications.

—— (2004) *Ideology and Theory in Indian Sociology*. Jaipur and New Delhi: Rawat Publications.

—— (2007) "Composite Culture, Community and Identity: Interface with Social Change in India", in Bipan Chandra and Sucheta Mahajan (eds.), *Composite Culture in a Multicultural Society*, New Delhi: Pearson/Longman, pp. 195–218.

—— (2009) "Social Praxis, Conceptual Categories and Social Change: Observations from a Village Study", *Sociological Bulletin*, Vol. 58, No. 2, pp. 178–95.

—— (2010) "Cultural Discourse in India: Identity and Development", in Yogendra Singh (ed.), *Social Sciences: Communication, Anthropology and Sociology*, Vol. XIV, Part 2, Delhi: Pearson/Longman, pp. 451–62.

Singhi, N.K. (ed.) (1996) *Theory and Ideology in Indian Sociology: Essays in Honour of Professor Yogendra Singh*. Jaipur: Rawat Publications.

Srinivas, M.N. (1996) "Indian Anthropology and the Study of Indian Culture", *Economic and Political Weekly*, Vol. 42, No. 44.

2

Transforming Sociology

A Modern Discipline Encounters Globalization

Devorah Kalekin-Fishman

The point of departure for this paper is "the difficult problem of the relationship between globality (or globalities) and modernity (or modernities)" (Robertson and White, 2005: 345–46). But it is important, to my mind, to note that an even more difficult problem underlies this one. While, as Robertson and White insist, there are issues related to globalization that only sociology can deal with, sociologists' awareness of globalization as a phenomenon arises from patently modern evidence. 'Things' do not fit well into the grids that block out modern life. Because of a pervasive feeling that life is changing, 'the modern' is giving way to 'the global' and part of the process is the development of a kind of industry of description and explanation. Throughout this paper I will take seriously the assertion that globalization signals a transformation of the world we live in, and that as part of the rush of a globalizing world, sociology, too, is undergoing a transformation. What I will do here is to sketch the principles that I think have to underlie this kind of analysis. I will begin by marshalling evidence that sociology is indeed a discipline of modernity. Then I will point out contemporary developments in sociology, which indicate how sociology is being transformed by globality.

Sociology as a Modern Science

Referring to the many discussions of the modern, Canclini (1995: 11, Note 3) reminds us that the morph 'modern' is treated in the social sciences in at least three different ways. *Modernity* is the term used to define a stage in history; *modernization* is the term for describing and explaining the socio-economic processes that lead to the construction of modernity as a historical stage with identifiable characteristics; and *modernism(s)* is the term for cultural projects that renew symbolic practices with an experimental or critical sense. Recognized as a scientific endeavour that emerged in at a particular historical time, *modernity* in sociology was established in order to describe and analyse society in ways that contrast with the kinds of social thought which came before. Its most important self-appointed task was to describe and explain socio-technical processes of *modernization*. Moreover, the forms of sociological research and writing are an expression of *modernism*. This is seen in the types of descriptions and explanations considered convincing – being publicized – canonized – awarded prizes. In the following, I will point out how sociology ties in with each of these aspects.

Modernity

According to Habermas (2007; 1980: 364), there have been proclamations of modernity throughout history but, until the 19th century, these were always declarations of differences with a normative tradition which soon reasserted itself. It remained for Romanticism, in his view, to produce "a radicalized consciousness of modernity that detached itself from all previous historical connections and understood itself solely in abstract opposition to tradition and history *as a whole*" (emphasis mine). Evidence of this position is to be found throughout the literature of sociology, where 'modernity' is consistently discussed as a fixed historical period. There is extensive theorizing about the characteristics of the modern; about whether modernity is past or passing; about whether it has been succeeded or preceded by a period of postmodernity (Jameson, 1991; Lyotard, 1989) or whether it is enjoying resuscitation as a second, or late modernity (Beck, 1992). While Jameson (1991) pointed out that a sense of 'ending', not merely chronological, indicates that modernity is giving way to postmodernity; Habermas (2007/1980) sees modernity as an unfinished project; and Latour (1993) argues that the modernity understood as a collection of well-defined qualities, has not yet been experienced at all. Giddens (1990) accepts modernity as a definition of the times, which are characterized by choices among conflicting dualities. In his optimistic view, these clashes can be resolved by the exercise of agency. Bauman (1992: 54), on the other hand, who claims that 'sociology emerged to theorize and service modernity' highlights the negative aspects of modernity, pointing out that the very conditions generated in modernity made the Holocaust possible. In the wider sense, these conditions have, to his mind, kept humankind from learning how catastrophes are caused when the state's political power overwhelms social and economic controls (Bauman, 1989: 217–18).

The very identification of a given historical period as that of modernity is an assertion of ascendancy in both a moral and a cognitive sense. Canclini (1995: 12) illustrates this conviction of pre-eminence when he cites "four basic movements that constitute modernity", namely, the *emancipating* project in which there is a "secularization of cultural fields" and the development of individualism; the *expansive* project, which focuses on the augmentation of knowledge through scientific endeavours and the increase of control of 'nature' through industrialization; the *renovating* project which undertakes to renew values in a world that is "liberated from all sacred prescription," and the *democratizing* project that is based on the spread of education and access to high culture. In the course of the development of these projects, the non-modern is relegated to a lesser position as 'traditional' dedication to 'popular' knowledge and popular arts, while the people who partake of the traditional and the popular are the 'subalterns' (Canclini, 1995: 145). Echoing the position that modernity is the realization of the Enlightenment project (see, e.g., Habermas, 2007/1980: 363), the founders of the sociological canon in Europe shared a world view which marked their enterprise as modern even though they asked different questions. All the projects explicated by Canclini are to be found in the sociology that was brought to a high point of development in the 19th and 20th centuries. On examination, it is clear that the work of sociologists exemplifies the principles and the norms that are attributed to modernity (see below).

Modernism

Sociological writings about the modern are, moreover, a form of modernism, "a cultural project that renews symbolic practices with an experimental or critical sense" (Canclini, 1995: 11). In defending a positivistic social science, Comte (2000/1855) already spelled out arguments about the ends of sociological practice that have coloured the pursuit of the modern as we know it and its description by Berlin (2006) more than 150 years later. The principles adopted, that (1) it is possible to find a single true answer to all valid questions related to value and fact; (2) it is possible to know the answers to such questions; and (3) together the answers contribute to a balanced understanding of the whole. Furthermore, Comte took it for granted that "Moderns (can) detach themselves from the Universe in order to examine it, probe it, penetrate it, fathom it, see of what it is made, understand how it works, explain it, control it, use it, and exploit it" (Howe, 1994: 514–15). With these conceptions of disciplined control and improvement through change, sociology was distinguished from the first by its normative orientation toward furthering the 'good life' in the modern sense. Sociological theorization took for granted the possibility of *emancipation* and *democratization* and their potential to enable lives where every individual is involved in an improving world.

Part of the search for emancipation and democratization was translated into an emphasis on 'doing the right thing', an idea that penetrated sociology in the form of a belief in doctrinaire methodology as the sine qua non for enabling viable research. It was understood that as a scientist, the sociologist could step outside the web of the social to observe developments neutrally and objectively, deploying honed concepts, asking the kinds of questions that signalled a distinct field of study and its capacity to achieve accurate prediction. The fruits of the sociologist's labour could then present a model for a liberated and democratic way of life, a way of life suitable to modernity. Building on the conception that science could contribute to human progress thanks to the careful management of observation and the cautious accumulation of data, Durkheim and Weber laid down principles that provided the foundation for the full flowering of sociology as a modernist endeavour in this sense. As part of the defense of sociology, but also as a clarification of the new discipline, Durkheim's (1964/1938) *Rules of the Sociological Method* grounded his conviction that an understanding of social phenomena as 'facts' required that they be observed statistically and analysed according to principles of statistical reasoning. By contrast, Weber (1968) emphasized that the point of departure for sociological analysis was the crystallization of an ideal type of any given social phenomenon. Comparing the unique qualities of each concrete appearance with the ideal type the researcher could come to conclusions about how and to what extent reality deviated from the researchers' idea. Harriet

Martineau, who translated Comte's books, dedicated herself to activist writings as well, but also felt it necessary to codify the rules that governed her systematic observations when she published analyses of the societies she encountered in her travels (e.g., Martineau, 1838, 2000/1838).

The extraordinary development of methodology reinforced the model of the sociologist as a modern – a neutral scientist in full control of the subject matter. Even more important, this literature underlined the unexamined and certainly unquestioned assumption that the world was an orderly collection of phenomena which could be described, analysed, and manipulated comprehensively. By following a well-defined methodology, every researcher would be capable of reaching unalloyed truths. Moreover, such truths could be communicated to researchers who would develop the science further, but also to laypersons who would benefit from applying their implications in their daily lives. In other words, a disciplined methodology could fulfil an expansive project: that of contributing to the enrichment of sociological knowledge, and also to achieving the moral goals sanctioned by the very existence of sociology as a discipline.

Modernization

Crystallizing a conception of how the world was changing meant applying neat methods for shedding light on the causes and ramified consequences of *modernization*. Guided by axiomatic values, sociologists bore witness to modernization as the realization of progress and the promise of further progress.

It is worthwhile in this connection to recall how central questions raised in the 19th century led sociologists in different directions. Dedicated above all to the *renovation* of social thought, Comte (2001/1855) and Spencer (1899) outlined their grasp of what constitutes a society and proceeded to ask about group formations and what kinds of 'mentalities' inspired them. Basing his analysis of the relations between religion and politics on his theory that mankind necessarily was progressing from eras where theological and later metaphysical reasoning prevailed, Comte deduced that humanity was now entering upon a 'positive' era in which rationality was configuring human action. Spencer, who conceived of evolution as the underlying logic of the physical world and of biological organisms as well as of culture and society relied on reports of travelers and missionaries. He interpreted human action and human mentality as gradually evolving phenomena.

Holding to positions as disinterested observers, Durkheim, Weber and Marx (still a canonical triumvirate) each combined questions about sociology as a science with questions about industrialization, the presumed objective core of the social changes they were witnessing. On the assumption that society existed thanks to forces of voluntary association, Durkheim (1895) studied social domains separately as evidence that sociology was indeed a science. He systematically looked at how groups dealt with the mental through religion, how a society ensures its continuity as well as the domains of law and education. But, the object of the differentiation was, of course, to study modernization by examining industrialization. In Durkheim's view, industrialization was providing a general basis for a new kind of 'organic' solidarity. Like the industrial plant where each worker is responsible for a single task that contributes to the production of the whole, the modernized society would be characterized by ties of mutual dependence, which were, to his mind, creating a new kind of 'shared consciousness'.

Although Marx's analyses derived from a sensitivity to the trials induced by industrialization, he conceived his task as a sociologist as a clarification of the principles underlying the economic framework in which these trials were embedded. In his search for an objective model of capitalist production as the key to an understanding of modernization, he examined how relationships between groups govern movements of prices and profits and derived an understanding of how capitalism develops and sows its own downfall. Taking his cue from a perception that conglomerates of individuals initiate societies, Weber proposed that it was necessary to understand the subjectively adequate motivations that impelled individuals to participate in groups. In Weber's view, motivations of different kinds made for the differentiation of institutions in the comprehensive social structure. In his search for the causes of the emergence of modern society, Weber (1963; 2002) examined correlations of industrialization and religious affiliation from a long range historical perspective, with an emphasis on the kinds of motivations different religions fostered. A related conception of how science expands was Simmel's search to establish a 'formal' sociology, a science based on models which could be applied to different domains. Focusing on the forms of human relations in daily life that were a consequence of industrialization, Simmel examined the nature of individual experiences of love and friendship, but also of estrangement, and the peculiar interactions that develop around the use of money (see Wolf, 1950).

Reviewing the work of Europeans from Spencer to Ratzenhofer and including discussions of the work noted above, Albion Small (1905) wrote a "syllabus", a textbook of *General Sociology* for American students with the express aim of helping them understand modernization. His goals were all in tune with what has come to be called the project of modernity. Small's ambition was to show that sociology as a science, albeit divided into separate domains, could be viewed as a unified science. In line with modern ways of thinking, he emphasized that sociology covered an area of study broad enough to include all aspects of group living, yet could not be accused of poaching on the domains of economics, history, theology, or even anthropology. Moreover, looking at modernization as a comprehensive set of processes attendant on human association, he defined the task of sociologists as that of studying process. Furthermore, while 'structures' might be interpreted as the stable aspects of the social, Small emphasized that in-depth analyses of the substance of structures lead to an explication of 'structure', too, as a complex of 'processes'.

Small followed the lead of the 19th century Europeans credited with marking the initiation of sociology as a science. They all approached the object of their interest as social developments during a particular stage of history – modernity; they examined the processes of modernization that marked their era; and they were careful to deploy clear-cut methods that bespoke the promise of modernity as a rationalist project. Yet, despite the shared principles of their approaches, and despite the fact that European sociologists were presumably all witnessing similar phenomena, their interpretations of what was impelling those processes were widely different. The trend toward differentiation can be traced in developments of sociology throughout the 20th century as well. Sociologists associated with the western canon of the 20th century showed that the pursuit of rationality and truth could take different forms.

Further Developments

After World War I, sociology was pursued in different ways in several central US academic institutions with each group of researchers and theorists intent on a rational organization of sociological knowledge. At Harvard, in the traditionally intellectual city of Boston, Parsons, involved in transporting sociology's theoretical heritage from Europe to the US, emphasized the emancipating project of modernity, elaborating on the symbolic possibilities of secularization. His goal was to work out a theory of the configuration of structures needed to support a society and to demonstrate the compatibility of social action within that configuration. To this end he devised clear-cut questions and provided models of dichotomous concepts with which it would be possible to propose unambiguous answers. While Parsons was busy almost exclusively with theoretical issues, research institutes at Columbia University in New York City were exploring another path toward building a science. There, in the 1940s, sociologists were establishing their authority as researchers who, by means of targeted questions, could use a minimum of theoretical baggage to derive useful measures with predictive power. Funded by the federal government, Stouffer's International Institute of Social Science focused on augmenting knowledge and extending control over groups through studying responses from soldiers during World War II. Exemplifying the type of sociology that would later be legitimated by Merton's (1957) vision of 'middle range theory', Lazarsfeld and his group in the Bureau for Applied Social Research, were oriented to public opinion research, including market research. The projects they undertook were distinguished by ongoing elaboration and re-elaboration of the questionnaire as a subtle instrument for testing hypotheses about a limited number of variables. Lazarsfeld's genius was realized in the range of approaches to data analysis, among them innovations such as "reason analysis, programme analysis, panel analysis, survey analysis, elaboration formula, latent structure analysis, mathematical sociology (especially the algebra of dichotomous systems), contextual analysis" (Lazersfeld et al., 1948; Lazersfeld and Barton, 1955; Jeřábek, 2001). In 1997, Abbott (1997) launched a detailed deprecatory critique of the 'variable paradigm' initiated at Columbia. For Hynek Jeřábek (2001), who speaks for many sociologists, however, Lazarsfeld deserves recognition as the 'founder of modern empirical sociology'. From the first, this paradigm had widespread influence. At the time, even though he criticized Lazarsfeld's empiricism (Jeřábek, 2001), Adorno adopted many of the techniques. When he moved to California, Adorno led a team that attempted to explain the attractions of Nazism based on questionnaire research that operationalized theoretically-informed hypotheses (Adorno et al., 1960).[1]

In Chicago, on the other hand, the Department of Sociology had an agenda that was quite different from those of Harvard and of Columbia. Extrapolating from the interpretations of Albion Small, head of the department for twenty years, most of the research was concerned with social process as an interplay of conflicting interests, which must be seen as social forms brought into complex contextual interrelation (Small, 1905). Substantively, sociologists at the University of Chicago followed the lead of Simmel's formal sociology and located analytical phenomena in urban life by examining groups particularistically. The idea was to seek out social types, carry out ethnographic observations, and analyse how they fitted into social structure. Implicit in their work was the modernity project of emancipation as this approach to sociology in effect broadened and deepened the 'muckraking' project of the beginning of the 20th century in which journalists deliberately undertook to improve the evolving American society. At that time, Lincoln Steffens (1987/1957) and Upton Sinclair (1906) wrote extensively about the immorality and corruption of big business and public institutions. Inheriting their fervour, sociologists such as Anderson (1928) studied homeless men, Cressey (1932) studied the exploitation of women in night clubs in the city, and Shaw (1966/1930) studied juvenile delinquents. They intentionally took on the task of describing and analysing recognized social problems in contextual detail so as to lay the basis for reforms (Barley, 1989).

In general US sociology developed a characteristic division of labour between the empiricist (who does research – preferably with questionnaires) and the theorist (who comments reflectively). By contrast with the variety of developments in US sociology, European sociologists sought legitimation for social sciences in different ways. Moreover, the departmentalization of theory and research does not hold in France or in Germany (Broady, 1996). Typical of the integrative perspective among French sociologists, is the work of Bourdieu who throughout his career based his theorizing on extensive research (Bourdieu, 1977; 1984; Bourdieu and Passeron, 1990). Similarly, Touraine (1988; 1996) theorized sociology as a science that demanded active participation of the objects of its research. To some extent this was also true of sociology in England (see Bell and Roberts, 1984)

In Germany, on the other hand, sociologists tended to focus on developing viable theory by constant reference to philosophical clarification (Meja et al., 1987). True, some sociologists went on in the direction of Lazarsfeld's empiricism (Jahoda et al., 1933), theorization flourished as the heart of the discipline's development. After his return to Germany, Adorno dedicated his research to analyses of cultural phenomena, especially music, and to the development of what has come to be called 'critical theory'. In a head on collision between theorists in Germany, the 'Postivismusstreit', Popper and Adorno (1969), each interpreting the meaning of 'criticism' differently, both contended that they were following a critical tradition in philosophy. Popper defended a social science which makes clear distinctions, develops hypotheses, and examines the claims of its findings by deploying formal logic. In his view, even though the truth cannot be grasped as a whole, the rules of logic enable sociologists to discover the failings of their researches and to ensure that they are constantly moving in the direction of true conclusions. By contrast with the reliance of logical positivists on verification, Popper insisted that it was possible to estimate how close to the truth outcomes are even though absolute truth is unattainable. Like the natural scientist, the social scientist starts from a problem, clarifies the differences between scientific and lay interests in contending with the problem, goes on to a critical examination of the question, consulting texts and colleagues, and with the aid of the laws of logic can check and re-check to see whether the hypotheses underlying the research can be falsified. Adorno et al. (1960) response, on the other hand, signalled a provisional denial of objectivity in the 'modern' sense. He rejected both strict distinctions and mathematical logic as tools for approaching any truth about society. In his view, social life is riddled with contradictions and facts elicited about it can never follow the rules of formal logic. Beyond this, it is necessary to study particularities in context, keeping in mind their relation to the general. Adorno's critical sociology is a sociology that insists on dialectical analyses, rather than on what he saw as the chimera of 'clarification'.

Although the Positivismusstreit (the positivism dispute) was aired more than 45 years ago, it can still be seen as belonging to the efforts of sociologists to find ways of coping with the discovery that the world that sociology examines is/was undergoing changes at an unexpected pace. On the one hand, modernism in sociology is evidenced by sociologists creating a language designed to make the social world transparently objective. In order to do this, sociological research ranged from examinations of phenomena designated as different levels of the social (macro-, meso-, micro-). Some found it necessary to resort to descriptions of the subjective world. But the four tasks of modernity that Canclini (1995) discusses all seduce sociologists into the trap of relying on the normative criteria embedded in what Habermas (2007/1980) calls 'the project of modernity'. Among others, the globalizing world seems to be evading efforts at making it transparent and challenges the possibility of objectivity.

A persistent bias of sociology as it developed in the 20th century is the understanding that ultimately it will be possible to systematize all the knowledge about the social that can be gathered. This was bolstered by an emphasis on methodology seen as a mode of neutralizing the non-rational qualities of the researcher as a person. Further means toward the end of compiling neutral social knowledge are prevailing prescriptions for choosing topics that can be formalized in hypotheses; and for deducing hypotheses from theory. These precepts fit in with the projects typical of modernism noted by Canclini: the projects of expanding knowledge through scientific endeavour, of emancipation, of the secularization of cultural fields, among them science. Beyond this, findings in the form of description and explanation are framed in articles and reports that compete for preservation as part of the sociological culture, in publications that serve as materials for distribution in the framework of the project of education.

From Modernity to Globalization

This sketch of disciplinary enclaves has pointed up the nature of sociology as a quintessentially modern undertaking, part of a project of finding out how industrialization was changing the way people in the 'West' lived. It is not by chance that the sketch is limited to how sociology was practised in a few limited milieus. With Africa, Latin America, and most of Asia neatly ruled by colonial powers in Europe (mostly the United Kingdom) and the United States, academic disciplines could be defined and outlined by the interests and the points of view of people who saw the world from the standpoint of the colonizing powers. Only the shifting sands of history could upset the conceptualization of the colonial natives as 'others' and the exclusivity of the sociological canon.

World War II led to a comprehensive re-division of the map of the world. Through a series of convulsive events, countries in Asia and Africa managed to attain self-determination and, at least nominally, freedom from the yokes of European colonist states. The Monroe doctrine, which had ensured US hegemony over Latin America since the 1820s was vigorously contested. Political upheavals reflected an ongoing reorganization of production, commerce and finances. Newly independent political units found themselves embroiled in contests for attaining a viable economic foundation as well as in struggles to establish national identities. Displaced people – moving in amorphous spaces in search of a place to stay and call home – threatened homogeneous identities in territories outlined by concise borders. The world market became a fact rather than an aspiration. The constant intensification of the flows of goods in that market, of financial arrangements via the global cities (Sassen, 2005), of people constantly in search, signals an era in which the fact of globalization cannot be ignored.

After all, throughout the 20th century, 'social change' has been taken for granted as a central concern of sociology with sociologists seeking ways to explain change in exhaustive ways as befits modern social scientists. In the final decades the change was given a name – 'globalization'. Just as did the 'fathers of sociology' of the 19th century, late 20th century and early 21st century sociologists are approaching the perceived massive political, economic, and cultural changes in different ways: among them new readings of modernity and its various versions, puzzling out the long-term implications of colonialism, descriptions of world systems, and the potential of globalization for differentiation. There is no possibility of sociology being able to rest on its laurels so to speak. All social phenomena – including the social sciences – are embedded in history and all the shifts that characterize a globalizing era, in the domains of the economy, international relations, politics or religion, require that sociologists reconsider the boundaries of their discipline. Yet finding descriptive and analytical tools for dealing with the subtleties of globalization has proved a daunting task. Indeed, sociologists are highly conscious of the limitations of their science.

Outgrowth of Modernistic Approaches

In an attempt to explain how non-western societies have developed during recent centuries, Eisenstadt (2004: 16) introduced the concept of 'multiple modernities', an insight based on the point that it is possible to "distinguish analytically between the structural dimension, especially the trends to structural differentiation – and the cultural dimensions ..." Hence, while throughout the world, it is possible to classify as modern all the societies in which structural modernization can be detected, phenomena that are culturally dominant will colour the way modernity is played out in each society. By insisting on emphasizing culture as an autonomous sphere influencing human action, Eisenstadt manages to preserve the notion that 'modernity' is an inevitable outcome of social evolution and thus, globalization is no more than an intensification of the structural trends of modernity.

Eisenstadt is not alone in insisting that modernity is ongoing and far from exhausted. Beck (1992, 1996) sees the increasing emphasis on individualization as a sign of the intensification of modernity and is developing research projects to investigate cosmopolitanism, an approach to the social which, he insists is imposed by the unforeseen outcomes of choices made in modernity. Giddens (1990) salvages an understanding of the era as 'late modernity', characterized first and foremost by reflexivity in the sense of a general re-vision of social process and of social structures that is imposed by the constant increment of information.

Emphasizing continuities, but over a much longer term, is the theory of world systems developed by Wallerstein (1974–89) who moves globalization forward to cover modernity so to speak. His Marxian-informed analyses trace the groundwork of global relations from the 16th century onward. But Wallerstein, too, accepts the notion that the object of his analysis is the '*modern* world system'. Moreover, with his description of the crisis that he perceives as having come to a head in the second part of the 20th century, he finds it necessary to describe what is happening by resorting to using modern terms, sharply distinguished from one another. Although he does not pretend to know the outcome of the crisis perpetrated by runaway capitalism and the awakening of the subalterns, Wallerstein conceives it with the help of clear-cut modern terminology.

Among Wallerstein's contributions to the progress of sociological theorizing were his insights into the origins of the hegemonic states and the global division of labour. These a basis for understanding how core capitalist societies have succeeded in perpetuating the variously dependent, deliberately underdeveloped peripheral and semi-peripheral societies in non-European areas (Frank, 1966). Significantly nuanced ideas about how modernity interfaces with globalization come out of neo-Marxist thinking about cities as a 'lens for social theory' (Harvey, 1985; Sassen, 2005). Among the most important perceptions is the perception of class as process (see, Schouten, 2008), a process of domination which, according to different historical configurations, may crystallize according to race, gender, ethnicity, as well as along lines of the various types of situatedness in the arrangements of the economy (Sennett, 2005).

What comes across in the literatures cited and in many more writings of the last several decades is a kind of panic among social scientists. Things are happening; they are gigantic; the world is changing – and we do not yet know how to describe and explain them in satisfactory ways. All of the theorists mentioned are trying to work within the bounds of sociology as an institutionalized discipline, i.e., as a modern science. Yet, their efforts often have the air of attempts to grasp the end of a thread that in unraveling will disclose the magical weave of structure and culture, of individual and group, of state and city and relieve the sociologist of the need to find different ways to approach each pole of what are clearly imagined dichotomies. The struggle has been marked by a series of challenges to some of the disciplinary traditions and to the sociological canon, each of which is marked by interests that cannot be aligned.

Challenging the Canon

Among those challenging the sociological canon as we know it, are postcolonialists (including 'southern' sociologists), students of science and technology, cultural studies adepts, feminist researchers, and philosophers of science. Partisans of each of these approaches present several kinds of challenges to sociology as it exists today. For one thing, there are challenges and suggestions as to what it should include rather than what are generally taken for granted as the classics. For another, there are challenges to the *intentionalities* that infuse sociology as it is implemented today and the role played by canonical methodologies in realizing these intentionalities. Further critiques settle on the *effects* of contemporary sociology, the practical outcomes of modernistic modes of investigation. The critiques derive from opposition to deprivation and include a substantiation of dispossession that is not evident to the deprived themselves. Another persistent challenge is one that is put to the *isolationism* of sociology with demands that the data of sociology – and its findings (sic!) include the insights of literature and the arts. Often, the challenges are – not always deliberately – mingled in different schools of thought.

Postcolonialist Sociologists

Sociologists who assume the mantle of postcolonialism, attack science in general, and sociology in particular, as the instrument of colonizers. In the variety of writings in this vein, there are declarations of general rebellion. In fact, what is actually evident is less an attempt to overthrow the canon than an assertion that we must be aware of its implicit and explicit *intentionalities*.

Sociologists studying developments in Africa and Asia have publicized injustices that were well hidden. During the 19th and 20th centuries most of the areas of Africa, like most areas of Asia, were subjected collectively to the trauma of colonialism. For Latin America, USA colonialism was disguised as protection against the ravages of invading European states. Whatever the justification, the arrangement meant complete subjugation to the economic ambitions of a European or American colonizing power, and constrained to serve the targets of that power. Representatives of the colonizing regimes enforced policies laid down 'at home' and cowed the 'natives' in order to establish the pre-eminence of the 'homeland' as well as that of the organizations that stood to benefit there. The project entailed persistent self-conscious pressure to erase native knowledge and tastes together with a deprecation of native morals and native values.[2]

Since the colonizing powers defined their goal as that of 'civilizing' the primitives, the very coining of the term 'colonialism' signaled the beginning of self-healing. Note, however, how the use of the term is connected with the theoretical basis in the description of postcolonialist sociology laid out in the brochure for a conference on postcolonialism in Toronto in 2002:

> "'Colonialism' is a term that critically refers to the political ideologies which legitimated the modern invasion, occupation and exploitation of inhabited lands by overwhelming outside military powers. For the local populations, it implied the forceful elimination of resistance, the imposition of alien rules, and the parasitic utilization of natural resources including manpower. This term appeared in the context of Marxism and became a cornerstone of the discourse of resistance during the 20th century. It was meant to counter the positive connotations attached to the use of 'colonization' – understood as a legitimate 'civilizing process' often reinforced by a religious agenda – calling attention to its actual economic motivations and denouncing its ruthless oppression." But the fact that the colonial powers were constrained to pull out of most of the colonized areas in the course of the twentieth century does not mean that their

intentions changed and, as the introduction goes on, "the new forms of economic and cultural oppression that have succeeded modern colonialism, (are) sometimes called 'neo-colonialism'. Post-colonialist theorists are able to warn about the current threat of cultural homogenization of ever larger areas of the globe."

Similarly, the idea of a 'southern sociology' developed by Raewyn Connell, explores the subtle colonialist thrust of the canon which relies on 'universalist abstraction'. Her argument for 'dirty theory' (2007: 207–08) is an account of postcolonialism as anti-positivistic science. "Our interest as researchers is to maximize the wealth of materials that are drawn into the analysis and explanation. It is also our interest to multiply rather than slim down the theoretical ideas that we have to work with. That includes multiplying the local sources of our thinking. ... A market society built on universal commodification involves universal abstraction as a fundamental part of its reality. It seems to invite representation by the placeless abstractions of neoclassical economics." In this view, deciding on what constitutes knowledge is necessarily dependent on how people live. The passionate description of how domination works suggests that it is possible to succeed in the struggle against commodification and to withstand the market society. In creating a society of struggle, it is presumed that as the sociologist retreats from 'placeless abstractions', she contributes to the preservation of the uniqueness of persons and groups.

In a word, despite different points of departure, postcolonialist theorists are united in promoting the idea that an epistemology which does not follow ontology is invalid; it is propelled by damaging intentions, and, obliquely, but perhaps because of that, highly effectively, it perpetuates the colonialist system. Critics fear that unless there is a concerted effort to ensure not only the prominence of subaltern experience but also to endow subalterns with realistic political and social privilege, the dominant capitalist narrative is lurking and ready to co-opt the postcolonialist struggle to the dominant narrative of beneficent capitalism (Mishra and Hodge, 2005: 397).

Moreover, the actual deployment of methods by postcolonialist sociologists, the basic approach to the reality 'out there' is not determined by local epistemologies. It is the locality as an object of inquiry rather than the locality as a way of thinking that is to be the source of 'truth'. One may well wonder whether the idea of being able to 'universalize' from local studies is a more virtuous approach to studying collectives, or is, in any significant way, ultimately the basis for 'another' sociology. And indeed many of the efforts at postcolonial sociologizing have dribbled into cultural studies with their concern with identities as expressed in literature, myths, and informal storytelling.

Cultural Studies

It is safe to say that since the writings of Williams (1971) and Thompson (1964) in the UK and Lévi-Strauss (1962), Althusser (1969) and Barthes (1970) in France, there has been an increasing interest in critiquing sociology from the standpoint of 'cultural studies'. In an early article, Hall (1980) points out that the field was initially based on two paradigms: the culturalist (which he attributes to the British) and the structuralist (which he attributes to the French). In his view, both paradigms are directed to overcoming the divide between base and super-structure that Marx pointed out but did not actually elaborate on. He describes the point of view of the culturalists (and I believe fairly) as one in which culture is understood as the interrelations between forms of energy and organization underlying all practices. Thus every way of life has a dimension of struggle and confrontation with opposed ways of life. In Hall's (1980: 63) words, "where and how people experience their conditions of life, define them and respond to them ... define why every mode of production is also a culture and every struggle between classes is always also a struggle between cultural modalities". Thus cultural studies which stem from a culturalist paradigm centre on *experience* as the ultimate key to understanding culture.

By contrast, taking Lévi-Strauss as the source of structuralism in cultural studies, Hall (1980: 64) interprets his view as one in which culture is a "collection of categories and frameworks in thought and language through which different societies classified ... their conditions of existence ... the relations between human and natural worlds". In this framework, culture is to be understood as analogous to language. That is to say, it has to be viewed in terms of the logic of arrangement, and the articulation of parts within a structure. This, of course, means that experience is not the 'terrain' of culture, but rather its effect. It is only possible "to live and experience one's conditions in and through categories, classifications, and frameworks of culture". By contrast, then, with the culturalists for whom 'ideology' is a term of less than central importance, in the structuralist paradigm ideology is embedded in unconscious categories through which conditions are represented and lived (Hall, 1980: 66). As Althusser (quoted in Hall, 1980) puts it, "Ideology is a system of representations but they have nothing to do with 'consciousness'. ... It is as structures that the representations impose on the vast majority of men, not via their consciousness. ... It is within this ideological unconscious that men succeed in altering the 'lived' relation between them and the world and acquiring that new form of specific unconsciousness called 'consciousness'". In Hall's (1980: 69) reading, both schools are mistaken. By focusing on how subjects are constituted, culturalism overemphasizes consciousness and experience. Structuralism, on the other hand, overemphasizes ideology, proposing a process without a subject.

Even in 1980, when this article was published, cultural studies had evolved beyond the paradigms that Hall identified. A constant challenge to cultural studies is the issue of the relationship between reproduction and change. This relationship is being investigated in increasingly diverse ways. One trend is that of 'reading' processes of reproduction and change from particularistic points of view. Thus, Mercer (1994) presents a point of view on 'black cultural studies'; Probyn (2004/1993) presents work on the self and a person's sexual location. Sasson-Levy's (2002) papers carry forward analyses of identity-formation and its relation to social structure. In her 2005 paper, Clare Hemmings expands the analysis of identity formation showing that by studying affect it is possible to attain a fuller understanding of shifts in cultural patterns as well as of shifts in identities. Cultural studies has also led to the development of a sociology that focuses on visuals in ways that vary from an analysis of pictures to a research method (Sooryamoorthy, 2007).

There are then significant points of contact between the orientation to the social that is emphasized in critical cultural studies, and postcolonialist sociology. The point of departure for both is an understanding of the uniqueness of specified collectivities. Cultural studies practitioners are increasingly committed to an examination of how individualities are constituted, while among postcolonialist social scientists, concern for the individual subaltern is the core of the analysis. Yet both orientations share professional convictions (a) that the 'establishment' of sociology is inadequate to unravel the workings of the social world, and (b) that by focusing on the particularistic it is possible to establish a universally valid social science.

Feminist Sociology

In feminist sociology, there are several ways of opposing the sociological canon. They range from the position that women 'can do it better' to a flaunting of the political centrality of gender, and an identification of the political implications of women's methodologies, along with a view of women as dynamic, multifaceted social agents.

Among the stories of women who have been 'doing it' and doing it better, that of Harriet Martineau (1802 – 1876) is outstanding in having penetrated the bastion of the 'fathers'. Significantly, in the 800 page *Blackwell Companion to Major Social Theorists* (Ritzer, 2000), she is the only woman whose work is quoted among the major theorists of the 19th century. Indeed, Martineau was an untiring researcher and her accomplishments were legion. She produced three volume studies of both *Society in America* and of *Eastern Life Past and Present* (on the Middle East) among other extended projects. Interestingly enough, she wrote about America before de Toqueville, modelled social structure before Spencer, analysed suicide before Durkheim, wrote extensively about motivation, and compiled a book about how to do social research before Weber. Martineau also translated ('freely' she admits) the works of Comte for readers of English, a translation that is still serviceable and, moreover, available on the internet. In addition, she wrote literally thousands of newspaper articles, and didactic short stories that she designed especially to enable the public to absorb sociological principles painlessly.

Pointing out the primacy of Harriet Martineau is important because she was indeed a major sociologist and a fascinating woman. But the claim that there are women who 'did it' before the 'fathers', or that women are 'doing it' better than men today, is not really a serious challenge to the male canon. A second way, of course, is the guiding theme that the state of women in society and their conditions deserve analysis in their own right; and that the relations between the genders are the key to an understanding of how society is run. Among others, Walby (1990, 2004; Walby et al., 2007) insists that only full recognition of women will enable increased productivity and political progress. Another development has been the emphasis – perhaps, given the Chicago school, one should say the re-emphasis – on qualitative modes of research. There are many books and articles discussing how qualitative methods have been and can be taken over into feminist research (Harding, 2006; Lather, 2004; Madriz, 2003; Reinharz, 1992; Reinharz and Chase, 2003). The feminist appropriation of qualitative methods was underlined not long ago in the edited proceedings of the Nutrition Society conference headed *Getting Quality in Qualitative Research: A Short Introduction to Feminist Methodology and Methods* (Landman, 2007).

But when all is said and done, the goals of feminist methods are no different from those of qualitative research in regard to every population. Lather (2004: 204) puts it this way: "As the concept of 'disinterested knowledge' implodes and collapses inward, social inquiry becomes ... a site of the surfacing of what it has historically repressed". Like people from the global South, women are certainly among the historically repressed, and qualitative methodologies – whether open interviews, or ethnographic observations, or focus groups – envisioned as means for ensuring the 'subjectification' of the sites of inquiry are suited to the goals of feminists as they are for all repressed groups. Moreover, in placing women's interests at the heart of inquiry, feminist researchers can expand their critique of social arrangements throughout much of history by showing how the gender divide has governed the patterning of relations in politics, economics, and religion. This strength of the feminist reading of qualitative research methods/methodology is at the same time an indication of what in the long run turns into a weakness of feminist epistemologies – whether postmodernist, standpoint, or empiricist (Harding, 1986). It involves a mindset in which the focus on socio-political goals tends to deactivate researchers' capacity for self-criticism as well as a capacity for creative innovation. This is not to gainsay the value of the goals and the usefulness of publications in furthering them. It is, however, recognition of the fact that these epistemologies are not evidence of new modes of coping with description and explanation of the social. But signalling the emergence of a truly globalizing sociology, there are indeed some significant new trends in feminist research.

From Modernity to Globality?

Intersectionality

Feminists have not remained indifferent to the inadequacies that pursue the agenda of bringing gender to the centre. Recent feminist research has turned to a concern with the multidimensionality of oppression; a renewed conceptualization of the intersecting of gender, class, race, and sexuality has opened women's studies and the discipline of sociology to new possibilities. According to Denis (2008), "Intersectional analysis ... *simultaneously* takes into account the intersection of multiple social locations, each socially defined, with the constraints or opportunities that such a definition can entail. What is important is the *configuration* of one's social location based in each element of the triad of class, ethnicity/race and gender as roots of oppression (and, in some cases, with other sources as well). Over time, ... the importance of contextualizing the different social locations in terms of time, place, and other intersecting social locations (has been accepted). ... The contextualization involves recognizing that the meaning of a social location – a social construction – is not static. It also involves recognizing that the salience of our various social locations, whether for ourselves or our social environment, is not static either."

Describing three distinct methodological approaches to intersectionality, McCall (2005) insists that the work being done, both quantitative and qualitative, is creating a new interdisciplinary field that is constantly distancing itself from the 'older' disciplines. To demonstrate the justice of this thesis, however, she confronts research approaches with criteria from the philosophy of science. Unfortunately, arguing in this vein leads her to voluntaristic conclusions, losing touch with structures and experience. But this does not detract from the potential of positioning sociological investigation as *necessarily* a study of intersects. The contribution of intersectionality lies above all in its insistence on the fact that what happens among human beings and human groups cannot be described or explained on the basis of shallow stipulations. Through the conceptualization of intersectionality, sociology gains insights into the making of human action which can only be accomplished because it is rooted in a (sometimes vast) number of collective institutions. Thus, all types of action have to be described in as many dimensions as present themselves, so to speak; and they have to be explained on the basis of the patterning of those dimensions in diverse spaces over time.

The concept of 'intersectionality' points to the possibility of fulfilling requirements for a sociological programme that extends far beyond the prevailing traditions of rationality and the modern. But to realize the potential, it is important to take into consideration two other kinds of theorization currently being developed – both of them delving into particulars in ways that lead to a sociology of the global.

Locating the Body in Another Sociology

Generally at the sidelines, an independent stream of research has been developing apace. In the course of the 20th century, studies of the social in relation to the body tended to focus on body image as an outcome of social factors (see *Body Image: An International Journal of Research).* Conversational Research, an outgrowth of ethnomethodology, developed an interest in the body as part of the conversational frame (Schegloff, 1998). The investigation of sport has also drawn on sociological analyses of the body (Connell, 1995; Hall, 1996; Williams, 2007). In the last several decades, new studies have attempted to locate the study of the body in the context of the sociological canon (see Shilling, 2005, 2007, 2008). A further development of interest is work that deals with the body as the medium for what is known as performative sociology (see Roberts, 2008, and the entire issue of *FQS* in which it appears). As a domain of research, however, the study of the body has often led to novel and disturbing angles of vision of the individual and of the disciplines.[3] But as a 'school', the study of the body in connection with the social seems disconnected from central sociological concerns and has not yet been accepted as a project that is worthy of inclusion in the shaping of sociology. And yet, there is increasing evidence of the need to take into consideration the interplay between the neurological and the social, the physiological and the social (see Pirani and Smith, forthcoming), as well as the crystallization of the relationship between the senses and the social (Low, 2009; Kalekin-Fishman and Low, forthcoming).

In connection with the last statement, it is important to point out that while the core of sociology is the concern with the relations that weave the collective into some kind of whole, these relations do not end at the skin. The subject is differentiated according to the uses of the body in the visible world, but is also differentiated in terms of how the world impacts the body – the relation of the body to the world through the differentiated world of the senses as well as its physiological and neurological reactions. For the world that is held together by and as collectives is made up of 'nature' and 'things' of all sizes from the gigantic to the minuscule, and of people in all their complexity in their stances vis-á-vis others, but also, in their complexity as clusters of highly differentiated subcutaneous systems. What we hear may be completely different from what we see, albeit the senses disclose their grasp of reality at the same time. The particulars of the senses are the markers of what is often meant by cultural differentiation and they have to be an element in any analysis of the global.

Science and Technology Studies: Actor-Network-Theory

The literature of 'actor-network-theory' points to still other aspects of an emergent sociology of globality. Growing out of studies of social aspects of science and technology (see, for example, Knorr-Cetina, 1993), ANT was heralded by the work of Latour and Woolgar (1986/1979) who carried out an extended ethnography in the Salk Laboratories, according to the ISCID Encyclopedia of Science and Philosophy:

> "Actor-Network-Theory (ANT) is an interdisciplinary approach to the social sciences and technology studies, and closely relates to research in terms of complexity and locality, activity theory, the sociology of knowledge and systems theory. ... The ANT perspective attempts to explain and interpret social and technological evolution using neither technical-material nor social reductionism, but rather it incorporates a 'principle of generalized symmetry', (namely) that what is human and non-human should be integrated into the same conceptual framework. As a result, humans and non-humans are sometimes both referred to as 'actants'."

Probably, because of uncomfortable controversies raised by the somewhat unruly group belonging to the ANT movement, Latour seemed to cut himself off from its stalwarts in a 1997 workshop titled: 'Actor Network and After.' He then noted that "there are four things wrong with Actor-Network-Theory: the words 'Actor,' 'Network,' 'Theory,' and the hyphen!" Still the thrust of the approach is alive and well in his recent work. Even before the book in which he reneges openly on the reservations (Latour, 2005), he implied his 'return to the fold' in a paper called "Where are the Missing Masses? The Sociology of a Few Mundane Artifacts" (Latour, 2001). There he critiques business and management from the point of view of science and technology studies, and from that of ANT. He draws encouragement for his project of ensuring the place of the nonhuman in analyses of the social from a notice about a door not being able to close properly because 'the groom (the hinge) is on strike'. Defending what would perhaps 'normally' be called anthropomorphism he shows that when human qualities are attributed to non-humans, the implications are immediately grasped. In relating to the actuality of the hinge and the door, Latour demonstrates that the hinge is not only unarguably the product of human action, but that it in turn shapes human action in the organization. The human action that creates the hinge involves *conceptualizing* the problem and the proposed solution, *drawing up* a design, *translating* the plans so as to *inscribe* them in a technological object that requires particular actions and rules out certain other actions, thus effectively changing the environment by contextualizing action. Central to the creation of action, then, is the use of paper and the translation of what is in and on the paper, to both what we recognize as the human and what, in daily parlance, we recognize as the non-human. With the 'hinge on strike', of course, many actions that are normal to the organizational environment have to be revised and minimally rerouted.

The careful description of two other pieces of equipment and their interaction with human beings furthers the argument by countering the common sense which reads the environment as stable whether it be 'nature' or an environment of artifacts. From the point of view of the sociologist, Latour describes a world of multifaceted interactions which cannot be explained by any of the theories that *exclude* objects. Latour's analysis indicates the possibilities of 'another' sociology as he shows the "political nature of (organizational) life; and unabashedly debunks conventional myths of the innate differences between the human and the nonhuman. The article superbly questions what we should consider as knowledge, and scrutinizes the reality that it draws from detailed investigation" as well as from exemplifying the very processes it describes (Editors' Introduction, *Organizational Studies,* Vol. 4, 2001).

Fathoming the social world as a complexity of people and things as diverse as trees and wolves, doors and detonators, as well as nano-structures, provides a completely different perspective on colonialisms and cultures, on women and language. As Donna Haraway (1994) says pointedly: "Human and nonhuman, all entities take shape in encounters, in practices; and the actors and partners in encounters are not all human, to say the least. Further, many of these nonhuman partners and actors are not very natural, and certainly not original." Echoing the complexities of intersectionality, the world of actor-network – theorizing provides conceptualizations through which to highlight the diverse tenors of the meetings of humans and non-humans for, among others, different genders, ethnies, classes, and geographical sites.

But more is implied by this view of the social. Taking on the challenge of 'reassembling the social', Latour (2005) examines dilemmas of the 'sociology of the social' and how they can be resolved. While acknowledging the accomplishments of modern sociology in making classifications and in measuring situations that stay put for a reasonable while, he argues that stability is not the topic of a useful sociology. In his perception, the social is to be recognized in assemblages (of human and non-humans) that are constantly on the move. With this idea of how society is regularly made and unmade, the sociologist has the deceptively simple task of tracking convergences and divergences as they take shape. These are myriad and present an endless challenge to the powers of description.

An Emergent Sociology

Clearly then, another kind of sociology is emerging. The institutional differentiation of what makes up identities and opportunities for oppression, which is the message of intersectionality developed by (but not exclusively meaningful in) women's studies, and the understanding that the relations among the different strands must be the focus of analysis are at the heart of this 'other' kind of sociology. The potentialities of investigating intersectionality are enhanced by the recognition of the socially constructed diversity of the ongoing relations with 'things' and with 'nature' which position us variously in different domains of our lives. And, these all have connections – form and are formed by – interactions in the body.

The emergent sociology may start from a set of questions such as: What are the connections between what happens 'inside' the body and the world that impacts that body – from language and ideology to categorization to experiences (whether as effect or as outcomes of interactions) in daily life. And, what are the lines of force to and from the body? How do these lines of force interconnect with the 'non-human' artifacts of common sense in the midst of which we operate, and how do they interconnect with the residues of 'nature' into which we venture from time to time? At which nexus is power exercised and what forms does oppression take?

Questions such as these stem from a comprehensive grasp of a highly heterogeneous reality, rather than from a particular canon. They express basic values of respect and appreciation for the formation of collectivities throughout our world. They can, in all fairness, be put to people everywhere; the responses sought 'subjectify' every topic of study; and the questions and the responses require reflection/auto-analysis on the part of the researcher-always-to-be-defined-as-a-student. Analyses of situations and of discourse can rely on systematic exploration of the *layering, the smooth narratives, the translations, hierarchies, rationalizations and explanations* that characterize the social situations in which we find ourselves (Law, 2006).

This attempt to mould an integrative type of sociology for a globalizing era rests on an empirical base in the sense that sociologists are going out of their way to cope with the impact of the social. After all, what is it that drives the efforts? Rarely is voice given to the 'personal' experience of the sociologist. And yet, in the case of moving from the modern science of sociology to one that is capable of coping with the events on a global scale or with their global conceptualization, one is drawn up sharply by the understanding that oddly enough (from the point of view of sociology), sociologists today, like those of the 19th century, start out from a keen sense of subjectivity betrayed. Almost two hundred years ago, sociologists felt the impact of industrialization as a mode of reducing subjectivity, to the point of the alienated person, the person who is being hollowed out by supplying labour power to the industrial behemoth. In the 21st century, that person is still hollowed out, but she is also spilling over, saturated with information, acquaintanceships, pounded by media of communication until the swirl of belonging and exclusion gives rise to a unique way of life, one that is an unending string of coming together in different kinds of assemblages. Oddly enough, the combined effect of intersectionality, the body, and ANT present at once a kind of reflection of Whitehead's (1929) metaphysics and of Foucault's (see, for example, 1975, 1988) diagnosis of social events as a mass of contingencies.

Is it worth doing? Following Lakatos (1970), I want to propose that the 'scientific' answer depends on whether what seems to be evolving is indeed a scientific programme. Even a superficial entry into the ramifications of the emergent social story discloses the possibility of a research programme which can be the starting point for a sociology complex enough to deal with the awe-inspiring and betimes devastating pressures being forged through globalization. Moreover, the kinds of theoretical statements that can be derived from such a programme may with luck be able to foretell some startling facts. No less should be demanded of 'another sociology', but at this point, no more need be demanded.

Still, the question of whether it is worth doing has several other facets. For one thing, the very extensiveness of the programme which is taking shape, its recognition of the inevitability of ambiguities at different levels or in different aspects of social action, of the necessary vagueness of attributions, of the scope of boundary practices, gives promise of alerting individuals and groups to the sources of alienation and exclusion in conditions of globalization. Thus, in this attempt at outlining an overarching (but far from 'grand') approach to social theory, there is also promise of clarifying the prospects for resistance.

In confronting the emergent sociology, there is no need to rely on philosophy for its legitimation. The point is to clarify and re-clarify what is happening in the world which is beginning at every moment. Sociologists equipped to amass particulars so as to lay out the designs of assemblages and to examine their inner facets, sociologists who can extrapolate to the threats of oppression from a host of virtual institutions are sighting the nature of the era and creating a veritable sociology of globality.

Notes

1. Actually members of the Frankfurt School were interested in doing empirical work and undertook important projects in which different methods were combined already in the 1920s (Horkheimer and Fromm, 1987; Fromm and Maccoby, 1996/1970).
2. It would be unfair to characterize these as 'traditional' because there is no reason to assume that native cultures were static.
3. Working Group 03, now Research Committee 54 of the International Sociological Association, presented their approach at the Barcelona Forum, September 2008. In January 2009, the Institució Milá I Fontanals, CSIC of Barcelona held an interdisciplinary conference on 'The Body: Subject and Object of the Humanities and Social Sciences'.

References

Abbott, Andrew (1997) "Of Time and Space: The Contemporary Relevence of the Chicago School", *Social Forces*, June 75(4): 1149–82.

Actor-Network-Theory (2008) *ISCID Encyclopedia of Science and Philosophy*. Retrieved on July 4, 2008 from http://www.iscid.org/encyclopedia/Actor-Network_Theory

Adorno, T.W., Frenkel-Brunswik, E. and Levinson, D.J. (1960) *The Authoritarian Personality*. New York: Harper and Brothers.

Althusser, L. (1969) *For Marx* (trans. Ben Brewster). New York: Pantheon Books.

Barley, S.F. (1989) "Careers, Identities and Institutions: The Legacy of the Chicago School of Sociology", in M.B. Arthur, D.T. Hall and B.S. Lawrence (eds.), *Handbook of Career Theory*, Cambridge: Cambridge University Press, pp. 41–65.

Barthes, R. (1970) *S/Z*. Paris: Editions du Seuil.

Bauman, Z. (1992) *Intimations of Postmodernity*. London/New York: Routledge.

— (1989) *Modernity and the Holocaust*. Ithaca: Cornell University Press.

Beck, U. (1992) *Risk Society: Towards a New Modernity*. London: Sage.

— (1996) "World Risk Society as Cosmopolitan Society?: Ecological Questions in a Framework of Manufactured Uncertainties", *Theory, Culture and Society*, Vol. 13, No. 4, pp. 1–32.

Bell, Colin and Roberts, Helen (eds.) (1984) *Social Researching: Politics, Problems, Practices*. London: Routledge.

Berlin, I. (2006) *Political Ideas in the Romantic Age: Their Rise and Influence on Modern Thought*. London: Chatto & Windus.

Bourdieu, P. (1977) *Outline of a Theory of Practice*. Cambridge: Cambridge University Press.

— (1984) *Distinction: A Social Critique of the Judgment of Taste*. Cambridge: Harvard University Press and London: Routledge and Kegan Paul.

Bourdieu, P. and Passeron, J.C. (1990) *Reproduction in Education, Society and Culture*. New York: Sage.

Broady, D. (1996) "The Epistemological Tradition in French Sociology", in Jostein Gripsrud (ed.), *Rhetoric and Epistemology* (papers from a seminar at the Maison des sciences de l'homme in Paris), September, pp. 97–119.

Canclini, N.G. (1995) *Hybrid Cultures: Strategies for Entering and Leaving Modernity*. Minneapolis: University of Minnesota Press.

Comte, A. (2000/1855) *The Philosophy of Auguste Comte* (freely translated and condensed by H. Martineau), Kitchener: Batoche Books.

Connell, R. (1995) *Masculinities*. Cambridge: Polity Press.

— (2007) *Southern Sociology: The Global Dynamics of Knowledge in Social Science*. London: Allen & Unwin.

Cressey, D.R. (1932) *The Taxi-Dancer*. Chicago: University of Chicago Press.

Denis, A. (2008) "Intersectional Analysis: A Contribution of Feminism to Sociology", *International Sociology Review of Books*, Vol. 23, No. 5.

Durkheim, E. (1895/1938) *The Rules of Sociological Method* (trans. S.A. Solovay and J.H. Mueller), New York: Free Press of Glencoe.

Eisenstadt, S.N. (2004) "Social Evolution and Modernity: Some Observations on Parsons's Comparative and Evolutionary Analysis: Parsons's Analysis from the Perspective of Multiple Modernities", *The American Sociologist*, Vol. 35, Issue 4, pp. 5–24.

Foucault, M. (1975) *Surveiller et Punir: Naissance de la Prison*. Paris: Gallimard.

— (1988) *Technologies of the Self: A Seminar with Michel Foucault*. Amherst: University of Massachusetts Press.

Frank, A.G. (1966) "The Development of Underdevelopment", *Monthly Review*, Vol. 18, pp. 4–17.

Fromm, E. and Maccoby, M. (1996/1970) *Social Character in a Mexican Village*. New Brunswick, NJ: Transaction Books.

Giddens, A. (1990) *The Consequences of Modernity*. Stanford, CA: Stanford University Press.

Habermas, J. (2007/1980) "Modernity: An Unfinished Project", in Craig Calhoun et al. (eds.), *Contemporary Sociological Theory*, Oxford: Blackwell, pp. 363–69.

Hall, M.A. (1996) *Feminism and Sporting Bodies: Essays on Theory and Practice*. Champaign, IL: Human Kinetics.

Hall, S. (1980) "Cultural Studies: Two Paradigms", *Media, Culture and Society*, Vol. 2, No. 1, pp. 57–73.

Haraway, D. (1994) "A Game of Cat's Cradle: Science Studies, Feminist Theory, Cultural Studies", *Configurations*, Vol. 2, No. 1, pp. 59–71.

Harding, S. (2006) 'Is there a Feminist Method?' *Philosophical Foundations of Social Research Methods*. INCOMPLETE

—— (1986) *The Science Question in Feminism*. Ithaca, NY: Cornell University Press.

Harvey, David (1985) *The Urbanization of Capital: Studies in the History and Theory of Capitalist Urbanization*. Baltimore, MD: Johns Hopkins University Press.

Hemmings, C. (2005) "Cultural Theory and the Ontological Turn", *Cultural Studies*, Vol. 19, No. 5, pp. 548–67.

Horkheimer, M. and Fromm, Erich (1987) *Studien über Autorität und Familie*. Frankfurt: Forschungsberichte aus dem Institut für Sozialforschung.

Howe, D. (1994) "Modernity, Post-modernity and Social Work", *The British Journal of Social Work*, Vol. 24, Issue 5, pp. 513–32.

Jahoda, M., Lazarfield, P.F. and Zeisel, H. (1933) *The Sociography of an Unemployed Community: Marienbad*. London: Tavistock.

Jameson, F. (1991) *Postmodernism or the Cultural Logic of Late Capitalism*. Durham, NC: Duke University Press.

Jeřábek, Hynek (2001) Three Examples of Cooperation between Qualitative and Analytical Research. (Lazarsfeld's Research Workshop). Prague: Institute of Sociological Studies, Faculty of Social Sciences, Charles University. www.cvvm.cas.cz/upl/nase_spolecnost (retrieved on 07/06/2009).

Kalekin-Fishman, D. and Low, K. (eds.) (forthcoming) *Everyday Life in Asia: Social Perspectives on the Senses*. Aldershot: Ashgate.

Knorr-Cetina, K. (1993) *Epistemic Cultures: How Scientists Make Sense*. Chicago: Chicago University Press.

Lakatos, I. (1970) *The Methodology of Scientific Research Programmes* (edited by J.A.C.G. Worrall), Cambridge: Cambridge University Press.

Landman, M. (2007) "Getting Quality in Qualitative Research: A Short Introduction to Feminist Methodology and Methods", *Proceedings of the Nutrition Society*, Vol. 65, No. 4, pp. 429–33.

Lather, P. (2004) "Feminist and Poststructural Perspectives: Science After Truth", in K. de Marrais and S.D. Lapan (eds.), *Foundations for Research: Methods of Inquiry in Education*, Mahwah, NJ: Lawrence Erlbaum, pp. 203–16.

Latour, Bruno (1993) *We Have Never Been Modern*, Cambridge, Massachusetts: Harvard University Press.

Latour, B. (2001) "Where are the Missing Masses? The Sociology of a Few Mundane Artifacts", in Warwick Organizational Behaviour Staff (eds.), *Organizational Studies: Critical Perspectives on Business and Management (Vol. IV – Evil Empires)*, pp. 1842–72.

—— (2005) *Reassembling the Social*. Oxford: Oxford University Press.

Latour, B. and Woolgar, S. (1986/1979) *Laboratory Life: The Construction of Scientific Facts*. Princeton, NJ: Princeton University Press.

Law, J. (2006) *After Method: Mess in Social Science Research*. London: Routledge.

Lazersfeld, P. and Barton, A. (eds.) (1955) *The Language of Social Research: A Reader in Methodology*. New York: Columbia University Press.

Lazersfeld, P., Berelson, B. and Gaudet, H. (1948) *The People's Choice: How the Voter Makes Up His Mind*. New York: Columbia University Press.

Lévi-Strauss, C. (1962) *La Pensée Sauvage*. Paris: Plon.

Low, K.L. (2009) *Scents and Scent-sibilities: Smell and Everyday Life Experiences*. Newcastle on Tyne: Cambridge Scholars.

Lyotard, Jean-François (1989) *The Lyotard Reader*. Edited by A. Benjamin, Oxford: Wiley-Blackwell.

Madriz, E. (2003) "Focus Groups in Feminist Research", in N.K. Denzin and Y.S. Lincoln (eds.), *Collecting and Interpreting Qualitative Materials*, Thousand Oaks/London/ New Delhi: Sage, pp. 363–88.

Martineau, Harriet (1838) *Retrospect of Western Travel*, 3 Vols. London: Saunders and Otley, Conduit-Street (accessed via Google Books, 7/06/09)

—— (2000/1838) *How to Observe Morals and Manners* (replica of 1838 edition by Charles Knight and Co., London) Elibron Classics.

McCall, L. (2005) "The Complexity of Intersectionality", *Signs*, Vol. 30, No. 3, pp. 1771–99.

Meja, B., Misgeld, D. and Stehr, N. (1987) *Modern German Sociology*. New York: Columbia University Press.

Mercer, K. (1994) *Welcome to the Jungle: New Positions in Black Cultural Studies*. New York: Routledge.

Merton, Robert K. (1957) *Social Theory and Social Structure*, New York: Free Press.

Mishra, Vijay and Hodge, Bob (2005) "What Was Postcolonialism?", *New Literary History*, Vol. 36, No. 3, pp. 375–402.

Pirani, B.M. and Smith, T. (eds.) (forthcoming) *Mapping the Body: The Bodily Factor in Memory and Social Action*. UK: Cambridge Scholars.

Popper, K. and Adorno, T. (1969) *Der Positivismusstreit in der deutschen Soziologie*. Neuwied: Luchterhand.

Probyn, E. (2004/1993) *Sexing the Self: Gendered Positions in Cultural Studies*. London: Taylor & Francis Group.

Reinharz, S. (1992) *Feminist Methods in Social Research*. USA: Oxford University Press.

Reinharz, S. and Chase, S.E. (2003) "Interviewing Women", in J.A. Holstein and J.E. Gubrium (eds.), *Inside Interviewing: New Lenses, New Concerns*, Thousand Oaks/London/New Delhi: Sage, pp. 73–90.

Ritzer, G. (ed.) (2000) *Blackwell Companion to Major Social Theorists*. Oxford, UK: Blackwell.

Roberts, B. (2008) "Performative Social Science: A Consideration of Skills, Purpose and Context (122 paragraphs)", *Forum Qualitative Sozialforschung/Forum: Qualitative Social Research*, Vol. 9, No. 2, Article 58. http://nbn-resolving.de/um: nbn: de: 0114-fqs0802588 (retrieved on July 4, 2008).

Robertson, Roland and White, Kathleen E. (2005) "Globalization: Sociology and Cross-Disciplinarity", in Craig Calhoun, Chris Rojek and Bryan Turner (eds.), *The SAGE Handbook of Sociology*, London: Sage, pp. 345–66.

Sassen, Saskia (2005) "The City: Its Return as a Lens for Social Theory", in Craig Calhoun, Chris Rojek and Bryan Turner (eds.), *The SAGE Handbook of Sociology*, London: Sage, pp. 457–70.

Sennett, Richard (2005) "The Culture of Work", in Craig Calhoun, Chris Rojek and Bryan Turner (eds.), *The SAGE Handbook of Sociology*, London: Sage, pp. 129–34.

Sasson-Levy, O. (2002) "Constructing Identities at the Margins: Masculinities and Citizenship in the Israeli Army", *The Sociological Quarterly*, Vol. 43, No. 3, pp. 357–83.

Schegloff, E.A. (1998) "Body Torque", *Social Research*, Fall. http://findarticles.com/p/articles/ni_m2267/is-3-65/ai-53461614 (retrieved on July 4, 2008).

Schouten, P. (2008) "Theory Talk #20: David Harvey on the Geography of Capitalism, Understanding cities as Polities and Shifting Imperialisms", *Theory Talks*. http://www.theory-talks.org/2008/10/theory-talk-20-david-harvey.html (09–10–2008).

Shaw, Clifford R. (1966/1930) *The Jack-Roller*. Chicago: University of Chicago Press.

Shilling, C. (2008) *Changing Bodies* (published in association with *Theory, Culture and Society*), London: Sage, p. 216.

—— (2007) *Embodying Sociology: Retrospect, Progress and Prospects* (Sociological Review Monograph Series), Oxford: Blackwells (Editor), p. 169.

—— (2005) *The Body in Culture, Technology and Society*. London, Newbury Park and New Delhi: Sage.

Sinclair, Upton (1906) *The Jungle*. New York: Grosset & Dunlap.

Small, Albion (1905) *General Sociology: An Exposition of the Main Development of Sociology from Spencer to Ratzenhofer*. Chicago: University of Chicago Press (retrieved from UCLA site, July 15, 2008).

Sooryamoorthy, Radhamany (2007) "Behind the Scenes: Making Research Films in Sociology", *International Sociology Review of Books*, Vol. 22, No. 5, pp. 547–67.

Spencer, Herbert (1899) *The Principles of Sociology*, Vol. I, New York: D. Appleton and Company.

Steffens, Lincoln (1987/1957) *The Shame of the Cities*. New York: Hill & Wang.

Thompson, E.P. (1964) *The Making of the English Working Class*. London: V. Gollancz.

Touraine, Alain (1988) *La parole et le sang: politique et société en Amerique latine*. Paris: Odile Jacob.

—— (1996) *Qu'est-ce que la démocratie?* Paris: Fayard.

Walby, Sylvia (2004) *Modelling Gender Pay Gaps* (with Wendy Olsen), Manchester: Equal Opportunities Commission.

—— (1990) *Theorizing Patriarchy*. Oxford: Blackwell.

Walby, Sylvia et al. (eds.) (2007) *Gendering the Knowledge Economy: Comparative Perspectives*. London: Palgrave.

Wallerstein, Immanuel (1974–1989) *The Modern World System*, 3 Vols. New York: Academic Press.

Weber, Max (1968) *Methodologische Schriften*. Frankfurt am: S. Fischer.

—— (1963) *Sociology of Religion* (trans. E. Fischoff), Boston: Beacon Press.

—— (2002) *The Protestant Ethic and the 'Spirit' of Capitalism and Other Writings* (trans. B. Baehr), USA: Penguin Classics.

Whitehead, Alfred (1929) *Process and Reality*. Cambridge: Cambridge University Press.

Williams, Jean (2007) *A Beautiful Game: International Perspectives on Women's Football*. Oxford and New York: Berg.

Williams, R. (1971) *The Long Revolution*. Harmondsworth (Middx.): Penguin Books.

Wolf, Kurt (1950) *The Sociology of Georg Simmel*. New York: Basic Books.

3

Sociology in India in the Context of Globalization

Issues and Challenges

Paramjit S. Judge

> The question of universalization or particularism of sociological categories in Indian sociology or social science as such remains open. A more enduring solution to this issue would probably come from accumulation of empirical knowledge through the findings of Indian sociologists and social scientists from studies conducted with self-awareness and scientific objectivity within their own ideological setting.
>
> — Yogendra Singh

For those who are familiar with the works of social scientists like Bruadel and Wallerstein, globalization is a recent term with some additional connotation of the notion of the world system. Some of the seminal works in history attribute the idea of globalization to the 19th century, which was the age of capital and imperialism. The experts opine that there is something distinct about the present phase of globalization. Since the objective of this paper is to situate the discipline of sociology in the age of globalization, it is relevant to understand the meaning and significance of globalization. Globalization is generally regarded as the movement of people and goods across regions and nations without hindrance. It may be understood as a process through which the people across state boundaries simultaneously experience certain forms of information, entertainment and market. This simultaneity of the experience continues to expand and seems like threatening to become total. Information and entertainment are combined in a number of ways. For example, the satellite media is a source of both entertainment and information. The Internet performs the same function. It is the market or the capital, which has the dominating influence. As it happened at the time of the collapse of the feudal world that the spatial and temporal boundaries of the estates were destroyed by the emerging capitalism, the globalization is undermining the state boundaries to create a uniform world system. Whether there are

This paper is a revised version of one available online on www.esocialsciences.com

chances of its success or not is a matter of discussion. This simultaneity of experience, however, has opened numerous possibilities for the individuals to transcend certain limitations imposed by their systems. At the same time, the simultaneity of experience is not universal. It has included as well as excluded certain groups and classes from it. In fact, the process of globalization assumes that two classes come to exist, one that interacts by overcoming the limitations imposed by the nation-state boundaries, and the other that is excluded from this interaction (Judge, 2003).

Indian society is passing through a rapid social change, induced by many international and national factors. The liberalization of the Indian economy and rapid technological changes have ushered in a revolution of a sort in the life of the people. Information technology has changed the meanings of trade and commerce and new notions, like e-commerce, have begun to capture people's minds. The rise of media and communication system has considerably altered the people's way of looking at the external world. The domination of market economy has initiated the process of globalization, which is cutting across the national boundaries. All these processes are going to have both desirable and undesirable social consequences. In this context, the role of social sciences becomes very crucial so as to examine and work out the measures to integrate society with the rapid economic and technological changes. Lyotard (1999) is of the view that postmodern thinking is a consequence of post-industrial society in which the nature and content of the pursuit of knowledge have radically changed. The pursuit of knowledge is no more an end in itself; rather it is asked, "what is the use of getting the knowledge?" The policy of the Indian state has made a definite shift in favour of privatization, liberalization and globalization. It is beginning to affect the university system as an activity of public sector sphere. The privatization of education and the challenge posed by the foreign universities have created the environment in which there is a need to have a fresh look at the state of affairs of sociology and other social sciences in the country.

Any exercise in mapping the current status of any social science discipline is a mammoth task, as it involves the normative concerns as well as the personal perceptions of the sociologist who treads this path. Instead of tracing the history of emergence of discipline of sociology in India, an attempt has been made to state and examine challenges that have been posed by the present circumstances. The expression "present circumstances" provides the clue that whatever is happening to the discipline of sociology is not entirely due to the process of globalization. The state of affairs of Indian society, polity and economy has a lot to do with what is happening. Let us begin by pointing out certain important facts with regard to social sciences in general and sociology in particular.

1. Social sciences have Western European origin. To put it in a more focused form, we may quote Singh (2004: 135), "Indian sociology, like most other social sciences in India, has grown through an encounter with the Western philosophical and scientific traditions". It is due to this historical fact that theory and method have remained predominantly western. Sociology emerged as a conservative reaction to the Enlightenment. At the same time, however, as Singh (ibid.: 135) points out, "sociology in India has also been

deeply influenced by the numerous internal processes which signify the passage of India from a colony of the British to the status of an independent republic". Oommen (2007: 2) makes an interesting observation when he writes, "In the West, anthropology and colonialism were inextricably intertwined; anthropology was perceived as the child of colonialism. In contrast, sociology is cognized as the offspring of modernity". Ironically, colonialism that controlled the world was also a child of modernity as capitalism made it possible for the British or French or any other imperial power to control and govern such a large and extend area.

2. With the revolution in biological sciences in the 19th century, the social sciences progressively got connected with positivist tradition. In this regard, claims of sociologists that sociology is a science began right from its emergence. As a result, sociology as a discipline developed peculiarities of its own in the sense that there has been a continuous attempt to claim the status of science as well as endeavour to devise methods of sociological research. Externality, constraint, social facts as things, causation, independent variable – all these expressions and concepts became popular in the struggle of sociologists to elevate sociology equal to the status of natural sciences.
3. Significant growth of social sciences took place after the end of Second World War. The post-1945 period has been characterized by the domination of the USA, which funded huge projects, particularly in the field of area studies (Wallerstein et al., 1997).
4. Within social sciences development was not uniform. As pointed out by Braudel (1981), economics felt less constraint because it had learnt to side with the state.
5. In India, the development of social sciences was linked with the colonial education and the purpose of colonial education was to create human resource suitable for the imperialists' needs.
6. India experienced tremendous expansion of universities and research institutes. This expansion was massive and reached its saturation point in the 1980s. Its saturation was not linked with the academic and research requirements, but with the financial capability and change in the perspective of the Indian state.
7. It is wrong to assume that in spite of the western origin of theory and method the growth of social sciences in India lacked autonomy. In this regard, the mode of production debate, which began in the late-sixties and continued in the following decade, may be referred as an example. It is important to remember that at the time of this debate the "development of underdevelopment" was the dominant thesis of discourse, which did not draw major attention of the scholars so as to generate a debate in India. What is notable about the mode of production debate in Indian agriculture is the participation of not only the economists (who in fact started it) but also of political scientists, historians, anthropologists and sociologists. The second instance of the autonomy of the Indian social scientists is the emergence of "subaltern

history", which may be stated as coming from historians predominantly educated from the western universities. But what is remarkable about them is their commitment to the understanding of Indian history by using empirical techniques, which are not as systematic as these are in sociology and it is always possible to doubt the validity of such findings on the basis of established and standardised techniques.

In the backdrop of above observations, it is worthwhile to explore and examine the state of sociology and its future in the country. It may be stated at the outset that though most of the issues raised in the preceding discussion can be observed and substantiated, but in terms of looking at the future, certain arguments offered here are conjectural.

Sociology and Social Sciences

It may be argued that that the past, present and future of sociology cannot be separated from those of other social sciences. However, all the social sciences cannot be put at the same pedestal, because the growth and development of all social science disciplines implicate different historical trajectories despite the fact that they have common origin in terms of space that is Europe. Certain social science disciplines, such as economics, have shown great expansion, and going by the arguments of Braudel, largely due to its intimate interaction with the state. Conversely, history has remained one of the most contentious disciplines in terms of the construction of national past and it is evident from the recent controversies that have recently come up with regard to medieval period in India. The Hindutva ideology is consciously constructing a past that is entrenched in singular tradition instead of the composite tradition. We can thus situate sociology and its growth in this unequal development of social science disciplines. The crucial importance of sociology has been a result of its fieldwork tradition. The distinction between anthropology and sociology with regard to field work became visible and sharp in 1960 when sociology began to shift towards, as Singh (2004) informs, 'tools and techniques of research'.

The new avatar of globalization, namely, the market, is emerging as the decisive element in the newly formed industry of higher education (ironically it already existed at the level of school education). Though Oommen (2007) rightly points out that the mode of conceptualization of the world in social sciences "has been changing in the last two centuries", but the present phase of globalization has accelerated this process of change. However, at the level the institutions of higher learning and the research priorities are also undergoing fast change. Two things are coming out as a result of this. First, new educational entrepreneurs are emerging who are trying to make quick buck. Secondly, certain courses are more market-friendly due to which the educational entrepreneurs are entering into specific disciplines. Placed in these two contexts are social sciences that are being ignored because of their low value in the market. This situation has its own dialectical consequence. On one hand, social sciences, particularly sociology, are not drawing the attention of educational entrepreneurs and, on the other hand, this low value may threaten their existence. So long as the institutions are sustaining certain social science courses and research, the future is secure. Over a period of time, the logic of market forces is going to eliminate those courses that are not useful in the sense the management courses are. In other words, sociology is faced with a threat of extinction if it does not prove to be marketable, but owing to its institutional context in India it has better life chances.

In recent years the environmental movements have made the states aware of their responsibility of safeguarding the environment of their territories. Now, an industrial project can only be cleared by the government if the environment is not adversely affected as well as the social survey of the population affected by the project for the purpose of proper rehabilitation is not carried out. This situation has made sociology useful. There are many other areas in which sociologists are finding themselves in competition with other social science disciplines to prove their worth. However, there are certain areas that should have been legitimately monopolized by sociologists, but it has not happened like this. The first is communalism largely dominated by historians and political scientists, whereas the other is farmers' suicide on which the economists are offering plausible but historically refutable arguments. Though such issues substantiate Wallerstein's argument in favour of interdisciplinary approach in teaching and research, yet sociological research tends to lag behind other disciplines in taking up new challenges.

Institutional Context

No social science discipline can grow without institutional context. Institutions are indispensable for achieving excellence in any area of research. Gone are the days when motivated individuals could pursue their research with passion. At present, this passion requires institutional base. Sometimes a scholar's institutional affiliation becomes an index of his being good/not so good/bad. To know the future trends of social science research, we must examine the nature and health of the institutions. There are two broad streams in the institutional context. First, there are universities and colleges that are engaged in teaching and research and, secondly, there are institutions, which are involved in research only. The University Grants commission (UGC) and the Indian Council of Social Science Research (ICSSR) are the two main apex bodies that fund the research in social sciences. Whereas the former is also the policy maker of the university system and in the process aims at ensuring high standards of teaching and research, the latter is exclusively involved in funding the research in the universities and the research institutes. In some of the ICSSR-funded institutes we also find M. Phil and Ph.D programmes being run quite successfully.

With few exceptions colleges are predominantly involved in teaching at the undergraduate level and the research orientation and practice remain poor. There are colleges that offer post-graduate courses and are expected to involve in research activities. At the college levels we have government as well as private colleges. Till recently, universities were autonomous bodies funded by the union or state government. The privatization and liberalization has opened the doors to the private universities on the line of the US. We now also expect the entry of foreign universities either independently or in collaboration with certain local institutions. Globalization process has transformed the education into a kind of industry.

What kinds of institutions are required to meet the challenge of globalization? What is the present state of affairs in India? In other words, are the Indian universities sufficiently equipped to meet this challenge? One of the most important features of an institution is its response to changing environment or its ability to adapt according to the situation with the sole purpose of achieving excellence so as to draw more and more "consumers". Indian universities, to begin with, are poorly equipped to meet any challenge (with few exceptions). One major reason is the bureaucratization of universities. If we divide the entire university staff between teachers and administrative staff, then we shall find that the proportion of teachers is far less than even half of the total. Most of the energy of the universities is expended in conducting examinations, evaluation and declaring results. Rajivlochan (2003) has identified examination system as the major reason for the decline in the educational institutions in the country. He is quite right, but that does not sufficiently explain the downward slide of universities.

It may be reminded that a university is an organization that is headed by its chief executive called the vice-chancellor. The appointment of the vice-chancellor is the function of the government – centre or state does not matter here. The governments have not worked out a transparent system of appointing a vice-chancellor so far. Political affiliations and influence work in the appointment – something that is quite prevalent in the Indian society at the higher levels. It is however possible to work out a system of transparency. In other words, universities, as is expected from educational institutions, do not present a picture of institutions of distinction. The vice-chancellors generally run the universities as organizations the running of whom is an end in itself. Instead of promoting academic excellence, most of the vice-chancellors get trapped in expending their energies in smoothly managing the universities. The consequences from such a scenario can be anticipated.

There has been a general opinion that shows the typical peasant consciousness (may be it is a part of our collective unconscious) that there is a decline in our standards in teaching and research. The issue would be discussed later on, but here its institutional context may be pointed out. The way the notion of decline is generally expressed is symptomatic of a tendency to glorify past. The view that emerges is that the British at the time of creating the universities, which, at that time, were nothing but instruments of conducting examinations, created the best. Such a notion is misplaced. Whatever might have been the rate of decline, these universities are still performing a crucial role. The crisis has emerged from the bureaucratization and bureaucratic control over the universities. This bureaucratization has made the universities non-responsive to the changing conditions and emerging challenges of globalization.

When we talk about research in the institutional context, it may not be assumed that the low quality of research is solely confined to the Indian universities. Let me inform you that even the research institutions created by the ICSSR do not score better than universities in this context. The only way they are better is that they are more efficient in churning out the reports after reports. These reports do not have much intellectual content. The case of the ICSSR, created in 1969, is quite interesting how the apex body of social science research undergoes a change. Chatterjee (2002: 3607) informs, "There is no doubt that the permanent staff of the ICSSR increased significantly through the 1980s and the expenditure on its own administration ate up a large part of the grants received from the government. In 1996–97, for instance, the ICSSR received a total grant of ₹ 9.69 crore from the Government of India. Of this, ₹ 4.64 crore, i.e., 47.9 per cent, went as grants to the ICSSR research institutes. Only ₹ 40 lakhs, i.e., just over 4 per cent, was given as research grants to scholars, while a whopping ₹ 2.25 crore, i.e., 23 per cent, was spent under various heads on the ICSSR's own administration".

The institutions, such as the UGC and the ICSSR, which fund major research projects do it so through the universities. Most of these universities have their own rules of conducting the projects. The researcher, who is the project director (principal investigator), ceases to be a researcher, but turns into an administrator acting through the maze of complex and tedious rules along with handling the university bureaucracy. Why do these organizations not fund the project directly by making the researcher accountable for carrying it out? The answer to this question is to be located in the way the Indian state has formulated the rules regarding accountability. Bureaucratization is the major crisis point in the ability of the Indian universities to meet the challenge of globalization through the entry of foreign universities. The process of globalization in which the emergence of the private universities and the entry of the foreign universities through collaboration would be taking place is not going to uniformly affect the existing system of teaching. It would largely depend upon the regional disparities in the academic institutions. The central universities have better chances of responding to the challenge in comparison to the state funded institutions.

Regional Disparities

The issue of regional disparities signifies the uneven development of the Indian society and it has much to do with the evolution of Indian state and its changing character from welfare approach to free market economy in which the educational institutions have also been covered. The discussion in this section, however, is confined to the teaching and research in sociology though it equally applies to other social sciences. The process of globalization is contributing to the accentuation of these disparities. What we are witnessing is the classical phenomenon of the formation of centre and periphery. Till the end of 1970s the teaching and research in sociology did not show much of polarization. There were a large number of universities around the country, which could be regarded as centres of excellence. Let us quote Deshpande (2005: 15) on this issue thus:

> Despite the 'spirit of the age' leaning in the direction of democratization and inclusionism, there is also an undeniable increase in all kinds of inequalities in the academy. The more obvious of these relate to the funding disparities mentioned above (we shall take up this issue in the next section), but a significant portion is due to other non-resource-related reasons that we need to study more closely. In other words, the overall gap between the handful of 'elite' institutions and the rest is much wider than the strictly resource-related gap, and has increased in recent times. ... The net effect of this is to increase the already wide gap between a few elite institutions, specially those in Delhi, and the higher education set up in the rest of the country.

Deshpande's observations on the state of affairs of the academic institutions are based on a wrong premise. In the age of globalization, it is not inclusionism but exclusionism, which is the guiding spirit. Thus disparities are a natural corollary to the privatization and liberalization. He has, however, presented the true picture of the state of affairs of academy. The reasons for few institutions in Delhi dominating are well known and there is no need to dwell upon the same. We may rather comment upon the way these institutions have been evolved and made to function. Let us start with the ICSSR-funded research institutions. It may be reminded that most of the ICSSR's institutes were created by eminent social scientists, mostly economists. There are two kinds of institutes that can be identified from the above perspective, namely, fully funded and partially funded. Most of the fully funded institutions are located in Delhi, whereas the partially funded institutions are situated in various states of India. In the case of the latter, the state governments do the rest of the funding. Such institutes face various kinds of problems in getting the funds as well in appointing the faculty. The net result is that the fully funded institutes do better than the others.

The university system also has the similar character, that is, we have central universities and the state universities. Whereas the former are fully funded by the Union Government of India, the latter get some grant from the UGC, but they survive on the state government funding. One may raise the question: what is going to be the future of these academic institutions as a result of privatization? It seems that this process least threatens the central universities. Since most of the central universities are located in the metropolitan centres, it is quite obvious that they are supported by elite and do not seem to have much problems in funding. However, the state universities have been experiencing the impact. Most of these universities have become market-oriented by introducing applied courses and are charging very high fees. In the process, the admission and tuition fees of the social science courses have also been raised. Privatization has turned the state universities into institutions that are catering to the needs of ambitious middle classes. The poor have been left out in this commodification of the higher education. Since subjects like sociology are thought to be not having much career options, the fee hike has led to the decline in the number of students seeking admission.

It is quite obvious that the process of globalization is leading to the widening of regional disparities, but the issue does not end here. It can also be observed that through the UPSC and the UGC–NET examinations the dominant centres have been deciding the course contents of sociology to be taught everywhere in the country invariably at the cost of certain local preferences. Simultaneously, there is a tendency to move to the elite institutions among the faculty as if only at places like Delhi and Mumbai their intellectual abilities would be fully realized and recognized.

It has neither been acknowledged nor being articulated that language has contributed most significantly in creating centre–periphery relations in this country. There is so much talk about teaching in one's mother tongue that it has become a kind of political issue. Sometimes, listening to the discourses of well-known social scientists in anglicized English about the need for using the mother tongue in higher education seems so farcical that one feels like treating it a tragedy. The visible decline in sociological research in certain regions of the country coincides with the introduction of the vernacular languages. Very limited attempts have been made by the universities in the country to write, prepare and translate the standard textbooks to be made available in the vernacular languages as a result of which the entire market was opened to the third rate help books. We thus have a centre speaking and writing in English with an international reach, whereas a majority is left with teaching and studying in vernacular languages at the periphery and is competing for jobs within the state creating necessary conditions for the emergence or reinforcement of nativism.

Interestingly, it is at the centre (not the periphery) that lots of discourses are found regarding the declining standards of research and teaching. Who are responsible for it? At least at the level of faculty it may be stated that most of the professors at the centre are responsible for it, because they are the most frequent members of the selection committees. If you ask them for their reason for making third-rate appointments, then you may hear them saying that local politics or the pressure of the vice-chancellors led to this or that appointment. Where does the buck stop?

Role of the State

Understanding the role of the Indian state requires explorations in different dimensions of the institutions and academic practices. Let us first begin with the institutions. We all know that in the post-independence period there was a tremendous expansion of the higher education in the world. In the case of the West this fact has been well noticed by Hobsbaum (1996). Similar kind of phenomenon could be observed in India though its reasons were different from those of the West, as the independent India was struggling to improve the quality of its human resource. According to Chitnis (1997), the enrolment in the institutions of higher education in India rose by 81.48 per cent between 1951 and 1961 and 108 per cent between 1961 and 1971. Shah (2005) has given an updated picture of the enormous growth of academic institutions thus: "During the 90 years, from 1857 to 1947, the number of universities increased from 3 to 19, it increased to about 320 in the 58 years between 1947 to 2005, i.e., roughly at the rate of five universities a year. Similarly, while the number of colleges increased from about 27 to 500 during 1857–1947, it increased to about 16,000 during 1947–2005, i.e., roughly at the rate of 268 colleges a year." Though Shah has not provided details according to the years and it is difficult to know at what point of time major expansion took place, yet we are familiarized with enormity of expansion of the academic institutions that has taken place after independence. So far as sociology is concerned, it is now taught in 100 universities (UGC, 2001). According to the University Grants Commission (UGC), about 10,000 teachers of sociology are involved in teaching at graduate and post-graduate levels and half of the departments of sociology in the country are unable to fill the quota of seats.

Most of the expansion took place till the end of 1980s. It is worthwhile to note that the UGC has been controlling all these institutions of higher education. According to Deshpande (2005), we have reached the stage of "end of state expansion" and "there are very wide disparities across states and disciplines, with many states having had to impose a ban on fresh recruitments and some having been unable even to pay salaries. So, the ultimate impact on institutions varies enormously, especially by degree of dependence on central versus state government funding". In the general context, the above observation is correct, but we have to seriously examine the underlying phenomenon. The Indian state is progressively withdrawing from its responsibility in education in general and higher education in particular that has been attributed to the LPG (liberalization, privatization and globalization). The economic interests of the political and economic elite are transforming education into industry. It is a kind of movement of education from social sector to the private market-oriented sector in which acquiring education is the responsibility of the individuals. The perspective of improving human capital through knowledge and skills so as to transform society in the direction of attainment of better quality of life and national progress has been pushed to the backseat.

Finally, the state, through the ICSSR, the UGC and other institutions, is the most significant in influencing the nature of research, particularly by funding that research which is in accordance with its priorities. For example, research in planning, land reforms, poverty eradication, futurology, etc., at different points of time since independence was a result of the interest, priorities and wishes of the Indian state. In the present state of affairs the role of social sciences with the possible exception of economics is being undermined by the state.

Transcending Local Limitations

We have so far talked about the negative dimensions and consequences of globalization on social sciences in general and sociology in particular. However, globalization has also changed the research and teaching of sociology in a big way. A considerable amount of literature is available on numerous websites that can be browsed through as and when a teacher/researcher/student finds difficulty in finding some books or journals in the university library. Let me elucidate this point through a personal experience. Recently, I came across a concept "root metaphor" in a book by an Indian sociologist, but I could not find any illustration of the concept. This led to the belief that it could be a very popular concept that escaped my attention. However, I did not remain ignorant for long as there were many websites elucidating this concept put forward by a philosopher Stephen Pepper. The present pleasant scenario may not remain so far long, as there is every possibility that one has to pay for getting the requisite knowledge and information through Internet. Even then what to find and where to find would remain the privilege of Internet surfer. In such a situation the division between regional and elite sociologies made by Jha (2005) seems to have become irrelevant.

Still more important for the academic institutions in India is that globalization has begun to destroy the feudal informal structure marked by patronage. It has started destroying the informal structures that were facilitating and impeding the academic interactions. Earlier when a social scientist who was doing research and publishing articles might not have got noticed because he did not have any informal patron/godfather. The western scholars used to help themselves by talking only about their own work. Now, the things have undergone a change. If a new scholar wants to work in a particular area, then what he/she has to do is to browse through the Internet to find the relevant material. In the process, he/she would come across all those who have done work in that area irrespective of whether they have godfathers or not. The globalization is making it possible for academicians to become global on the basis of their own work.

The revolution in information technology has transcended national boundaries and we may now look forward to the formation of transnational identities. The process though has taken place through various academic bodies that are basically voluntary organizations, like International Sociological Association, even prior to the current changes, yet what is happening now is quite phenomenal. According to Deshpande (2005), intensification of international interactions has occurred due to globalization, but it is more with the western countries. Obviously, any interaction that is mediated by technology would benefit those who are more advanced in technology.

Research: Current Status and the Issue of Indigeneity

To what extent the paradigms of social science knowledge are shifting and expanding. The Indian sociologists have started debating the issue of indigeneity of sociology. Is it a case of glocalization under the impact of globalization? The issue requires examination at different level of sociological practice, the foremost being theory and method. Mukherji (2005) emphasizes five points with regard to the entire issue. Firstly, sociology has remained "ideographic" in its approach and has remained confined to "micro-realities". Secondly, there is a need to understand and conceptualize changes in the age of globalization. Third, the "rigour of methodology" is necessary for research. Fourth, the issue of basic and applied research must be weighed properly for public policy issues. Finally, we must get involved in the comparative research. It is quite clear that Mukherji (ibid.) does not want to confuse indigenization with parochialization. Béteille (2002) makes it quite clear that there is something universal about the concepts, methods and theories of sociology. The western practice is based on certain universal principles of rationality that are being continuously questioned, re-examined and revised in the light of emerging realities in both natural sciences and social sciences. However, the issue of indigeneity may be understood in terms of the object of analysis, which is the Indian society. Do theories and methods of western origin prove to be adequate, effective and useful in understanding the Indian society? In other words, we have begun to raise doubts about the globalization of theory and method that took place during the colonial period. Sociology as a discipline was introduced in India during the colonial period and, in the beginning, ethnography was the method with considerable theories about two issues, namely, caste and the village communities. Sociology and social anthropology intertwined with each other in a way that not much difference could be discerned in the initial stages. In the post-independence period, social anthropologist moved to sociology and it still took a long time to introduce the empirical techniques developed and refined by the American sociologists. Even now strict boundaries do not exist between the two; nor are they desirable.

How should we go about the evaluation of the sociological research hitherto done in India? However, despite the increase in the number of Ph.Ds the quality has declined considerably (Deshpande, 2005). Anybody involved in the evaluation of Ph.D dissertations would know it better than others. It is not simply the quality of the research done at the level of Ph.Ds that requires serious pondering, but also the way such a research is accepted and positively evaluated. The first culprit is the compromise of the honourable professors who appointed non-deserving people on faculty positions. The second reason is the development of networking among the mediocrity. There are clicks that help each other out and the consequence is the transformation of various departments into Ph.D manufacturing units and some teachers becoming expert in guiding students in efficient manner. Most of such individuals could have done well in business. It has also come to the notice that one can buy Ph.D from the market, as one buys a toothbrush. Obviously, the price is quite high, but it is not as high as the value of a scooter. In other words, we also have got Ph.Ds valued in the market situation. Such dissertations, written by ghostwriters, can only go through if the networking helps in viva voce examinations. One can imagine the fate of the institutions that would employ such Ph.D degree holders. If you reject a thesis in the viva voce examination or a local candidate in the selection committee, you will become unpopular and may not be invited in future for such assignment. Or if you are regarded as strict, you will be avoided. Globalization can do nothing wrong to such institutions!

Despite all these limitations, sociology has grown as one of the major social science disciplines in the country. The number of books and articles giving evidence of high standard research has increased. Many regional associations are publishing their own research journals. A considerable proportion of the articles published in the journals show an evidence of research of high quality. On top of this many universities are bringing out the social science journals. Similarly, the research institutes and some departments of sociology are also bringing out their own journals. The kind of analysis Chatterjee (2002) has made on the basis of two journals is an indicative of elite perspective. He has ignored a considerable number of journals published in English in the country. We should also not ignore the journals published in the regional languages though the mainstream sociologists ignore such efforts and fail to make an assessment of the value and quality of such research.

Concluding Remarks

The market orientation in the age of globalization will be progressively premised on the question of the usefulness of sociology vindicating Lyotard's (1999) views on knowledge. The students have already started asking how pursuing sociology will help in their career orientations. However, a lot depends upon the level of research and the issues taken up by the discipline that address the practical problems of our society without ignoring the production of basic knowledge. To what extent privatization will be of help is the moot question that requires serious thinking. Chatterjee (ibid.: 3612) is of the view that "privatisation cannot be the answer to the problems that social science research faces in South Asia today. The type of research that private sponsors, consisting mostly of international development agencies, need from developing countries has no intellectual content. These sponsors have no interest in funding institutions that can only promise to produce new knowledge and a new generation of trained social scientists in 10 or 20 years". However, providing solution to the declining standards of research and teaching in various universities may be a quixotic exercise, as most of the steps required to reform the system are known to everybody. One may go along with Deshpande (2002) that the declining interest in social sciences is due to the withdrawal of the middle class elite form the social sciences, but it does not provide any solution, because the middle classes cannot be dissuaded from its present orientation. In his recent article, Shah (2005) has already shown how various strategies of the UGC have miserably failed. I would like to end the discussion with a note of caution. In the process of criticizing the discipline we should keep in mind that that in fact at certain levels sociology has grown well and there is much more number of good researchers now than in the past.

Anywhere the role of state has remained crucial in influencing the quality of education and excellence in research in sciences. What we are witnessing in India is that the state has started withdrawing from education. Ironically, in the recent economic crisis worldwide the market has not been allowed to correct the situation by the states. The private capital has been given the state support in most of the developed countries. It has become clear that free market is a myth when it comes to the issue of the survival of the private capital at the time of crisis. The present economic crisis has convincingly shown that neither the market nor the state is a self-propelling system. Both survive and thrive on each other's support. In such a scenario the future of social science research should be examined within the framework of the structure of relevance. The structure of relevance is being constructed in terms of instrumental rationality and the reasons for governance in which how social sciences in general and sociology in particular could be useful to both the market and the state is the moot point. We are thus entering an era in which the likelihood of marginalization of social sciences with the probable exception of economics exists. It is easy to talk about the declining standards of social sciences and institutions of higher learning, but difficult to reorganize the same for higher standards. At this moment the structure of relevance is oriented towards further marginalizing the social sciences through the use of the rationale of declining standards. Interestingly, sociology is a discipline that can survive because it is our own society that we study and it has its unique features that could be distinguished from other societies. With earnestness and commitment the sociologists can make themselves relevant in this fast changing world. The resilience of local cultures and social practices in the age of globalization has made it clear that the relevance of sociology would continue to grow in future. The need is to make ourselves professionally and ethically committed to our craft.

References

Béteille, André (2002) *Sociology: Essays on Approaches and Method*. New Delhi: Oxford University Press.

Braudel, Fernand (1981) *Civilization and Capitalism 15th–18th Century, Volume I: The Structure of Everyday Life*. London: Fontana Press.

Chatterjee, Partha (2002) "Institutional Context of Social Science Research in South Asia", *Economic and Political Weekly*, Vol. 38, No. 35, August 31, pp. 3604–12.

Chitnis, Suma (1997) The Crisis in Higher Education. I.P. Desai Memorial Lecture: 10, Surat: Centre for Social Studies.

Deshpande, Satish (2002) "Social Science Research Capacity in South Asia: Some Questions for Discussion", *Economic and Political Weekly*, Vol. 38, No. 35, August 31, pp. 3628–30.

—— (2005) 'New Anxieties and Old Predicaments: Sociology in a Globalized South Asia', paper presented in the South Asia Workshop on *State of Sociology: Issues of Relevance and Rigour*, held on February 23–25, at Suraj Kund, Haryana, organised by the Indian Sociological Society.

Hobsbaum, Eric (1996) *The Age of Extremes: A History of the World, 1914 –1991*. New York: Vintage Books.

Jha, Hetukar (2005) "Indian Sociology in Crisis: The Need for Regional Orientation", *Sociological Bulletin*, Vol. 54, No. 3, September-December, pp. 396–411.

Judge, Paramjit S. (2003) "Introduction: Globalisation and Social Dynamics", in Paramjit S. Judge et al. (eds.), *Development, Gender and Diaspora: Context of Globalisation*, Jaipur: Rawat Publications.

Lyotard, Jean-Francois (1999) "The Postmodern Condition", in Anthony Elliott (ed.), *Contemporary Social Theory*, Malden: Blackwell Publishers, pp. 317–26.

Mukherji, Partha (2005) "Sociology in South Asia: Indigenisation as Universalising Social Science", *Sociological Bulletin*, Vol. 54, No. 3, September-December, pp. 311–24.

Oommen, T.K. (2007) *Knowledge and Society: Situating Sociology and Social Anthropology*. New Delhi: Oxford University Press.

Rajivlochan, M. (2003) 'History of Improving Higher Education', paper presented in the UGC Golden Jubilee Seminar on "How to Complete the First Cycle of Access and Accreditation", September 26–27, Punjab University, Chandigarh.

Shah, A.M. (2005) "Higher Education and Research: Roots of Mediocrity", *Economic and Political Weekly*, Vol. 40, Nos. 22 and 24, pp. 2234–42.

Singh, Yogendra (2004) *Ideology and Theory in Indian Sociology*. Jaipur: Rawat Publications.

UGC (2001) Report of the Curriculum Development Committee in Sociology, New Delhi: UGC.

Wallerstein, Immanual et al. (1997) *Open the Social Sciences: Report of the Gulbenkian Commission on the Restructuring of the Social Sciences*. New Delhi: Vistaar Publications.

4

Late Modernization in the Age of Globalization

East Asia and Beyond

Volker H. Schmidt

The breakthrough to modernity marks a world historical turning point, giving rise to a new societal formation that differs fundamentally from its evolutionary precursor. Once this had happened somewhere, the environments of all other societies were altered, pressuring them to react and adapt. Modernity was from its earliest beginnings a globalizing phenomenon, as none of its constitutive features are "naturally" confined to any particular world region. On the contrary, as Marx was perhaps the first to point out for the case of the capitalist economy, its function logic drives it beyond all socially constructed (hence economically arbitrary) boundaries in the quest to draw the entire globe into one world market. Today, we can discern similar tendencies in the sciences, in the media, in religion, in medicine, in education, and, to a slightly lesser degree, in the more nationally circumscribed spheres of politics and law as well. Initially, the spreading of modernity beyond northwest Europe took place through processes of colonization. But colonization, driven by the aim to exploit the colonized, was no good developer. It should therefore come as no surprise that many of the benefits associated with modernity reached the non-western world other than Japan only after the Second World War and the collapse of colonialism. Global modernity has been in the making for centuries. But for the majority of the world's population, it is only just becoming a reality (Schmidt, 2007), with what has been labelled the age of globalization a key force behind its rapid diffusion.

Globalization occurred in several waves, with its earliest manifestations dating back to the late 15th century European "explorations". But compared to the enormously growing integration of the world witnessed during the past few decades earlier phases of globalization remained relatively confined phenomena. Still, modernization continued to be a very uneven process, penetrating different world regions to different degrees. Nowhere has the process been as thorough and successful as in East Asia, where several countries transformed themselves from poor "third world" nations to rich, highly developed economic power houses within a few decades. Failed processes of state building and development in the early postcolonial years had given rise to widespread pessimism concerning the possibilities of late modernization. East Asia proved this pessimism wrong.

The aim of the present paper is to reconstruct some of the key determinants of East Asia's modernization. It concludes with a few speculations as to its implications – for the world and for sociology.

II

As is well known, the first East Asian country to engage in full-scale modernization was Japan. Japan's modernization occurred in response to pressures of the United States and other western powers to (re-)open its sea ports for unrestricted (asymmetrical) trade. When American and European warships appeared off the shore of Japan in the 1850s and 60s, the country was in no position to militarily resist the might of the foreign intruders. The authorities were forced to sign a number of treaties similar to those that had earlier been imposed on China following its defeat in the two Opium Wars. This undermined the legitimacy of the Tokugawa shogunate that had ruled Japan for two and a half centuries. In what came to be known as the Meiji Restoration, in 1868, it was overthrown by a faction of the ruling elite with the aim to reorganize and empower the country's government, economy and military in such a way that its sovereignty could be defended. As the new rulers soon found out, accomplishing this mission involved nothing less than a complete transformation of Japanese society (Landes, 1998).

The term 'modernization', as it is used here, has two interrelated meanings. On the one hand, it simply refers to the dynamic aspects of modernity, the processes and products of change that accompany the transition from pre-modern to modern society and beyond. On the other hand, it signifies conscious efforts on the part of influential societal actors to set in motion, by means of rational planning, developments that result in what is understood as modernity (or high or advanced modernity) at a particular point in time.[1]

Historically, one of the most important, though by no means only, aspects of modernization has been industrialization of the economy. In countries that industrialized first, especially in Britain, the main driving forces were private entrepreneurs and (increasingly free) markets, coupled with state protection of domestic businesses against foreign competition, forceful opening of (distant) markets and decreed trade rules. Industrial latecomers, by contrast, often mobilize the state apparatus as the key agent and coordinator of the modernization process (Bendix, 1970). Whereas the earliest expressions of modernity were primarily emergent phenomena, the unintended and unanticipated effects of unplanned societal evolution, later modernizers, through the example of reference societies that are ahead of them, tend to have relatively clear ideas as to where they are headed and how to get there.

The best known cases of late modernization are those of Germany and Japan. In both cases, strong, authoritarian and bureaucratically organized central governments played a key role in the process and initiated many of the requisite steps. In the early phases of modernization, both countries relied on foreign know-how to build up their industries, which they "borrowed" by various legal and illegal means. Since Germany was ahead of Japan in several respects,[2] it also served as one of the models that the Japanese modernizers drew upon: in the military, in the bureaucracy, in science and (higher) education, in the legal sphere. Other similarities abound, among them both countries' rise to colonial powers around the turn to the 20th century, their roles in the Second World War, and their economic performance in the first few decades after that war.

Modernization theories tend to view economic development as the prime mover of societal modernization (see Lerner, 1968: 388), modernizing agents often do likewise. They have thus a tendency to prioritize economic growth over other policy objectives. That is certainly true of the leading cases of East Asian modernization, namely, Japan and the four tigers, but it also holds for other late industrializers in the region, especially for China. The results have been spectacular.

Beginning with the Industrial Revolution, the West experienced unprecedented economic growth. From 1820 to 1870, Britain's GDP increased by 1.2 per cent annually; 30 times faster than the world average between 1500 and 1820 (Maddison, 1995: 62; 20). It took the country 50 years to double its per capita income. Given that no country had ever achieved such rapid growth before, contemporary observers were understandably impressed. But what they witnessed was little in comparison to the growth rates achieved by East Asian economies during the second half of the 20th century. Japan's per capita income rose almost ten-fold between 1950 and 1973 and nearly 28-fold between 1820 and 1992. From the early 1960s onwards, the above tigers grew at double-digit rates for two to three decades in a row and continue to perform well to the present day. In the early 1970s, a third generation of high growth economies (comprising mainly Malaysia, Thailand and Indonesia) followed in their footsteps, with China joining in around the turn to the 1980s.

Because modern economic growth reached the non-western world other than Japan only after 1950, global (cross-regional) economic inequalities, which had been relatively moderate until the 18th century, exploded following the Industrial Revolution. East Asia's modernization has reversed that trend (Firebaugh, 2003). For most of recorded history, China's economy was the largest in the world. As late as 1820, the Middle Kingdom accounted for nearly a third of global GDP, with India contributing another 16 per cent (Maddison, 1995). By 1950, China's share had shrunk to 5 per cent. Conversely, the West's share of global GDP increased unabated for almost 200 years, peaking around 1950 when Western Europe, North America and Oceania (Australia and New Zealand) together controlled 57 per cent of the world's economic product. Thereafter, it dropped steadily; by 1998 the West's share of global GDP was down to 46 per cent, while that of Asia had more than doubled (to 37 per cent, up from 18.5 per cent in 1950; cf. Maddison, 2001: 263). This trend continued through 2008.

Both the West and East Asia performed well in the second half of the 20th century, but East Asia grew more than double the rate of the West. As long as the region's rise was confined to Japan and the four tigers, it did not affect the overall weights in the world economy very much, for with a combined population of (presently) just over 200 million people, they were in no position to challenge the West's dominance. China, on the other hand, represents more than one-fifth of the world population. If a country of this size takes off economically, then it is bound to shake the world.

It has already begun to do so (Kynge, 2006). Following the introduction of market reforms in 1979, China's increasingly open economy exhibited an average annual growth rate of approximately 10 per cent for 30 years. If past trends of cross-regional development continue, then China's economy may overtake that of the United States within the next 35 years; when comparing countries on the basis of purchasing power parities, which reflect the actual buying capacity of local incomes, this could happen as early as 2017 (*The Economist*, 2005: 86). Using market exchange rates, the measure at which firms trade and repatriate profits, China already replaced Germany as the world's number three in 2007. As a result, two of the world's three largest economies are now located in East Asia – a region that was economically marginal just a half century earlier. By 2025, this region may account for 40 per cent of the global economy, the share it held in 1820 when its long-lasting decline began (Gill and Kharas, 2007: 2). Another 15 years later, around 2040, China alone could be responsible for 40 per cent of the world's GDP, with the 15 countries comprising the EU in 2000 down to 5 per cent and the United States down to 14 per cent. If this prediction came true, the joint economic output of the West's core countries would be less than half that of China and less than a third that of Asia as a whole. With 12 per cent of global GDP, even India would only be slightly behind the United States, but significantly ahead of the EU (see Fogel, 2007).

East Asia's economic rise follows a similar pattern throughout the region. Except in the city-states of Singapore and Hong Kong, wide-ranging agricultural reforms aimed at raising the productivity of the primary sector generally preceded the industrial take-off. Based on a broad vision of how best to catch up with the industrialized world, highly interventionist governments then sought to find a niche for their country in the global system and promoted particular industries deemed strategic for that goal; additionally or alternatively, some of them established special economic zones and/or took various other measures to encourage foreign direct investment (as in the cases of Singapore, China and Vietnam) as a means to compensate for a dearth of experienced industrial entrepreneurship and as a vehicle of job creation and technology transfer. To foster indigenous industrialization, select local (often state-owned or controlled) businesses were supplied with cheap credit by the development bank, the "flagship of the developmental state" (Amsden, 2001: 285). In the domestic market, they were protected from foreign competition through import tariffs and quotas. Industrialization usually began with import substitution and then moved on to emphasizing trade and export. State subsidies to particular industries and businesses were not provided on a permanent basis but conditional on performance, measured by the ability to compete in international markets and to export the output (Grabowski et al., 2007).

Labour-intensive industrialization at the early stages of transition to a modern economy enables businesses to absorb abundantly available cheap labour. This at once reduces dependency on (usually scarce) capital and keeps unemployment low, thus contributing to political and social stability. In Japan, starting in the late 1880s, the simplest tasks were often performed by young country girls/women recruited from poor peasant households in distant areas (Sugihara, 2003: 99) – today that pattern is repeating itself in China and elsewhere in the region. As a country climbs up the technology ladder, mature, labour-intensive industries migrate to less developed neighbours, creating a regional division of labour wherein the advanced countries take the lead and concentrate on capital-intensive, complex, high-value added production processes that require a workforce with better skills. Over time, wages increase in both settings, thus reinforcing this "flying geese" pattern of development and extending its range geographically as well as to a growing number of industries.

Initially depending on the imitation and adaptation of techniques from the West, Japan had become a world leader in important technologies by the 1990s, setting the parameters of change for others (Katzenstein, 2003: 216ff.); other East Asian "miracle" countries likewise quickly transformed themselves from low-wage economies making simple commodities to globally competitive producers of high technologies. Taiwan, for example, needed less than two decades for this transformation, and from 1995 to 1999 its information industry was the third largest in the world, only to be overtaken by China in 2000 (Greene, 2007: 145). China itself, while still the world's workshop, meanwhile also moved beyond the stage of purely assembly-driven, low-technology mass production that characterized its economic profile in the 1990s; if it had not, it could not have surpassed Taiwan in this high-tech domain. In fact, "China's export bundle is (now) that of a country at a level of per capita income three times higher than the country's actual level" (Gill and Kharas, 2007: 98). Currently, massive efforts are undertaken by businesses and the government alike to achieve a position of technological leadership within the next few decades (Zhou, 2008). The examples of Japan and the four tigers show that this ambition need not be illusionary.

The state's role in the modernization process goes well beyond the nurturing and governing of what despite massive intervention are nevertheless market economies. It invests heavily in infrastructures, in the formation of human capital, in research and development, in the provision of (basic) public welfare, in recreational facilities – in short, in well-rounded development that, while privileging core groups, includes all segments of the population through policies of "shared growth". Policy-designation tends to be pragmatically-oriented rather than driven by ideological concerns or uncompromising commitment to deep-rooted moral convictions. After earmarking a problem for regulation, the first step usually consists in a "systematic scanning of the relevant environment" (Katzenstein, 2003: 224) to identify best practices for emulation, as well as pitfalls to be avoided, at home. The lessons drawn from these exercises are then translated into locally adapted policies. Recruitment into and promotion within the civil service are based primarily on technical skills and competence (rather than on social status and capital, i.e., connections, as is often the case in developing countries), and leading government officials are benchmarked against the performance (in Singapore even pay levels) of business leaders. Bureaucracies tend to be powerful and relatively uncorrupt by global standards – although significant intra-regional differences exist in this respect.[3] They often draft, and usually have the capacity to implement, formally adopted policies, although that too varies between countries. China's central government, for instance, is in many ways far less effectual than that of other late East Asian modernizers, owing partly to the country's enormous size, partly to its lower level of development, and partly to other factors.

Using the United Nations' Human Development Index (HDI) as a measurement rod, Japan and the four tigers are now in the same league as their (erstwhile) western models. If Israel is treated as a part of the West, then no single non-western country from outside East Asia is ahead of any of the region's star performers, whose (as yet) "weakest" member (South Korea) ranks 26 among a total of 177 countries. China too improved its HDI steadily (from 0.527 in 1975 to 0.768 in 2004; UNDP, 2006: 289). One of the poorest countries in the world in 1978, it has been a lower-middle income country since 2003 (Independent Evaluation Group, 2007), with the upper-middle income level slowly coming into reach. And, while the growing wealth is spread very unevenly across regions, China no longer has a single province that falls into the United Nations' "low development" category; the whole country is now either in the "high" or "medium" group (Ministry of Foreign Affairs of the People's Republic of China, and the United Nations System in China, 2005). Equally instructive as the comparison with its own past is that between China and India. While both countries started from roughly similar levels of development after World War II (Drèze and Sen, 2002), today China is about twice as rich as India and 47 places ahead of the subcontinent in the HDI (UNDP, 2007: 229ff.).

Public education is a key to human development (for an emphasis on the region, see Tilak, 2002). Because people are the only readily available resource in the region, governments made sustained efforts to develop it. In a cultural environment that holds learning in high esteem public education is also a very popular service (Jones, 1993). As in most other dimensions of change, Japan was the first East Asian country to institute (compulsory) mass education (soon after the Meiji Restoration). Once released from their colonial masters, the tiger countries followed suit,[4] and so did China after the Communist Revolution. Since industrial work requires at least basic literacy and competency in science and mathematics, the initial emphasis was on guaranteeing universal enrolment in elementary schools. Later, this was complemented by rapid expansions of secondary and tertiary education, as well as the introduction of various on-the-job training and skill enhancement schemes. Today, the educational systems of Japan and the four tigers are considered to be amongst the best in the world, with students from these countries repeatedly scoring high in international performance evaluations (see, e.g., Martin et al., 2008a; 2008b). In South Korea, up to 70 per cent of school leavers now undergo tertiary education, a rate matched only by a few other countries (e.g., Australia and some of the Nordic countries; see OECD, 2007), thus putting South Korea into a global leadership position. China, while obviously far behind such levels, has also made enormous progress in educational enrolment and attainment. By 1980, its adult literacy rate stood at 69 per cent, roughly equivalent to that of the East Asian tigers at the time of their economic take-off (Drèze and Sen, 2002: 76). By 2003, the primary school enrolment rate had reached close to 99 per cent, and in 2004, the adult literacy rate stood at 91 per cent (UNDP, 2006: 324). At the same time, enrolment ratios in both secondary and tertiary education have also rapidly expanded. In the

1980s, only 2 to 3 per cent of school-leavers went to university, in 2004, the figure was 19 per cent (National Bureau of Statistics of China, 2005). In 2006, more than four million students graduated from university, up from just over one million five years earlier. The expansion at the doctoral level is even faster than for undergraduates: between 1999 and 2003, nearly 12 times as many doctorates were awarded as in the period from 1982 to 1989 (*The Economist*, 10 September 2005). The upward trend has since continued.

As indicated before, East Asia's innovation capabilities were relatively limited until recently. Innovativeness is largely a function of research and development (R&D) efforts, which tended to be concentrated in the West. Hence, the dependence of industrial latecomers on imported western technology. Japan was the first East Asian country that tried to emancipate itself from this dependency by committing substantial financial resources to the development of technology. The country now devotes over 3 per cent of its GDP to R&D spending – more than most western nations except the Scandinavian countries (Frank, 2006). South Korea, Taiwan and Singapore, whose R&D efforts were negligible until the 1970s, now spend between 2.2 and 2.6 per cent, a level comparable to that of the United States and other leading innovators, and China, while still trailing behind with 1.5 per cent, more than doubled its R&D expenditure between 1995 and 2004, the aim being to catch up with the United States by 2020. By 2006, China had already become the world's second largest spender on R&D. The investments are clearly paying off. Using patenting as an indicator of innovativeness, the average annual number of patents granted to the region's leading R&D countries more than doubled in the past decade. Topping the group of the four tigers, Taiwan now generates 30 patents per 100,000 population, about as many as Japan and the United States, the two world leaders (Gill and Kharas, 2007: 154). South Korea and even China have also made enormous progress in recent years, with both countries ranking among the top ten patenting nations in the world (World Intellectual Property Organization, 2007). It is expected that by the end of the next decade the United States will have lost its globally dominant position in R&D, owing mainly to a significant shifting of R&D activities to Asia, especially to China and India (*Financial Times*, 15 October 2007). This expectation is mirrored by other sources believing China and India may significantly narrow the gap between their and the American national innovation system(s) within the next ten years (National Intelligence Council, 2008).

Once again, government initiatives were (and continue to be) crucial to set the development in motion. Throughout the region, billions of tax dollars are spent on the building of science and technology parks, the creation of research centres and laboratories, the expansion and upgrading of universities, the awarding of scholarships, the luring back of native talent sent abroad for advanced studies and/or the hiring of foreign researchers, etc. Yet, like in the West, the bulk (60%) of R&D is carried out within the business sector, while only 20 per cent is conducted by governments and another 20 per cent at universities and other institutions of higher education (Gill and Kharas, 2007: 24). And, while East Asian R&D used to have a strong bias toward prioritizing applied research aiming for small, incremental improvements of established technology, of late a growing portion of R&D has begun to be devoted to basic research as well. This augurs well for the region's future innovative capability, which is already high by global standards, but taking East Asia as a whole still significantly lower than that of the West.

Much basic research takes place in universities that are also responsible for the education of future researchers. Around 1900 academic research was highly concentrated in North America and Europe; outside the West, only Japan and a few other countries were building up their own scientific infrastructures. But whereas Japan had no more than 33 chairs in all academic fields at the turn of the century, German universities had as many as 2,667 members of academic staff (Cozzens, 1997). Today, Japanese universities score better in global rankings of top universities than their German counterparts (which lost their global leadership position in the first decades of the 20th century; Ben-David, 1971, ch. 7), and all of the tiger countries have several world class universities. In fact, East Asia is now the only non-western region with a sizeable number of globally renowned universities (Shanghai Jiao Tong University, 2007; Times Higher Education, 2008), and that number is almost certain to increase with China's further ascent.

The findings reported here and in many other publications on East Asia's post-World War II development confirm a view held by many modernization theorists that successful modernization is a systemic process, affecting all institutional sectors of society and including the whole population whose living conditions change dramatically in a short span of time. Within a matter of a few decades, industrialization and urbanization transformed a rural way of life that had dominated the experience of the overwhelming majority of humankind for thousands of years. Even in Japan, the workforce was still predominantly agrarian in the early decades of the 20th century. Between 1950 and 1975, the proportion of city dwellers almost doubled from 38 per cent to 67 per cent due to a massive rural-to-urban migration wave (Sugihara, 2003: 108). After the Second World War, most South Koreans were still farmers working tiny plots of land; by 1975, a majority lived in cities (Mason et al., 1980: 9), and today that is true of 82 per cent of the population (UNDP, 2007: 243). China lags behind the earlier late modernizers in East Asia, but is presently undergoing the same transformation. Before its transition to capitalism, 82 per cent of the population lived in rural areas. Over the past three decades, this share has shrunk to 58 per cent (National Bureau of Statistics of China, 2005). Prior to 1978, China's economy was predominantly agrarian, with over 70 per cent of the workforce engaged in the production of food and the primary sector accounting for nearly 40 per cent of the GDP. Today, the two figures are 46 per cent and 13 per cent, respectively. The trend continues. Each year, some 20 million rural workers move to the modern sector of the economy, with 300 million more expected to follow in the next 15 to 20 years (Gill and Kharas, 2007: 98).

Industrialization has raised incomes and reduced poverty enormously throughout East Asia. Japan and the four tigers are now amongst the richest countries in the world despite lacking significant natural resources, thus mirroring the situation of (most) wealthy western nations. They also resemble them in other ways. Their economies are highly competitive; their political systems all excel in "good governance"; their legal systems function well and are becoming increasingly autonomous; they all have welfare systems in place that protect the most vulnerable; and their educational and (with some qualification) medical systems are top of the global league.

In the past thirty years, China has made enormous strides toward catching up with its East Asian and western role models, but while much of the Middle Empire has been fundamentally transformed, it still has a long way to go to reach their levels of development. Whether this is at all possible for a country of China's size and complexity, and whether the country will be able to tackle the enormous problems facing it on its further way up, is an open question. But, while caution is certainly sensible, history has proven many skeptics wrong – even the most farsighted 19th century observers of industrial capitalism in Europe and North America had no presentiment of the advances that the 20th century would bring to those parts of the world, and when the East Asian tigers embarked on their route to affluence, they were not only in desperate conditions but widely viewed as doomed to fail.

III

For a millennium and more antedating the modern age, Asia "was the world" (Gordon, 2008), if by that phrase one means the centre of economic gravity, of courtly and political culture, of travel and trade, of innovation and human self-reflection. The arrival of modernity, first in Europe and later in what gradually was to become "the" West, ended Asia's pre-eminence, turning the erstwhile centre into a peripheral part on the margins of the West-centred "world system". Asia's "march to modernity" (Mahbubani, 2008), beginning with Japan's transformation after the Meiji Restoration, but picking up speed only in the second half of the 20th century, is reversing the course of history and bringing Asia back onto the world stage. If current trends continue, then Asia may well become "the" world again – the centre of the world economy, the centre of world politics, the centre of world science, the centre of world culture – in short, the centre of modernity.

That is the first implication of (East) Asia's rise. Regardless of whether (East) Asia becomes the next centre of modernity, the region's development brings to a close an era that lasted roughly 500 years – the era of western domination and supremacy. A new world order is in the making, and its emergence means that, in the words of the United States National Intelligence Council (2008: vi), "the international system – as constructed following the Second World War – will be almost unrecognizable in 2025". And, while nobody can predict with certainty how the new system will look like, it is clear that it will be very different from the old one. New players are emerging on the global stage, and that alone alters not only the composition of the world's "steering bodies", but also their agendas, because the new player's interests are not the same of those of the established parties that are no longer able to dictate the rules of the game. The policy takers of the past are becoming active policy makers, so future rules will reflect a wider spectrum of interests and values. Moreover, as the world becomes more multi-polar, more and more world trends will emanate from Asia in particular, and from other non-western world regions in general.

A second, and related, implication of East Asia's rise is that the region has become a model of development – for other parts of Asia, for instance for the Middle East and South Asia, but also for other parts of the world, notably Africa and Latin America, where Asia is rapidly gaining influence. Successful modernization of East Asia means the less developed world no longer needs to look to the West as the sole role model. For better or for worse, that alone is a "liberating" moment as it frees many countries from dependence on the West. Equally liberating is the boost in confidence that East Asia's rise offers: yes, it can be done if only the right measures are taken. Learning from East Asia has already stimulated policy changes in several parts of the world, and the success of many emerging economies partly reflects such changes.

A third implication, related to both the first and second ones, is that underdevelopment can no longer be blamed exclusively on external forces (preferably "the West"), as East Asia's shows that development is possible even in the face of rather adverse conditions. The positive lessons to be drawn from East Asia's modernization shed light on the failures of less successful developers, on internal policies and structures that are detrimental to development and that must be overcome if development is to become a reality.

A final implication to be mentioned here is academic and concerns the lessons to be drawn for the social sciences. One such lesson is that a resumption of modernization research might be desirable. Modernization theory – the theory that guided much of this research in the past – was abandoned in the early 1970s due to various real and invented problems associated with it. Since then, sociology has taken many turns, not the least of which is a parochial turn as a result of which most sociologists concern themselves primarily, if not exclusively, with "domestic" issues. One consequence of this parochial turn is that sociology now stands empty-handed before the above transformation of world order that, while being widely debated among historians, political scientists and economists, does not yet seem to have emerged on sociologists' radar screens. For decades some of the discipline's leading figures preached development is not possible. Modernization theory could not only have taught them otherwise, but could also render intelligible what some believe signals "one of the biggest revolutions in history" (*The Economist*, 17 November 2007) – if it were finally taken note of.

Notes

1. Since modernity is a societal formation that differs not only from its evolutionary precursor but, due to constantly accelerating change, at any given point in time also from itself in earlier "incarnations", the notion of "the modern" is far from fixed. Instead, it co-varies with ongoing social, cultural, institutional, technological change that turns what counts as an instance of advanced modernity today into a matter of the past tomorrow. Needless to say, modernity is also an "essentially contested" concept whose analytic meaning cannot be fully separated from normative and political content.
2. Under the leadership of Prussia, German law was rapidly modernized in the early decades of the 19th century. A reform of the universities at about the same time laid the foundations for the rise of German science to global pre-eminence (in the late 19th and early 20th centuries), and the earliest beginnings of industrialization can be traced back

to the 1830s. Especially after 1871, the modernization of the economy was strongly guided by what in hindsight might well be called (one of) the first developmental state, a term coined by Chalmers Johnson (1982) for Japan's case. Interestingly, Prussia was also ahead of other European countries in basic education, one of the key determinants of successful (late) modernization.

3. For instance, South Korea performs less well in its control of corruption than do the other East Asian tigers, and in some studies China's corruption problem is assessed to be worse than India's (see Kaufmann, Kray and Mastruzzi, 2007).
4. This statement needs to be qualified insofar as all four tiger countries were educationally relatively well developed long before they reached independence from colonial rule (or, in the case of Hong Kong, became a special administrative region within China).

References

Amsden, Alice H. (2001) *The Rise of 'the Rest': Challenges to the West from Late-Industrializing Economies*. Oxford: Oxford University Press.

Ben-David, Joseph (1971) *The Scientist's Role in Society: A Comparative Study*. Englewood Cliffs, NJ: Prentice Hall.

Bendix, Reinhard (1970) "Preconditions of Development: A Comparison of Japan and Germany", in Ronald Dore (ed.), *Aspects of Social Change in Modern Japan*, Princeton, NJ: Princeton University Press, pp. 27–68.

Cozzens, Susan E. (1997) "The Discovery of Growth: Statistical Glimpses of Twentieth-Century Science", in John Krige and Dominique Pestre (eds.), *Science in the Twentieth Century*, Amsterdam: Harwood Academic Publishers, pp. 127–42.

Drèze, Jean and Amartya Sen (2002) *India: Development and Participation* (second edition), Delhi: Oxford University Press.

Firebaugh, Glenn (2003) *The New Geography of Global Inequality*. Cambridge: Harvard University Press.

Fogel, Robert W. (2007) *Capitalism and Democracy in 2040: Forecasts and Speculations*. Cambridge: National Bureau of Economic Research, NBER Working Paper No. 13184.

Frank, Simona (2006) "R&D Expenditure in Europe", *Eurostat. Statistics in Focus. Science and Technology*, Vol. 6, pp. 1–7.

Gill, Indermit and Homi Kharas (2007) *An East Asian Renaissance: Ideas for Economic Growth*. Washington, DC: World Bank.

Grabowski, Richard, Sharmistha Self and Michael P. Shields (2007) *Economic Development: A Regional, Institutional, and Historical Approach*. Armonk: M.E. Sharpe.

Greene, J. Megan (2007) "Taiwan's Knowledge-Based Economy: A Historical Perspective on Higher Education, Manpower Planning and Economic Development", in Robert Ash and J. Megan Greene (eds.), *Taiwan in the 21st Century: Aspects and Limitations of a Developmental Model*, London: Routledge, pp. 128–51.

Gordon, Stewart (2008) *When Asia was the World*. New Haven: Yale University Press.

Independent Evaluation Group (2007) *Development Results in Middle Income Countries: An Evaluation of the World Bank's Support*. Washington, DC: World Bank.

Johnson, Chalmers (1982) *MITI and the Japanese Miracle: The Growth of Industrial Policy, 1925–1975*. Stanford, CA: Stanford University Press.

Jones, Catherine (1993) "The Pacific Challenge: Confucian Welfare States", in Catherine Jones (ed.), *New Perspectives on the Welfare State in Europe*, London: Routledge, pp. 198–217.

Katzenstein, Peter J. (2003) "Japan, Technology and Asian Regionalism in Comparative Perspective", in Giovanni Arrighi, Takeshi Hamashita and Mark Seldon (eds.), *The Resurgence of East Asia: 500, 150 and 50 Year Perspectives*, London: Routledge, pp. 214–58.

Kaufmann, Daniel, Aart Kray and Massimo Mastruzzi (2007) *Governance Matters VI: Aggregate and Individual Governance Indicators 1996–2006*. World Bank Policy, Research Working Paper 4280, July, Washington, DC: World Bank.

Kynge, James (2006) *China Shakes the World: The Rise of a Hungry Nation*. London: Weidenfeld & Nicholsen.

Landes, David (1998) *The Wealth and Poverty of Nations*. New York: Norton.

Lerner, Daniel (1968) "Modernization", in D.L. Sills and R.K. Merton (eds.), *International Encyclopedia of the Social Sciences*, New York: Macmillan, pp. 386–95.

Maddison, Angus (1995) *Monitoring the World Economy 1820–1992*. Paris: OECD.

—— (2001) *The World Economy: A Millennial Perspective*. Paris: OECD.

Mahbubani, Kishore (2008) *The New Asian Hemisphere: The Irresistible Shift of Global Power to the East*. New York: Public Affairs.

Martin, Michael O., Ina V.S. Mullis and Pierre Foy (2008a) *TIMMS 2007 International Science Report*. Boston: TIMSS & PIRLS International Study Center, Lynch School of Education, Boston College.

—— (2008b) *TIMMS 2007 International Mathematics Report*. Boston: TIMSS & PIRLS International Study Center, Lynch School of Education, Boston College.

Mason, Edward S. et al. (1980) *The Economic and Social Modernization of the Republic of Korea*. Cambridge: Harvard University Press.

Meyer, John W. et al. (1997) "World Society and the Nation State", *American Journal of Sociology*, Vol. 103, pp. 144–82.

Ministry of Foreign Affairs of the People's Republic of China, and the United Nations System in China (2005) *China's Progress towards the Millennium Development Goals 2005*. Beijing: Ministry of Foreign Affairs.

National Bureau of Statistics of China (2005) *China Statistical Yearbook 2005*. Beijing: China Statistics Press.

National Intelligence Council (2008) *Global Trends 2025: A Transformed World*. Washington, DC: US Government Printing Office.

OECD (2007) *Education at a Glance*. Paris: OECD.

Schmidt, Volker H. (2007) "One World, One Modernity", in Volker H. Schmidt (ed.), *Modernity at the Beginning of the 21st Century*, Newcastle: Cambridge Scholars, pp. 205–28.

Shanghai Jiao Tong University (2007) *Academic Ranking of World Universities – 2007*. http://www.arwu.org/rank/2007/ranking2007.htm.

Sugihara, Kaoru (2003) "The East Asian Path of Economic Development", in Giovanni Arrighi, Takeshi Hamashita and Mark Seldon (eds.), *The Resurgence of East Asia: 500, 150 and 50 Year Perspectives*, London: Routledge, pp. 78–123.

The Economist (2005) "The World in 2026", *The World in 2006*, London, p. 86.

Tilak, Jandhyala B.G. (2002) *Building Human Capital in East Asia: What Others Can Learn*. Washington, DC: World Bank, Stock No. 37166.

Times Higher Education (2008) *Times Higher Education – QS World University Rankings 2008*. http://www.topuniversities.com/worlduniversityrankings/results/2008/overall_rankings/fullrankings/.

UNDP (2006) *Human Development Report 2006*. New York: United Nations Development Programme.

—— (2007) *Human Development Report 2007/2008*. New York: United Nations Development Programme.

World Intellectual Property Organization (2007) *PCT Newsletter No. 02/07*.

Zhou, Yu (2008) *The Inside Story of China's High-Tech Industry: Making Silicon Valley in Beijing*. Lanham: Rowman & Littlefield.

5

Technological vs. Political Modernization

Interactions and Feedbacks

Lech W. Zacher

It should be noted that *modernization* is a de facto everlasting process of making everything modern (i.e., counter-traditional). Modernization is the creation, introduction and diffusion of novelties or *innovations* of all types – scientific, technological, organizational, institutional, social, political, cultural, environmental, and so on. Many models and methods are related to innovation processes. It is rather clear that innovation processes are, to some extent, stimulated, controlled (by rational choices, strategies, and politics), and to some extent they are spontaneous, and chaotic. Figure 1 below schematically illustrates this situation:

Figure 1

Conceptual Scheme of the Structure of Factors Influencing Innovation Processes

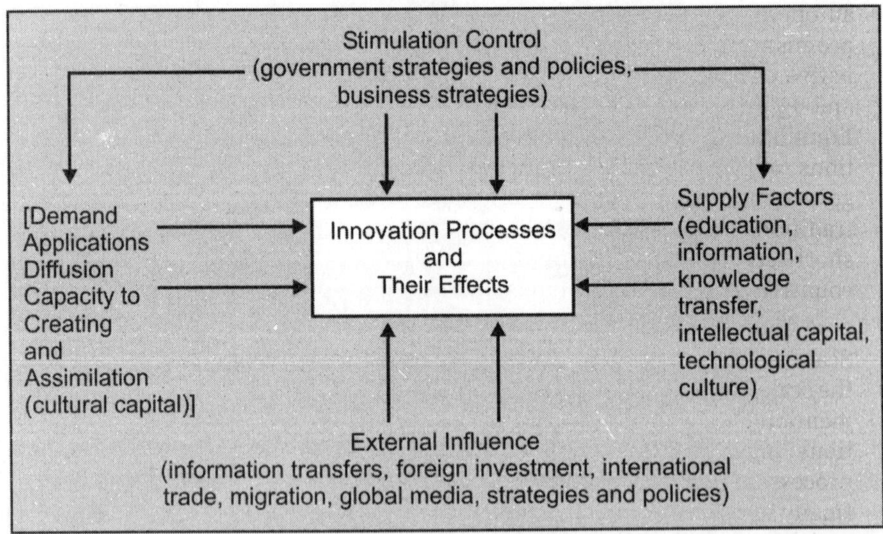

In the case of all types of innovation, there is both demand (not necessarily only domestic) and supply. Moreover, some possibilities for the stimulation and control of supply and demand exist; however, they are very different from one nation to another as well as across time. Separation of external influence is important in the time of ongoing globalization. Global technological competition, technology imports and exports, technological information flows, foreign patterns of technology creation, application and diffusion, international technological cooperation (and also espionage), and the technologically upgraded skills of returning emigrants are impacting governments' choices, strategies and policies.

Possibilities for deliberate and effective influence on innovation processes have, to varying extents, all decision-making subjects at interest, including governments and their agencies, companies and business associations, citizens and their organizations, social movements, and so on. It seems that in the current situation, referred to as the information revolution (embracing civilization, society, economy), all subjects gain increasing amounts of power, so eventual clashes of visions, interests, and attitudes lead to contradictory viewpoints. ICTs (information and communication technologies) make all subjects more powerful – governments may more effectively manipulate people, businesses may also do so via marketing and ads, and above all, the production of ICTs can make all parties dependent on these technologies. Finally, citizens are also dependent when gathering, protesting, and organizing (even worldwide).

The coordination of decision-making subjects' decisions and behaviour regarding innovation processes is not easy. The area of choice is limited, information is notoriously incomplete, interests are very differentiated, and implementation capacities vary. Uncertainties and risks make it difficult to create coherent and stable innovation systems. In spite of the old idea of a national innovation system (the concept was introduced by Freeman in the 1980s), it is not easy to make a country's innovation activity systemic, especially in the case of large (in terms of area and population) countries.

To realistically make innovation systems work, it is necessary to ensure the autonomy of universities, decent financing of R&D, support of the most promising fields (e.g., ICTs, biotechnologies, nanotechnology, biomedicine, alternative energy sources, and so on), and a constant goal of reaching a consensus among state, business, and civil society in regards to priorities and funding. Equilibrating various interests can be difficult since the aspirations and expectations of segments and groups of society are not the same. For example, governments can be military-oriented, while people, especially local, may have traditional low technological culture, and businesses can be focused on short-term profits. Situation is hard in large complex systems, such as in big countries or regional groupings (like the European Union).

There are many stakeholders of innovation (or modernization at large). Scale and time are also important dimensions. What is practically important is the scale of risks, costs, and expected gains, as also their social distribution, not to mention their distribution in time and space. Social, spatial, and time distributions must be considered in strategies and policies. However, innovation processes are not only subjects of choice and deliberate, planned actions of policy (many sectoral policies have their own rationale, such as scientific, technological, social, economic, educational, environmental, financial, investment, foreign, migration, cultural, etc.). Market mechanisms (domestic market, global one, conjuncture, etc.) are extremely important, especially in countries applying a neo-liberal economic approach to development and policy. However, the present de facto world crisis (not only financial) can, to some extent, redirect attitudes and policies toward innovation processes and their use for growth. The role of the state can be expanded. The problem, however, is how to include the innovation activity of TNCs in national innovation systems. Perhaps this question should be reversed – how can national innovation systems (their parts perhaps) be included in global innovation networks designed and controlled by TNCs? The answer is unknown, and will probably differ according to the subject in question.

It seems worthwhile to point out that the ideal, de facto democratic model of innovation processes (or modernization) presumes information, consent, participation, perhaps some social justice is not performed worldwide. Conversely, some countries that have been quite successful in modernization (many historical and present examples) were rather authoritarian or even totalitarian, what is very hard for social scientists to explain.

External influences are, as a rule, connected with bigger risks and fuzziness, which is why innovation processes are seen by "an external observer" as beyond any effective control. Of course, according to ideological convictions and the preferred type of policy, two attitudes regarding innovation processes are possible: *reactive* (the processes emerge autonomously or are induced or transferred) or *proactive* (while attempting stimulation and control). Complexity of the discussed problematique is even greater when considering all potential negative side effects, as these are difficult to predict or even imagine. For example, such as connected with electronization of politics in the form of e-administration, e-government, or e-governance.

II

It is rather common in the social sciences to not properly consider the role of technology, in general, and technological innovation, in particular, in modernization processes, as well as in the sphere of politics. The main cause is probably the constant appeal of rather obsolete concepts and theories – seen often by many scientists as relevant forever in spite of the hard fact that they refer to totally different realities than the times we live in. Meanwhile, the development of technology generates many radical and profound changes in virtually all spheres of human and social life. Of course, technological impacts "touch" various social phenomena and change in differentiated ways, and are not necessarily total and unequivocal (sometimes they are not evident and difficult to identify). Our thesis is not connected with any type of *technological determinism*; it points out only the empirically evident fact that technology has been, throughout human history, a dominant driving force of development and its transformations. There was not a period in history without technology, technological innovation, and their applications (of course the scale, span, and effects vary spatially and in time).

Therefore, it seems quite justified to connect the stages of modernization with the subsequent stages of technological development. The great industrial revolution of the 18th century, which was based on new inventions and radical industrial technologies, generated the emergence of new social classes, professions, institutions, work organizations, political solutions, and so on. Indeed, it produced a new type of society called the *industrial society*. Much later, as the result of political transformations in the leading countries, a new term – *industrial democracy* – appeared in the scientific and political discourse. Industrial democracies composed the so-called *industrial world* in contrast to the pre-industrial or semi-industrial one. Democracy was often short where industry was lacking.

In turn, the *scientific-technological revolution* – professed by J.D. Bernal at the end of the 1930s – meant great breakthroughs in science and technology as well as new and intense interactions and feedback in addition to multifaceted, profound consequences and effects (including negative and undesirable effects). This revolution is historically situated in the middle of the 20th century and is characterized by crucial innovations and their applications, especially in the field of new materials, nuclear energy, and automation. Somewhat later the ICT, biotechnology, and nanotechnology came to the fore. Industrial societies together with their institutions and constituting features commenced to transform – first of all in the civilizationally leading countries – into an *information society*. So, the era of information is replacing the industrial era (of course never totally and everywhere). This development meant the colossal transformation and modernization of virtually everything, including the sphere of politics.

The ongoing *information revolution* (also known as cybernetic, computer, telematic, and digital) is an actual form of scientific and technological revolution, but it has not yet ended, so its milestone achievements are marked by inventions and innovations which resulted in products such as computers, telematic networks, mobile phones, television, DVD, blu-ray, Mp3s, iPods, and so forth. It is interesting that modernization processes are the fastest in these new areas of technology and their applications, while societies are lagging behind technology (as Ogburn ascertained some time ago). What should be added here is that there are accompanying processes such as the digitalization and convergence of mass media (often already global) which may have an immense impact on politics (media become so-called the fourth power).

New technologies in addition to their vast applications and wide diffusion require strategies, policies, and some control, involving all actors and stakeholders of modernization. Such arrangements (political, institutional, etc.) continue to emerge, in spite of frequent declarations of a totally free market, non-interventionism of state, autonomy of scientific centres, and so on. One example is that the European Framework for R&D is centrally funded, as are other national projects requiring governmental (public) financing; research projects strongly conditioned by uncertainty and risk, which require the development of public-private partnerships; and sometimes government agencies take a part in risk (technical and financial), assuring some type of aid to businesses (e.g., Advanced Technology Programme conducted by the American Department of Commerce Technology Administration and National Institute of Standards and Technology). Negative side effects (existing or expected) are also the subject of government regulations and parliamentary legislation. Various agencies and offices exist for such a purpose, such as the former US Congress Office of Technology Assessment (1972–1995) and the German Bundestag TAB (Technikfolgen Abschätzung Büro). The concept of technology assessment was potentially a great invention for ameliorating the effects of modernization.

The development of technology and its many multifaceted applications, by their very nature, get entangled in politics, decisions (governmental, business, and citizens not only as consumers), stakeholder conflicts, the sometimes complicated process of social acceptance, and so on. They are therefore tied to political systems, the principles and mechanisms of democracy (in its various forms and levels), the articulation of business interests, and the political activism of citizens, NGOs, and social movements, especially environmental, eco-feministic, anti-globalistic, or alter-globalistic (see, e.g., the works of Klein, 2007).

III

Contemporary times include many revolutionary technologies and mass revolutionary applications (computers, especially PCs, laptops, and netbooks, more and more advanced mobile phones, electronic mass media, the Internet, emerging VR technologies, etc.). We are therefore experiencing *great transformations* (but different than the description of Polanyi) that include "things" like mass networking, network individualization, electronization and globalization of mass media, radically growing access to information, immediate online communication, virtualization of life, and a shift of a considerable part of human life to cyberspace (which becomes an additional social space). There are multiple consequences of these processes, phenomena, and events, i.e., modernization of politics (the latter becomes more and more *post-politics*), new occurrences called teledemocracy and telepresident, new possibilities of total surveillance of societies (Orwell redivivus!), and contemporary technological possibilities of mass citizens' participation in political processes (also with reference to modernization, including its directions, pace, costs, distribution of risks, and gains), not to mention negative things such as computer and Internet crimes as well as cyber-terrorism. The social sciences do not focus much on the risky and detrimental results of development (e.g., issues such as Internet crime, computer-aided world organized crime, or national and global network security).

The important, perhaps even principal, field of politics is military research, the so-called defense industries and also wars (von Clausewitz called this an extension of politics). Today, wars are info- or cyber-wars, and the most modern equipment and technologies are used (e.g., in Iraq), including advanced computers, robots (automated battlefields), intelligent missiles and ammunition, spying satellites, and the like. Today's wars (Gulf war, Iraq, Afghanistan) require not only immense funds (see the book by Stiglitz), but also long-term research programmes (e.g., SDL, Defence Shield) which must be stimulated and controlled politically. Therefore, the modernization of armies, equipment, command facilities, equipment for special forces, military telecommunications (including satellite systems), and espionage are extremely costly and very politicized areas of modernization, especially in countries having military ambitions or unfriendly neighbours (like some Asian or Latin American nations).

The effects of revolutionary changes in science and technology and their massive use are real challenges for politics and people's lives. These changes not only cause the general "acceleration of everything" (discussed by Gleick, Eriksen, and Virilio), but also impose adaptation. Those which are unable to adapt are excluded and, as a result, are alienated from modernization processes. Those countries, regions, societies, groups of people, and even individuals become a "burden" to development, and at the same time constitute a potential power of resistance and even destruction (in the form of new Luddites).

As a result of the above-mentioned breakthroughs, changes, and transformations – besides univocally positive impacts – specific "developmental fuzziness" or a kind of "new opaqueness" (to paraphrase Habermas) is emerging, leading to the negation of old insights and theories concerning our permanently changing reality as well as new approaches attempted, for example, by postmodernists like Lyotard, Baudrillard, Virilio, and Bauman. Some thinkers have prophesied a *decline of civilization* (e.g., Eco) or its total catastrophe (some ecologists). Consumptionism steering through advertisements, narcissism, the artificial world of mass media and cyberspace, and ideological and political manipulation – all of these can put societies or parts of societies to sleep, or can make them infantile, give them cheap popular entertainment (or infotainment), or political (post-political) one. However, technological trends will more or less stay the same.

Paradoxically, emerging societies – informational, networked, digital, mediumistic, and relational – aspire to be (or at least aspire to be called) *knowledge societies*. As a result of rather autonomous cognitive processes of research and technology, the level of knowledge is constantly raised, stimulating production, growth, and education. The leading economies are increasingly based on knowledge, new knowledge, and scientific knowledge adapted in the course of production for practical needs (of industry, services, politics, and society). This mode of knowledge production has been called Mode 2 (by Gibbons et al., 1994) in contrast to the traditional academic Mode 1.

The question is whether postmodern societies are really becoming knowledge-based societies. Economies are surely increasingly, but societies? A new gap may be appearing – a knowledge gap due to a separation of knowledge between elites (cognitariat) and the masses, which have differentiated access to information (the digital divide is an illustration). Technology increasingly becomes, even more so than before, an *ideology* (what was discussed by Habermas some time ago). It becomes a principal transformational force and a powerful instrument of authorities and their manipulations. These challenges are often overlooked by the social sciences in many less advanced countries, especially if their societies are traditionally-oriented, rather than focusing on and investing in the future.

Modernization, especially when successful, is not automatic (as we know some civilizations, empires, states, industries, and professions declined and finally fell down). Differentiation of modernization processes is significant, throughout history and today, and probably in the future as well. There are *pioneering* countries (societies) and *imitators*, as well as countries *lagging behind* and countries already *excluded*.

It should be noted, however, that all of these situational structures are, as a rule, not fully closed and clearly separated. Usually, one can find enclaves of all situations; however, the dominant one determines the place in the aforementioned classification.

We deal with a great variety of models of modernization, including its ways, strategies, policies, and effects and impacts (including negative impacts). Comparative studies show a phenomenon which can be called *shallow modernization*. Shallowness means that, in spite of formal access to information and despite the proactivity of decision-makers (political, businesses, and citizens), it is not possible to obtain a desirable level and effectiveness of modernization goals typical for the leading countries. Of course, shallow modernization often has historical roots. Its present expression can be an inability to coordinate all factors and forces of modernization (technological, political, economic, social, cultural, psychological, and institutional). Overcoming shallow modernization, similar to the enclave modernization, is difficult, costly, and lengthy. Big political ambitions and big plans are often present in countries which are afflicted with this inability. There are many countries, parts of countries, or whole regions (e.g., Eastern Europe, Latin America, Asia) in which modernization was (or sometimes still is) shallow. This situation can be called a *modernization divide*.

In theories of modernization it is often presumed – implicitly or explicitly – that there is *one common pattern* for all. Therefore, countries having delayed developmental take-off (or in other words, late comers) or countries with shallow modernization or other problems in development should initiate the universal patterns of the leading countries (societies). The *idea of progress* (invented by Condorcet in the 18th century) required tracing out a proper direction practically chosen and designed by the West (by Europe, then together with the US). That is why terms such as westernization or Americanization occurred. Even the colonial conquests were considered to be a form of the externally induced western modernization. Beyond a doubt there were some ideological and political dimensions of such approach, as market and democracy had to ensure the proper direction of development and its success. Some futurists (e.g., Kahn in the 1970s) forecasted successful imitatory growth in the following decades.

Therefore, the civilizational and socio-economic reality did not want to evolve according to simplistic theoretical concepts or ideological convictions. Instead of the presumed total universalism and in spite of some uniformization and levelling of globalization, it appears that what is dominating is the great variety of models of development, methods, strategies, and policies, not to mention the diversity of barriers, consequences, impacts, and negative side effects (e.g., unemployment or brain drain). That is why theories of dependence and domination, of centres and peripheries, of neo-colonialism, and so on were developed. Adding to the diversity, some not very democratic countries unexpectedly achieved developmental success (e.g., Chile, Asian "tigers", China, Russia and Brazil). However, the universalistic mythology of modernization is still vivid. It often masks the ideology of the expansionistic hegemons (formerly the Soviet Union, and of course the USA). It is necessary to underline that the "only right" western patterns were rejected (at least politically) by a number of countries, such as Islamic nations (called, following Huntington, the *clash of civilization*). Moreover, it was already announced – certainly with some exaggeration – the Post-American World (see Zakaria, 2008), the decline or an end of the West and Christianity and even the white race. Changes in the proportions of the forces and influences in the world and its progressive reconfigurations have become a hard fact. Even the traditional mainstay of the western patterns – Europe – seeks something different than the American Dream (see Rifkin, 2004). Europeanization, the unionization of Europe, and growing multicultural immigration to Europe may fructify with new ideas and modernization patterns. It seems that our traditionally universalist *mindset* and *world view* are changing, which is a benefit for the social sciences and political practice.

IV

Technology, technological innovations, and their massive, diverse applications play a great role in the stimulation of political modernization (not only in the leading countries). They transform societies as well as their structures, consciousness, attitudes, aspirations, and visions, not to mention education, skills and behaviour. New modernized societies require *a new type of governance*, and new rules and principles because they have immense access to information (immediate, online, and transborder in spite of some censorship sometimes). Moreover, some new possibilities for interactions among, and feedback from, "government, business and civil society" (to use the western cliché) are emerging. Political systems, party systems, new institutions, networks and relations, and procedures are originating, changing, and influencing, all thanks to technological feasibility. Political modernization (of systems, structures, institutions, activities like voting, referenda, dialogue with citizens, and participatory decisions) is basically the effect of the use of technology and technological innovation. The great technological breakthroughs disturb the linearity of development and make it more fuzzy, chaotic, and unexpected. This is also related to political modernization. It seems that the social sciences (political ones in particular) underestimate it and as a result lag behind. It should be added that, in this context, the radical transformations (not only in terms of technology) which we witness have important *generational dimensions* (new generations educated in the digital environment are different, and have different understandings of technology and technological procedures and skills, such as being connected with *e-politics*).

Cultural ability regarding the creation, application, and diffusion of technological, organizational, and political innovation becomes a key condition in all domains, including science and research on modernization processes. The mediatization of politics (terms such as *mediumistic societies* or *netocracy* are used) and its technologization ought to be subjects of intensive study. In present societies (technological, technologized), massive, comprehensive technological applications probably influence people more so than ideologies and religions because they are experienced daily, and are not only ceremonial. Positive cultural ability is connected with features and properties of societies (of people) such as innovativeness, creativity, activism, entrepreneurship, prospective orientation, raising aspirations, and favourable norms and values, as well as the quality of politics and governance, citizens' behaviour regarding risk, trust, cooperativeness, and striving for success. Leaders and agents (actors) of modernization are also part of this cultural ability, as they can be enlightened and charismatic political leaders, entrepreneurs, innovators (to recall Schumacher, 1973), organizations and institutions, citizens, including individuals and NGOs, social movements, and so on. All of these parties determine real possibilities of modernization, and are also political since there are multiple feedback loops among innovations and between technological and political modernizations. The latter should be a subject of research and deliberated activities of political and societal actors.

The role of the cultural ability of societies to modernization change is very important. It is heavily conditioned by their history (the moment of take-off to development), their past failures, various gaps, institutional barriers, unfriendly impacts of the external environment, possibilities connected with various resources, social capital, and so forth. Important elements of this ability are human individuals and groups, organizations (companies and corporations), and institutions which want and are able to act as agents of modernization, including their leaders, actors, and stakeholders. Some elements disturb and delay the processes of modernization such as various oppositional groups, people with obsolete skills, people unable to assimilate to new technologies, some conservative fundamentalists, socially excluded people, those on the social margin, and diverse hostile saboteurs (industrial, military, scientific and technological espionage).

Historically, many countries were able to modernize technology, infrastructure, economy, society, and politics in their developmental processes. Of course, modernization factors (or rather their sets) were historically diversified, for example, positive inertia ("innovation impetus"), ideas (independence, anti-colonialism, postcolonialism), aspirations (imperial), interests (big business, TNCs), impositions (political and social implied by access to global information, tourist experiences, migration), and external impacts (foreign trade, globalization, cooperation possibilities, direct investment).

Modernization is a *multi-trajectory* and *multi-level* process. Its processes are predominantly seen in the military sector, industry, banking, transportation, education, mass media, entertainment, public administration, and households. Their level of advance, depth, transformational ability were diversified. Mutual influences, interactions, and feedback loops can lead to systemics and synergy when there are deliberate and rational strategies, policies, and activities. It is neither easy nor automatic because economic and societal systems are greatly complicated and complex. What is really needed is not exactly to imitate pioneers or foreign leaders of modernization but critical, reasonable use of their experience and taking advantage of cooperation and the transfer of knowledge and skills, rather than imitating pioneers or foreign leaders of modernization.

History and comparative analyses indicate that modernization, as a *multifaceted*, *multi-trajectory* and *multi-level* process of creating, introducing, and diffusing innovation, has various scales, pace and effects. Therefore, it is possible to use terms such as *evolutionary modernization* (gradually "levelled"), *revolutionary modernization* (big scale, deep changes, crucial impacts and effects) and *halted modernization* (examples are Iran and China). Modernization can also be *regressive* (when introduced changes indicate a retreat, such as an increase in religious fundamentalism and the resulting influence on politics, social customs, education, etc.). Each case of modernization has both endogenous and exogenous characters, although in varying proportions. *Induced modernization*, in turn, is rather frequent in many countries and regions. Its carriers were historically involved in conquest, colonization, and trade (especially import of new commodities and technologies), and are presently involved in "things" like FDIs, foreign capital, TNCs, global media, immigrants, and so on. As a rule, modernization processes generate ambivalent impacts (both positive and detrimental, though not necessarily at the same time). These processes also cause various negative side effects that are difficult to predict. Visions of modernization or modernization projects are important because they mobilize and shape efforts not only of main actors of development but also of whole societies, countries, and regions. Modernization processes may run spontaneously, inertially, or chaotically. They can also be, if possible and feasible under the given conditions, stimulated, planned, monitored, and controlled. All of this depends on the assumed ideology, politics, knowledge, social consciousness, and so on.

Figure 2

Conceptual Model of Modernization Policies: Main Factors, Driving Forces, Conditions and Contexts

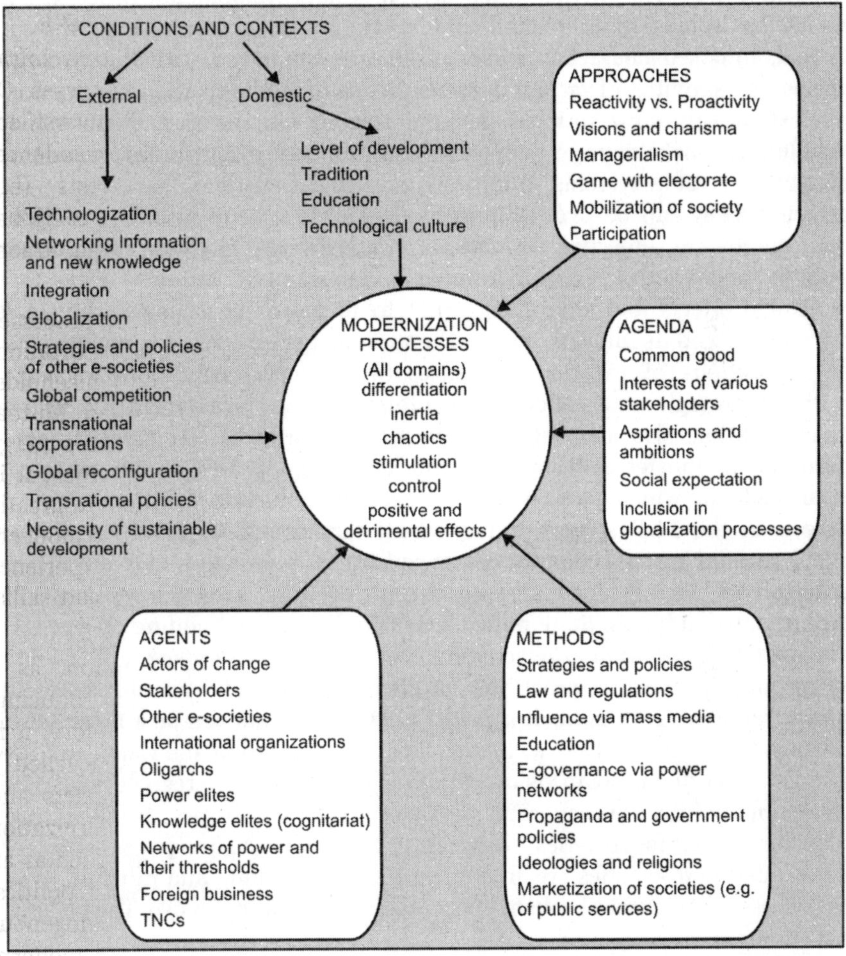

Thus, modernization is composed of an extremely complex class (assemblage) of processes, all which are interconnected and mutually conditioned, and generated both domestically and externally. It is worthwhile to form theoretical models enabling a structuration of problematique and its understanding, and aiding in the programming of practical activities. Figure 2 shows the conceptual model of the modernization policy, which is often grounded in great ideas and projects, such as de-colonization, obtainment of independence, self-reliance, access to integrational grouping (like the EU), also in striving for global competitive advantage, and maintaining or attaining hegemony, whether it is military or political, aimed toward technological leadership, ideological, or a cultural mission.

Modernization policy on a national scale, however, may be notoriously confronted with difficulties and resistance. Let us name some possible disturbing problems: network individualism, cosmopolitanism, non-political attitudes, de-politicization, post-politics, particularization of interests, internationalization and globalization of critical and opposition movements, complexity of problematique hindering elaboration of strategy and consensus seeking, and the competition of others and their impacts on internal developmental processes. It is evident that some conditions and contexts of modernization have an objective, external, imposed character, while others are connected with the strategies, policies, and activities of various domestic actors of modernization, so they are, to some extent, subjective, rational, planned, steered, monitored, and controlled (if possible). The behaviour of people, in addition to their attitudes, aspirations, expectations, value systems, traditions, and social customs, have yet another character. They can be *pro-* or *anti-*modernization, or eventually *indifferent*. Thus, there are objective conditions, impositions, chaotics, adjustments, creativity and control, coordination and management, but also little to no predictable effects and side effects (not to mention the changeability of the environment and its impacts, e.g., in the form of a crisis). What is important are the *proportions* of external influences and internal conditions related to creativity, strategies and policies, and cultural abilities for efficient and effective implementation. Also, a model of *passive* modernization based on mechanisms of international transfer of technology and knowledge as well as on market and global trade in which particular (and egoistic) interests dominate (e.g., the interests of the R&D sphere, industrial-military complex, private media, and various societal groups) could be developed. Then assimilation to modernization challenges will be imposed externally and the eventual success a result of many uncoordinated subjects. State policy is usually limited to building proper infrastructure (transportation or telecommunications), the development of education and training, supporting practically profiled research, and possibly correcting "market failures". It is difficult *a priori* to evaluate what can be a more serious challenge for modernization: a chaotic, lack of coordination and vision and these "failures" and often utopian vision of politicians or excessive regulation of development and political-bureaucratic mistakes of state authorities. Needless to add in conclusion that for societies – apart from the modernization per se – its multifaceted effects on societies are, in fact, limitless, important, and valuable, even if this process is sometimes broken, unsuccessful, or even regressive. The balance is what counts.

References

Anderla, G. et al. (1997) *Chaotics: An Agenda for Business and Society in the 21st Century*. Westport, CT: Adamantine Press.

Berger, P. and Huntington, S.P. (2002) *Many Globalizations: Cultural Diversity in the Contemporary World*. New York: Oxford University Press.

Bijker, W.E. and Law, J. (1992) *Shaping Technology/Building Society*. Cambridge: The MIT Press.

Drucker, P.F. (1994) *The Age of Discontinuity*. New Brunswick, NJ: Transaction Books.

Gibbons, M. et al. (1994) *The New Production of Knowledge*. London, Thousand Oaks and New Delhi: Sage.

Harrison, L.E. and Huntington, S.P. (eds.) (2000) *Culture Matters: How Values Shape Human Progress*. New York: Basic Books.

Katz, E., Light, A. and Thompson, W. (eds.) (2003) *Controlling Technology: Contemporary Issues* (2nd edition), Amherst, NY: Prometheus Books.

Klein, N. (2007) *The Shock Doctrine: The Rise of Disaster Capitalism*. New York: Metropolitan Books.

Mack, T.C. (2006) *Creating Global Strategies for Humanity's Future*. Bethesda, MD: WFS.

—— (2007) *Hopes and Visions for the 21st Century*. Bethesda, MD: WFS.

Misa, Th. J., Brey, Ph. and Feenberg, A. (2004) *Modernity and Technology*. Cambridge: The MIT Press.

Negri, A. and Hardt, M. (2004) *Multitude*. New York: Penguin Books.

Polanyi, K. (1944) *The Great Transformation*. Boston: Beacon Press.

Pool, R. (1997) *Beyond Engineering: How Society Shapes Technology*. New York: Oxford University Press.

Rifkin, J. (2004) *The European Dream*. New York: Tarcher.

Rycroft, R.W. and Kash, D.E. (1999) *The Complexity Challenge: Technological Innovation for the 21st Century*. London: Pinter.

Schuler, D. and Day, P. (2004) *Shaping the Network Society*. Cambridge: The MIT Press.

Schumacher, E.F. (1973) *Small is Beautiful: A Study of Economics as if People Mattered*. London: Vintage.

Seidensticker, B. (2006) *Future Hype: The Myths of Technology Change*. San Francisco: Berrett–Koehler Publishers.

Smith, M.R. and Marx, L. (1994) *Does Technology Drive History? The Dilemma of Technological Determinism*. Cambridge: The MIT Press.

Tainter, J.A. (2006) *The Collapse of Complex Societies*. Cambridge: Cambridge University Press.

Taylor, P.A. and Harris, J.L. (2005) *Digital Matters: Theory and Culture of the Matrix*. New York: Routledge.

Urry, J. (2000) *Beyond Societies: Mobilities for the Twenty-First Century*. London: Routledge.

Wagner, C.G. (2008) *Seeing the Future through New Eyes*. Bethesda, MD: WFS.

Wellman, B. (red.) (1999) *Networks in the Global Village*. Boulder, Co.: Westview Press.

Zacher, L.W. (2007) "E-Transformations of Societies", in *Encyclopedia of Digital Government*, Vol. II, Hershey – London – Melbourne – Singapore: Idea Group Inc.

—— (2009) "Information Society Discourse", in *Encyclopedia of Information Science and Technology*, Hershey, PA: IGI Global.

Zakaria, F. (2008) *The Post-American World*. New York: W.W. Norton.

6

Modernization of Indian Tradition and the Gandhian Way

Towards a Sociological Invitation

Anand Kumar

It may not be inappropriate to suggest that the challenge of understanding modern India cannot ignore the twin needs of explaining modernization of Indian tradition and contextualizing the Gandhian way as they are intertwined in so many ways. But, most of the social scientists have adopted the path of avoidance about it by separating the processes of the making of Indian modernity and the rise of Mohandas to 'Mahatma Gandhi'. Often there is overemphasizing of the structural–functional aspect of modernization of India by separating the historical from the sociological in it. Similarly, there is too much focus on the biographical and episodic aspects about Gandhi and his way, and ignoring his immediate and long-term socio-political and ideological impacts. It was not unexpected about Gandhi; Albert Einstein had already predicted that people world over may scarcely believe that such a one as this ever in flesh and blood did walk upon this earth (Wolpert, 2001: 268, Hardiman, 2003).[1] But, it is definitely a big deficit in the sociological accounts of the making of society, polity and culture of modern India. It looks more intriguing when we do have significant examples of attempts to study and explain the links between the making of Indian modernity and the Mahatma by such outstanding scholars like Arnold Toynbee (1948),[2] Nirmal Kumar Bose (1948),[3] Gunnar Myrdal (1968),[4] Erik Erikson (1969),[5] Louis Dumont (1964)[6] and A.K. Saran (1969).[7] There is no simple answer to this question.

Given such a setting, it is very significant that this togetherness of Indian modernity and Gandhi has been recognized, analysed and critiqued by Professor Yogendra Singh by constantly visiting this theme in his analysis of modernization, stratification and social change in India since 1973 (Singh, 1973, 1977, 1993, 1997).[8] His analysis has been based upon historical facts as well as sociological theories. It has underlined the continuities and changes promoted by Gandhi through his unique ideological approach, political methodology and civilizational vision. By focusing on the role of Gandhi in the making of Indian modernity and identity, Yogendra Singh has been able to underline the existence of not one but two orthogenetic processes of change in the Indian tradition oriented towards different directions: (i) Sanskritization and (ii) Renaissance (or reformation movements). He argues that Sanskritization is more existential than ideational. It is a process of change oriented to cultural synthesis rather than resistant encounter. On the other hand, orthogenetic Renaissance changes are not neutral to modernization. It is more ideational than existential. The Renaissance or reformation movements, with few exceptions, have been focused upon the need of maintaining the basic values of the traditional world view by marginal adaptations. The core values are never compromised. Adjustments are proposed at the periphery, without making major changes in the hierarchy of goal orientations.

Orthogenetic Cultural Renaissance and the Gandhian Alternative

In the assessment of Yogendra Singh, the contribution of Gandhi in presenting a sharp contradiction to the western or modern way of life and its basic value premises is quite systematic and complete from a sociological point of view. To quote, "In fact, the model presented by Gandhi is not a product of aggressive reaction to alien religious or cultural patterns. It is also not an angry protest against the pathology of some Hindu cultural and ritual practices which is paramount in the writings of Dayanand. It does not emerge from a deep sense of resentment at the comparative lack of development or dynamics in the Hindu society vis-à-vis, the west, which unconsciously or consciously motivated Vivekanand. Gandhiji's contribution is much more comprehensive, dispassionate and fundamental. It presents a total alternative world view to the two of the most basic world views of the contemporary times: first that of hedonistic liberalism of the so-called modern, free world, and second that of hedonistic-collectivism (Marxism) of the socialist society. Gandhism, thus, should be treated as an expression of orthogenetic, cultural Renaissance par excellence. It is a fact that in independent India, Gandhism has become a mere sect instead of being a cultural force with a dimension of mass mobilization, which it once has generated. The failure of Gandhism in India opens a vast window on the problem of cultural change and modernization in this country which should be analysed."[9]

What are the critical elements of the Gandhian alternative system of values and social order? According to Yogendra Singh, the Gandhian model has at least six basic aspects: (i) Gandhi has reiterated the concept of social and cultural order based on dharma or moral obligation. It implied a conscious rejection of the western theory of social order based on power. (ii) Next, the Gandhian principle of non-violence (derived from the hierarchy of five means of self-control in the Hindu tradition and Jain and Buddhist philosophy) is an effort towards restoration of moral society. (iii) He has emphasized the superiority of agrarian and handicraft economy and rejection of mass production-oriented machine-based industrial civilization. (iv) His theory of trusteeship in property was a simultaneous non-legitimation of private gain and profit promoted by capitalism as well as of state ownership of property as practised in communism. (v) The Gandhian scheme of decentralized system of administration through a hierarchy of representative bodies for creating a communitarian society was in opposition to the modern atomistic form of representative democracy borrowed from the British polity. (vi) Gandhi practised and preached respect for all religions (*sarva dharma samabhav*) to take human civilization towards the path of tolerance and spirituality and away from different kinds of individualistic and collective hedonism.

Critical Contributions of Gandhi

The studies about the interrelations between modernization of Indian tradition and the Gandhian way by Yogendra Singh have acquired a new relevance in the 21st century India because of accurateness of some of his conclusions, reflections and evaluations of the strengths and weaknesses of the ideological, structural and institutional aspects of Indian modernity as well as the Gandhian way. They caution us to recognize that nationalism and democracy in India have come into being in a special historical context which separates the Indian trajectory of modernization from the western experience. The role of colonialism or economic and socio-cultural factors of 18th and 19th century India, particularly interjecting a set of western institutional innovations in the Indian body politic in a highly compressed form, have created far greater cultural stresses for India than the processes of Reformation and Enlightenment caused in the West. Furthermore, Indian democracy has been based upon Indian nationalism and the nationalistic consciousness was oriented towards the Indian traditions. He asserts that the national leaders were for modernity but not at the cost of traditional cultural identity. In the rise of Indian nationalism, the role of Gandhi has specially been of great historical significance, which renders Indian political process of modernization quite unique.[10]

Gandhi was the architect of a mass-oriented national movement, which had followers of three major political ideologies – communal conservative, moderate liberal and radical populist. He created a space for conversations among the elites of all the three trends by emphasizing on the need of maintaining the traditional cultural identity in its essential form with due moderation. It harmonized with his 'uncanny' skill of projecting to Indian masses the many humanistic values of the modern West through traditional cultural symbolism. For example, secularism for Gandhi did not mean a-religiosity but the spirit of religious tolerance which he presented on the basis of universalistic ethic of Hinduism itself. His advocacy of nationalism was rooted in Hindu tradition without allowing itself to become an instrument of communalism, of ethno-centricity or xenophobia. His conception of the postcolonial Indian polity was entirely indigenous and non-communal and yet not secular in the strictly western sense of the term.[11] He also reinforces the ideology of self-sufficient, morally and economically integrated village community as the elemental organic unit of the superstructure of the Indian society.[12] According to Yogendra Singh, "Freedom movement ushered in a new political culture of modernization. At its centre was the personality of Mahatma Gandhi whose one foot was always deeply embedded in tradition. His emergence during the peak of westernization process in India signifies an orthogenetic response of Indian tradition to the new challenge of social change. Gandhi successfully mobilized Indian people for the attainment of freedom, but he could not, however, avert one serious breakdown in the process – in the partition of India into two independent nations ... it followed from the uneven growth of sub-cultural traditions of modernization in Hinduism and Islam, each conditioned by unique historicity of their own. The quest for a separate nationhood by the Muslim community in India reflected a crisis of aspiration along with that of confidence."[13] Here, Professor Yogendra Singh also demonstrates his objectivity as a sociologist by bringing in the counter perspectives of such other scholars particularly Louis Dumont who considered Gandhi more as neo-Hindu than a holistic Indian who was motivated by 'twin objectives of winning freedom and saving Hinduism'.

Yogendra Singh is cognizant of the ideological plurality, with due significance of Gandhism, inherent in Indian modernity. According to him, Marxism, democratic liberalism and Gandhism stand out as three ideological systems which inform the processes of political and cultural modernization in India. Of these three, only Gandhism offered a truly alterative model of modernization in conformity with the Indian ethos. Why and how? Because it took notice of both types of western cultural challenges – the Marxist and the liberal democratic. The chief elements forming the value framework of the Gandhian alternative model included (i) asceticism, (ii) egalitarianism, (iii) activism, (iv) mass participation or populism, and (v) theism and non-individualism in political life. He did not believe in (i) the parliamentary form of democracy, (ii) individualistic constitutionalism, or (iii) welfare socialism. He was believer of (i) ethical egalitarianism through collective mobilization, (ii) radical economic changes to eliminate mass poverty and conspicuous consumption, (iii) total alternation of the structure of social and economic relationship, and (iv) decentralization of political and economic power along with the creation of pluralistic functional institutions. Gandhi did not accept the theory of progressive structural and cultural differentiation as a unilinear universal of modernization.

It is interesting that after all these elaborations, Yogendra Singh also alerts that "the structure and process of political modernization, its ideology as it subsequently evolved has deviated in essentials from the Gandhian ideology, despite projections of symbolic affinity to Gandhism in free India."[14] Thus, Professor Singh creates a framework of dialogue and debate to go further in making sense of changing role of Gandhi and his ideas and movements in the rise of wave of political and cultural modernization in both the phases of the 20th century India: (i) during the British Raj, and (ii) after freedom from it.

Drifting Away of Independent India from the Gandhian Way

Any understanding about the role and impact of Gandhi in the context of Indian modernization project includes a clear analysis of the similarities and differences between the approaches of Gandhi and Nehru. Most of the analysts have kept it away from their focus. A few others have adopted the official line of the postcolonial power elite that Gandhi appointed Nehru as his successor who made suitable updating of the goals and plans of the Indian National Movement during his role as the first Prime Minister of independent India. In case of Professor Yogendra Singh this is not sufficient for a sociological understanding of either dynamics of modernization or role of Gandhi or Nehru in it. He has opened the issue with several serious observations about the differences between the approaches of Gandhi and Nehru for further interrogations. In the understanding of Yogendra Singh they belong to two different frameworks because Gandhi was a proponent of synthesis ideologies whereas Nehru was a rationalist liberal.[15] First of all, he makes it clear that Gandhism was never rationally accepted by the majority leadership in the Congress party including Nehru. Secondly, it was disowned by Independent India whereas the liberal democratic tradition was consolidated under the leadership of Jawaharlal Nehru.

What is the significance of these two facts of modern India? According to Yogendra Singh, the shift of emphasis from the mass politics of Gandhi to the elite politics of Nehru has been an important structural change in India's political modernization which took place following independence. This elitism was most clearly reflected in the elimination of a significant choice for the Indian people between the mobilization system of Gandhi and constitutional democracy. As a consequence, the emerging contradiction indicates that if constitutional democracy is not made more effectively socialistic and the precepts of socialism, equality and freedom are not translated into practice, *there will definitely emerge forces of political radicalization which will be hard to counter* (emphasis added).[16]

Yogendra Singh further inferences that the problems of political modernization are rooted in the process whereby a society predominantly governed by status groups takes one long and sudden jump to introduce party system of democracy and rejects the non-party model of political modernization offered by Gandhi, who essentially symbolizes the reawakening of the Indian and Asian consciousness. *In this choice lies our historic problem for modernization – social, cultural as well as political. We have preferred the elitist system of political modernization over the mass mobilization system of Gandhi* (emphasis added).[17]

Why was it so critical to be alternative about distancing from the Gandhian way soon after independence? Did Gandhi not become irrelevant as he failed to keep national movement united and above the pressures of communalism, casteism and the class questions towards the end of his life? The answer from the writings of Yogendra Singh suggest that it was the personality of Mahatma Gandhi which had successfully synthesized the two ideologies of the sceptics (who had a deep regard for the India traditional system and many apprehensions about the European ideologies) and the proponents of techno-scientific world view with great trust in the economic radicalism of the industrial society.[18] Gandhiji's politico-religious philosophy had enabled the Indian elite to stir the masses. However, after independence, the political elites had lost their touch with the masses. Their eclectic and ambivalent ideologies carry little conviction with the people. This greatly impedes social change in India.[19]

Yogendra Singh further argues that it was the effort of Gandhiji to preserve the cultural identity of India by purposeful and selective rejection of many cultural values of the West such as the abstract dehumanizing elements in the western techno-scientific system and the notion of abstracted individualism. The preeminent place, according to the village-oriented ideologies in Gandhiji's social and economic agenda was for reconstruction of Indian society, was probably in recognition of the historical distortion that emerged during the colonial period in country–town relationship. Ironically, the process of modernization in India took a highly segmentry form as a result of colonial disruption as it grew mainly from urban metropolitan centres and had a narrow base in class and caste structure in specific areas of the economy. His emphasis was on equality, community and to a certain measure also on historicity of culture norms. Hence, he emphasizes the need of an indigenous model of cultural development in India. Gandhiji's thrust was upon egalitarianism and corresponding policies of transformation in the economic, social and cultural institutions of the country. He had identified the agrarian structure, ownership pattern of property, uplift of the suppressed castes, especially those of the so-called 'untouchables' and of the backward classes of women, for basic changes. This emphasis had endowed his movements a radical socio-cultural character. He was not merely a political leader because his movements had introduced several irreconcilable contradictions between some older Indian cultural values and the new ones, where the new values would logically lead to the disintegration of the traditional principle of hierarchy, thus rendering the former autonomy between social stratification and social norms fundamentally obsolete. Therefore, the movements led by Gandhiji prepared the ground for a collective self-awareness with an ideological shape among a variety of emerging social groups. A strategy, not only for political independence but social, economic and cultural modernization of society, was evolved.

The emphasis on the involvement of women, members of the weaker sections, peasants and workers reflected this ideological perspective. Political leadership at the local, regional and national levels emerged. *Leadership also emerged among the weaker sections, women and tribal groups.* He does not deny the segmentry character of this process of social change as the national movement itself had it despite periods of mass mobilization.[20] He reminds that Dr Ambedkar's confrontation with Gandhi on the issue of communal electorate for the Scheduled Castes (SCs) resulted into the 1932 Puna Pact which averted a major process of political and social schism in the nation's body politic. But it could not entirely rule out polarization between the forces of segmentation and the SCs. Gandhi stood for an integrative ideology with respectable place for the SCs in the social system. This commitment proved invaluable in the national drive to do away the social disabilities of the SCs with the provision for special constitutional safeguards for them. His approach also facilitated the dominating role played by Dr Ambedkar in the process of constitution-building.[21] He also points out that India's strength in nation-building lies in its legacy of the non-violent tradition raised to the level of a political craft by Gandhi which set the foundation of the strategy of reconciliation.[22]

Conclusion

Studying about modernization and its historical route in India has been a great contribution of Professor Yogendra Singh. He has educated three generations of Indian academicians and policy makers through his teaching, research and writings about its strengths, contradictions and challenges. It will be very meaningful for anyone who wants to understand India's journey from a colony to an independent nation-state, from tradition to modernization, from hierarchy conscious social formation to egalitarianism-oriented society, to engage with his writings about it as they are an open-minded invitation for a better understanding and further exploration. In the context of modernization, he has consistently approached the complexity of the process by looking at the historical, economical, cultural and civilizational factors to provide a sociological understanding. This is best exemplified by his objectivity in interpreting the interrelationship between the modernization of Indian tradition and role and impact of Gandhi.

Acknowledgement

I am thankful to Professor I.P. Modi to include me among the contributors of this volume in honour of Professor Yogendra Singh. I also thank my wife Dr Manjula Rathaur in providing moral and intellectual support for it. I am grateful to Ashish Kumar Das who has helped me in putting it together in the present form.

Notes

1. See Wolpert, Stanley (2001) *Gandhi's Passion: The Life and Legacy of Mahatma Gandhi*. Delhi: Oxford University Press and Hardiman, David (2003) *Gandhi in His Time and Ours*. Pietermaritzburg: University of Natal Press.
2. Toynbee, Arnold (1948) *A Study of History*. Vol. III, London: OUP.
3. Bose, Nirmal Kumar (1948) *Selections from Gandhi*. Ahmedabad: Navjivan Publishing House.
4. Myrdal, Gunnar (1968) "Gandhi as a Radical Liberal", in S. Radhakrishnan (ed.), *Mahatma Gandhi: 100 Years*, New Delhi: Gandhi Peace Foundation.
5. Erikson, Erik (1969) *Gandhi's Truth: On the Origins of Militant Non-Violence*. New York: W.W. Norton and Company.
6. Dumont, Louis (1964) "Nationalism and Communalism", *Contributions to Indian Sociology*, No. 7, March.
7. Saran, A.K. (1969) "Gandhi's Theory of Society and Our Times", *Studies in Comparative Religion*, Vol. 3, No. 4 (Autumn). Also included in Fred Dallmayr and G.N. Devy (eds.) (1998) *Between Tradition and Modernity: India's Search for Identity*. New Delhi: Sage.
8. See the following books of Prof. Yogendra Singh for further details – *Modernization of Indian Traditions* (Delhi: Thompsan Press, 1973), *Essays on Modernization in India* (New Delhi: Manohar Publications, 1977), *Social Change in India: Crisis and Resilience* (New Delhi: Har-Anand Publications, 1993), and *Social Stratification and Change in India* (New Delhi: Manohar Publications, 1997).
9. Singh, Yogendra (1973/2009) *Modernization of Indian Tradition* (Jaipur: Rawat Publications, p. 58 and pp. 44–45).
10. Ibid., p. 114.
11. Ibid., p. 115 and 136.
12. Ibid., p. 184.
13. Ibid., pp. 203–4.
14. Singh, Yogendra (1978) *Essays on Modernization in India*. Delhi: Manohar Publications, pp. 12–13.
15. Singh, Yogendra (1997) *Social Stratification and Change in India*. New Delhi: Manohar Publications, p. 82.

16. Singh, Yogendra (1978) *Essays on Modernization in India*. Delhi: Manohar Publications, pp. 48–49 and p. 60.
17. Ibid., p. 74.
18. Ibid., p. 170.
19. Ibid., p. 174.
20. Ibid., p. 45.
21. Singh, Yogendra (1997) *Social Stratification and Change in India*. New Delhi: Manohar Publications, p. 50.
22. Singh, Yogendra (1993) *Social Change in India: Crisis and Resilience*. New Delhi: Har-Anand Publications, p. 166.

7

Modernity, Postmodernity and Global Development

P.N. Pandey

Auguste Comte (1798–1857) perceived a rationalist progression of society from theological to metaphysical to scientific stage.

Henri de' Saint Simon (1760–1825), the master of Auguste Comte and one of the founders of sociology, initiated his quest in 1816 when he began publishing, though irregularly, the periodical *L' Industrie* (popularizing the word 'industrialism') and describing in it the society of the future. Past society, said Saint Simon, had been military society in which the chief figures were priests, warriors and feudal lords, the parasites and consumers of wealth. The new industrial society, he said, would be ruled by producers – the engineers and the entrepreneurs – the "coming men" of the times.

Writing in 1840, Alexis de Tocqueville (1966: 666–67) predicted the possible outcome of the new mass democracy in the emergence of modern society. Thirty years later, the historian Jacob Burckhardt (1871: 151–58), observing the transformation of German society, wrote a letter mentioning that the military state would be turned into "industrialist". Fifty years after Burckhardt, Thorstein Veblen (1921), returning to Saint Simonian theme, i.e., 'Revolution in the Twentieth Century', said, it could only be on "industrial overturn". He also observed in his *The Engineers and the Price System* (1963) that if a revolution came in the United States of America, it would be led by production engineers who were indispensable "General Staff" of the industrial system.

One skeptic Clifford Geertz (1974) has remarked that the category "transitional society" may become a permanent category in the social sciences. As a matter of fact, we began using the term 'transitional society' since the end of the World War II (1945) and fifty years after we still prefer to denote our society with the same adjective.

For Ralf Dahrendorf (1958: 272–76, 301–03), we are living in a "post-capitalist society". It was authority not ownership that counted in industrial society. With the denunciation, in legal ownership of means of production, there is a break between economic and the political order. In post-capitalist society relation to the instruments of production no longer decides dominance or power or privileges in society. No doubt, economic and property relations still generate their own conflicts but they no longer become the centre of conflict in society. Who constitutes the ruling class of post-capitalist society? Our answer to this is that it is head of bureaucratic hierarchies, the authorized ones who give the directives to the administrative staff. Outside the portals of an industry, a manager (administrative staff) is simply a citizen while a worker of the factory may happen to be a member of the parliament and a minister and here lies the authority of direction.

According to George Lichtheim (1963: 194), the contemporary industrial society is increasingly "post-bourgeois". The 19th century class struggle is ending with institution of private entrepreneurship on which it was pivoted because of social welfare legislation, human rights legislations and income distribution which are getting associated with the operation of market economy.

For Amitai Etzioni (1968: 8), we are in a postmodern era. It is from his book *The Active Society* that we find a heralded pronouncement of "postmodernism". A new conceptual reference to connote the unprecedented transformation of the societies of West, particularly the USA, Germany, France, Italy, the UK and other Western European societies. He says that the modern period has ended with the radical transformation of the technologies of communication, knowledge and energy that followed the Second World War. Now, the societies have moved on towards super technologies, computers, electronics and wonderlands of knowledge and ideologies. The so-called postmodern societies are conducted, controlled and geared up by technocrats, knowledge elites, computer scientists, and electronic and nuclear experts.

Modernization, Modernity and Modernism

Frequent expressions of modernization, modernity and modernism have been synonymous in common parlance. Modernization and aspiration to modernity are probably the most penetrating features of the contemporary scenario. Most nations are now-a-days caught in the web of becoming modern. Historically, modernization is a process of change towards those types of social, political and economic systems that have developed in Western Europe and North America from the 17th century to the 19th century to the South American, Asian and African continents (Eisenstadt, 1969: 1–2). It is a process of change, a total transformation of traditional or post-traditional societies proceeding with techno-economic changes which necessarily produce changes in the socio-political order.

Modernization is essentially a process – a movement from traditional or quasi-traditional order to certain desired types of technology and associated form of social structure, value orientations, motivations and norms (Dube, 1968: 33–45). Two other terms are sometimes used almost synonymously with modernization. They are: westernization and industrialization. But, modernization denotes a broader perspective and scope than westernization. The West and things western do not have entirely happy connotations for most of the developing societies. Many of these countries have gone through an intense anti-colonial phase, and have lingering memories of ruthless domination and exploitation by the West. The choice of the new world order of international goodwill and welfarism requires a less emotionally changed term – modernization. The term 'modernization' in such a situation soothes their healing. Further, the westernization seems to be direction-bound, limited and releasing generally a smell of British colonialism and imperialism. There are several models with British model overshadowing. Modernization is neutral, direction-free and keeps the choice open. Thus, as a concession to the sensitivity of developing societies and as an aid to conceptual clarity, modernization is to be preferred to westernization. Modernization, too, has several models. Japan and South Korea and recently China have developed their own indigenous models. The advancements in Japanese technology and electronics are superseding all over the world and rank matchlessly in the western markets. As regards industrialization, it is an important part of modernization; it does not encompass the entire process. The connotations of industrialization are overtly technological. Social and cultural processes are considered under it only by implication. Modernity denotes the common "behavioural systems" historically associated with the societies of Western Europe, North America as well as those of Japan. In a sense, thus, modernity refers to the state and situation of having been modern. It denotes common behavioural systems historically associated with urban, industrial, literate and participant societies of Western Europe as well as those of Japan. Modernization, on the other hand, is a wave, a tendency towards adoption of contemporary style of life and systems of developed societies of the West. It has been an overwhelming choice, a contemporary scenario, a call of the people, a taste of the time as well as a pronouncement of the present era. A number of brilliant analyses in the works and writings of particularly Daniel Lerner (1962), G.A. Almond and J.S. Coleman (1960), D.C. McClelland (1967) and S.C. Dube (1968) appeared in regard to the process of modernization during the end of sixties. Now, the period of full-fledged modernization has already reached its saturation point during the first half of the 20th century in the western world. Now, these societies are showing an upward march beyond modernization to be termed in this present discourse as postmodern.

In the process of modernization both the developed and developing societies are apprehensive of their identity loss and that is why they attempt to put their alternativeness on the agenda of modernity. If we look in the context of the developed countries of the West, we find that the European Union, which presently a federation of 28 European countries, has a common economy, polity and social structure and is showing a collectivist identity of Western Europe. Despite the emerging new scientific attitude, the national objectives and goals and the evaluation of the policies of science and technology are done on the basis of purposive rationality as against communicative rationality in terms of Habermas' perception.

Most of the classical sociologists were engaged in an analysis of the critique of modern society. Such analysis is clear in the work of sociological theory of Marx, Weber, Durkheim and Simmel. All were working at the point of emergence of modernity. In the perception of Marx modernity was defined by the capitalist economy.

The city is where the modernity is concentrated or intensified. The money economy involves extension and expansion of modernity. The detailed description which Georg Simmel has made in his *Philosophy of Money* (1975), perceives modernity as 'epiphany'. Simmel deals with the powerful effect of money on modern society, especially, alienation. This, in turn, brings us back to the central issue of Simmel's sociology of modernity, that is, "tragedy of culture", the growing gap between objective and subjective culture or as Simmel puts it, "the atrophy of individual culture" and "hypertrophy of objective culture" (Frisby, 1992: 69).

Anthony Giddens defined modernity in terms of four basic institutions. The first is capitalism, characterized by commodity production, private ownership of capital, properties as labour and a system of class based on these characteristics. The second is industrialism which involves the use of inanimate power to source and machine to produce goods. Industrialism is not restricted to workplace only; it also affects transportation, domestic life and communication. The third institution is surveillance capacity. It refers to the supervision of the activities of subject population in the political sphere and the final institutional dimension of modernity is military power or the control of the means of violence.

Giddens has described the modern world (its origin in 17th century) as a juggernaut. More specifically, he is using this term to describe an advanced stage of modernity – radical, high or late modernity. Among others is Ulrich Beck (1992), who perceives modern society in terms of "risk society". Beck has a perspective on modern society. He wants to explain that modernity is followed by industrial society which emerged by eliminating the 19th century feudal order of society. Now, he discerns that it is a new phase of modernity. Beck recognizes this risk society in terms of new modernity as a reflexive project in which the modern society is getting rid of the structural web work and allows the people to develop their personality according to their choice and they are making the society also reflexive. His ideas are quite akin to the ideas of Giddens. To Zygmunt Bauman, modernity is associated with holocaust where he describes how the so-called modernized technology of the modernity with all their systems and programmes were applied by the German Nazis to weed out the Jews. They were transported by the military, police authority and the railway officers in a planned way to the gas chambers of the factories and were reduced to ashes. In other words, it was application of irrationality of the rationality. What he means to say is a negatively planned application of apparatus, machinery and resources of modernity to bring an end to a species of humanity. Jurgen Habermas described modernity as an unfinished project employing that there is a move to return in modern world before we can think about the possibility of such a world. The progressive stage of modernity to him appears as a colonization of the life-world by the system.

From Modernity to Postmodernity

The very concept of postmodernity or postmodernism has emerged as a wave of change or an ideology of impression from western/modern developed societies, viz., the USA, France, Germany, Italy and the UK. The postmodern development, as a matter of fact, refers to the changes emerging in these societies which have attended the zenith of their urbo-industrial development. Zbigniew Brzezinski (1967) observes American society as the first 'technotronic society'. The so-called postmodernity refers to the unprecedented changes that have been brought about in the form of culture. Malcolm Waters (1992) defines postmodernity in terms of 'post-cultural development'.

The contemporary debate on postmodernity has also resulted in some contradictory remarks. The intellectuals, the architects, the cultural entrepreneurs all have shown their concern about the unprecedented changes that have emerged in modern society as a result of excessive bureaucratization, computerization and commodification of knowledge. Most of the social theories perceived this trend of change as an emerging cultural practice. There are others who distinguish this phenomenon as objective discussion. In contemporary writings, the concept has emerged as a warm game or as a dazzling point of debate. Kellner (1989) perceives this phenomenon as an extremely hot subject.

The postmodernism may be seen as a dazzling variety of styles that can be mixed and matched with various packages. To Lyotard, this postmodernity refers to a historical epoch that is generally seen as following the modern era. J.F. Lyotard (1984) characterizes postmodernity as changes in the structure of feeling and sensitivity of the human beings. He starts with his working hypothesis that the status of knowledge is altered as society enters what is known as post-industrial stage and culture enters what is known as postmodern stage. Lyotard basically involved himself in the study of postmodernity with reference to art, literature and problem of communication and cybernetics. To him, postmodernity is incredible to meta-narratives and grand-theories.

Frederic Jameson (1984) characterizes postmodernity as a cultural logic of late capitalism. He describes this new formation as cultural dominant. It may also be considered a new systematic cultural norm. It is made up of quite heterogeneous elements (ibid.: 7). In Jameson's understanding, this postmodernity can be characterized by superficiality and lack of depth. It is depthless, a-historical, timeless and immediate. It conceives of the social world as technological entity. It is more concerned with simulacrum. This postmodernity ignores historicity and, therefore, the loss of historicity tends to random cannibalization of all styles of past (ibid.: 65–66). The result leads us to another key term in postmodernity theory, i.e., pastiche. Jean Baudrillard in his *Mirror of Production* (1975) characterizes postmodernity as a shift from mode of production to code of production and more to speak he adds a number of inputs as against adjectives as implosion, seduction, simulation, de-differentiation and hyper reality. Baudrillard is an extreme postmodern theorist. Habermas observes it in terms of colonizing the life-world of individual by the system, ascendancy of purposive rationality (in Weberian term 'Zweckrationalitat'), over communicative rationality (in Weberian term 'Wertrationalitat'). There are some theorists who characterize postmodernism as a chaotic, mass-mediated, individual preference-based phenomenon. David Harvey (1989), for example, depicts postmodernity with fragmentation, ephimerality and discontinuity.

The debate on modernity and postmodernity has not ended. There are proponents of both postmodernity and modernity. Among the defenders of modernity mention may be made of Giddens, who perceives the existing situation as advance modernity that is radical, high or late modernity. Bauman and Beck are the other theorists in this group. Habermas is another name who observes modernity as an unfinished project. Bauman characterizes it in a different way. Instead of discussing about postmodernity, he uses the term 'liquid modern society' and more to say the present trend of modern development as 'posthumous modernity'. Among the proponents of postmodernity, the names of Kellner (1989), Lemert (1994), Lyotard (1984), Jameson (1984), Harvey (1989) and Baudrillard (1975) may be cited.

Unfortunately, there is no discussion of technologies of communication, knowledge and energy or a clear specification of what exactly postmodern societies are in the discussion of Etzioni. No doubt, he talks of continued increase in the efficacy of knowledge and technology as a central characteristic of modern period. So, the postmodern period or society is not a discussion, but only a question in his book. He is skeptic in his views. He says that the efficacy of the technology of production and ever-growing super systems of technology pose a challenge to the primacy of values they are supposed to serve. He fears to predict about the future whether the society is to be the servant or the master of the instruments it creates.

Similarly, Samuel Beer (1969: 426) talks of 'post-collectivist politics'. He feels the collectivist model of British politics, which was partly divided as feudalist society and as oriented to the welfare state may be coming to a close. The post-collectivist tendency is a "reaction to the increasing scale and intensity of rationalization in both government and society".

And so a debate moves with the above prologue on 'postmodernism'. It used to be that the great literary modifier was the word 'beyond', e.g., beyond tragedy, beyond culture, beyond society, and so on. But we seem to have exhausted the "beyond" and today the sociological modifier is the prefix 'post' (Bell, 1974: 53). Sydney E. Ahlstrom (1970), a theologian, has described the religious scenario in the United States in 1960 as 'post-Puritan', 'post-Protestant' and 'post-Christian'. Lewis Feuer has sub-titled his work on *Marx and Intellectuals* as a "Set of Post-Ideological Essays".

John Leonard (1970: 26), in *The New York Times*, has talked of the 'post-literature culture' as being heralded by McLuhanite age. For S.N. Eisenstadt and Eric Hobsbaum (1971: 36) the new states have become 'post-tribal societies' for though they are no longer bound by the norms of the past and they seek consciously to change, they live in a suspended world with little approximation to the modern societies of the West. Hobsbaum has obviously written about 'post-tribal societies'. Similarly, Roderick Seidenberg (1950), foretelling the victory of rationalism, had described a 'post-historic man' in which we move from periphery in which instinct-dominated intelligence through the transitional period in history into post-history in which intelligence dominates instinct.

Daniel Bell (1974: 54) observes that the concept of 'post-industrial society' emphasizes the centrality of theoretical knowledge as the axis around which new technology, economic growth and the stratification of society will be organized. Empirically one can try to show that this axial principle is becoming more and more predominant in advanced industrial societies. To Bell (1974: 112), the post-industrial society is a continuation of trends unfolding out of industrial society and many of the developments were foreseen long ago.

Since the phenomena of the so-called postmodernism and post-industrialism are evolving and continued, therefore, no scientific parameter can be applied to bifurcate the modern from postmodern and the industrial from the post-industrial in absolute sense of distinction.

As it has been discussed in the preceding pages the essential division in modern society is not between those who own the means of production and undifferentiated 'proletariat' but the bureaucratic and authority relations between those who have powers of decision-making and those who have not in all kinds of organizations social, economic and political. The basic attribute of post-industrial societies can be observed as (i) a change in the economy denoting a shift from good producing to service economy, (ii) pre-eminence of a professional or technologically expertized section, (iii) centrality of theoretical knowledge as source of innovation towards control, (iv) modern technology and technological assessment, and (v) creation of a new "intellectual technology" for decision-making.

Zbigniew Brzezinski (1967: 18–21) is one of the contemporary social scientists who has made his observation of American society in regard to post-industrial development and has pointed out that America is in the midst of transition, that is, both unique and baffling and is being shaped to an over increasing extent by technology and electronics and, thus, is going to be the first 'technotronic society'.

Sociologically, it appears that the theoretical knowledge of modern technology, electronics, nuclear resources and computer science formulates the very edifice of the post-industrial social structure of societies in the western world. Bell (1967: 24–39, 102–19), in his study of the post-industrial society, stresses on the functional significance of the knowledge derived in the areas of techno-electronic resources in the system of electronic production and shift from manufacturing economy to service economy.

Observations and Postulates

In order to proceed towards the interpretation of the subject matter, we have formulated certain sociological postulates as follows:

1. The concepts of postmodernism and post-industrial society as referred to social and economic structure of those industrially developed capitalist societies which are being conducted, regulated and controlled by technological, electronic and computerized machines, instruments and resources. Such societies in the writings of social scientists like Alain Touraine, Daniel Bell, Albrecht Wellmer, Zbigniew Brzezinski, Stephen Crook, Jan Pakulski and Malcolm Waters and Robert Hollinger are termed as post-industrial societies.

   Our postulate in this regard is that the more there is application and dominance of technological and electronic resources, the greater there shall be an upper hand of dominance by technocrats and knowledge elites and they will emerge as experts and 'house ideologues' in the service of the ruling class.

2. The perspective on the postmodernism and post-industrialism is limited and cannot at the same time be applied to societies or nations of the third world.
3. Our observation in regard to super industrial societies is that there is still the dominance and importance of property ownership in such societies but the capitalist class has failed to continue its dominance as it did in the industrial societies because of the emergence of technocratic elites as an important component possessed of a power-oriented mentality in these societies.

The Indian Context

India is an old society but a new nation which is a living example of multicultural pluralism comprising all major religions, languages, castes, cultural, sub-cultural, ethnic and parochial networking. Religion in India has played a pivotal role from times immemorial. Therefore, all the scientific developments and technological innovations had to be associated with religion and morality. Religion without science is lame and science without religion is blind. Therefore, modern technology has to be associated with the values of tolerance, righteousness and morality otherwise, it will create catastrophe in society. The social, economic, cultural and political systems in India have evolved out of its traditions.

Therefore, the application of technology of the developed societies without indigenous concerns will impede the growth. The traditional bonds in India are such that we are not ready to put one step forward without looking two steps backward. The process of social transformation in India is ongoing and, therefore, modernization of the country requires a well-organized national endeavour. But, in the process of modernization, we perceive that the situation is elusive and full of dilemmas, for example, 'dharma', 'karma', rebirth, spirituality, caste system and secularism, universalism and particularism, ascription and achievement can be taken as dilemmatic situations. It can be said that such dilemmas have not emerged in India only but in the other developing societies as well. They are facing the dilemma of tradition vs. modernization. On the one hand, there is the lure of ascription while on the other, there is a craze of achievement. Similarly, the dilemma of universalism vs. particularism, self-interest vs. collective interest, affectivity vs. affective neutrality can also be traced. In addition to the above, the concept of 'dharma', rebirth, the notion that this world is a mirage, happen to be the major constraints in the implementation of the national programmes of modernization. If we look at the programme of family planning and population control through medico-technological resources, for example, one can easily perceive that religious sanctions and cultural taboos in certain sections of society create major constraints.

Modernization proceeds with secularization, rational outlook and accelerates democratic values. At the same time, the age-ridden iron laws of caste system impose the bars of stratification. Westernization and the articles of western origin in India might have created temptations to adopt them but their pronouncement and appreciation by civil and intellectual society is not very much appreciable because they bear the smell of last 200 years British colonial and imperial domination and exploitation.

In such a backdrop, a neutral process like modernization, undoubtedly, happens to be more acceptable and sooths the healings of the past. But, the problem is that there is no single model of modernization before India. Most of the developed nations, viz., the USA, France, Germany, Italy and the UK at the one end and Japan, Korea and China at the other have developed their own models of modernization. In such a situation, India has also to evolve its own model aided by indigenous resources.

Further, what should be the ultimate destination of man in the process of cultural development through modernization? The debate still remains unanswered by the American and European social scientists. The western exponents of modernization and industrial development have presented the parameters such as gross domestic product (GDP) and per capita income. They are basically the economic parameters and not social or cultural. Development and modernization do not mean merely increasing productivity. These also imply qualitative changes such as improvement in lifestyle, easy accessibility to health, hygiene, education, recreation and rehabilitation.

In my perception, the parameters of cultural development in terms of modernization are yet to be developed. Most of the social scientists in India had accepted the paramount role of education and media of mass communication in the process of modernization in developing societies. The informatics and cybernetics have played very significant role in defusing the value of modernity. The unprecedented changes being brought about in agricultural economy and political and cultural developments are very optimistic signs which show that India is emerging as one of the most powerful nations of the world, but at the same time, the regional voices emerging as ethnic movements in India are obsessive. The claims for retaining specific identities are yet another obsession.

In such a situation, the rational application of science and technology with indigenous resources is essential and while projecting development, the regional, territorial, cultural, ethnic and geopolitical priorities should be put in limelight for an enduring modernized society. The indigenous models and patterns of development should be taken into account while proceeding towards modernization. As a matter of fact, India has to emerge as fully modernized society which should be socially egalitarian, culturally sensitive and environmentally sustainable.

Globalization

Globalization is a multidimensional concept that refers to the transformations of trade, technology, industry and economy in a universalizing direction. It is a cultural process as well but more specially, it is focused by the western industrially developed countries, i.e., the USA, France, Germany, Italy and the UK as a worldwide trade mechanism. In cultural terms, it refers to both as compression of the world and intensification of the consciousness of the world as a whole (Robertson, 1992). It is a process that transforms institutions of modernity in universalizing directions (Giddens, 1991). Capitalism, industrialism, surveillance and monopolization of means of violence are its major institutions.

Globalization, as a worldwide trade mechanism, is a new approach but its roots lie in last six decades of post-World War II period. The decades of 1960, 1970 and 1980 started with the agenda of growth, modernization, social transformation, development and sustainable development and finally at the turn of the 20th century led to globalization with emphasis on liberalization and privatization (Pandey, 1997). The chief motivators for globalization are: (i) search for market place, (ii) multinational investments, and (iii) new tools of technology and electronics with computer network. Most paradoxical aspects of globalization are disparity, inequality, injustice, insecurity prevailing in the economy, polity and social structure of different societies of the world. The industrially developed countries of the world represent 20 per cent of the world population and hold control over 80 per cent of the world resources while the developing world represents 80 per cent of the world population with 20 per cent of the resources of the world. The US, the UK, France, Germany and Italy are moving towards post-industrial economy from manufacturing to service economy. They are in urgent need of market place for their products. It is developing countries of Latin America, Africa and Asia which appear as alternative grounds for market. These countries are apprehensive of identity loss. They do not want techno-electronic imperialism.

Sad Impressions of Modernization, Development and Sustainable Development

The so-called sad impressions of modernization, development and sustainable development have created more disparities, discrepancies and discriminations, though the slogans of globalization are more attractive.

The outcomes of the western developmental programmes have disheartened the developing nations. The ever-increasing social and economic disparities, discrepancy, differentiations and the egalitarianism and equity have proved elusive and dilemmatic to the societies of Asia and Africa (Hudson and Goulet, 1971; Bauer, 1972; Mende, 1973; Hayter, 1971; Béteille, 1993; Wallerstein, 2000).

Western developed countries have created adverse consequences in these countries. Tibor Mende (1973: 36) has traced out that a tendency of strong resentment and protest has been evoked among the developing nations against the developed western countries. The developing nations are realizing that foreign aids are instrumental in perpetuating long-term dependency in the developing nations and as such is a strategy to place the developing societies in the grip of their trade and technology. The profiteering motives and interference in the economy and polity of the developing countries by the western nations will always put them in the subservient condition. Hence, they are threatened about their identity loss. In this state of affairs, the developing countries must evolve their own indigenous models and parameters to their social and economic development. This will help them restore their identity. Teresa Hayter (1971: 151–152) goes a step forward and emphatically argues that the policies and programmes initiated by development agencies such as International Monetary Fund, World Bank, United States Agency for International Development and Inter-American Development Bank accord and approve the international and national character of western capitalist countries and aim at maintaining their supremacy over these countries. These agencies motivate for creating free market, trade and technology and to rely on them with a sense of attachment and commitment. P.T. Bauer (1972: 49–68) is another social scientist who has given a critical assessment of the nature and form of western aid and has concluded in his investigations that the western developed countries have attempted more to create a vicious poverty circle in the third world countries rather than improving their economy and social standards of life. Immanuel Wallerstein, in one of his works entitled *After Liberalism* (2000), has expressed apprehension about the immanent crisis sprouting out of the late capitalism. A contemporary economist of the US George Soros in one of his latest works entitled *The Crisis of Global Capitalism: Open Society Endangered* (2000), is very vocal and clearly highlights that globalization is an inevitable outcome of the crisis of post-industrialization in the western world. A well-known Canadian economist Sislia Ostry (1999) observes that the western industrially developed capitalist countries are facing crucial problems in the sale and consumption of their products and are setting their eyes towards the countries of Asia and Africa. The excessive technologized production in the West requires a large and wide market place for effective sale and consumption. The increasing demand of consumption is a decisive factor for the success of technologized production and this is feasible only when there is extensive market place for consumption. In this context, the third world countries appear as the only alternative market place for the West.

The principles of justice, associated with socialist welfarist states, are ridiculed in the agenda of globalization. The nature and quantum of availability of electronic appliances, computer, email, internet, etc., are not equally available to all the countries of the world. Research and development (R&D) is lifeblood in any economy. The initiatives are taken by multinationals more frequently, hence, infringement of powers and capacity in policy-making. It means multinational corporations will have upper hand in the developing nations. Globalization proceeds with consumerism while 80 per cent of the world is in need of productive economy. Globalization is elusive to the need and expectation of the poor and the weaker sections. It widens the gap between the rich and the poor. Accepting globalization means accepting the primacy and rule of integrated minority over a huge majority of the world. At the structural transformation level, the programme of globalization is against participatory democracy as 80 per cent of world population has little representation and interference in its policies and decision-making. Apparently, the developing nations at Seattle in the US and also in Geneva at the WTO summits denoted that they are not ready to accept the terms and conditions of WTO as bindings on their social and economic liberty. The theft of intellectual property by multinationals and putting on their patent is nothing less than imperial exploitation. It has shattered the nerves of the egalitarian ideology and obsesses the poor countries with ruthless domination and super bossism of the West. The western industrially developed countries show deceptive crocodile sympathy to developing countries which have different culture, history, tradition, national ethos and ideology. This programme of globalization is the outcome of western crisis of post-industrialization and is devoid of human concern and issue of uniformity. The third world countries must come out in a consensual way to make a forte of their own and also to face the challenges in the new millennium.

The Process of Cultural Change

The most recent theoretical debates about culture centres on the issue whether culture has taken a new turn or entered a new phase at the end of the 20th century. The cultural registers analysed by the neo-Marxist and neo-Weberian scholars are essentially modern in character. If society prefers to be dominated by a single set of ideas, then Gramsci of Frankfurt School can investigate how these ideas, are manufactured, or if society is divided by men into a small and fixed number of classes, the Bourdieu or Abercrombie, Hill and Turner can investigate whether culture exhibits similar internal differentiations.

The hardest Marxist version comes from F. Jameson (1984). He interprets cultural change as the 'cultural logic of late capitalism'. He proposes a three-fold perception of capitalism, which comes originally from Mandel:

1. Market capitalism, which involves markets within nation-states.
2. Imperial or monopoly capitalism, in which the capitalist states establish colonies, so that they could catch both suppliers of raw materials and international markets.
3. Multinational consumerist capitalism which establishes a new integrated global place for capitalist expansion and within that expands markets by expanding individual acquisitiveness.

This expansion of capitalism into global arena is percolated by global expansion of culture which liberates it from particular social context. There is a prodigious expansion of culture throughout the social realm. This is so-called postmodern culture. The postmodern culture, which focuses on the centrality of the global space and dislocates individuals from the realities of their own situation, has four characteristics:

1. It is depthless (i.e., what you see is what you get) which has risen on the collapse of grand narratives and meta-theories.
2. It is a-historical and immediate: It provides no reference back to human suffering and struggle. Traditions can be mixed and matched in pastiche rather than drown upon or resisted.
3. It is timeless. It focuses on organization of fragments of culture meanings in space. The time relations of these fragmentations are not signified.
4. It conceives of the world as a technological entity rather than as a natural one. It also conceives of social network as a computer network, rather than an ecological balance.

If we count Jameson (1984) and Harvey (1989) along with Habermas (1981) as critics of postmodernism, then among its advocates must be Lyotard (1984) and Baudrillard (1975). The move from modern to postmodern knowledge parallels social development. The status of knowledge is altered as societies enter what is called as the post-industrial age and culture enters what is known as postmodern age. The post-industrial developments are the computerization and commodification of knowledge. Increasingly, performativity, the capacity to deliver outputs at the lowest cost, replaces truth as yardstick of knowledge. Modern culture is highly differentiated but post-culture moves towards hyper differentiation. Postmodern culture can be seen as a dazzling variety of styles which can be mixed and matched with various packages. Modern culture is highly rationalized pattern of technical cultural expertise located either in tradition or its transcendence. Postmodern culture is so hyper intensified that their can no longer be any claim to expertise or any development of tradition. Modern culture is highly commodified, postmodern culture is so hyper commodified that material commodities are subsumed by signs which represent them.

Information Technology and Global Change

The media of mass communication revolutionizes culture and the knowledge of science, technology and electronics enhances it to give wider coverage to the global space. The society is transferred into a 'technotronic' culture with computer networking. The 'culture specifics' are attempted to be subsumed into multiethnicity and multiculturalism as smaller clenches with secondary importance. In addition, printing press, radio, film, television, the computer networking, the cybernetics and informatics are controlling the global network. The information technology and telecommunication systems with digital codifications are reducing the vast pool of human knowledge to a codified structure embedded into the computer websites.

In the words of Habermas, this process of globalization is going to de-couple the integration of life-world and the system and is tended to proceed towards internal colonization. In the modern techno-electronic set-up, individuals are forced to go through purposive rationalization (in Weber's term 'Zweckrationalitat'). The purposive rationality is marked with contractual morality, i.e., non-critical, object-oriented and not by communicative rationalization, i.e., critical reasoning (in Weber's term 'Wertrationalitat'). The character of this so-called postmodern culture which is emerging can be termed as Disethesized and shameless. The individual is emerging as a client leaving aside his real identity and the whole world system is being regulated by purposive rationality and is going to emerge as a computerized networking rather than a natural entity; a technological entity rather than an ecological balance.

The developing countries in general, and India in particular, have a long historicity of grand-narratives, meta-theories, legends and myths. Globalization cannot assimilate all of them. In my assessment, India and other developing countries of Asia and Africa will ever manifest a peculiar blend of their historical identity even in the global modernizing attempts.

References

Ahlstrom, Sydney E. (1970) "The Radical Turn in Theology and Ethics", *The Annals*, January.

Almond, G.A. and Coleman, J.S. (1960) *The Politics of Developing Area*. Princeton, NJ: Princeton University Press.

Baudrillard, Jean (1975) *The Mirror of Production*. St. Louis: Telos Press.

—— (1990) *Seduction*. New York: St. Martins'.

—— (1993) *Symbolic Exchange and Death*. London: Sage.

—— (1994) *Simulation*. New York: St. Martins'.

Bauer, P.T. (1972) *Dissent on Development*. Cambridge: Cambridge University Press, pp. 49–67.

Bauman, Zygmunt (1989) *Modernity and the Holocaust*. Ithaca, NY: Cornell University.

—— (1991) *Modernity and Ambivalence*. Ithaca, NY: Cornell University.

—— (1991) *Postmodern Ethics*. Oxford: Blackwell.

—— (2005) *Liquid Life*. Cambridge: Polity Press.

—— (2007) *Consuming Society*. Cambridge: Polity Press.

Bech, Ulrich (1992) *Risk Society: Towards a New Modernity*. London: Sage.

Beer, Samuel H. (1969) *British Politics in Collectivist Age* (Epilogue edition), New York: Vintage.

Bell, Daniel (1967) "Notes on Post-Industrial Society", *The Public Interest*, No. 6 (Winter) and No. 7 (Spring), pp. 24–23 and 102–48.

—— (1974) *The Coming of Post-Industrial Society*. New Delhi: Arnold-Heinemann Publishers, pp. 3–29, 49–54 and 113–19.

—— (1979) *The Cultural Contractions of Capitalism*. London: Heinemann.

Béteille, André (1993) *Equality and Inequality*. New Delhi: Oxford University Press.

Birbaum, Norman (1971) *Towards a Critical Sociology*. New York: Oxford University Press.

Boulding, Kennith (1964) *The Meaning of Twentieth Century*. New York: Harper & Row.

Brzezinski, Zbigniew (1967) "The American Transition", *New Republic*, Vol. 157, No. 23, December, pp. 18–21, also reprinted in Alain Western (ed.), *Information Technology in a Democracy*, Cambridge: Harvard University Press, pp. 161–67.

Burckhardt, Jacob (1871) Letters to Von Preen, April 96. Alexander Dru (ed.) (1955), pp. 151–52.

Crook, Stephen, Pakulski, Jan and Waters, Malcolm (1992) *Postmodernization: The Change in Advanced Societies*. New Delhi: Sage.

Dahrendorf, Ralf (1959) *Class and Class Conflict in an Industrial Society*. Stanford, CA: Stanford University Press. See Chaps. VII and VIII "Classes in Post Capitalist Society (i) Industrial Conflict (ii) Political Conflict", pp. 272–76, 301–02.

Dube, S.C. (1968) "Human Problems of Economic Development", in *Economic Development and Cultural Change*, New Delhi: Raj Kamal Prakashan.

—— (1976) "Modernization and its Adoptive Demand on Indian Society", in M.S. Gore, I.P. Desai and Suma Chitnis (eds.), *Sociology of Education in India*, New Delhi: NCERT.

—— (1994) *Tradition and Development*. New Delhi: Vikas Publishing House, pp. 1–16 and 17–44.

Eisenstadt, S.N. (1969) *Modernization, Protest and Change*. New Delhi: Prentice Hall of India, pp. 1–2.

Etzioni, Amitai (1968) *The Active Society*. New York: Free Press, p. 7.

Frisby, D. (1992) *Sociological Impressionism: A Reassessment of Georg Simmel's Social Theory*. London: Heinemann.

Geertz, Clifford (1974), cited in *The Coming of Post-Industrial Society* by Daniel Bell.

Giddens, Anthony (1990) *Consequences of Modernity*. Cambridge: Polity Press.

—— (1991) *Modernity and Self Identity*. Cambridge: Polity.

Habermas, J. (1981) "Modernity versus Postmodernity", *New German Critique*, Vol. 22 (Winter), pp. 3–14.

—— (1984) *The Theory of Communicative Action, Vol. 1, Reason and Rationalization of Society*. Boston: Beacon.

Harvey, David (1989) *The Condition of Postmodernity: An Enquiry into the Origins of Cultural Change*. Oxford: Blackwell.

Hayter, Teresa (1971) *Aids as Imperialism*. Harmondsworth: Penguin Books, pp. 151–52.

Hobsbaum, Eric (1971) "Social History and the History of Society", *Daedalus*, issue entitled 'Historical Studies Today', Winter, p. 36.

Hollinger, Robert (1994) *Postmodernism and the Social Sciences: A Thematic Approach*. New Delhi: Sage.

Hudson, Michael and Goulet, Denis (1971) *Myth of Aid*. NY: Orbis Books, pp. 13–64.

Jameson, F. (1984) "Post Modernism or the Cultural Logic of Late Capitalism", *New Left Review*, No. 146, pp. 53–92.

Kellner, Douglas (ed.) (1989) "Introduction: Jameson, Marxism and Postmodernism", *Postmodernism/Jameson/Critique*, Washington, DC: Maisonneuve Press.

Lemert, Charles (1994) "Social Theory at the Early End of a Short Century in Sociological Theory", by George Ritzer (1996).

Leonard, John (1970) "Post-Literature Culture", *The New York Times*, November 26.

Lerner, Daniel (1962) *The Passing of Traditional Society*. Glencoe: The Free Press.

—— (1963) "Toward a Communication Theory of Modernization", in Lucian W. Pye (ed.), *Communications and Political Development*, Princeton, NJ: Princeton University Press, p. 11.

Lichtheim, George (1963) *The New Europe Today and Tomorrow*. New York: Praeger, p. 194.

Lyotard, J.F. (1984) *The Postmodern Condition*. Manchester: Manchester University Press.

McClelland, D.C. (1967) *The Achieving Society*. Princeton, NJ: Van Nostrand Co.

Mende, Tibor (1973) *From Aid to Re-colonization: Lessons of a Failure*. New York: Pantheon Books, p. 36.

Ostry, Sislia (1999) *The Crisis of Global Trade*. New York.

Pandey, P.N. (1991) "Science Technology and Changing Power Structure in Industrial Society", *Journal of Social and Economic Studies*, New Series, 3rd Issue, New Delhi: Harshad Publication, pp. 21–27. A previous version of the paper was presented in XVIII All India Sociological Conference held on March 3–5, 1989 at Haryana Agricultural University, Hissar, Haryana.

—— (1997) "Dilemmas of Development: A Case of the Third World", *Samajiki, Journal of UP Sociological Society*, Vol. 10, Joint Issue 1–2.

Pool, Ithiel de Sola (1963) "The Role of Communication in the Process of Modernization and Technological Change in Industrialization and Change", in Bert F. Hoselitz and Wibert Moore (eds.), *Industrialization and Society*, Paris: UNESCO-Mouton.

Robertson, R. (1992) *Globalization*. London: Sage.

Seidenberg, Roderick (1950) *Post-Historic Man*. Chapel Hill, NC: University of North Carolina Press.

Simmel, Georg (1907/1978) *The Philosophy of Money* (ed. and trans. Tom Bottomore and David Frisby), London: Routledge and Kegan Paul.

Simon, Henri de Saint (1816) *L'Industrie*, cited in Daniel Bell, *The Coming of Post-Industrial Society*, New York: Basic Books, p. 49.

Soros, George (2000) *The Crisis of Global Capitalism: Open Society Endangered*. New York: Free Press.

Tocqueville, Alexis de (1966) "Democratic Nations Have to Fear", quoted in Daniel Bell, *The Coming of Post-Industrial Society*, New York: Basic Books, pp. 666–67.

Touraine, Alain (1971) *The Post-Industrial Society*. New York: Random House, p. 3.

Veblen, Thorstein (1921) *The Engineers and the Prince System*. New York: Harbinger.

Wallerstein, I. (2000) *After Liberalism*. New York: New Press.

Waters, Malcolm (1992) *Modern Sociological Theory*. New York: Columbia University Press.

Weinstein, Deena and Weensteen, Michael A. (1993) *Postmodern(ized) Simmel*. London: Routledge.

Wellmer, Albrecht (1971) *Critical Theory of Society*. New York: Herder and Herder. See also Max Horkheimer (1968) *Critical Theories*. Frankfurt: Frankfurt School of Sociology.

8

Globalization: Where Lies the Choice?

Partha Nath Mukherji

The phenomenon of globalization has raised a whole host of issues including whether it is a historically new phenomenon or has a long antiquity; whether it is an extension of modernity and derives basically from a capitalist logic; whether it is a homogenizing force across economies, cultures and societies; and so on. The discourse and debates had for long taken the form, in a conspicuous manner, of votaries and antagonists across the fence. While one has come to live with globalization, its consequences still evoke strong reservations, particularly since the global market meltdown. To my mind the initial confusion iies in the different perceptions of globalization in the wake of the sudden and rapid release of new forces of change that have had compulsive and unanticipated consequences for countries, cultures and societies.[1]

Although the process of what we call globalization had set in much earlier, the term or concept was virtually unknown before May 1, 1983. According to Richard Tomkins, the term was introduced by the marketing guru Theodore Levitt, Professor at the Harvard Business School in an article published in the *Harvard Business Review*. The sum and substance of Professor Levitt's message, according to Tomkins was: "As new technology extended, the reach of the global media brought down the cost of communications, the world was shrinking. As a result, consumer tastes everywhere were converging, creating global markets for standardized production on a previously unimagined scale" (Tomkins, 2003).

Professor Levitt had proclaimed, "(t)he world's needs and desires have been irrevocably homogenised. This makes the multinational corporation obsolete and the global corporation absolute" (quoted in ibid.). Why? "Because old fashioned multinational companies that made different products to local tastes were doomed, whereas global corporations that offered the same products, in the same way, everywhere, benefiting from enormous economies of scale in production, distribution, marketing and management, would undercut the MNC's" (ibid.).

Tomkins observes, in fact, the opposite happened. Barring some product categories in the purely technology, culture-free area, the paradox of globalization is that it has led not to a convergence of tastes, but to a vast increase in the number of choices available to consumers. People around the world started demanding more local sovereignty and greater protection of their cultural identity. The 'one-size-fits-all' model had to be replaced by 'think local, act local'. Coca-Cola, which took Professor Levitt seriously, had to beat a hasty retreat to their 'multi-local heritage' (ibid.).

I will argue that there are two aspects to the phenomenon of globalization. One is the aspect of irreversibility; the other, that of choice of alternative paths in an era of globalization.

Post-War Modernity

It would be instructive to compare the previous watershed in history, viz., the post-World War II era of modernization. When the concept and theories of modernization found sudden universal currency, much the same way that globalization has in present times, there was hardly any dilemma on whether or not to modernize. The problem lay in the western capitalist model of modernity, claiming for itself a unilinear, historical inevitability. For, there existed a parallel competing Soviet socialist model of development, which was also premised on a unilinear, historical model. The co-existence of these two powerful, parallel models, with their separate institutional structures of the economy and polity, provided the scope for mixed models. Postcolonial countries tended to draw from both. Ours resulted in the adoption of the socialistic pattern of mixed economy.

Whichever of the two dominant models, the common underlying assumption was that of modernity, which was counterposed against tradition. Objections were voiced against such theorizing in India almost from the beginning. Gandhi was not against appropriate technology but was severely critical of the capitalist industrialism of the West. D.P. Mukerji, delivering the first Presidential Address of the Indian Sociological Society in 1955, declared that it was wrong to view tradition as nothing, but conservative. In the ultimate analysis, the study of tradition involved unveiling those symbols which "under certain conditions and on particular levels, are explosively creative and dynamic, and, therefore, the values and norms retain and enrich their noetic (intellectual or mental – meaning provided by author) connection with specific social structures and concrete historical situations" (Mukerji, 1958: 228–41).

Amongst later scholars, Joseph Gusfield was quick to point out that the tradition-modernity polarity was misplaced. Yogendra Singh expanded on the theme of modernity of traditions and the traditionalization of modernity. It became established that there was not one single model of modernization, but multiple models.

More recently, Immanuel Wallerstein (1997) has questioned this 'presumed intellectual problematic of modernity' in the social sciences – what it was, what social problem it caused, "how we might better understand its evolution. This explicit or implicit assumption of linear evolution could no longer be stated as a truism, but it must have to be defended as a controversial intellectual position."

The fact remains that economies and societies of all developing countries, deciding to modernize by introducing modern western institutions did not, as postulated, replicate the 'take-off' as the western and some other countries had done historically. The pattern variables of Talcott Parsons, which had signified invariant attributes of transition from tradition to modernity, did not work out for many developing countries. And yet, it has to be accepted that the modernity model was so compelling and so pervasive that it was hardly a matter of choice – whether or not to modernize. In a fundamental sense, it was driven by technology and industrialization. The developing world was, in fact, infatuated with modernity.

It will be useful to recall how India fell in for the Community Development Programme, modelled on the Tennessee Valley Authority. The Ludhiana Agricultural University was modelled on the Land Grant Colleges in the USA to usher in a Green Revolution. We also went in for the High Yielding Variety (HYV) Strategy in agricultural production, but this distracted us from concentrating on drought-resistant varieties. The multipurpose dams of the Damodar Valley Corporation withdrew our attention from our traditional tank irrigation, which needed to be re-discovered. The relevant question remained: what development path to choose and how to go about it, rather than look for pre-packaged recipes of modernization.

Globalization: From Fordism to Flexible Accumulation

Unlike the open-arm welcome to modernization, globalization has met with a turbulent reception, although it will generally be conceded that it is, by and large, an extension of modernization. What are significantly different, are the scale, speed and intensity of far-reaching changes. There is, however, one fundamental difference. While modernization largely operated at the 'inter-national' level, globalization has a 'trans-national' terrain. It has been a process of *transformation with continuity*.

I would like to draw attention to four historic moments that are associated with the transformation from the era of modernization to globalization. These are: the unresolvable tensions introduced by the Vietnam war and the oil shock in the early seventies and the emergence of petro-dollars; the extension of the application of the revolution in information technology revolution from the confines of military technology to the wider arena of the world economy; the collapse of the Soviet Union and the socialist economy; and the neo-liberal rationalization of the world economy signalling the end of the Keynesian era. To appreciate this transition, we need to retrace out steps to the Fordist era and follow its evolution.

In 1914, Henry Ford, the father of the automobile industry, introduced the $5, 8-hour-a-day work schedule for his automated car assembly line factory. This became the model for the restructuring of the modern world economy.

Three features of this new economy were:

(a) long-term and large-scale fixed capital investments in mass production, on the presumption of stable growth and invariant consumer markets,

(b) labour markets, labour allocations, and a deeply entrenched working class power, and

(c) state commitments to social security, pension rights, etc.

Two successive devastating world wars and the Great Depression of 1929, led to debilitating trauma for Europe and the world. This trauma, in turn, led to the historic UN Monetary and Financial Conference at Bretton Woods in New Hampshire in July 1944 even before the war had finally ended. The specific objectives of the conference were: (a) to rebuild a war-ravaged Europe, and (b) its long-term goal was to 'save the world from future economic depression' (Stiglitz, 2002: 11). The Bretton Woods System (BWS) gave birth to (a) the International Bank for Reconstruction and Development (World Bank), which has been assigned the task of reconstructing the European and world economy, and (b) the International Monetary Fund (IMF), whose duty was to ensure against any future economic depression.

John Maynard Keynes, the intellectual godfather of IMF, provided its theoretical foundation. He felt very concerned that markets can fail and might generate persistent unemployment. If that happened, the economic downturn in one country could affect other countries, as one country's imports were linked to one or more countries' exports. An economic downturn (i.e., unemployment) would lead to loss of purchasing power in that country, thus affecting countries exporting to it because of cutbacks in imports. He argued that economic downturns were a consequence of aggregate demands. In such situations, government policies were required to stimulate such demand. Both monetary (e.g., credit, interest, money supply and banking) and fiscal (e.g., tax relief, expenditure, management, public debt, deficit financing, borrowings) policies needed to be applied to restore and re-invigorate the economy. Embedded in this kind of state intervention lay the logic for 'global collective action' (Stiglitz, 2002: 196; discussion with Atul Sarma). Thus, the original mandate for the IMF was: (a) to put 'pressure on countries to maintain their economies at full employment', and (b) to provide 'liquidity for those countries facing downturns that could not afford expansionary increase in government expenditures, so that global aggregate demand could be sustained' (ibid.).

The operations of such a mechanism required a monetary system that could "provide monetary services in sufficient amounts to enable member governments to maintain exchange rates for their currencies at pre-determined values". This required stabilization of a monetary system that could be achieved "by tying every currency to a non-monetary asset". Member-states "were anchored by tying every currency to the dollar, which in turn, was tied to gold, and the major powers informally coordinated their economic policies" (Gilpin, 2000: 59). The IMF was designed to play this role. This was the Keynesian era of modernization of developing nations in the postcolonial period.

The system began experiencing strain of high inflation from the late sixties that climaxed in the seventies and totally transformed the BWS by the eighties. The circumstances that brought about this change were:

- The hidden costs of the Vietnam war and the other factors cumulatively manifested themselves during the Nixon régime (1969–1974). This forced him to devalue the overvalued dollar on 15th August 1971, in the face of 'ballooning of the American trade deficit' (ibid.: 68–69).
- The Eurodollar (not to be confused with Eurocurrency – the Euro of the European Common Market) appeared as early as 1949 when the Chinese government sought protection of its dollar earnings from the reach of the American state. These dollars were deposited in a Parisian bank: Bank

Commerciale pour l'Europe du Nord, which paradoxically was owned by Soviet Russia. The Russians too took the cue from China and began depositing their own dollars. Subsequently, the Moscow Narodny Bank came up in London to serve the same function. Other governments and multinational corporate entities keen on not repatriating their dollars to the US 'led to the institutionalization of a set of money and credit market that were effectively beyond the authority of any rational or international regulatory authority' (Dubey, 2004: 62, 59–63).

- The rising inflation in the US due to the Vietnam war led to the dollar rapidly losing its value and the US buying dollars in exchange for gold.[2]
- Simultaneously, in August 1971, with the devaluation of the dollar, the dollar was no longer freely convertible into gold, effectively signalling the end of fixed exchange rates and the demise of Bretton Woods. Henceforth, in theory, the "value of currencies (was) set by global market forces, that is, worldwide demand and supply of a particular currency" (Held et al., 1999: 202).
- Close on the heels in 1972, petroleum-producing countries of the Middle East (OPEC) suddenly withdrew their oil supply, eventually quadrupling the price of oil. This resulted in a "huge transfer of funds from oil importing to oil exporting countries". The large surpluses of leading oil exporters, an estimated $50 billion between 1974–76, suddenly found entry into the international monetary markets, increasing the liquidity of international banks (Gilpin, 2000: 71; Held et al., ibid.). The scale and speed of international financial flows expanded so much by the late 1970s that it irretrievably transformed the international economic system by integrating the monetary and financial systems of national economies on a global scale as never before (Gilpin, ibid.: 74). This was an unintended trigger effect of the oil crisis.

Certain unanticipated implications of these developments were: (a) if a country increased its interest rates to control domestic inflation, money would flow instantly from low interest areas to neutralize it; and (b) international financial flows became an important determinant of exchange rates adding to its volatility (ibid.: 74–75).

The era of Fordism, anchored in 'fixed capitals' gave way to the new era of 'flexible accumulation'. This flexibility extended to "labour processes, labour markets, products and patterns of consumption. It (was) characterized by entirely new sectors of production, new ways of providing financial services, new markets, and above all, greatly intensified rates of commercial, technological and organizational innovation" (Harvey, 1990: 147).

The Information Technology Revolution, the Socialist Collapse and the Global Economy

The information technology (IT) revolution, by its function of space and time compression, enabled the accelerated transformation of economic globalization. Satellite communications and reduction in transport costs shortened 'time horizons' of public and private decision-making covering wider and wider geographic areas. Electronic banking and plastic money revolutionized transnational money transactions in a manner that made it difficult for states to have much control over them. States moved from the concept of *control* to that of transnational regulations of an increasingly globalizing economy. The sudden and dramatic collapse of the socialist economies was interpreted as the triumph of neo-liberal market fundamentalism, overtaking the Keyensian era.

There was a gestalt change in the new patterns and processes of production and consumption. Sub-contracting, outsourcing, just-in-time delivery systems and small-batch production reduced the turnover time in sectors such as machine tools, automobiles, construction, clothing, and so on, leading to higher rates of skilling and de-skilling of labour. It led to mega mergers of large corporations, their downsizing of the labour force to cut on cost of production for increasing margins of profitability and market share. It introduced volatility and ephemerality in the products of mass consumption with a premium on consumerism, fuelled by aggressive advertisement and image-building, seeking to manipulate desires, tastes and opinions. It resulted in a burgeoning service sector, re-introduced artisanal models of production and introduced flexible work regimes and labour contracts. With the integration of the global financial market and liberalization in trade, capital became mobile seeking out spaces over wide geographic areas for better profits and rapid accumulation. Globalization introduced new dimensions of accumulation of wealth and inequality, and poverty within nations and worldwide. In the perceptive words of Harvey, "Economies of scope have beaten out the economies of scale" (ibid.: 155).[3]

The Global and the National: Contestations over the Nation-State

Two questions may be addressed at this stage: (1) Does globalization signal the redundancy of the nation-state? (2) Does economic globalization per se circumscribe only the neo-liberal incarnation?

I shall briefly summarize from the excellent review of the contending positions on the status of the nation-state in a globalizing world by David Held and his co-authors, and then comment. According to Held, the hyper-globalists (including Wriston, 1992, Ohmae, 1995, Gill, 1995, Strange, 1996, Cox, 1997, Gray, 1998, all mentioned in Held) believe that the transnational networks of production, trade and finance are giving rise to new forms of social and economic organization that are already supplanting, and in course of time, will supplant the traditional nation-states. The roles of the nation-states would be reduced to that of managing the consequences of globalization (Held et al., 1999: 3–5). To the skeptics (including Gilpin, 1987, Gordon, 1988, Callinicos, 1994, Hirst and Thompson, 1996, Hirst, 1997, all referred to in Held) globalization is a new form of economic interdependence, by no means historically unprecedented. It is yet another phase of western imperialism, which is leading to the further marginalization of the South, and playing on the deeply rooted patterns of inequality and hierarchy, pushing the world towards regressive fundamentalism and aggressive nationalism, threatening clash of civilizations. They assign the role of the national governments as the prime architects of internationalization.

The transformationalists (including Giddens, 1990, Rosenau, 1990, Camilleri and Falk, 1992, Scholte, 1993, Ruggie, 1903, Keohane, 1995, Linklater and Macmillan, 1995, Castells, 1996, Murphy, 1996, Hoogvelt, 1997, all referred to in Held) strike a middle course. They acknowledge that the contemporary process of globalization is historically unprecedented, in as much as the distinction between the domestic and the international has become blurred. Globalization, however, is regarded as a long historical process, with its attendant contradictions and conflicts. In its contemporary phase it is in the process of reconstituting the power, functions and authority of national governments, as national economies no longer coincide with national territorial borders. The emerging global pattern of stratification is linked with the de-territorialization of economic activities, as production and finance acquire global transformational dimension. The earlier 'pyramidal analogy' of the world social structure is veering towards the analogy of 'concentric circles' cutting across national boundaries, representing the 'elites', the 'contented' and the 'marginalized'. A new 'sovereignty regime' is replacing the traditional conceptions of statehood as it negotiates with the emergence of powerful, non-territorial forms of economic and political organizations (multilateral corporations, transnational social movements, international regulatory agencies). Complex global systems from financial to ecological connect the fate of communities in one locale to the fate of communities of distant regions of the world. 'Sites of power and subjects of power may be literally oceans apart'. This does not imply the 'end of the state', but rather a more 'activist state', engaged in a variety of adjustment strategies. Consequently, in one or more respects, every country has virtually become functionally a part of the larger global system (Held et al., 1999: 7–9).

Paradoxes of Globalization

On the one hand, there is considerable theorizing that pre-figures the demise or the weakening of the nation-state. On the other hand, there is an equally strong and pervasive argument that countries act on the basis of their 'national interests'. So strong are the domestic interests that they contribute to the shaping of international trade and international relations.

The assumption that trade conducted free from any fetters, charts out a dispassionate course of action for all actors in the market, has never been allowed to hold. The operation of a free market is a myth. That is why, 'trade liberalization' has been considered a more appropriate concept to 'free-trade' (Gilpin, 1987: 89).

This contentious issue is not confined to the developing countries. Votaries of trade liberalization themselves have sometimes been most defensive in lifting protection. The US, in the face of oil crisis, threatened by increased imports from Japan and other developing countries, imposed the Multi-Fibre Arrangement in 1973, slapping quantitative restrictions on textile and apparel imports in violation of the GATT principle of non-discrimination (ibid.: 81). The protests in Doha and Cancun suggest that developing countries are on the defensive.

The nation-state, in fact, is demonstrating stronger resilience against its being reduced to a manager of consequences flowing from global economics or politics. The 9/11 episode was a threat to the US nation leading to its unilateral invasion of Iraq, where a nation-state was sought to be put back in place, both by Iraqis and the US with different national motives. Political processes are aiming at bringing about democratic nation-states in Palestine and Afghanistan. No matter how much global integration takes place in the economic sphere, it is unlikely that the structural concept of the nation-state will just wither away into political insignificance in the absence of alternative globally authentic institutional structures to which all peoples of the globe lend legitimacy. The crux of the problem lies in the fallacy of the mindset that the western form of representative democracy is the only viable form of democracy. This leads to pressuring the external constructions of one-size-fits-all democracies of the West to culturally different contexts, by the West.

Globalization: Irreversibility and Alternatives

The inexorable logic of globalization is embedded in the phenomenal compression in time and space that the revolution in information technology has brought about. Communication has become dramatically instant and economically affordable for many. The cell phones are being used with profit by all and sundry. Almost all that happened 'really' now can happen 'virtually'. The continuous advances in software are opening up new opportunities for more efficient communications and transactions. The reaches of the local and the global have become reciprocal. This is the fundamental factor of globalization, which is irreversible. The context of the 'glocal' is the outcome.

The unprecedented and rapid integration of the financial markets following the petro-dollar accumulations during the oil crisis; the cross-border flow of finances; the trans-nationalization of jihad; the diasporic construction of Hindu fundamentalism; the global reaches of cultural products like yoga, meditation, classical Indian music and dance; the social movements reaching out for transnational solidarities; and the myriad other aspects of society reaching out to global lengths, have been rendered possible on account of this revolution in technology.

The fallacy lies in conflating the globalization of neo-liberal economy of market fundamentalism with globalization per se. It is important to remove this fallacy. While globalization is not reversible, neo-liberal market fundamentalism is. As observed earlier, this was very much in evidence during the multinational protests at Doha and Cancun, where the neo-liberalizers were on the retreat, whilst the marginalized were on the offensive. Besides, globalization is not just economic globalization. It is well nigh impossible to accept that the entire world, for all times to come, will get homogenized into a single-brand world economy, subscribing to a single culture of consumerism, within an overarching global governance, moving from a rich plurality to monotonous singularity, with docility. One can argue that the same forces of production that have globalized geographic space, are globalizing plurality, cultures, conflicts, contesting ideologies, beliefs, and so on. Location/context-specific phenomena are into their global extensions. The diasporas do not necessarily submit to easy assimilation in the distant host cultures but are introducing multiculturalism in their host countries. The ramifications of the conflict in Afghanistan, Palestine, Iraq and Sri Lanka have become transnational.

The challenges that the globalization of the neo-liberal variety pose in India are meeting with new offensives from grass roots levels mobilizations, building up on coalitions of like-minded mobilizations to create new bottom-up pressures that compel the state to respond. D.L. Sheth, recently, in an excellent paper, documents the dramatic changes that have taken place amongst many NGOs since the mid-1990s, as they jerked out of their 'stable', 'comfortable' existence pampered by international donor agencies, to confront the challenges faced by the neo-liberal hegemony. Observes Sheth:

> Accordingly, they now view development as a political struggle for people's participation in defining development goals and devising means to achieve them. Their view of development is thus a non-hegemonic, pluralistic process, in articulating which they use inductively arrived insights and criteria evolved through their own struggles. (2004: 45–48)

According to Sheth, the principles of participatory democracy transacting democracy from the grass roots levels upwards, enunciated by Gandhi and elaborated by Jayaprakash Narayan, which were dismissed as archaic and unrealisable are surfacing as visible demonstrations of politics of everyday life in their confrontation with challenges from remote national and global ends. He cites the movements and initiatives by Aruna Roy of MKSS on the Right to Information, which culminated in state legislation; Rajendra Singh of the Tarun Bharat Sangh in Alwar who successfully regenerated dried up streams with people's participation against opposition from the state administration, but finally legitimized their collective action; the Chatra Yuva Sangharsh Vahini, which was able to appropriate 10,000 acres of land from the illegal possession of a powerful temple trust in Bodh Gaya and got this distributed amongst the poor and landless tillers of the land through non-violent action; SAMTA in Vishakhapatnam, a conglomerate of 50 action groups, which waged a relentless struggle to resettle the tribal population that was displaced by the calcite mines, ultimately extracting a judgment by the Supreme Court in their favour.

Let me conclude with the words of Fidel Castro, the world's most resilient communist:

> In our view, globalisation is nobody's whim; it is not even anybody's invention. Globalisation is a law of history. It is a consequence of the development of productive forces – excuse me, please, for using this phrase which might still scare some due to its authorship – it is a consequence of scientific and technologic development ... I believe globalisation is an irreversible process and that the problem is not globalisation per se, but the type of globalisation. (Castro, 1999, quoted in Dubey, 2004: 61)

Here lies the choice: globalization can take multiple forms – capitalist, Gandhian, socialist or any other. The neo-liberal hegemony on globalization is not the end of history but only the beginning of a new era of struggles and transformations ahead. The critical question is: not how to do away with it, but how to engage with it, for globalization has defined the conditions under which we have to chart out our existence. The choices lie here.

Notes

1. The discussions at the XXVII All India Sociological Conference held at IIT Kanpur in December 2003, and the multinational World Social Forum held in 2004 reflect the many concerns flowing out of globalization.
2. It is stated that during the Tet offensive in Vietnam (March 1968) the outflow of gold from the US to London led to the collapse of the weighing room in the Bank of England!

(Dubey, 2004, 62; reference from Garcy O'Callahan, 1993, 'The Structure and Operation of the World Gold Market', Occasional Paper No. 105, IMF, Washington, September, Special Issue on Globalization, 503, July 2001).

3. For an interesting and serious discussion on the early phase of globalization, see David Harvey (1990: 147–55; 184–85; 285–95).

References

Castro, Fidel (1999) *On Imperialist Globalisation: Two Speeches*. New Delhi: Leftword Books (quoted in Dubey, 2004: 61).

Dubey, Abhay Kumar (2004) "Globalisation: In the History Workshop", *Economic and Political Weekly*, Vol. XXXIX, No. 1, January 3–9.

Gilpin, R. (2000) *The Challenge of Global Capitalism: The World Economy in the 21st Century*. Princeton, NJ: Princeton University Press.

— (1987) *The Political Economy of International Relations*. Princeton, NJ: Princeton University Press.

Harvey, David (1990) *The Condition of Postmodernity*. Massachusetts: Blackwell.

Held, David et al. (1999) *Global Transformations: Politics, Economics and Culture*. Stanford, CA: Stanford University Press.

Mukerji, D.P. (1958) *Indian Tradition and Social Change in Diversities*. New Delhi: People's Publishing House.

Sheth, D.L. (2004) "Globalisation and New Politics of Micro-Movements", *Economic and Political Weekly*, Vol. XXXIX, No. 1, January 3–9.

Stiglitz, Joseph E. (2002) *Globalisation and its Discontents*. London: Allen Lane (an imprint of Penguin Books).

Tomkins, Richard (2003) "Happy Birthday, Globalisation", *Business Standard*, May 7.

Wallerstein, Immanuel (1997) Letter from President, International Sociological Association, April.

9

Globalization and Modernity

Indian Scenario

Jaikant Tiwary and Manish Tiwari

While delivering the inaugural address in the International Seminar on Structure of Poverty in SAARC Countries, Yogendra Singh (2007) inquired, "Who is happy with globalization?" During his address, he comprehensively discussed the economic, social and regional structure of poverty, but the axis of his arguments centred around the theme: in what manner globalization could be more inclusive? The synchronization of social science on globalization is a striking instance of how developments in the world economy keep impinging on societal processes and institutions, induce new pattern of change and necessitate reassessment of the adequacy of concepts and approaches in social sciences for understanding complex social reality. The globalization debate, in general, is focused largely on more recent developments, whose impact is not confined either to a single nation or to a subcontinent. Consequences of the global economic integration are seen spread over a wide range of non-economic spheres of life all over the world. It is commonly understood as a process that rapidly transforms the world heterogeneously, yet at the same time it intensifies consciousness of the world as a whole (Robertson, 1992: 8).

Conceptualizing Globalization and Modernity

Globalization is a widely used term which has been defined in different ways. According to Oxford English Dictionary, the word 'globalization' was first employed in a publication entitled *Towards New Education* in 1952 to denote a holistic view of human experience in education. Since the later half of 1980s, the term achieved widespread use by economists and other social scientists.

In social sciences perspectives, the term 'globalization' includes fast movement of people which results in greater interaction, information technology revolution, emancipation from intrusive social, economic and political processes, etc. Today, the concept of globalization revolves mainly around social consequences of integration with the world economy via the market and multinationals. Friedman and Kaplan (2002: 64) define globalization "as a process of integration of markets, finance and technology, especially information technology in a way that shrinks the world to a miniature in size and enable people from different parts of the globe to reach around the world faster, deeper and cheaper". This characterization of globalization, however, projects it as if it is confined to the market and economic activities alone. E. Anitat (2000: 4) talks of globalization as the "process through which an increasingly free flow of ideas, people, goods and capital leads to the integration of economies and societies". Anitat further argues that such global integration has boosted growth and incomes and has thereby helped to raise general standard of living in less developed and underprivileged parts of the world. With globalization not only sophisticated technologies have become available to developing countries, but also marked improvements in average literacy, quality of health and general life expectancy and above all greater integration have taken place and these have promoted human freedom. Guy Brainbant says that the process of globalization not only includes opening up of world trade, development of advanced means of communication, internationalization of financial markets, growing importance of MNCs, population migrations and more generally increased mobility of persons, goods, capital, data and ideas but also infections, diseases and pollution. Neverthemore, the leading Marxist-feminist-deconstructionist Gayatri Chakravorty Spivak (2011) argues that only capital and data globalize, all the rest is a damage control.

Some sociologists approach the problematic of globalization via considerations of modernity. Anthony Giddens (1990: 64), for example, defines globalization as intensification of worldwide social relations which link distant localities in such a way that local happenings are shaped by events occurring miles away and vice versa. Giddens emphasizes four dimensions of globalization: the nation-state system, the world capitalist economy, the world military order and the international division of labour. Each of these four, according to him, is an extension of societal modernity and an offshoot of its basic institutional features. He, therefore, states modernity as inherently globalizing and hence today's globalization is no more than the fundamental consequence of modernity project of the West.

Almost similar logics were propounded by enlightenment theorists of modernity, who characterized it in terms of rationality, reason, empirical, scientific, progress, universalism, individualism, tolerance, freedom, secularism, uniformity in human nature. The theories of Issac Newton, John Locke, Rousseau, Montesquo, David Hume, Adam Smith, Immanuel Kant, Peter Hamilton, etc., established that modernity is based on scientific knowledge, empiricism and rationality. Max Weber, the classical sociologist, argued that modernity emancipated human beings from the iron cage of irrationality and created the ethos of rationalization.

Modernity, in social parlance, refers to social conditions, processes and discourses consequent to the age of enlightenment. Giddens (1998: 94) describes modernity as a shorthand term for modern society or industrial civilization. It is associated with (a) a certain set of attitudes towards the human intervention, (b) a complex of economic institutions, especially industrial production and a market economy, and (c) a certain range of policy institutions, including the nation-state and mass democracy. Largely, as a result of these characteristics, modernity is vastly more dynamic than any previous type of social order.

Shmuel Noah Eisenstadt (2003) introduced the concept of multiple modernities, which broadens the definition of modernity from exclusively denoting Western European culture to a cosmopolitan culture. In a similar fashion, Delanty (2007) argues that modernity is not westernization, rather its key processes and dynamics can be found in all societies. In a nutshell, modernity is aimed towards a progressive force promising to liberate humankind from ignorance and irrationality. Modernity is interpreted in a different perspective in postmodern sociological theory. Ulrich Beck (1992), for instance, calls modern society as 'risk society'. To him the modernity in classical era of 19th century was industrial whereas the modernity of second phase is individualistic, which has created manufactured risk, health risk and socio-cultural risk such as inequality, etc. Advanced industrial society, which is primarily a politicization of nature, has created environment pollution and various risks. Zygmunt Bauman (1989) considers modernity as a holocaust. He cites the destructions in Second World War as an example. The Nazis in Germany massacred thousands of Jews by throwing them into gas chambers, Bauman argues that this genocide was neither an act of irrationality nor it was barbarism of pre-modern society. Rather it was well-planned act of modern bureaucracy, who wished to get rid of Jews and rebuild Germany. He also argued that such holocaust is not merely confined to Germany, several illustrations can be cited all over the world, which claims to be civilized, in fact, lacks ethics. Modernity is dehumanization. The notion of modernity, thus, has different connotations in classical and postmodern sociological theories.

Implications of Globalization

There have been both positive and negative impacts of globalization on economy, society and culture. It has brought cheers to people's life by opening new vistas of employment; making life fast, comfortable and enjoyable through scientific and technological innovations; making inroads in the cultural heritage of the country through international exposure of multiculture; synchronizing the distances of time and space, etc. The waves of globalization have also influenced the polity in addition to economy and society. The Human Development Report, 2002 shows that democracy has been spreading, including in the developing world. The number of authoritarian regimes declined from 67 to 26 between 1985 and 2000, while the number of nations categorized as 'most democratic' rose from 44 to 82. The recent mass movements in countries like Egypt and Libya reveal that the process of democratization is on the increase.

Institutional reorganization through globalization indeed is meant to deny the relevance of social concerns in defining economic activities. There is an accent on recovery of costs and abandoning the soft corner for those who cannot pay for using public utilities. Mercerization of social issues is the new concern/characteristic of globalization era. What is accomplished, thus, is not really the separation of social and economic issues but a reversal of their relationship. Social concerns are not expected to interfere with economic processes of state or market, but market principles are supposed to become the defining rule of social issues. Thus, health, education, housing, employment of common man, job security, etc., should be privatized and made to run with profit motive as the guiding norm. This is meant to increase efficiency. The question of access to this efficiency is not considered important. Access comes to be defined as an individual problem and not a social concern. The social content of economic issues is, thus, easily dismissed. Many social problems are simply dismissed as individual problems, calling for individual solutions. Unemployment becomes a problem of acquiring skills, insecurity in job a matter of upgradation of skills, health and education more a subject of consciousness rising. Structural content of problems facing the society is thereby delinked from everything except market opportunities. Market themselves become an important social concern when redefinition of issues creates legitimacy for them.

Globalization and Indian Economy

According to the World Bank, in the past decade, the number of poor in the world rose by more than 100 million. The World Bank also holds the view that the impact of growth on poverty has varied according to the pattern of investment. For example, in India, a given growth rate has cut poverty in some states by four to five times as much as in others. Those states which invested heavily in education and health saw a much higher rate of reduction in poverty.

The developing world has not received a fair share of benefits because the rich have not kept their part of agreement reached at the Uruguay round, under which they had pledged to reduce subsidies to their agriculture by 36 per cent in return for lowering of tariffs on agricultural imports by the developing countries. While the developing countries reduced their tariffs by 50 per cent, the rich countries subsidies remain unchanged.

Agriculture and textiles together account for 70 per cent of the poor world's exports. Developing countries lose nearly $100 billion a year due to rich countries' export subsidies and trade barriers. In rich countries, tariffs on goods from poor countries are four times higher than on goods from rich countries. If poor countries' goods get free excess to rich country markets, and if the later remove all subsidies, it would add $1.5 billion by 2015 to poor countries' income and lift 300 million people from the rank of the poor.

The liberalization of the domestic economy and the increasing integration of India with the global economy have helped step up GDP growth rates in the past two decades. India's position in the global economy has improved from eighth in 1991 to fourth in 2001.

The implications of globalization for a national economy are many. Globalization has intensified interdependence and competition between economics in the world market. As a result, domestic economic developments are not determined entirely by domestic policies and economic conditions. Rather they are influenced by both domestic and international policies and economic conditions.

Digital Divide

The most important manifestation of the globalization process is reinforcing existing social division besides creating a new one called digital divide. The term 'digital divide' denotes the ever-growing gap between the people and communities who have access to information and communication technology, especially internet technology, and those who do not. In other words, the society today is characterized by 'new' imbalances and inequities, christened as the 'digital divide'. The internet has the potential to empower its users with new skills, new perspectives and new opportunities in life. Those groups which remain isolated from this technology are further segregated into the periphery of public life. The facts reveal that the diffusion of internet technology is highly uneven. Internet users are predominantly urban and located in certain regions. Developments in digital technologies over the last decade have generated a period of extraordinary social and cultural change by creating huge benefits like improvements in communication, information, knowledge, entertainment and opportunities. But these benefits are not enjoyed by all. Inequality in the use and application of digital technologies is a new driver of social exclusion in the 21st century, which risks accelerating existing social divides and creating new ones.

The recent (2010) edition of *Measuring the Information Society* reports that by the end of 2009, there were an estimated 4.6 billion mobile cellular subscriptions. Likewise, globally, internet use has continued to expand, albeit at a slower pace. In 2009, an estimated 26 per cent of the world population (1.7 billion people) were using internet. In developed countries the percentage remains much higher than in developing world, where four out of five are still excluded from the benefits of being online.

The report also features the latest Information Communication Technology (ICT) price basket which combines 2009 fixed telephones, mobile cellular and fixed broadband tariffs for 161 economies into one measure and compares these across countries, and over time. It reveals that people in developed countries have to spend relatively less of their income (1.5%) on ICT services than people in developing countries (17.5%). This shows that, with a few exceptions, ICT services tend to be more affordable in developed countries and less affordable in developing countries, especially the least developed countries (LDCs).

Deepening of Disparity

Global markets are inherently disequalizing, making rising inequality in developing countries more rather than less likely. There are at least three reasons:

1. The tremendous economic gains associated with deeper and more efficient global markets are not equally shared. Markets reward those who have the right assets – financial capital, human capital, entrepreneurial skills.
2. Global markets are far from perfect. They fail in many domains. The classic example of a market failure is that of pollution, where the polluters capture the benefits of polluting without paying the full costs. At the global level, high greenhouse gas emissions of the United States of America are imposing costs on poor countries.
3. Global markets tend to be disequalizing because trade, migration and intellectual property regimes at the global level naturally reflect the greater market power of the rich. Today's battle to reduce rich countries agricultural subsidies and tariffs that discriminate against poor countries is a good example.

Human Development Report, 2001 reveals the growing disparities between the rich and the poor over the years after introduction of globalization. In the decade of 1960–70, the ratio of difference between the 20 per cent richest and 20 per cent poorest people in the world was 30: 1, which increased up to 74: 1 by the year 1999–2000. According to an estimate, 143 richest persons of the world have acquired wealth equaling to aggregate wealth of LDCs of the world. The savage inequality of the world is exhibited by the fact in 1999–2000, the poorest 10 per cent of the world's people had only 1.6 per cent of the income of the richest 10 per cent, while the richest 1 per cent of the world's people received as much as the poorest 57 per cent. The richest 10 per cent of the USA population (around 25 million people) had a combined income greater than that of poorest 43 per cent of the world's people (around 2 billion people). The evidences suggest that globalization is deepening disparity. According to ILO World of Work Report 2008, the income gap between the rich and poor households has widened significantly over the years. India is among the worst performers in terms of rising income equality. ILO study found that between 1990 and 2006, the share of labour in India's national income fell as the annual growth rate of 1 per cent lagged behind productivity growth of 4.5 per cent.

Growing Ethos of Consumerism

The globalizing process accelerated the interaction of native people with global forces of consumption. The process of consumerism, defined by Philip Salzman (1993: 7) as the 'catching of consumption as an appropriate orientation', has now permeated much of rural India. Consumer goods, such as television, electric fans, irons, motorcycles, telephones, mobile phones, VCD and VHS players, satellite dishes, etc., are becoming very common in village homes. The role of advertisement is critical in promoting this new ethos of consumerism. The study by Johnson (2006: 4) reveals how the advertisement has reversed the notion of happiness in a rural family. Happiness, which has always been linked to one's relationship to one's family, to one's faith and to one's work, now appears to be based on consumption of goods. Each advertisement of TV tells us "Drink a coke and you will be happy" or "Wash your clothes with a particular detergent and your husband will love you". From soap to toothpaste, from hair removal cream to exercise equipment, the message is always the same: happiness is gained through the purchase and consumption of objects. In other words, happiness comes from the market.

According to Samir Amin (1997: 128), globalization is the ideology of capitalist superpowers that labour a utopian vision of running the world like a market. The market forces led by globalization destroy the indigenous culture and generate consumerism. The cultural invasion through films, music, games, toys, T-shirt fantasies, etc., disseminate global dream which undermines the indigenous value, culture, interpersonal and intercommunity relations and cultural heritage, commodification of culture according to alien tastes generate an ornamental hoax. Dhanagare (2003: 15) remarks that the final aim of globalization is to render nation-states as economically parasites, politically powerless and socio-culturally faceless before bulldozing power to the market with MNCs driving from the back seat.

The growing trend of ethnic conflicts and religious fundamentalism has to be understood primarily as a repulsive response to the pernicious impact of the global consumer culture on diverse, even unique, local cultures. Local communities feel both unstable and unsafe in the face of global market forces bolstered up by media that too are controlled by MNCs. The media impact on local communities and cultures is so shattering that the consumer culture has pushed them to the threshold of extinction. Local economies are being swallowed gradually by the global capitalism and traditional cultures are being displaced by the ever-expanding global market and consumer culture. Local communities in the developing world are silently, somewhat, helplessly, watching their plentiful raw material and natural resources are getting depleted and these are replaced by scarce imported materials produced by TNCs. At the same time, local communities are experiencing a study and systematic undermining of their self-esteem.

This kind of erosion of local cultures by the process of homogenization, and particularly by the promotion of global monoculture, has disastrous consequences. To achieve development at any cost, many developing economies are pressurized to make structural adjustments, introduce neo-liberal measures, reduce social sector spending and undertake massive programmes of infrastructure development that is unsustainable in the long run. Much of the development initiatives in developing countries is geared to serve the needs of global capitalism to exploit their cheap labour, material resources and vast markets (Dhanagare, 2003: 24).

Global inequality in consumption, while reducing, is still high. World Bank Development Indicators, 2008 reveal that the wealthiest 20 per cent of the world accounted for 76.6 per cent of the total private consumption, the middle 60 per cent consume 21.9 per cent, whereas the poorest 20 per cent share merely 1.5 per cent of the total private consumption. More specifically, the richest fifth consume 45 per cent of all meat and fish, 58 per cent of total energy, have 74 per cent of all telephone lines, consume 84 per cent of all paper, and own 87 per cent of the world's vehicle fleet, whereas the poorest fifth consume mere 5 per cent meat and fish, less than 4 per cent energy, 1.5 per cent telephone lines, 1.1 per cent paper, and less than 1 per cent world's vehicle fleet.

Pathetic Condition of Farmers

Indian farmers' experience with the globalization reveals that they are not able to cope with the new competitive environment after economic reforms. Over the last decade we have been hearing from different parts of country that farmers have been committing suicides or eating raw meat. Why do farmers take this extreme step? Is income from cultivation not enough to meet consumption and other expenditures? Are farmers heavily indebted due to lower income from cultivation and increased cost of cultivation? Answers to these questions have finally come from the survey initiated by Union Ministry of Agriculture, which is known as Situation Assessment Survey (SAS).

The National Sample Survey Organization (NSSO) carried out the SAS of farmers during 2003 (January–December) covering 51,770 households spread over 6,638 villages across the country. The NSSO (2005) report reveals dreadful condition of farmer households – be it income, expenditure or indebtedness of farming households (see Table 1).

Table 1 Income, Expenditure and Indebtedness of Farmer Households (July 2002–June 2003)

(in Rs)

State	Annual Cultivation Income	Annual Total Income	Annual Cultivation Expenditure	Annual Consumption Expenditure	(2)-(4)	(3)-(5)	Incidence of Indebtedness (per cent)	Extent of Indebtedness
(1)	(2)	(3)	(4)	(5)	(6)	(7)	(8)	(9)
Andhra Pradesh	8916.00	19,698.00	12,085.00	28,632.00	–3169.00	–9024.00	82.00	23,965.00
Assam	21,504.00	37,932.00	3370.00	32,568.00	18,134.00	5364.00	18.10	813.00
Bihar	10,152.00	21,720.00	6809.00	29,508.00	3343.00	–7788.00	33.00	4476.00
Gujarat	13,968.00	32,208.00	11,456.00	37,524.00	2512.00	–5316.00	51.90	15,526.00
Haryana	17,928.00	34,584.00	18,270.00	52,968.00	–342.00	18,384.00	53.10	26,007.00
J&K	29,112.00	65,856.00	6342.00	49,308.00	22,770.00	16,548.00	31.80	1903.00
Karnataka	15,192.00	31,392.00	10,344.00	31,296.00	4848.00	96.00	61.60	18,135.00
Kerala	13,440.00	48,048.00	7793.00	51,000.00	5647.00	–2952.00	64.40	33,907.00
M.P.	11,952.00	17,160.00	8886.00	28,068.00	3066.00	–10,908.00	50.80	14,218.00
Maharashtra	15,156.00	29,556.00	10,793.00	32,268.00	4363.00	–2712.00	54.80	16,973.00
Orissa	4032.00	12,744.00	3143.00	20,364.00	889.00	–7620.00	47.80	5871.00
Punjab	3864.00	59,520.00	25,945.00	58,080.00	7919.00	1440.00	65.40	41,576.00
Rajasthan	4308.00	17,976.00	7668.00	39,456.00	–3360.00	–21,480.00	52.40	18,372.00
Tamil Nadu	7908.00	24,864.00	8597.00	30,072.00	–689.00	–5208.00	74.50	23,963.00
U.P.	10,032.00	19,596.00	9151.00	34,788.00	881.00	–15,192.00	40.30	7425.00
W.B.	8844.00	24,948.00	8429.00	32,016.00	415.00	–7068.00	50.10	5237.00
All India	11,628.00	25,380.00	8791.00	33,240.00	2837.00	–7860.00	48.60	12,585.00

Source: NSSO (2005).

According to the survey, at the all-India level, the average annual income of farmer household was ₹ 25,380 which includes cultivation, wages, farming of animals and non-farm business income. What is interesting is that income from cultivation accounts for only 45 per cent of the total income and the remaining receipts are from other sources, including wage income, which alone accounts for almost 39 per cent. Clearly, the annual income from cultivation comes to only about ₹ 11,628 per farmer household, after excluding the other sources. The condition of individual state is not very much different from the national level average. Obviously, with such low income of the farmers, the basic issue arises: Can the farmers survive with this low income? Do farmers have any incentive to remain in farming? Is it possible for farmers to meet the consumption expenditure with this income?

The survey also provides that average expenditure on cultivation comes to ₹ 8,791 per household at the all-India level. We notice a wide variation in the expenditure on cultivation across states, the highest in agriculturally developed states like Punjab, followed by Haryana and Andhra Pradesh and the lowest expenditure in Orissa. The situation is bleaker while comparing the annual income with the average annual consumption expenditure of the farmer households (ACEFH). The average ACEFH for the country as a whole was ₹ 33,240. The highest ACEFH was reported in Punjab, followed by Haryana and Kerala, while the lowest annual consumption was in Orissa. This clearly suggests that farmers are in severe distress and the income that they get from all sources is not even enough to meet the consumption expenditure of the households. The situation leads them to take loans from various sources so as to meet the consumption as well as the productive expenditure of the households.

The incidence of indebtedness as well as the extent of indebtedness is found to be higher in all states where consumption expenditure exceeds the income of farmer households. The data concerning indebtedness status of the households reveal that the debt per farmer household is very high in all the states except Assam and Jammu & Kashmir. Farmers from Andhra Pradesh, Haryana, Karnataka, Kerala, Madhya Pradesh, Maharashtra, Punjab, Rajasthan, Tamil Nadu and Uttar Pradesh are heavily indebted possibly because the income of household is not enough to meet the consumption expenditure. In fact, the average debt per household varies from ₹ 24,000 to ₹ 42,000 in the relatively developed states like Andhra Pradesh, Haryana, Kerala, Punjab and Tamil Nadu.

The results of SAS prove that the farmers are not getting enough remuneration from their produce. This could possibly be because of a sharp deceleration in the growth of price of many agricultural commodities and increase in the cost of cultivation after the introduction of reforms. It is reported from various parts of the country that the use of spurious inputs (seeds, fertilizers and pesticides) in cultivation is one of the major reasons for high cost. Another reason for the low income of farmer households could be dominant role played by the middlemen in the market. Studies reveal that farmers were not able to get even 40 per cent of the money that the consumer pays for various agriculture commodities in the market. Despite the significant increase in the flow of institutional credit, the SAS data shows that still over 42 per cent of rural credit supply comes from the non-institutional sources like moneylenders, where the rate of interest is not only exorbitant but the terms and conditions of the loans are often exploitative.

All these facts clearly suggest that the farmers are in great distress. SAS report (NSSO, 2005: 11) also indicates that given a choice 40 per cent of the farmers would quit agriculture and take up some other career. The situation can aggravate further, if adequate measures are not taken immediately to improve the income level of the farmer households. Potentially, this can harm the growth of agriculture and food security of the country (Narayanamoorthy, 2006: 472).

Plight of Working Class

Conditions of working class, in both organized and unorganized sectors, in developing countries seem to be not better under a globalizing economy. Throughout the history, working class movements and trade unions have always sought to influence and humanize capitalist system within the nation-states framework. In the globalization phase of capitalism, however, MNCs and TNCs have undercut the capacities of national governments to regulate them, particularly in developing countries (Ross, 2000: 1–2). Consequently, the labour is facing new problem under globalization, as markets keep expanding in their reach and power beyond labour organizations will and capacity to affect MNCs.

The most important challenge Indian labour is facing as a result of globalization is that traditional industrial working class is practically pushed into the background and is likely to become invisible soon because of four processes, namely, tertiarization, feminization, casualization and precarization (Dhanagare, 2003: 18). These processes unleashed by globalization are adversely affecting labours and their unions that hither to depend on the traditional support base of organized blue-collar workers.

The Future of Nation-States

The triumph of TNCs and their finance capitalism over microcosms of nation-states raises the question whether globalization will strengthen or weaken nation-states? A more optimistic view is that globalization actually strengthens the state by redefining its role in changed economic conditions resulting from global interaction via market and finance capitalism. The other, more pessimistic, view is that globalization process will not only weaken but will hasten the demise of the nation-state.

The dominant market-oriented and state-limiting ideas have come from the proponent of public choice theory, most predominantly by Milton Friedman, James Buchanan, Gordon Tullock, William Nisakenen, etc., Friedman argues that market is more effective than government in achieving social goals. Once a technology-driven globalization sets in, it starts shrinking the world. As the need for morality of order gets reinforced naturally then everyone is willing to give up a share of one's independence for the sake of 'world government'.

In the context of growing anxiety over the future of nation-states, Martinelli (2002: 9–11) views globalization process as eroding the very foundation of sovereignty and autonomy of nation-states. This is largely because global finance capitalism compels nation-states to adopt neo-liberal economic policies to stay in the competitive world market. Sovereign states have, therefore, no option but to come to terms with gradual loss of sovereignty and erosion of their power. The consequence is that the vulnerable strata of society will be deprived of the benefit of nation-state. Bhambhri (1996: 263) rightly opines that without state intervention, social equalization cannot take place and if the state does not control national economic and productive resource, it cannot implement welfare programmes, like food security and job guarantees, etc. The evidences of economic history of the world reveal that market has never been a pro-poor institution.

David Held and Anthony McGrew (2001) have suggested that the implications of globalization can be separated into three frames: (1) Hyperglobalists hold that autonomy and sovereignty of nation-states have been eclipsed by contemporary processes of economic globalization. (2) Sceptics hold that intensity of contemporary global interdependence is considerably exaggerated and that the hyperglobalists ignore the continued primacy of national power and sovereignty. (3) Transformationalists emphasize the way in which globalization has brought about the spatial reorganization and rearticulating of economic, political, military and cultural power.

Peer Fiss and Paul Hirsch (2005) identified three main frames of interpreting discourses on globalization: positive, neutral and negative. The positive frame points to the potential gains and benefits, the neutral frame portrays globalization as a natural, evolutionary and largely inevitable development although avoiding moral judgements, whereas the negative frame points out the increasing potential for economic crisis, the threat to the livelihood of workers and the growing income inequality caused by globalization. Apart from these three frames, an emerging constructive frame supports global cooperation and interaction while opposing some of the negative effects of globalization.

The positive frame, mainly comprised of neo-liberal thinkers, claims that globalization increases economic prosperity as well as opportunity, especially among developing nations, enhances civil liberties, leads to a more efficient allocation of resources, lower prices, more employment, higher output and higher standard of living. Proponents of laissez-faire capitalism and libertarians see globalization as the beneficial spread of liberty and capitalism. The most encouraging aspect is that for the first time poor nations are trying hard with desire and commitment to realize the potential of their huge labour to break into world markets for manufactured products and services. Since the initiation of globalization, manufacturers have witnessed a rise from less than 25 per cent to 80 per cent. Marshall McLuhan and Bruce R. Powers (1992) presented the optimistic view of globalization through his conceptualization of global village, which suggests that people from all countries will become more integrated and aware of common interests and shared humanity. A large body of literature also points out the value of international cooperation in solving problems of mutual concern ranging from human rights to environmental concerns.

The neutral frame, largely characterized by financial community, has become less prominent as the issue of globalization has become increasingly politicized. Examples of this frame would include books on international finance, articles on globalization in financial journals like *The Wall Street Journal*, etc.

In the negative frame, the critics of globalization take two different forms of concern: (a) concern over economic well-being in developed countries, and (b) concern over impact from environmental issues to issues like democracy, national sovereignty and the exploitation of workers, etc.

The constructive frame involves a synthesis combining elements of all three frames. It believes that international cooperation can provide solutions to important problems. At the same time, it recognizes the negative aspects of globalization, and proposes ways to mitigate their impacts. Beginning in 2001 with the World Social Forum, there has been a movement consisting of individuals trying to bring about this type of synthesis. It is associated with the term 'alter-globalization', a positive spin on the term 'anti-globalization'. Members of this movement support the international integration of globalization, but demand that values of democracy, economic justice, environmental protection and human rights be put ahead of purely economic concerns. Some people, who are labelled anti-globalist or skeptics, consider the term to be too vague and inaccurate. Anti-globalization movement is an umbrella term which encompasses a number of separate social movements such as nationalists and socialists. According to Joseph Stiglitz and Andrew Charlton (2005), the term 'anti-globalization' is a misnomer, since the group represents a wide range of interests and issues. Some members aligned with this viewpoint prefer instead to describe themselves as the global justice movement, anti-corporate globalization movement, the movement of movement, the alter-globalization movement, etc. Noam Chomsky (2002) believes that the term 'globalization' has been appropriated by the powerful to refer to a specific form of international economic integration, one based on investor rights, with the interests of people incidental. Accordingly, other forms of globalization are described as anti-globalization, though it is a term of propaganda and should be dismissed with ridicule.

However, globalization should not be accused for loosing share of the low income countries. These countries suffer from internal problems like rapid rise in population, infrastructure bottlenecks, weak financial markets, and so on. To get a share of global capital, technology and output, developing countries have to upgrade their social and economic institutions through administrative, legislative and legal reforms.

For instance, conventional wisdom holds that notable increases in inequality and steep declines in poverty rate for India and China in recent decades can be explained by the simultaneous and deepening interconnectedness within the global economy. Bardhan (2007), by contrast, asserts that inequality has risen and poverty has fallen because of internal forces, such as domestic policy and population changes. For example, the decline in China's poverty rate is most likely the result of increased agricultural production following land reform during the 1980s.

Globalization should not be thought of as solution to everything. It merely provides opportunities. Globalization is not supposed to produce equality of outcome but it produces equality of opportunities for those with right mindset. Hence, the developing countries have to focus on economic restructuring, building market-supporting institutions and create efficient regulation mechanisms. It is true that left to themselves, the low income countries can not travel long. What, in fact, needed is the international assistance and a support mechanism so as to facilitate their participation in the process of globalization.

References

Amin, Samir (1997) *Capitalism in the Age of Globalization*. Delhi: Madhyam Books.

Anitat, E. (2000) "Surmounting the Challenge of Globalization", *Finance and Development*, March, pp. 4–7.

Bardhan, Pranab (2007) "Inequality in India and China: Is Globalization to Blame?", Yale Global Online, October 15, Yale Centre for the Study of Globalization.

Bauman, Zygmunt (1989) *Modernity and the Holocaust*. Ithaca, NY: Cornell University Press.

Bhagwati, Jagdish (2004) *In Defense of Globalization*. New York: Oxford University Press.

Bhambhri, C.P. (1996) "Globalization, Liberalization and the Welfare State", *The Indian Journal of Public Administration*, Vol. XLII, No. 3, July–September.

Beck, Ulrich (1992) *Risk Society: Towards a New Modernity*. London: Sage.

Chomsky, Noam (2002) *The Croation Feral Tribune*, 27 April, ZMAG Org./znet 07 May.

Delanty, Gerard (2007) "Modernity", in George Ritzer (ed.), *Blackwell Encyclopedia of Sociology*, Malden: Blackwell Publishing.

Dhanagare, D.N. (2003) "Globalization: Towards an Alternative View", *Sociological Bulletin*, Vol. 52, No. 1, March.

Eisenstadt, Shmuel Noah (2003) *Comparative Civilizations and Multiple Modernities*. 2 vols., Leiden and Boston: Brill.

Fiss, Peer and Hirsch, Paul (2005) "The Discourse of Globalization: Framing and Sensemaking of an Emerging Concept", *American Sociological Review*, Vol. 70, No. 1, February, pp. 29–52.

Friedman, T. and Kaplan, R. (2002) States of Discord (A Debate), *Foreign Policy*, March–April.

Friedman, Thomas L. (2005) "It's a Flat World After All", *New York Times Magazine*, April 3.

Frank, A.G. (1998) *Reorient Global Economy in the Asian Age*. Berkeley: University of California Press.

Giddens, Anthony (1990) *The Consequences of Modernity*. Stanford, CA: Stanford University Press.

—— (1998) Conversations with Anthony Giddens: *Making Sense of Modernity*. Stanford, CA: Stanford University Press.

Held, David and McGrew, Anthony (2001) "Globalization", an article in Joel Krieger (ed.), *Oxford Companion to Politics of the World*, New York: Oxford University Press.

Human Development Report (2001) *Making New Technologies Work for Human Development*. UNDP, Oxford University Press.

Johnson, Kirk (2006) "Globalization at the Crossroads of Tradition and Modernity in Rural India", *Sociological Bulletin*, Vol. 54, No. 1, January–April.

Martinelli, A. (2002) 'Market, Government, Communities and Global Government', Presidential Address delivered at the XV World Congress of Sociology, Brisbane, July 7–13.

McLuhan, Marshall and Powers, Bruce R. (1992) *The Global Village: Transformations in World Life and Media in the 21st Century*. New York: Oxford University Press.

Narayanamoorthy, A. (2006) "State of India's Farmers", *Economic and Political Weekly*, Vol. XLI, No. 6, February 11–17.

NSSO (2005) *Situation Assessment Survey of Farmers: Indebtedness of Farmer Households*. Report No. 497 and 498, 59th Round, Ministry of Statistics and Programme Implementation, Government of India.

Robertson, R. (1992) *Globalization: Social Theory and Global Culture*. London: Sage.

Ross, G. (2000) "Labour versus Globalization", *Annals of the American Academy of Political and Social Sciences*, Vol. 570, July.

Sachs, Jeffrey (2005) *The End of Poverty*. New York: The Penguin Press.

Salzman, Philip (1993) 'The Electronic Trojan Horse: Television in the Globalization of Para-modern Cultures', paper presented at the 13th International Congress of Anthropological and Ethnological Sciences, Mexico City.

Singh, Yogendra (2007) 'Inaugural Address', International Seminar on Structure of Poverty in SSARC Countries, M.G. Kashi Vidyapith, Varanasi, February 17–18.

Spivak, Gayatri Chakravorty (2011) An Aesthetic Education in the Era of Globalization (unpublished book) quoted in 'Conversation, Bulan Lahiri: Speaking to Spivak', *The Hindu, Literary Review*, February 6, Sunday, p. 1.

Stiglitz, Joseph and Charlton, Andrew (2005) *Fair Trade for All: How Trade Can Promote Development*. Oxford: Oxford University Press, p. 54.

Stiglitz, Joseph (2006) "Dialogue with Nathan Gardels", *The Hindu*, September 29, p. 11.

World Development Report (2001) *United Nations Development Programme*. Oxford: Oxford University Press.

10

Globalization, Marginalization and Social Transformation

The Context of Indian Rural Society

Ishwar Modi

Globalization is the most often used and talked about contemporary phenomenon. But it is equally true that not much empirical work, which could assure us of its impacts, whether good or bad, has been done so far. Everyone is borrowing from every other person and has been repeating what many others have already said. It is mostly epistemological. We are still not very sure of its ground realities and its ontological paradigms are still by and large conjectural or else ideologically influenced and loaded.

I would like to begin my short contribution by observing that the importance of rural society in understanding India and its society in its totality, and as a whole, can hardly be overemphasized. It also need not be overstressed that real India lives in its villages both in terms of its ethos and also demographically speaking. In spite of growing urbanization, growth of urban centres, large-scale migrations, etc., rural life is the principal pivot around which the whole Indian social life revolves. Its long history, entrenched customs and traditions, complex social organization and unity in diversity, etc., can be understood only through the study of rural life. One can encounter the persistence of many a custom and tradition as also the complex social organization of Indian society in its villages in spite of the fact that Indian rural society has undergone considerable change in the recent past, particularly since independence.

Though vestiges of the monarchical-feudal social structure remained until independence and to some extent even later, the intervening period of British rule brought many changes in the traditional cultural patterns and social structure of India (Singh, 1973; Modi, 1985). The period of British rule was the period of transition. Its impact was not the same in every part of the country. The pace of

---

Valedictory address delivered at the National Seminar on "Indian Rural Society: Globalization and Emerging Crisis", Department of Sociology, Osmania University, Hyderabad, February 27–28, 2009.

change, however, was rapid. The changes that took place in the structure of society in the post-independence period may be treated as a sequel to the change taking place before independence.

However, the pace of change became extremely rapid and critical after the impact of globalization started being felt in India mainly during the 1990s.

Understanding Globalization

Globalization is on the tip of every tongue in the world today. But, most of those who talk about globalization are not aware of its fundamentals. Nevertheless, there is a red-hot debate about this much circulated concept in academic corridors, board meetings and even bedrooms (Prabaharan, 2007).

Globalization is a complex phenomenon that has had far-reaching effects. Not surprisingly, therefore, the term 'globalization' has acquired many emotive connotations and become a hotly contested issue in current political discourse. At one extreme, globalization is seen as an irresistible and benign force for delivering economic prosperity to people throughout the world. At the other, it is blamed as a source of all contemporary ills.

The effects of the new technology have also given a distinctive character to the current process of globalization, as compared to similar episodes in the past. The natural barriers of time and space have been vastly reduced. Not only cost of moving information, people, goods and capital across the globe has fallen dramatically, global communication is also cheap and instantaneous and becoming ever more so. This has vastly expanded the feasibility of economic transactions across the world. Markets can now be global in scope and encompass an expanding range of goods and services.

In a recent book *Global Transformations,* David Held and associates suggest that globalization may be thought of initially as the widening, deepening and speeding up of worldwide interconnectedness in all aspects of contemporary social life, from the cultural to the criminal, the financial to the spiritual (Held et al., 1999: 2).

Most observers could probably agree with this emphasis on 'interconnectedness', but beyond this there are fundamental differences. For some observers, globalization is a process of fundamental transformation, leading humanity into a new epoch, which coincides with the start of the third millennium. For others, globalization is much more limited, referring mainly to issues of trade and investment, and containing little which is qualitatively new. For some, globalization offers huge opportunities for economic growth and improved living standards. Other commentators argue that globalization erodes the autonomy of the nation-state, removing its ability to protect its citizens by means of economic management and welfare policies.

However, there is an almost unanimous consensus that globalization is a complex and multidimensional process. It can be viewed through a variety of lenses. The first characterizes it as a process in which the barriers to cross-border flows are being reduced, not just for economic flows, but also for the global extension of knowledge, information, belief systems, ideas and values. But this perspective lacks agency, so globalization can also be seen in relation to the ambitions and actions of key global actors, including firms and groups seeking political and religious hegemony. Further, globalization is an outcome of technological advances, and of the natural curiosity of the human species, fuelled by increasingly cheap and sophisticated communication system. In short, globalization may be characterized by systematic reduction in the barriers to the cross-border flow of factors (labour, capital), products, technology, knowledge, information, belief systems, ideas and values (Kaplinsly, 2005).

Causes of Globalization

Let us also have a look as to what has brought about globalization? We find a great variety of explanations in the literature. Virtually all analysts draw attention to the rapid growth in global economic flows, particularly of trade and capital. In both hyperglobalist and sceptical views on globalization, economic factors are usually seen as predominant. Ohmae (1991) celebrates the power of TNCs and global markets in overcoming anachronistic nation-state boundaries. Similarly, authors with social-democratic or neo-Marxist perspectives such as Reich (1991), Hopkins and Wallerstein (1996), and Beck (1997) emphasize economic changes, although the latter goes on to show how alleged economic imperatives are often a cloak for new forms of political control. An analysis by an inter-governmental body (OECD, 1997) stresses economic causes, but goes on to examine social consequences. The main skeptical accounts, such as Hirst and Thompson (1996), and Weiss (1997) also focus on trade and investment.

Other authors see the main driving force elsewhere. Castells (1996), for example, stresses scientific innovation, especially the rapid development of information technology: globalization goes hand-in-hand with the spread of an 'informational mode of production' which is replacing the industrial mode. However, all this takes place in the context of a restructured capitalist 'mode of regulation' of the world economy. Capitalism has not exhausted its potential for change, and the profit-motive remains the dominant motivating force. Other writers emphasize the importance of global media which diffuse a new global culture, largely based on US values – McDonaldization or Disneyfication of the world (e.g., Martin and Schumann, 1997). New forms of urbanization are seen as important by some observers, notably Saskia Sassen with her analysis of 'the global city' (Sassen, 1991). Giddens (1990) stresses the importance of 'time-space compression' the way in which new forms of communication and transport speed up flows and transactions to the point that old barriers become meaningless. Bauman (1998) takes up this notion, and shows how new forms of global stratification are emerging, especially the class division between those who have the resources and knowledge to become mobile and participate in global markets for employment, social good and cultural symbols; and those confined to a purely local (and therefore disempowered) existence.

Some accounts of globalization focus on international relations and the development of global and regional forms of governance. Strategic and military criteria are seen as equal in importance to political economy. The end of the Cold War and the collapse of the Soviet bloc are crucial in creating the political conditions for globalization. An extreme view on this is provided by Fukuyama (1992), his idea of 'the end of history' implies that liberalism, having defeated communism, is now a universally-accepted model for economic and political cooperation. By contrast, most international relations scholars argue that the end of the bipolar world has opened the way to new types of fragmentation and conflict, which present major threats to democracy and social order. Castells (1997) and Huntington (1993) – from widely differing perspectives – stress the emergence of new forms of identity politics. McGrew (1997) examines the future perspectives for democracy and the state and supra-state levels. Links between international relations, regionalization and globalization in the Asia-Pacific region are explored in Berger and Borer (1997).

Some of the most interesting discussions of the origins of globalization put it in a long historical perspective. If globalization represents a major social transformation for the whole world, does this mean that it is a new phase of modernity, or the emergence of postmodernity, or the beginning of an altogether new 'global age'? Such discussions are pursued at length by such authors as Albrow (1996), Giddens (1990), Lyotard (1984), Robertson (1992) and Bauman (1998). This topic may seem somewhat abstract, but in fact has considerable significance. If we accept the idea of a new age or epoch, it implies not only major economic and political changes, but also the need for new philosophical principles and cultural values appropriate to a new type of civilization. The changes would be as major as those between the ancient and the medieval world, or between the medieval and the modern world.

Effects of Globalization

There is no one single effect of globalization. It is a multiple-effect phenomenon impacting differently the various sectors. Those countries who master the art of combating adversities and succeeding in the battle can be called the good boys and those who fail in this fight are called the bad boys of globalization. India is neither totally good nor totally bad. There is a mixture of benefits and problems affecting the long standing Indian society. People swing sweeping remarks in this or that way. Very few have understood the differential consequences of globalization in India (Prabaharan, 2007).

Generally globalization can be understood as a process which compresses the world into a small space where business and technology play a predominant role in ushering new social relations. Although globalization has started with relaxation of economic rules to accommodate free market principles and foreign players, now, it has grown beyond the comprehension of even the economists. Today, it is a massive social process demanding an altogether different method to understand the developments in culture, society, religion, polity and personal relations. These factors and characteristics of society need massive in-depth research and analysis to know and understand globalization fully well (ibid.).

The effects of globalization on the Indian economy in the post-globalization years are clearly visible in the foreign sector – foreign exchange reserves, international trade, inflow of foreign capital, etc. However, structural changes in the domestic economy are not significant. The source-wise structure of savings and capital formation has changed, but trends in the macro-economic indicators such as national income are more or less traditional. The relative contributions of agriculture and industry to national income have followed the historical trends.

The contribution of area under cultivation to production also remains largely unchanged (Mishra and Nayak, 2006).

Although economic in the core, globalization has pervasive effects on society. It has its impact on the social structure, values, social institutions and attitudes. India is a multilingual, multiethnic and multicultural society. Globalization has impacted noticeably on cultural identity and social harmony among various social groups. The Indian social structure is basically pluralistic, replete with a multitude of enclaves of several types and strata. There are enclaves making rural–urban, men–women, caste–dalits, organized–unorganized, formal–informal, and so on. Globalization has led to an increase in disparities among these enclaves (ibid.).

Social scientists have differed with regard to the historicity and the processes of globalization. While some believe that globalization is in a new and contemporary process, others hold that it has been there ever since. Throughout history, adventurers, generals, merchants and financiers have constructed an ever-more-global economy. "It can be seen in the arrival of Christopher Columbus in the Americas or in the period 1870 to 1930." However, the new wave of globalization, which began between 1970 and 1980, includes new dimensions that Christopher Columbus probably never dreamed of: shrinking time, shrinking space, and disappearing borders – linking people more closely than ever before, and enabling multinational corporations to make decisions that have an immediate impact on people around the world (Capdevila, 1999).

Today, unprecedented changes in communications, transportation and computer technology have given the process new impetus. As globally mobile capital reorganizes business firms, it sweeps away regulation and undermines local and national politics. Globalization creates new markets and wealth, even as it causes widespread suffering, disorder and unrest. It is both a source of repression and a catalyst for global movements of social justice and emancipation. But for billions of the world's people, business-driven globalization means uprooting old ways of life and threatening livelihoods and cultures. The global social justice movement, itself a product of globalization, proposes an alternative path, more responsive to public needs. Intense political disputes will continue over globalization's meaning and its future direction (ibid.).

As such, it is apparent that globalization is a complex concept and depending on who is addressing the topic, the opinions and views remain quite conflicting. Globalization has several dimensions: political, technological, human, environmental and cultural. These dimensions can reflect or contribute to the exclusion of the economically and educationally poor people, especially in developing countries, and environmental degradation, as well as the growth of prosperity and peace in some areas. Proponents and opponents of globalization have described and emphasized these different aspects. Others believe in the opportunities for social and economic progress, alongside the major problems associated with asymmetrical development (Pais, 2006).

Judging Globalization

In any case, globalization has to be judged by what it delivers. Although many of the ills of the world today – poverty, the lack of decent work, the denial of human rights – existed long before the present phase of globalization, there has been growing exclusion and deprivation in certain regions of the world. For many, globalization has dislocated traditional livelihoods and local communities, and threatens environmental sustainability and cultural diversity. As the current process of cross-border interaction and interconnectivity gathers speed, there is increasing debate not only about inequalities between countries but also about inequalities within countries, and its effects on people, families and communities. These concerns lie at the heart of politics. The debate on globalization is fast becoming a debate on democracy and social justice in a global economy (ILO Report, 2004).

Besides the several negative impacts of globalization, it is also recognized that globalization has opened the door to many benefits. It has promoted open societies and open economies and encouraged a freer exchange of goods, ideas and knowledge. In many parts of the world, innovation, creativity and entrepreneurship have flourished. In East Asia, growth lifted over 200 million people out of poverty in a single decade. Better communications have enhanced awareness of rights and identities, and enabled social movements to mobilize opinion and strengthen democratic accountability. As a result, a truly global conscience is beginning to emerge, sensitive to the inequities of poverty, gender discrimination, child labour, and environmental degradation, wherever these may occur (ibid.).

Yet there is growing concern about the direction globalization is currently taking. Its advantages are too distant for too many, while its risks are all too real. Its volatility threatens both rich and poor. Immense riches are being generated. But fundamental problems of poverty, exclusion and inequality persist. Corruption is widespread. Open societies are threatened by global terrorism, and the future of open markets is increasingly in question. Global governance is in crisis. As such we are at a critical juncture, and we need to urgently rethink our current policies and institutions (World Commission on the Social Dimension of Globalization, 2006).

There are deep-seated and persistent imbalances in the current workings of the global economy, which are ethically unacceptable and politically unsustainable. They arise from a fundamental imbalance between the economy, society and the polity. The imbalance between the economy and society is subverting social justice. The benefits of globalization have been unequally distributed, both within and between countries. There is growing polarization between winners and losers. The gap between rich and poor countries has widened (ibid.).

Impact of Globalization on India

Now, let us have a look that how these key characteristics and enabling conditions of globalization have impacted India. According to the report of the ILO World Commission on the Social Dimension of Globalization (2004), the impact has been mixed in India. There had been winners and losers.

India's globalization is a conscious and deliberate effort to permit the factors of production, the produce and the socio-economic forces to permeate across the national boundaries and remove any obstacle to such permeance. In short, it has been a deliberate decision to open up a national economy to the forces of product, factor and money markets, followed by a sequence of requisite policies and actions, leading to structural reforms (Mishra and Nayak, 2006).

Unlike how the presently developed economies expanded and went global in their hoary past, the main reform initiatives in India (like in many other developing countries) were undertaken after a fiscal and foreign exchange crisis which brought it to the verge of default on the foreign loans. Thus, the Indian globalization is a result of the decadence within and the pressure from without (ibid.).

As is well known, globalization in India started with the new economic policy in July 1991. Globalization, liberalization and privatization constituted the trinity under the structural adjustment programme (SAP) pushed by the World Bank and International Monetary Fund (IMF) in a crisis situation. The first generation economic reforms are over. As of now, India is engaged in the second generation reforms. This period has witnessed a mix of political stability and instability, affecting the reforms one way or the other.

The lives of the educated and the rich had been enriched by globalization. During the last 15 years, globalization has hardly lived up to its promise. It has benefited only 5–10 per cent of the affluent sections of business and industry and highly qualified professionals in disciplines such as information technology (software), management, engineering, medicine, etc. Even during the pre-globalization period, majority of highly qualified professionals graduating from prestigious institutions like IITs, IIMs and AIIMS used to migrate to USA and Western Europe. The globalization has, however, greatly enlarged these opportunities and numbers with larger emoluments and perks, recessions like in software industry notwithstanding. Software industry and manpower, textiles, tea, some engineering goods, diamond (cutting/polishing) and food grains are some of the areas in which India has an edge. Accordingly, some benefits have already accrued and more may follow, depending on the policies, environment and efforts (Tripathi, n.d.).

The information technology (IT) sector was a particular beneficiary. But, the benefits had not yet reached the majority, and new risks had cropped up for the losers – the socially deprived and the rural poor. Significant numbers of 'non-perennial' poor, who had worked hard to escape poverty, were finding their gains reversed. Participants at the dialogue feared that globalization could erode values such as democracy and social justice. Power was shifting from elected local institutions to unaccountable transnational bodies. Western perceptions, which dominated global media, were not aligned with local perspectives; they encouraged consumerism in the midst of extreme poverty and posed a threat to cultural and linguistic diversity.

Globalization is associated with rapid and significant human changes. The movements of people from rural to urban areas has accelerated, and the growth of cities in the developing world especially is linked to sub-standard living for many. Family disruption and social and domestic violence are increasing. For example, The 2004 New Delhi Police Report indicates that deaths in the city of about six women everyday are dowry-related. Concepts of national identity, and of family, job and tradition are changing rapidly and significantly. There is concern that competitiveness introduced by globalization is leading to more individualistic societies. On the other hand, rapid change can encourage fundamentalism, a desire for the past, and a loss of tolerance for differences in religion and culture. The nation-state is losing influence relative to global economic pressures, and in some countries there is a failure or hesitation to develop social policies. All of these changes increase the likelihood that vulnerable people will be exploited, and threats to the human rights of less able people will increase (Pais, 2006).

On the whole, the life for the rural poor in particular and masses at large has become far more painful and insecure due to the panic and penury resulting from globalization. Just as Asia is home to two-thirds of the world's poor, India has over 433 million people living on less than $1 a day and 36 per cent of the total number of the poor in the world. About 72 per cent of Indian population is rural. About 58.4 per cent of the total workforce is employed in agriculture – 31.70 per cent as cultivators and 26.69 per cent as agricultural labourers. Only about 4.07 per cent of the workforce is employed in household industry and the remaining 37.53 per cent is engaged in other occupations (Census 2001). It is, however, pertinent to underline that as of now, the unorganized sector contributes 92 per cent of the total employment in India, besides contributing 59 per cent of the GDP. And it will continue as a major source of employment in the foreseeable future. Whereas organized sector contributes only 8 per cent of the total employment – 5.5 per cent in the public sector and 2.5 per cent in the private sector (Tripathi, n.d.).

Accordingly, the key issue in rural development in India is the eradication of poverty and unemployment. However, hi-tech jobless profit-driven growth in globalization provides little help in this regard. As a result, during this period of globalization, in spite of higher overall GDP, there has been a decline of 1.63 per cent in the overall annual growth of employment (ibid.).

If international trends of employment, inequality and poverty as a consequence of globalization are any indicators, then it may definitely be said that India as a whole and the rural India in particular has done poorly. For the world, as a whole, latest ILO estimates show that open unemployment has increased over the last decade to about 188 million in 2003. However, employment performance over the past two decades has varied across regions. It is also noticeable that within the developing world unemployment rates have increased since 1990 in Latin America and the Caribbean and South-East Asia, and since 1995 in East Asia (ILO Report 2004). Similarly, there has been a rise in income inequality. Besides these economic impacts, there have been many social impacts also.

Globalization, Social Development and Marginalization

The talk of globalization will be meaningless if it is not examined in the context of development. Most often the dialogues on development have centred around economic development. The re-examination of the concept of economic development has led to its broadening into the concept of social development. Today, development is explained in terms of an overall change including social progress, economic growth and change in perception and attitude. As P.G. Jogdand has put it, "Development means an upward change in social, economic and cultural conditions of a person or a group of persons or community. It also includes greater political participation and more access to power" (2006: 182). Jogdand further argues that "in case of the Dalit, development is to be understood in terms of bringing them out of their degraded social status, utter poverty and exploitation" (ibid.).

As on today, we cannot do any meaningful sociology in India and talk about social development without our concern for the dalits, the adivasis, and the indigenous and vulnerable marginalized people and their all-round development.

Poverty in case of the marginalized people is not only an economic state but is basically a process of social exclusion and marginalization. This process of marginalization excludes certain groups or communities more than the other and reduces the choices available to these groups/communities to come out of poverty. As most of these groups/communities are based in rural areas and are directly more dependent on the natural resources for their livelihoods and sustenance, the globalization has hardly done any good to them. On the contrary, in many cases, they are now uprooted from their native habitats and sliding into acute poverty.

Amitabh Behar and his co-authors (2007) have very perceptively pointed out:

> The journey of postcolonial India presents a mixed but depressing picture. Despite significant achievement in some sectors and dimensions of economic development, the state has massively failed in addressing basic human needs like food, shelter, education and health. However, the biggest failure is that the poor, marginalized and deprived groups and communities have remained excluded from the fruits of economic, social and human development. This failure sharply highlights the persistence of widespread inequality. India's low level of human development also reflects the extensive nature of human deprivations, suggesting a denial of rights and the absence of freedoms along critical dimensions of human life. Illiteracy, ill health, malnutrition, insufficient earnings, social exclusion, and lack of say in decision-making – all these have to be viewed as a 'set of un-freedoms constituting human poverty'.

Development indicators for excluded groups continue to be grim, despite constitutional guarantees, political rhetoric of successive governments and state interventions through targeted programmes and policies. As expected the women, dalits, adivasis and children have remained the most marginalized in the developmental process. Significantly, marginalization in addition to caste and gender has a strong regional dimension.

As such, social development and marginalization are directly related to social transformation. No social transformation more so a desired social transformation is possible unless social development of the marginalized groups, particularly that of rural India, is undertaken in an earnest spirit and sustained manner since the marginalized and the excluded groups are still, and going to remain, at the lowest level of society. The spirit of social transformation must adhere the way it has been defined: "Social transformation may be defined as a multidimensional process of accelerated social change, as also the radical change in the mindsets, lifestyles, ways of thinking and doing, and creating a desire to achieve an egalitarian social order with improved quality of life and happiness" (Modi, 2008).

Examined from this perspective of social transformation, the condition of the marginalized and the excluded groups, more so in the rural India, is rather pathetic. Excluded groups are often faced with double and triple discrimination. A dalit or adivasi woman faces discrimination on account of gender as well as caste, leading to increased vulnerability and exclusion from the process of development. For example, the male literacy rate in India is 75.3 per cent compared to the much lower female literacy rate at 53.7 per cent. This disparity is in itself alarming. However, it is the low rate of literacy among the SC and ST females at 41.9 per cent and 34.8 per cent respectively, which reflects the double disadvantage faced by the dalit and adivasi women (Behar et al., 2007).

We not only have a large number of marginalized groups in India but their size is also enormous and dispersed. While problems of poverty, discrimination, illiteracy, malnutrition, and that of ill-health and exploitation are almost common among all the marginalized groups – be they scheduled castes, scheduled tribes, women, children, aged persons, unorganized sector workers, slum dwellers, destitute or the minorities – each of these groups has its own specific problems and as such deserves special attention and developmental plans. India cannot be empowered without empowering its marginalized people.

The impact of globalization on culture – not only of the urban people but also the rural – has been significant. Technology has now created the possibility and even the likelihood of a western-dominated global culture. Its sweeping impact can be felt all over – be it dress, food or the drinks, songs, music or the dance, the various art forms, as also the norms and values. The impact of globalization on all these components of culture is apparent and visible even in the villages. However, it is yet to be assessed in a comprehensive manner.

The impact of globalization on various social institutions, both in urban and the rural areas, is also clearly visible. Large-scale migrations under the impact of globalization are not only creating new trends in marriages but also in the structure of families. The male earners, followed by their spouses and children, are migrating from rural areas leaving behind the older members of the family. As such, not only the joint family is breaking but also the problems of the care of the old, which were hitherto almost unknown or very limited, are surfacing and increasing in a big way. Migrations to urban areas are also leading to divorces and the spread of HIV/AIDS. However, there is still very limited impact of globalization on caste due to political reinforcement and alignments on caste lines.

Let us also briefly reflect upon the impact of globalization on leisure and tourism – the two phenomena which of late have gained great social value in the wake of their phenomenal growth. Globalization has drastically changed the patterns of leisure. While in the traditional society subsumption of leisure in culture was integral to its world view and the activities called leisure in such a society were hierarchical, group institutionalized, group participation-oriented, normative and rhythmic, these are now becoming more egalitarian, individualistic, secular and recurring. The impact of the mass media, particularly that of TV, films and the internet, on leisure is apparent. Under the impact of globalization, the mass movement of people, both as international and domestic tourists, is also causing degradation of the fragile ecosystems in the country impacting the environment.

However, globalization is now a fait accompli in Asian region including India. Hence, its proponents describe it as irreversible, whereas the opponents, especially social activists, have been vehemently opposing it for its adverse impact in the region, especially on the disadvantaged sections of the society. Therefore, the basic challenge is: How to humanize globalization and harmonize it with regional, national and local situations, needs, perceptions and aspirations, leading to a happier situation (Tripathi, n.d.).

The report of the ILO World Commission on The Social Dimension of Globalization (2004) is a positive but critical message for changing the current path of globalization. It says that the potentials of globalization, in terms of growing connectivity and productive capacity, are immense. However, current systems of governance of globalization at national and international levels have not realized such potentials for most of the world's people and in many instances have made matters worse. "Seen through the eyes of the vast majority of men and women around the world, globalization has not met their simple aspiration for decent jobs, livelihoods and a better future for their children." In 2003, official figures for global unemployment reached a record high of over 185 million people. Unofficial figures would be much higher, especially if one includes the underemployed and the working poor.

We like it or not, globalization has come to stay. No wishful thinking or protest can turn it around. India cannot remain away and aloof from globalization when practically the whole world has been overtaken by it. Isolation is neither expedient nor feasible. A lot of give-and-take has been taking place in this already globalized world in economic, political, socio-cultural and even spiritual areas for many centuries. Accordingly, the process of globalization, if rationally redesigned, will yield much better, positive and acceptable results. Let us ponder over the basic question: Why globalization? The obvious natural response in Indian context as in that of other developing Asian countries shall be to address rapidly and effectively the vital issues such as poverty and unemployment, access to basic needs such as food, clothing, shelter, drinking water, health and education, reduction of inequalities, environmental concerns, and in sum needs of the many rather than greed of a few in the spirit of 'vasudhaiva kutumbakam' (the world is but one family) while ensuring democracy, good governance and human rights.

Therefore, as emerging from the experience and rational analysis of the impact of globalization so far, gradual, decentralized, locally appropriate and acceptable, participatory, people-centred and shock-free reforms are more likely to be successful. Decentralized democratic system, along with the restructured Panchayati Raj in India, provides a ready framework for the proposed redesigned humanized globalization to be harmonized with local, national and regional situations, needs, priorities, aspirations and perceptions, especially of the disadvantaged sections of the rural population and rural development at large. It will hopefully lead to a desired social transformation and a developed and happier India, Asia and the world.

References

Albrow, Martin (1996) *The Global Age: State and Society beyond Modernity*. Stanford, CA: Stanford University Press.

Bauman, Zygmunt (1998) *Globalization: The Human Consequences*. Cambridge: Polity Press.

Beck, Ulrich (1997) *Was ist Globalisierung?* Frankfurt: Suhrkamp.

Behar, Amitabh, Subrat Das and Debdulal Thakur (2007) Reaching the Excluded. http://www.india-seminar.com/2007/574/574_amitabh_behar_at_al.htm

Berger, Mark T. and Douglas A. Borer (eds.) (1997) *The Rise of East Asia: Critical Visions of the Pacific Century*. London and New York: Routledge.

Capdevila, Gustavo (1999) Globalization a Double-edged Sword, says UN. http://www.atimes.com/global-econ/AG14Dj01.html

Castells, Manuel (1996) *The Rise of the Network Society, The Information Age: Economy, Society and Culture*. Vol. I. UK: Blackwell.

—— (1997) *The Power of Identity, The Information Age: Economy Society and Culture*. Vol. II. UK: Blackwell.

Fukuyama, Francis (1992) *The End of History and the Last Man*. New York: Avon Books.

Giddens, Anthony (1990) *The Consequences of Modernity*. Cambridge: Polity Press.

Held, David et al. (1999) *Global Transformations: Politics, Economics and Culture*. Stanford, CA: Stanford University Press.

Hirst, P. and G. Thompson (1996) *Globalization in Question: The International Economy and the Possibilities of Governance*. Cambridge: Polity Press.

—— (1996) *Globalization in Question*. Cambridge: Polity Press.

Hopkins, Terence K. and Immanuel Wallerstein (eds.) (1996) *The Age of Transition: Trajectory of the World-System, 1945–2025*. London: Zed Books.

Huntington, Samuel P. (1993) "The Clash of Civilizations?", *Foreign Affairs*, Vol. 72, No. 3, Summer.

ILO World Commission (2004) *The Social Dimension of Globalization*. Geneva: ILO Office.

Jogdand, P.G. (2006) "Social Development of the Dalits: Some Prevailing Trends", in P.G. Jogdand and S.M. Michael (eds.), *Globalization and Social Movements: Struggle for a Humane Society*, Jaipur: Rawat Publications.

Kaplinsky, Raphael (2005) *Globalization, Poverty and Inequality: Between a Rock and a Hard Place*. Cambridge: Polity Press.

Lyotard, J.F. (1984) *The Postmodern Condition*. Minneapolis: University of Minnesota Press.

Martin, Hans-Peter and H. Schumann (1997) *The Global Trap: Globalization and the Assault on Prosperity and Democracy*. Leichhardt: Pluto Press.

McGrew, Anthony (ed.) (1997) *The Transformation of Democracy: Globalisation and Territorial Democracy*. Cambridge: Polity in association with the Open University.

Mishra, S.K. and Purusottam Nayak (2006) Socio-Economic Dimensions of Globalization in India. http://papers.ssrn.com/sol3/papers.cfm?abstract_id=899709

Modi, Ishwar (1985) *Leisure, Mass Media and Social Structure*. Jaipur: Rawat Publications.

—— (2008) "Leisure and Social Transformation". Invited presentation at the Common Session: CS 01: Social Changes and Social Problems, First ISA Forum of Sociology, Barcelona, Spain, September 5.

Ohmae, Kenichi (1991) *The Borderless World: Power and Strategy in the Interlinked Economy*. Hammersmith: Fontana.

Pais, Shoba (2006) 'Globalization and its Impact on Families', paper presentation at the 4th Viennese Conference on Mediation, Vienna, Austria. http://www.bildungsmanagement.at/download/Konferenz%202006/Pais.pdf

Prabaharan, A. (2007) Essentials of Indian Globalisation. http://prabaharan.wordpress.com/category/globalisation/

Reich, Robert B. (1991) *The Work of Nations*. London: Simon and Schuster.

Robertson, R. (1992) *Globalisation: Social Theory and Global Culture*. London, Newbury Park and New Delhi: Sage.

Sassen, Saskia (1991) *The Global City: New York, London, Tokyo*. Princeton, NJ: Princeton University Press.

Singh, Yogendra (1973) *Modernization of Indian Tradition*. Delhi: Thomson Press.

Tripathi, P.M. (n.d.) Impact of Globalisation on Regional Development in Asia: Focusing on India. www.angoc.ngo.ph/.../Impact-of-Globalisation-on-Regional-Development

Weiss, Linda (1997) "Globalization and the Myth of the Powerless State", *New Left Review*, Vol. 225, pp. 3–27.

World Commission on the Social Dimension of Globalization (2006) *A Fair Globalization Creating Opportunities for All*. New Delhi: Academic Foundation.

11

Globalization and the Future of Cultures

Yogesh Atal

Theories of social change are relatively recent entrants into the domain of the social sciences. Prior to the advent of social sciences, our understanding of the society was guided by the perception of sages and savants, who mixed descriptions of the 'actually existing social situations' with prescriptions regarding desirable social structure, norms of behaviour and cultural patterns. These native philosophers did not make distinction between 'what is' and 'what ought to be'. In fact, the treatises, particularly of the Indian sages, were couched in terms of a 'desirable' future of our culture. While this may not be that true of the western societies, it is more generally true of the ancient civilizations of the East. However, it can be said that the introduction of the social sciences brought focus on the present, leading to the description of the 'is' – the 'present' – of the societies.

Such exercises logically led some of the scholars to ask the pertinent question: How has the present emerged?

Search for answer to this question took them to the corridors of the past, and, in the absence of objective evidence, to the realm of conjectures. Some scholars focused on the entire humanity, and talked of change in 'evolutionary terms'; some others confined themselves to their own societies, and to the known past, and laid foundations of social history. The prescriptive protocols were assumed by several scholars as continuance of prevailing practices.

The fact, however, is that the early social theorists – the pioneers of modern social science – gave prime attention to the understanding and analysis of the existing social structures, using historical, ideological, or structural-functional approaches. It is only recently that changes brought about by the processes unleashed by industrial revolution, and accompanied by the colonization of the non-western societies and cultures, began attracting the attention of the social scientists. And since this change was so very prominent in the West – which is now called the North – early studies of change focused on the industrializing societies and built theories regarding change based on that experience. In the face of startling pace of change in the West, the cultures of the non-West, falling under the colonial net, were viewed as no-change, or, at best, slow-change societies. Darwinian influence of evolutionism came handy to prove the point of their superiority, justifying the colonization as *struggle for existence* and *survival of the fittest*. Built on these premises, a staircase theory of unilinear evolution, and later a modified version of it as multilinear evolution, was promulgated which remained in use for long. These were then replaced by the newer simile of an escalator – some sort of self-propelling yet necessitating coverage of all the stairs in the ladder. Newer forms of change, however, did not oblige old theories of change, and scholars introduced the concept of 'leapfrogging' to accommodate newer patterns of change that do not require the same following. Many of the present-day changes occurring worldwide illustrate this new pattern of change.

Needless to say that the story of Indian Social Science is no different. For long, Indological treatises fed us on the structure of our society. But all this was the description of the past, or the prescription by the likes of Manu on the do's and don'ts of the Hindu society. The plural, or multicultural, character of our society came to be highlighted in the orations of our leaders who led the freedom struggle. The same could be noticed in our teaching of the Indian social system – even in the 1960s. Until then, our orientation remained Indological, as is evident in the writings of, for example, G.S. Ghurye, K.M. Kapadia, or P.H. Prabhu. There are some who still follow the same line ignoring the fruits of recent research. Such scholars and teachers equate, rather misleadingly, Hindu society with the Indian society.

It is important to remind here that the era of empirical studies, which began somewhere in the late 1950s, took our anthropologists to the tribal societies, and our sociologists to urban and rural India.[1] These exercises greatly helped in redrawing the contours of our society in multicultural terms. Initial studies dwelt on the descriptions of the 'present' that made our society look different from the indological model. Of late, the focus has shifted to the changes that were brought about with the initiation of planning and directed culture change. Introduction of the Community Development Programmes in India, in the year 1952, drew the attention of the entire nation towards our villages. Both sociologists and anthropologists got interested in the study of planned cultural change, with a view to (i) recording the present that was subjected to the forces of change, and (ii) assessing the impact of changes brought from without.[2] The major concern was to document the prevalent pattern of social relationships and of culture before it gets lost in the theories of change. It was realized that the then prevalent western theories of change – which were mostly civilizational in character – were not adequate to capture the new processes of directed change operating at the micro or meso levels. Scholars engaged in such micro-level studies at the village or block level soon realized the existence of rural–urban continuum, and some of them thus were drawn again to the urban centres. They started investigating the processes of industrialization and urbanization alongside of community development-related changes in the villages. In doing so, they employed the umbrella concept of 'westernization', which later got redefined and rechristened as 'modernization'. These processes were impacting both the rural and the urban societies in several ways. The two-step flow of communication was easily noticed by them and led some to investigate the role of mass communication vis-à-vis, personal communication in influencing public awareness and public opinion on a variety of issues, including economic and political. Even modern technology – particularly relative to agriculture – arrived in the villages via this route. That is how the isolation of the village was broken. Village was no longer conceived as an 'isolate', although it was 'isolable'.

It was towards the last decade of the 20th century that the realization came that all that we had achieved in the previous decades would soon become a past tense. And that the time has come to look towards the future, and to build it on the achievements of the past. The future began to be fashioned by those living their present and leading the processes of social and cultural change. In fact, the previous decades of development were seen not as improving the present by 'catching up the Joneses', but as deliberate and planned attempt at bringing about a desirable future for the coming generations.

Scholars and political and social leaders, thus, shifted their orientation from the 'past' and the 'present' to the 'future'. The newer scholarly interest was, however, not only focused on 'what will be?' but also on 'what should be?' our future. Rather than entering into an uncertain future, the need was felt to fashion a future of our liking by stemming the unwanted trends and initiating the desirable ones. The magic figure of the year 2000 somehow prompted the review of the past, on the one hand, and instigated the intellectuals to construct the images of the future, on the other.

This shift to future is indeed a shift of the paradigm. Of course, it remains linked with our commitment to development. Began as a process of decolonization – which was negative in its orientation – development became, in the countries of the so-called Third World, an ideology for rapid, planned and directed culture change. Newly independent nations began to move in the predetermined direction with defined goals and targets, and preconceived strategies. The planners and administrators took on the role of the 'fashioners' of future. Developing countries got involved in the 'revolution of the rising expectations'. The West served as the reference group that even proxied many decisions on behalf of the governments of the newly independent countries. In such a context, *westernization* and *modernization* became synonymous of *development*.

In this manner, orientation to change has also changed. Rather than focusing on the past, and reconstructing the journey from the past to the present, social scientists began investigating the changes in contemporary world. And, as we approached close to the 20th century, the focus of change shifted again – this time from the present to the future. I submit that the concept of *globalization* is the product of this last phase.

Understood this way, we must admit that this is the period of understanding the process of globalization, and not of passing judgement on it. It is a new coinage passed on to us from the international political arena. As a concept, it is still being sculpted. Collapse of communism, leading to the liberalization of the economies and increasing democratization of polities, has created new conditions for international interactions in almost all the fields. But, depending on our subject specialization, we view this process as economic, political, cultural, or a total mix of all these aspects of our life.

Like the previous concepts of westernization and modernization, globalization is also used in two distinct senses – as an ideology and as a process. When the process is deliberately planned – with manifest intentions and clear-cut goals – its ideological stance gets prominence. This can be said about westernization, which was a part of the ideology of colonization, and was thrust upon the colonies by the colonial masters. The latter regarded the colonies as 'primitive' and 'backward' compared to their own societies and, therefore, took steps to 'westernize' the colonies through education, imposition of a foreign language, and implantation of western institutions of management and administration to bring them to the realm of 'modernity'. The colonies were at the receiving end; there was a single source of external influence that was designed to bring out radical changes in the cultures of societies ruled by them. Switching over from westernization to modernization, in a way, was an acknowledgment of the process with no deliberate design of any ideologue.

I share the view that globalization is a process, and not a deliberate ideology imposed by some agency. We continue to be one world with many voices, and with several cultures, and yet all the societies of the world are in the grip of this overwhelming process of globalization.

I am aware of the advantages that are inventoried and also the fears that are expressed about the ill-effects of this new process, which has become a word of common parlance. Since the process is so new, and since it has not touched all the societies in the same manner, and to the same extent, it is rather early in the day to pass a judgement over its role. No doubt, there is affluence of 'literature' on this process, doubling much faster, but large volume of this is journalistic and is in the nature of impressionistic political commentary; very little is based on systematic scientific research, and is, therefore, cannot become the basis for any profound generalization. Social sciences are not yet ready to either denounce or endorse this phenomenon. I might also say that it is *not* the function of the social sciences to pass judgments on the desirability or otherwise of an emerging phenomenon. Objectivity demands such restraint.

If I were to encapsulate the trends of discussion on this issue in various fora – seminars and symposia and even published articles in good journals – I would list four major emphases:

1. *Discovery of ideological underpinnings*

   Globalization is alleged, by many, to be the conspiracy of the West designed to spread the capitalist ethos, and to highlight the changing role of the state versus the market.

2. *Recounting of failures*

   Writers allude to the failure of the prevalent developmental paradigm that converted the rising revolution of expectations into a rising revolution of frustrations while debating the advantages of globalization. The growing disenchantment with the development paradigm is supported by the deteriorating state of our environment, particularly the tribal forests, the increasing rate of unemployment even amongst the educated, death of cultural traits, and uprooting of people as a result of newer trends of migration. And all these trends are now being attributed to the process of globalization, which is just in the offing.

3. *Anticipation of fear*

   Many vociferous opponents of the process of globalization, particularly those who regarded this as a process 'directed' by some interested countries of the developed world, express the fear that this is 'intended' to hegemonize the world, and that it would in due course 'engulf' indigenous cultures and civilizations to establish a homogenized world culture.

4. *Attribution of current social disorders to the process of globalization*

   Reinforcement of ethnic identities, racial violence, migration to other countries, adverse effects of media, lower levels of morality, etc., which are now widely seen in all societies, are all regarded by some 'concerned' scholars as consequences of globalization.

Authors of the South lay blames for all this to the countries of the North, as if they were to derive all the benefits from this process by extending their markets, locating their industries, killing local enterprises, and engulfing national cultures.

It is difficult for me to join such a chorus against globalization. If we subsume all the past processes of change, particularly those coming from without, as globalization, and regard this as a process that began centuries ago, then I have no problem. But if this were to be seen as a new process, then certainly doubts can be raised about its alleged negative role that is exemplified by the trends that have a long history. This is a process that has hardly begun, and that has as yet to reach the remote locations – rural and tribal; as such, it cannot be given credit for things that have happened even prior to its arrival. It would indeed be interesting to see the literature on westernization and modernization that was produced in this country in the 1960s and 1970s and compare it with what is being written today on the process of globalization. One would find almost verbatim the same allegations against those processes. One wonders whether we are not lifting those criticisms and pasting them on the new phenomenon. Similarly, it would be presumptuous to blame the process of globalization for the many new changes that are occurring today and are regarded as dysfunctional; their causation may have a different history.

As a precaution, let me hasten to mention that I am not arguing a case in favour of globalization, nor am I suggesting that its consequences are all *eu*-functional or *non*-functional.[3] I am only saying that this remains to be found out through sustained empirical research. It should be the part of a newly prioritized agenda.

As long as the countries are pursuing the old western paradigm of development, even when the processes of globalization have begun impacting, perhaps the criticism of the old paradigm in vogue may still remain valid. But that should be seen as the criticism of the continued paradigm of development rather than that of globalization. If the latter is a new process, it is too early to assess the damage wrought by it; the fears expressed may only serve as a caution, but need not be taken for the truth.

II

The collapse of communism, accompanied with the end of Cold War era and universal acknowledgment of the need to focus on social development, are the features that emerged with dramatic revolutions in information technology and rapidly expanding market culture that broke the various *insulators* and opened out several *apertures*[4] to link the various nations. Liberalization of the economy, democratization of the polity, and an urge for peace became global trends. They are being summed up as globalization. However, different scholars accentuate one aspect or the other rather than talking of the total baggage that ought to define this overarching process.

We are in the midst of that process. While people are writing on this process and debating its relative merits and demerits, it must be admitted that no consensus has emerged on its definition. The word 'globalization' connotes different meanings to different people. There is a need for conceptual clarity. Rather than attempting a social scientific definition of the concept, most discussions on globalization are in the nature of the perceived 'ill-effects' of this process on the cultures and societies of the developing world.

I am of the view that globalization signifies a major turning point in development. Broadly speaking, one can say that change goes through three phases: (i) endogenous change, (ii) change influenced from the outside as a one-way traffic, and (iii) the reciprocal processes of change. It is true that as long as change was only from within, it was not so noticeable mainly because of its slowness. But once, societies came in contact with each other, the pace of change became faster. Thus, what was new was not the fact of change, but its pace.

The pre-colonial period was characterized by the first kind of change. The second phase of change is associated with the advent of colonialism, when the colonizing countries began influencing their colonies and brought about radical changes in them through imported system of administration, introduction of modern (i.e., western) education, improvements in transportation and communication, etc., to make these societies 'similar' to the cultures of the colonizers. Since there was more of a give by the colonizers, it was a one-way traffic, with the colonies at the receiving end. Anthropologists called this a process of *acculturation*. Even after the attainment of independence, this process continued with the difference that developing countries identified more than one reference group outside their cultures and had the possibility, at least in principle, to decide what to receive, from where, and when. Colonization and acculturation gave way to development and modernization, but still keeping the developing countries at the receiving end most of the time. But, the development that has taken place in the past four to five decades has changed the scenario and has created conditions for the new phase, which is now called globalization.

To sum up, it can be said that the pre-colonial phase was a phase of *self-dependence* – of endogenous or orthogenetic growth with minimal of addition from the outside world. The colonial phase can be characterized as period of *dependence* – colonies heavily dependent on the colonial master and hegemonized by the outside culture from a single source (*single aperture model* of interaction). The postcolonial phase that lasted for about five decades was a period of *independence* – colonies becoming politically independent and making choices for the receipt of outside elements from a wide variety of sources (*multiple aperture model*) generating an ambivalence between tradition and modernity while pursuing either the western paradigm of development or the socialist–communist mode of growth, or a mixture of the two. That was the phase of *modernization* and *westernization*. With the collapse of communism in the Eastern Europe, and the end of the era of cold war, the world has entered the phase of *interdependence* that is characterized by the process of *globalization*. Interdependence in this context implies reciprocity on more or less equal footing, leaving behind the verticality of previous relationships.[5]

Societies of the so-called 'Third World' (a term that has lost all its meaning with the end of the Cold War era) are becoming 'modern' without being 'western'. But this phase is not the phase of 'West versus the Rest'. All the societies are engrossed in this process of mutual give and take. The globe is entering in each of the cultures, and each of the cultures is entering in different ways in most other cultures through a variety of routes – directly or vicariously. And, the globe as a whole is experiencing problems that are common – environmental pollution, population explosion, violence and crime, deficits in social development as exhibited by rising rates of poverty, expanding unemployment, and threats to the integration of societies. Despite this commonality, what is significant to observe is the fact that these trends have their distinguishing profiles in each country. Commonality of the problems does not mean identical profile of the emergent situation. The etiology, the gravity, and the extent of each of the problems differs from country to country and, therefore, calls for country-specific cataloguing of the 'burden of disease'[6] and culture-specific strategies for their amelioration. It is this fact that has brought the cultural variable to the centre stage. We have come to realize that common problems need uncommon solutions. Each culture has to work out solutions to the problems that it confronts. Leaders of society are to think globally and act locally.

Globalization can be understood as a process of making the world a 'global village' in the sense in which Marshall McLuhan[7] used the concept. Geographical distances notwithstanding, communications are playing their role in bringing closer different parts of the globe as an interacting and communicating community. The essence of this is that things happening in any part of the world influence, albeit in different degrees and in different ways – positive and negative, all the parts of the rest of the system. In other words, isolation of individual communities and countries is broken. Thus, not only India is affected by what happens in the US or in Singapore, but Singapore and the US are also affected by what happens in India. This is how the process of globalization has brought the entire world to India and taken India to different parts of the world. And this is made possible by advances in the technologies of transportation and communication. Even when individuals remain stationary in their homesteads, the information technology – technology of the mass media – transports them to distant lands. This revolution has taken away the monopoly of information from the state by opening alternative channels of information. In the 1970s, some of the authoritarian states used to censor all the arriving mail and the printed magazines and books. Today, one can ignore the postal system and get the mail and magazines through the electronic medium. The happenings at the Tiananmen Square and the brutal military attack on democratic protestors in Thailand were witnessed by people all around the world because of the presence of the foreign media. The fact that they were banned on the national channels did not serve the intended purpose of the state to withhold information. I tend to believe that the IT revolution was responsible for the collapse of communism in the Eastern Europe as it opened apertures to the outside world, which the state was unable to prevent.

What we witness today is, to use Jan Nederveen Pieterse's phrase, the 'Cultural Turn in Development'.[8] Pieterse argues that culture figured in development first as part of western ethnocentrism. That was the "*implicit* culture of developmentalism" which "is no longer adequate in the age of 'polycentrism in a context of high interaction' or globalization" (p. 60). As the paradigm of westernization/modernization has lost its relevance, the author feels that the "questioning Western itineraries is now no longer an anti-imperialistic preoccupation but a matter of soul-searching in the West". With the end of Cold War and the emergence of religious and ethnic movements, culture is now assuming a novel prominence. In earlier analyses, culture (that is, local culture) was brought in as an explanatory variable to suggest how it obstacles the introduction of innovations from abroad. The emphasis is now shifting to national culture in a pluri-cultural context – the effort to bring about a convergence toward a single national culture. Pieterse makes a reference to Fanon's book titled *Wretched of the Earth* (published in 1967 by Penguin) wherein three phases in the cultural development of the colonized people are listed. These are: (1) assimilation of the culture of the colonizer, (2) recollection of original cultural resources, but removed from the masses, and (3) combat, revolution and formation of a national culture in which the artist 'rejoins the people'. The question of cultural identity, subsumption of culture under a political agenda, and politicians serving as custodians of culture are the new issues that are emerging. A reconnect between development and anthropology is being tried. In Germany, a new journal is devoted to this area, which is named *Entwicklungsethnologie*.

The concept of 'culture' has to be defined in broader terms, that is, in the manner in which modern cultural anthropology defines it. The narrow specialists of culture – the so-called 'culture people' such as prehistorians, archaeologists, the traditionalists, and the fundamentalists – are at best 'preservationists'. They have mostly engaged themselves in the rediscovery of the past and its glorification through sheer adumbrationism. They are worried about the dilapidation of the physical structures (such as monuments) because of their gross neglect, or about the damages done to them by natural hazards or by irresponsible human actions. Their guiding motto is: 'preserve', 'protect' and 'renovate'. 'Change' does not exist in their vocabulary; culture, to them, is a mere museum of tradition. Most of the first-generation anthropologists, for example, regarded all forms of culture contacts with the outside world as disruptive to the 'primitive' way of life and, therefore, they wanted the primitives to maintain their *status quo;* they were dubbed as advocates of *anthropological zoos*.

Those committed to the 'safeguarding of culture' employ three prominent strategies:

(i) *Reservationist strategy:* Protection of sites, insulating people from outside influences, 'caging' the cultures in museums, or zoos.

(ii) *Display:* Putting the 'culture' on stage. Cultural performances for outsiders where they are torn out of context, and become a 'show'.

(iii) *Displacement*: Through thefts of cultural artefacts, or their faking, some aspects of a given culture get displaced. Acquisition of these artefacts results into *museumization* of the drawing rooms in other settings. Bereft of their cultural meaning, such traditional artefacts from other cultures become symbols of modernity in the developed world. In some sense, modernization partly involves 'transfers of traditions' – western traditions of long standing (including Christianity) came to the non-western cultures as part of the modernization package; and similarly, material cultural elements from the primitive and other non-western societies enter the western drawing rooms to modernize them. Modernization has, thus, displaced and dislocated traditions.

It is with this kind of orientation that the so-called cultural specialists, including old-style anthropologists (propagating separation between sociology and anthropology[9]), hold the view that the cultures of the developing countries have been the victims of development. The development specialists, on the other hand, have attributed all the failures of planned development programmes to culture; they regard culture as an obstacle to development. Both the perspectives see culture of the non-western people as unchanging or as unchangeable.

The manner in which culture has responded to change, or culture contact, has defied all such prognostications. Protests against culture contacts notwithstanding, what has happened even in regard to the tribal groups the world over is quite astonishing: no tribe has remained completely *insulated* from the outside world maintaining its pristine, exotic existence; and many of the material cultural traits of various non-western societies have travelled far and wide to become showpieces in modern drawing rooms. There is a discernible trend towards, what may be called, 'museumization' of the drawing rooms. This has influenced current thinking regarding the concept of culture in social sciences.

Questions concerning culture, such as the following, are being raised in the context of rapidly enveloping process of globalization: Will economic and technological progress destroy the cultural diversity and bastardize our cultures? Will we witness a return of intolerant chauvinism that would make cultures retreat to their shells? Will there be a judicious fit between the old and the new? Where are we going? Where shall we reach? What will be the fate of our cultures? These questions should be answered in a broader sociological perspective.

It needs to be stressed that a living culture cannot be treated as a mere museum of tradition, or as an anthropological zoo. There is a need to adopt a broader definition of culture – as a way of life of a given people. To talk of only material culture, or sophistication (arts, music, dance, literature), is to take a narrow view of culture. In this sense, cultures are not likely to return to their shells by isolating themselves and insulating from each other. Cultural oysters are no longer possible. The opening out of cultures, the inter-cultural dialogue, and the cross-cultural fertilization have brought into play two seemingly contradictory processes of globalization and localization or *indigenization*. The co-existence of these processes is, in fact, indicative of resilience of cultures. There is a need to know how these twin processes relate and operate in different cultural settings and how new equations are worked out. The fact remains that while cultures are no longer completely *insulated*, their opening out of *apertures*[10] has not uprooted them. They are able to maintain their core and retain their identity. How should that core be defined? And how does a culture maintain its core? are the questions that need examination. Researches carried out with such a paradigmatic orientation will look at those aspects of culture that have screened the entry of outside elements and assimilated those gaining entry without losing their own identity.

What appears striking is the fact that despite so much of give and take occurring between cultures – call it by whatever name such as westernization, modernization, or even globalization – cultures have maintained their identities, and the globe is characterized by the heterogeneity of cultures. In the midst of sea change experienced by non-western societies, one notices a reassertion of their respective cultural identities. The resurgence and revival of traditions are manifestations of this assertion.

This leads us to ask the following questions: What is the function of cultural identity? Does it create solidarity among the people who belong to that culture? Or, does this process lead to the emergence of sub-regional loyalties which may become secessionist? What happens when a person is sandwiched between dual loyalties – for example, religious identity versus cultural identity? How does culture give identity to its people? Can newer identities be created by manipulating cultural symbols? Do identities really empower? Or, are they fictitious?

In our analysis of globalization, very little attention has been paid to these worrisome queries.

The question of cultural identity is closely associated with the question of cultural values. Granted that it is not very easy to define and identify 'core values'. Nevertheless, cultural values are brought in as explanatory variables when evaluating the success or failure of an innovation. It is important to note that values of the outsiders are a major source for distorting the reality or misreading it. They are also used to condemn a reality. Both insiders and outsiders have their own angles to view reality and to judge its significance. What is good or bad depends upon these perceptions. What an outsider regards bad may be a highly cherished value amongst the insiders, and vice versa. So, whose values should or would prevail? Who should fashion the future – the outsiders or the insiders? Should a futurist impose his/her own ideological predilections while predicting or prescribing future? Or should he/she accept value diversity and acknowledge the powers of living cultures to find their own ways of moving ahead?

In this context, the concept of *resilience* of cultures seems quite important in explaining the phenomenon of continuity in societies that are going through a phase of rapid transformation. The retention of cultural identities alongside modernization can be explained in terms of resilience. But this concept is still vague and is used in a variety of ways, for example:

(i) Accounting for the unchangeables in society.

(ii) Capability of a culture to 'withstand shock' so as not to allow 'deformation', 'rupture', or 'fracture' of the cultural and social system. Resilience can be equated with the pliancy of the bamboo – 'bending with the storm but not breaking'.

(iii) As a synonym of 'homeostasis': springing back to former position: recidivism, cultural resurgence, fundamentalism, and conservatism.

(iv) Resilience as a synonym for adaptability, integration, accommodation, and plasticity.

(v) As a creative response to cope with change: symbiosis, encapsulation, cultural reinterpretation, and indigenization.

(vi) As opposite of stability.

It remains to be found out whether resilience occurs in all societies, or only in certain societies – for example, developing Asian societies. If the latter is the case, then what are the contexts that give rise to resilience? Questions also need to be raised in regard to the measurement of resilience, spheres of its manifestation, role of exogenous and endogenous forces in invoking resilience, types of processes through which resilience manifests itself, and the manipulability of resilience.

One also notices a trend towards indigenization of social sciences[11] by promoting the use of native categories of thought. Is this a form of cultural resistance? Or of cultural resilience? If knowledge becomes *parochialized* and the culture gets *insulated*, then resilience stands for a retrogressive step.

Another significant feature of the era of globalization is increasing mobility of people across the cultures. This has led to the formation of, what I have named, *sandwich cultures*.[12] Increasing geographical mobility and resettlement of migrant groups in different lands has made most cultures plural societies. The migrant groups evolve their own mechanisms to preserve their cultural identity and yet develop interfaces with the culture of the host society. The emerging culture of the immigrants is the result of sandwiching between the forces of the host culture and the parent culture. Since host cultures vary, the sandwich cultures of peoples originating from the same country, but settled in different countries, also differ. The existence of sandwich cultures makes native cultures more diverse and heterogeneous. Only the broad contours of this phenomenon have been drawn by me in a prefatorial to this possible theory. But systematic empirical research of the phenomenon of sandwich cultures as they emerge in different country contexts is badly needed to enrich our understanding of the impact of globalization.

III

Anthropological literature exhibits a peculiar ambivalence towards 'change'. It is significant to note that while ethnological theories have focused on 'evolution' and 'diffusion', earlier ethnographies of particular tribal groups did not assign any space to the description and analysis of change occurring in them. These monographs were written in the idiom of eternal present; the tribal communities were regarded by them as *no-change* or *slow-change* societies. It is only in the late 1940s that some anthropologists began ending their ethnographies with a postscript on change. Fuller studies of change in tribal and village communities are rather recent, started somewhere in the mid-1950s when newly independent countries initiated an era of planned and directed socio-cultural change. The term, 'directed culture change', was evolved to signify exogenous changes – changes brought from without. The analysts of directed culture change either attributed costly failures of any innovation to the 'neglect' of the 'cultural' factor, or impressed upon the planners and administrators to have a holistic view of culture and assess the ramifying influence of change brought about in a particular sector of social life. But interestingly enough, whatever we have by way of literature on culture–development interface[13] is mainly anecdotal. There are narrations of stories of (mainly) failures highlighting the importance of the cultural factors. But no guidelines exist as to how to plan a change that will not meet a failure. Wisdom of the hindsight can only provide an awareness of the importance of the cultural variables but cannot equip a social scientist to offer readymade recipes to planners of change. Similarly, the planners have also not yet improved their planning protocol to incorporate the cultural variable in the planning process to ensure that it will not cause hindrance. We all recognize that there is a cultural dimension to development but we feel ill-equipped to handle it.

There is a need to establish a relationship between the concepts of 'change' and 'future'. In my view, both concepts are diachronic, but change is past-oriented and future is forward-looking. One is rooted in history; the other is dependent upon our powers of prediction. Analysts of change often indulge in the glorification of the past; prognosticators of future tend to exaggerate the glory of their vision of future or decry the prospects of an unwanted future. Those concerned with future either talk of *appropriating* the PAST, or of *displacing* the PRESENT, or of *colonizing* the FUTURE. Are our visions of future, and their propagation, an attempt towards the colonization of the future? And can we really colonize it given the existence of several variables that tend to influence any cultural change? Who determines what is good or bad for a given society? The conspiracy allegation implicit in our critiques of the past and the present is based on our wisdom of the hindsight. How can we say that our imposition of the vision of the future is not yet another conspiracy that may be condemned by the coming generations? There has been ample criticism of the West as a colonizer responsible for destroying cultures of the developing countries; but the fact is that the West itself is disintegrating in some respects and that despite a spate of changes in non-western cultures, their cores are still intact.

There seems to be an agreement on the point that 'development' did not succeed in homogenizing the world. Traditions did not oblige their obituary writers. The process of development, in fact, created greater disparities, broadened the divide between the rich and the poor, and falsified many tenets of modernization. Alongside the process of modernization grew the process of revival and resurgence of tradition, and even of religious fundamentalism.

Those who take a pessimistic view of the future of cultures feel that all cultures would lose their pristinity through hybridization and would be reduced to their ornamental roles. The optimists, on the other hand, feel that cultural communities would plunge into their indigenous roots and come up with their own recipes for survival and advancement.

The universal desire for change notwithstanding, societies are making an equally emphatic assertion of their respective cultural identities. The forces of change have not transformed cultures or made them as look-alike societies. Industrializing Thailand cannot be mistaken for Taiwan, or the roaring tiger of Korea for Japan. India has remained India although it is a much different India than what it was fifty years ago.

What one witnesses in developing countries is a growing heterogeneity – a queer mixture of tradition and modernity: jumbo jets and bullock carts, mosques and temples alongside the science laboratories, traditional attire and western paraphernalia. Our saints and Swamis are becoming national icons via the electronic media. Through the exposure to the wider world, each culture has certain elements of a global culture which itself is now greatly differentiated rather than being merely 'western'. The migration of people and their settlement in other cultures has given rise to *sandwich cultures* – sandwiched between the forces of parent culture and the pressures of the host society. It is not only Japan or China that has come to, for example, India, but India has also reached these destinations. Chinese restaurants in different lands, to take another example, have popularized Chinese food, but in each country Chinese food tastes differently because of its adaptation to the local taste. So is the case with Indian food in other countries. Tandoori dishes served in India, particularly in Punjab, have a different flavour that one cannot get when one orders them in Paris or in London. Similarly, the Chinese food served in Indian restaurants hardly matches in taste and standard to what is served in Beijing, or in Singapore. The way English is spoken by people of different countries demonstrates cultural ingenuity to adapt outside cultural elements.

Countries are becoming heterogeneous in their cultures and plural in their social structures. No doubt, cultures are also losing some of their traits. But disappearance of certain traits does not amount to destruction of a culture. Similarly, accretion of new traits contributes to cultural enrichment and not to its impoverishment.

Culture should not be viewed as a museum of tradition. As a living entity, it is a continuously growing phenomenon. The opening out, the inter-cultural dialogue, the cross-cultural fertilization, and the modernity–tradition negotiations contribute to the growth of cultures and reinforce their resilience. Cultures are like bamboos which bend but do not break when winds blow fast.

Fears do exist in terms of the possibilities that open out with every technological advancement. Some people argue that growth of science heralded the end of nature, and that genetic engineering now heralds the end of culture, and that robotics in future would cause the death of species. This is a horrible scenario for the future in which no one would like to enter. However, it must be stressed that whatever is technologically feasible is not always socially desirable and culturally acceptable. To the same innovation, different cultures respond differently. While it is true that technology has helped in widening the cognitive horizons and enlarging the range of choices, its global hegemonic blanket is incapable of enshrouding all cultural specificities. To what uses a given technology is put, is still very much dependent on the people. The resurgence and revival of tradition alongside of development puts question marks on the 'conspiracy' theory that alleges the West for all the ills of development.

There are several unintended consequences of the development process. Reinforcement of cultural identity is one of them. Modern media have done a great deal to revive and diffuse tradition. People have become mobile – both physically and psychologically. Not only do they cross the cultural boundaries, they are enabled to travel into the corridors of their own cultural past.

There is nothing strange in culture change. What a culture retains and what it gives up, or what it receives and what it rejects from the outside is governed by a process of thorough cultural screening and redefinition. Living cultures do not oblige spectators who would like to put the culture on stage, or make it a show piece, or an anthropological zoo. It is common knowledge that tourists arriving in traditional societies to observe 'exotic' cultures have been primarily responsible for disturbing the status quo of the tourist site. But those who live that culture may not regard such disturbance as 'dysfunctional'.

Surely, their culture will not remain the same, but changes in it need not be seen as symptomatic of an impending demise. And views may differ within a given society as to what is good or bad. What the outsiders may like to retain may be the ones that the insiders would wish to discard, and vice versa.

It can be said that all cultures in future will look different from what they are today, with changes in the profiles of their demography and literacy, and with the continuing onslaught of technology and its attendant ramifications. But they will remain, and remain different with their own identities. Similarities in material culture – the externalia – will not obliterate differences in values and ways of life.

Neither will there be a single future for the globe, nor a single global culture. Multiple cultures will have multiple futures. Heterogeneity will continue to prevail.

Change has now become a key concept and its inevitability is recognized. It is acknowledged that the desire for change is universal; all societies – big or small, modern or primitive, western or non-western – share this desire. At the same time, one also notices a newfound attachment to one's own culture; there is in evidence an effective assertion of cultural identity. No society would wish to lose its cultural roots. No culture would allow itself to be engulfed by another dominant culture. These two tendencies – desire for change and keenness to maintain identity – have resulted into increasing modernization of the societies, on the one hand; and revival and resurgence of tradition, on the other. Forces of change have not homogenized the globe into a common culture. The individual cultures have certainly changed and expanded, both in material and non-material terms, but they have not all become even look-alike societies. Religion and tradition have constantly tried to establish new equations with external forces of change. There is an accretion of new cultural elements – either invented within or innovated from the outside; simultaneously, there is also an attrition of some old cultural traits – deliberately or otherwise.

One may ask: Does disappearance of certain cultural traits amount to the destruction of a culture? If the answer is in the affirmative then we may pose the question: how does the culture grow? Or, is culture just another name for the deadwood? I would submit the point that changes occurring in the ambit of culture do not always erase its identity; it may, however, confuse its identification. Accretion and attrition are the processes that operate in all living cultures; that is how they grow and express their vitality.

The phenomenon of cultural continuity has challenged the 'homogenization' hypothesis. While individual cultures are experiencing vast changes, they are not becoming similar, not even look-alike. Even the homogeneity of the western societies has suffered; they are becoming heterogeneous both in terms of their demographic composition and cultural constitution. The so-called world culture's monocultural stance is no longer tenable. The plausible perspective is to view both culture and future in their plurality. No single future can be imposed on all cultures. Cultures have their ingenuity to respond to changes and bring about new equations between the old and the new.

In this sense, we cannot talk of 'future' (in singular) of 'cultures' (in plural). Of course, there will be a single, empirical future of a given culture, but scholars may present alternative scenarios – these would be in the nature of 'prescriptions' and not as 'predictions'. Similarly, predictive futurists may sound optimistic or pessimistic depending upon the premises of their prediction. That is why I suggest that we use both culture and future as plurals in this discourse. Plurality goes even further: most nation-societies are plural – both in terms of ethnic composition and in cultural constitution, thanks to decades of culture contact which is now greatly accelerated by the modern means of rapid transportation and communication. Each society consists of multiple layers of culture. At least three strata can be easily identified:

(i) universal, international (global) culture of science and technology, modern industry, bureaucracy, transport and communication, emerging Infosphere;

(ii) emergent national culture, deriving civilizational base and giving the country its cultural identity; and

(iii) regional and local, parochial cultures; *sandwich cultures* – cultures of migrant groups which emerge as a result of sandwiching between the forces of the parent culture and the host country culture.

While we may not be in a position to predict the totality of our future scenario, what can be predicted, however, is the outcome of irreversible trends – trends that cannot be halted, and therefore prediction of what is inevitable to happen. For example, in case of India, it can be said that it is inevitable that literacy levels will rise in the near future; that urbanization and industrialization processes will further accelerate; that information revolution will transform the styles of management – both of government, and of private business; that environmental pollution and depletion of natural resources will increasingly become difficult to stem; that there will be more people inhabiting the country and its surrounding region; and that there will be more scientism in our mode of thinking.

IV

The challenge before us is to investigate the new phenomenon of change as it occurs in our society and brings about transformation of our cultures without erasing their identities. As social scientists, we must move away from mere rhetoric and superficial criticism or ideological tirades; we must, instead, develop a protocol for sound empirical research to assess the manner in which the society and culture are responding to the new waves of change, their desirability or otherwise notwithstanding. For this, we need a new paradigm, the contours of which are broadly indicated in this paper.

We must work out an agenda for research that provides us with comparable insights. There is scope both for macro- and micro-level studies, and there lies the virgin territory of entire range of new concepts that would be needed to mount a theory of change suited to contemporary trends.

Notes

1. In the initial phase, a person's academic degree did not define a person's status as a sociologist or an anthropologist. People with degrees in Economics, Philosophy, Political Science, or Philosophy took studies that were either sociological or anthropological. In fact, tribal studies were a synonym for anthropological work and urban studies or the studies of scriptural texts were considered as sociological. But when it came to rural studies, both – who had degrees in sociology or anthropology – undertook such exercises following more or less the same methodology.
2. S.C. Dube did the pioneering work by publishing *India's Changing Villages* in 1958, as the first Principal of the National Institute of Community Development. Based in Hyderabad, he was instrumental in sponsoring several studies in rural change; using the concepts of westernization and modernization, such studies focused on directed culture change and also examined the processes of industrialization and urbanization.
3. In the sense in which Robert Merton used these terms while proposing the paradigm for functional analysis. See his *Social Theory and Social Structure*, Illinois: Free Press of Glencoe, 1968; especially the chapter on 'Manifest and Latent Functions'.
4. For the concepts of *insulators* and *apertures*, see, Yogesh Atal, chapter one of *Building a New Nation: Essays on India*, New Delhi: Abhinav Publications, 1981.
5. It is interesting to note that India has begun refusing 'development aid', and has become a donor for several smaller countries – Afghanistan, for example. It has joined that group of 'developing countries' who are ready to accept help under the UN auspices, but who insist on implementing the projects themselves, i.e., without outside expertise – a change that suggests improvement in India's technical manpower.
6. Though this phrase is used in the health context, but here it is employed in a much broader sense about all societal and environmental ailments.
7. McLuhan argued that while print media detribalized us, electronic media is retribalizing us. The electronic media is reconstituting an oral tradition. McLuhan said that the present world is gradually becoming a *global village*, a theatre of simultaneous happening where time and space are vanishing. The electronic media is beginning to put us back in touch with the tribal emotions which print had divorced us from.
8. Jan Nederveen Pieterse, *Development Theory: Deconstructions/Reconstructions*, New Delhi: Vistaar Publications, 2001.

9. To be sure, there are sociologists also who wish to perpetuate such an image of anthropology to demarcate the boundary of the two disciplines. Fortunately for India, such distinction between sociology and social anthropology is gradually being discarded.
10. For use of the concepts of *insulators* and *apertures*, see Yogesh Atal, *Building a Nation: Essays on India*, New Delhi: Abhinav Publications, 1981, Chapter 1: "Insulators and Apertures: Dynamics of Nation Building".
11. See Yogesh Atal, "The Call for Indigenization", *International Social Science Journal*, Vol. XXXIII, No. 1, 1981, pp. 189–97.
12. See Yogesh Atal, "Outsiders as Insiders: The Phenomenon of Sandwich Culture – Prefatorial to a Possible Theory", *Sociological Bulletin*, Vol. 38, No. 1, 1989, pp. 23–41.
13. See, for example, Yogesh Atal (ed.), *Culture–Development Interface*, New Delhi: Vikas Publishing House, 1991.

References

Atal, Yogesh (1981) *Building a New Nation: Essays on India*. New Delhi: Abhinav Publications.

—— (1981) "The Call for Indigenization", *International Social Science Journal*, Vol. XXXIII, No. 1, pp. 189–97.

—— (1989) "Outsiders as Insiders: The Phenomenon of Sandwich Culture – Prefatorial to a Possible Theory", *Sociological Bulletin*, Vol. 38, No. 1, pp. 23–41.

Dube, S.C. (1958) *India's Changing Villages*. London: Routledge and Kegan Paul.

Fanon, Frantz (1961) *The Wretched of the Earth*. London: Penguin Books.

Ghurye, G.S. (1950) *Caste and Class in India*. Bombay: Popular Prakashan.

Kapadia, K.M. (1947) *Hindu Kinship*. Bombay: Popular Prakashan.

—— (1955) *Marriage and the Family in India*. Bombay: Popular Prakashan.

Pieterse, Jan Nederveen (2001) *Development Theory: Deconstructions/Reconstructions*. New Delhi: Vistaar Publications.

Prabhu, P.N. (1954) *Hindu Social Organization*. Bombay: Popular Prakashan.

12

Globalization, Culture and Change

Chandan Kumar Sharma

Though the conventional understanding of culture projects it as an innocent, apolitical phenomenon, the recent cultural theories have forcefully brought out the political character of culture. The political potency of culture was recognized long before by the Marxist theorists when they identified it as an important weapon of class struggle. This understanding also forms the basis of celebrated Marxist theorist Antonio Gramsci's critical analysis of folklore and popular culture (1978).

The collective identity and the world view of a community finds its expression through its culture. That is why, appropriating the culture of a people has always been an important agenda for forces seeking to establish hegemonic dominance over a people. This appropriation, however, has never been so much subtle in design, endemic in scale, and successful in execution under the contemporary process of globalization.

This essay explicates the economic interest underlying the process of globalization and its exploitation of culture to further these interests. Thus, it argues that the much-celebrated propaganda of change globalization is said to have brought about needs to be accepted with circumspection.

Defining Globalization

Globalization refers to the process that seeks to establish a world that is characterized by networks of connections that span multi-continental distances. It entails a dynamic shrinking of distance on a large scale. Though as a phenomenon globalization is not new in that international trade and commerce, empires, military expeditions, cultural influences, etc., existed even in the ancient times, it will be hard to contend that these processes encompassed the lives of the people

---

This is a much revised version of another paper entitled 'Globalization as the Political Economy of Cultural Anarchy: Implications for North-east India' published in A. Dutta (ed.), *Human Securities in North East India: Issues and Policies*, Anwesha, Guwahati, 2008.

of those times in the same degree that they do now. In other words, globalization has become much more intense today. It now refers to a more advanced stage of the above processes of development steered by what is described as a global economy. As Manual Castells explains:

> the global economy concept must be distinguished from the notion of a world economy ... Capitalism has accumulated since its beginnings, on a worldwide scale. This is not to say that capitalist economy was a global economy. It is only now becoming such. By global economy we mean an economy that works as a unit in real time on a planetary scale. It is an economy where capital flows, labour markets, commodity markets, information, raw materials, management, and organizations are internationalized and fully interdependent throughout the planet, although in an asymmetrical form, characterized by the uneven integration into the global system of different areas of the planet. (1994: 21–22)

The forces of globalization, therefore, tend to erode the integrity and autonomy of national or local economies. It is the imperative of relentless expansion of business and profit under capitalism that forms the driving force behind globalization. This is the age of multi-national capitalism. The newly emerging and consolidating multi-/trans-national corporations (MNCs or TNCs) are the propelling force behind the process of globalization. Where TNCs in the past operated across a number of national economies, economic globalization now requires corporate interests to treat the world as a single entity, competing in all major markets simultaneously rather than sequentially (Robins 1996: 345).

Globalization as a New Face of Imperialism

The advocates of globalization project it as a mutually benefiting process for all societies throughout the world. But it has been widely described as imperialism in a new garb. J. Petras and H. Veltmeyer, for example, argue, "the existing world economic order is in the process of being renovated so as to create optimal conditions for the free play of greed, class interest and profit-making" (2001: 8). As an instrument of that economic order, globalization involves a "widening and deepening of the international flows of trade, capital, technology and information within a single integrated market" (ibid.: 11). They, therefore, arraign globalization as politics in the service of a particular vision of economics, the result of a consciously pursued strategy which ensures that the profits generated in the emerging global economic regime still remain concentrated in the imperialist centres. Castells concurs this when he says, "the global economy embraces the whole planet, but not all regions and all people on the planet. In fact, only a minority of people is truly integrated into the global economy ... This global economy increasingly concentrates wealth, technology, and power in 'the North' ..." (1994: 22).

Recounting the real nature of globalization, Petras and Veltmeyer have identified the TNCs as the motor and principal beneficiaries of globalization (2001: 34, 36). They show that the US-based TNCs continue to strengthen their grip on global economic activity. They laid bare the fact that to the degree that these TNCs control the world economy, it is largely the US that has re-emerged as the overwhelmingly dominant power (ibid.: 62). Anthony Giddens, the eminent

British sociologist, not particularly known as a critic of globalization, highlights the nature of contemporary globalization when he says, "(G)lobalisation, of course, isn't developing in an even-handed way, and is by no means wholly benign in its consequences. The share of the poorest fifth of the world's population in global income has dropped from 2.3 per cent to 1.4 per cent over the past 10 years. The proportion taken by the richest fifth, on the other hand, has risen from 70 per cent to 85 per cent. In Sub-Saharan Africa, 20 countries have lower incomes per head in real terms than they did two decades ago ... As one writer put it recently, rather than a global village, this is more like global pillage" (1999).

It may be noted here that it is not only the disparities between nations but also within them, rich or poor alike, which underlie the process of globalization. For example, while a poor country like India is churning out billionaires, some among the 'richest in the world', the poorer section of the population is facing increasing pauperization and the country ranks a dismal 119 in the UN Human Development Index Report published in 2010. This quashes the argument of the apologists of globalization that despite such inequalities there would be a decline in poverty as a result of the 'trickle-down effect'.

Further, the economic processes of globalization have seriously undermined the capacity of individual nation-states, as Petras and Veltmeyer note, "to pursue and advance their national interests, not to mention to control their own destiny" (2001: 18). This has the most damaging effects on the developing countries of the world including India. These countries have a colonial past and are in need of considerable investment in the social sector. For such investments they have been traditionally dependent either on the international financial institutions under the control of the world imperialist powers or the individual imperialist states. The governments in these poor countries are now enjoined to withdraw from the social sector. Directives come from the global capitalist powers and the financial institutions under their control for corporatization of the most vital areas of social sector like health, education, power, transport, and so on. The concept of welfare state that emerged out of the crisis era of the World War II committing itself to state provision of support and services for improving the quality of people's lives is being steadily decimated. Though the concept was essentially a capitalist one, it provided the much-needed succor to the common masses, both in rich and poor countries. Under the neo-liberal regime of today, however, capitalism has openly expressed its rapacious character.

As a result, today, we witness large-scale withdrawal of the responsibility of the state from the crucial social sectors. Further, under the influence of the global capital, the developing states like India today are steadily moving toward adopting a 'hire and fire' policy for its workers. Such a policy is being implemented understandably to do away with the 'welfaristic' labour policy for the benefit of the international as well as the national big capital. However, such economic policies are also poised to trigger intense social disturbance among the millions of impoverished people in the poor countries. In fact, the pernicious effects of such withdrawal of state responsibility and the subsequent corporatization of the social sector are already unfolding.

Culture as an Instrument of Imperialism

It is in order to control such possibilities that the global capital has taken recourse to the power of culture through the agency of the mass media. The ultimate objective of this process is to overwhelm the collective identities of the masses of these countries embedded in their cultures so that they lose the force to resist the economic expansionism and the political aggrandizement of the big capital.

Thus, under the control of the global capital, the media today is engaged in progressive marginalization or even trivialization of the local cultures. This is carried out, on the one hand, by outright debunking or parodying or suppression of the ingenious elements of the local cultures and, on the other hand, by producing an unhealthy obsession toward the conservative elements of the latter. Simultaneously, the task of imposition of mostly the cheaper version of the western (mainly American) popular cultural products, again controlled by the TNCs, on the third world masses is underway. Starting with the Hollywood, almost the entire western (again primarily American) media, especially its electronic version, today is engaged either in spreading vulgarity or obscurantism or in distorted representation of facts. The media in the developing countries, either owned by the global capital or dependent on the latter for advertisement revenue and so forth, is largely playing the role of a loyal collaborator despite its outward show of courage, commitment and neutrality.

Parallel to this, the media is also engaged in the proliferation of a culture of consumerism, the primary driving point of which is infinite avarice and meaningless competition for acquisition. On the pretext of offering 'free choice' to consumers the neo-liberal economy of today is generating a class of impulsive buyers, commonly described as shopaholics. What Thornstein Veblen (1899) censured in the late 19th century actually looks innocent in comparison to the irrational economic behaviour that has engulfed the contemporary affluent class.

The perpetrators of the consumer economy, posing as the defender of individual right, declare that nobody has the right to decide for others which goods are 'necessary' for living and which are not. However, what is conveniently ignored is that consumerism itself is created through extensive advertising and media influence. It hardly arises from people's natural ideas regarding the kinds of things they need. This has led some critics, notably the French thinker Bernard Stiegler, to argue that capitalism today appears to be governed not by production but by consumption, and that the advertising techniques used to create consumer behaviour results in an addictive cycle of consumption, leading to hyperconsumption (Stiegler, 2006).

This has obviously worked in favour of the big capital. However, such obsession for individual acquisition and status has today threatened the very concepts of society or community. Simultaneously, and more significantly, with this, the ultimate objective of the project of a consumerist culture, i.e., the de-politicization of culture is also being largely accomplished. The projection of culture merely as a means of cheap entertainment segregating it from its actual context has had a corrosive effect on it which has progressively stifled not only the ingenuous creative potential of culture but has also undermined its most important role as a unifying and mobilizing force. This has produced a new threat to the developing societies and the danger of becoming subservient to the global imperialist design looms large on many of them and for many it has already become a reality. Thus, culture in the contemporary world has become an important component of domination – both of and within developing societies. Culture has become not only a mask to hide but also a sword to achieve imperialist goals (Panikkar, 1995: 374).

Indeed, the culture industry in the capitalist West during the last couple of decades has undergone transformation beyond recognition. A very large quantum of capital has gone into this industry. Aided by the revolutionary advances in the field of electronics, the cultural products created by the capitalist industry have reached nooks and corners of the globe transcending national boundaries like never before. The manner in which capital transcends national boundaries in pursuit of more profit, cultural products also need to be transmitted across nations. This cultural aggrandizement is intimately related with economic exploitation and political and military domination. Hence, cultural imperialism is the order of the day.

Culture as Commodity

That culture can be used to such an effect is pointed out much earlier by Theodor Adorno and Max Horkheimer when they coined the term 'culture industry' in their critique of 'mass culture', the *Dialectic of Enlightenment* (1947). They conclude that the total effect of the culture industry is one of anti-enlightenment, in which, enlightenment, that is, the progressive technical domination of nature becomes mass deception and is turned into a means for fettering consciousness. It impedes the development of autonomous, independent individuals who judge and decide consciously for themselves. In his important essay, 'Culture Industry Reconsidered', Adorno writes:

> ... The culture industry fuses the old and familiar into a new quality. In all its branches, products which are tailored for consumption by masses, and which to a great extent determine the nature of that consumption, are manufactured more or less according to plan ... made possible by contemporary technical capabilities as well as by economic and administrative concentration. The culture industry intentionally integrates its consumers from above. To the detriment of both, it forces together the spheres of high and low art, separated for thousands of years. The seriousness of high art is destroyed in speculation about its efficacy; the seriousness of the lower perishes with the civilisational constraints imposed on the rebellious resistance inherent within it as long as social control was not yet total. Thus, although the culture industry undeniably speculates on the conscious and unconscious state of the millions towards which it is directed, the masses are not primary, but secondary, they are an object of calculation; an appendage of the machinery. The customer is not king, as the culture industry would have us believe, not its subject but its object ... (1991/2000: 85)

Though one may question Adorno's separation of culture into 'high' and 'low' in the light of the expositions of the contemporary cultural theories, the trivialization of culture and the nature of its relationship with masses that Adorno identifies can hardly be ignored. Adorno also clearly points out the role of the mass media in the process when he said, "the very word mass-media (is) specially honed for the culture industry ..." (ibid.: 85) in which "neither is it a question of primary concern for the masses, nor of the techniques of communication as such but of the spirit which sufflates them, their master's voice" (ibid.: 85–86). Under the culture industry regime, the cultural commodities of the industry are governed by the principle of their realization as value, and not by their own specific content and harmonious formation. The entire practice of the culture industry transfers the profit motive naked onto cultural forms.

Project of Cultural Homogenization

Culture is thus turned into a commodity just like any other commodities in the market. Obviously, the expansion of demand for uniform cultural products on a planetary basis has brought rich dividend for the big capital. The US being the predominant contemporary imperialist power has profited most from the contemporary cultural globalization. It is not a mere coincidence that almost all the major players in today's culture industry from visuals to victuals (Hollywood, Disneyland, Coca-Cola, McDonald's, etc.) are American ["Many of the most visible cultural expressions of globalization are American" – Giddens (1999)] and in the name of global culture what is being imposed on us is actually the American culture, and mostly its trivial, version.

In the very first page of his most well-known work *Primitive Culture* (1871/2010), the British anthropologist E.B. Tylor provides an all-inclusive definition of culture as follows: "Culture, or civilization, taken in its broad, ethnographic sense, is that complex whole which includes knowledge, belief, art, morals, law, custom, and any other capabilities and habits acquired by man as a member of society". The constituents of culture, however, do not take shape in vacuum. They emerge out of the prolonged interaction of man with his specific environment, both physical and social. Hence, though culture is universal, it is also space and time specific. Therefore, any attempt at arriving at a definition of a 'global' or 'world' culture is a problematic exercise, if not untenable. However, though the postmodern wisdom does not allow us to speak of anything essential, one may still argue for a global culture as an expression of the universal human spirit running through numerous local cultures. In this sense, the existence of the so-called global culture can be perceived only through local cultures. This is because while the global culture is an abstract concept the local cultures can be perceived through its various elements, tangible or intangible.

Besides, it is to be recognized that the local cultures are not innocent, undifferentiated categories. They too have dominant, elite elements as opposed to subaltern, folk elements in them representing prevailing social hierarchies. To ignore such realities would be tantamount to endorsing a notion of global culture which would accentuate the process of domination of not only of one culture over others but also within particular cultures. Yet, the project of cultural globalization, seeks to homogenize all cultural differences and diversities through standardization of human tastes, values and preferences in the mould of the dominant culture. One can well imagine what a homogenized 'global' culture would be like without any substantive linkage with the specific geo-economic contexts that characterises culture.

Here, it is relevant to recall T.S. Eliot's attempt at conceptualizing 'world culture' more than six decades back. He contends:

> (A) world culture which was simply a uniform culture would be no culture at all. We should have a humanity de-humanised. It would be a nightmare. But on the other hand, we cannot resign the idea of world-culture altogether. ... We are therefore pressed to maintain the idea of a world-culture, while admitting that it is something we cannot imagine. We can only conceive it as the logical term of relations between cultures. ... We must aspire to a common world culture, which will yet not diminish the particularity of the constituent parts. (1948: 62–63)

Referring to the significance of local cultures in a national context (in this case that of England), he says:

> (T)o many it has never occurred to reflect that the disappearance of the peripheral cultures of England (to say nothing of the most humble local peculiarities within England itself) might be a calamity. We have not given enough attention to the ecology of cultures. It is probable, I think, that complete uniformity of culture throughout these islands would bring about a lower degree of culture altogether. ... For a national culture, if it is to flourish, should be a constellation of cultures, the constituents of which, benefiting each other, benefit the whole. (Eliot, 1948: 58)

Surely, Eliot's treatment of the term 'peripheral cultures' as a constituent of 'national culture' betrays his own conservatism as he ignores the fact that the 'national culture' itself might well be a 'hegemonic local culture'. Nevertheless, it is quite clear that Eliot was opposed to the treatment of 'world culture' as a 'uniform culture' in the mould of the above-mentioned dominant culture.

However, it appears that the phrase 'dominant culture' may not necessarily be located in the cultural life of a particular people. However, the cultural symbols of the latter may appear to be most prominent in it as the case with what is called the 'American culture'. The 'dominant culture' in the context of cultural globalization is constituted mostly by the cheaper, trivialized version of western popular cultural products produced and disseminated by the mass media, controlled by the big capital and dedicated to the service of the latter. The real spirit of the western culture does not have much to do with it. It is noteworthy that globalization has scarcely promoted the serious elements of the western/American culture or the alternative discourses within it. In other words, the 'dominant culture' is created and used by the ruling class of the west (implying generally the US) "in order to reorder the values, behaviour, institutions, and identity of the oppressed peoples to conform to the interests of the imperial class" (Petras, 1993: 140).

The advocates of globalization would argue that many of the cultural forms and artifacts that are being globalized today are not American (Giddens would go as far as to describe this phenomenon as 'reverse colonization'). Neither Salsa nor Shakira's music, for example, are American but Latin American. While apparently that is true, a little reflection would make it clear that though both these cultural forms are of the Latin American origin, and especially Salsa in the US imparts a Latino identity to its immigrants from northern South America, their commercial proliferation all over the world would not have been possible without the support of the US media which benefit the most from such proliferation. Besides, the character of these cultural forms is such that with little modification they can be made fully congruent with the dominant cultural domain that the US imperialist capital seeks to create and promote across the globe. In other words, though these cultural products are of Latin American origin they have been fully appropriated by the US capitalist interest. Again, it is also to be noted that what is being disseminated in different parts of the world as Latino product, the case of Salsa, for example, has hardly retained their original form and content. Suffice it to say that Salsa, a popular cultural product in northern Latin America which often functions(ed) as a symbol of Latino pride, becomes a cultural identity marker for the *nouveau riche* in the countries like India. Perhaps more importantly, these cultural products have now returned to their roots with totally new import!

Nevertheless, refuting the allegation that globalization will lead to a levelling and degradation of culture, to a diminution of cultural diversity, Tyler Cowen, for example, an eminent proponent of globalization, along with Eric Crampton, contends that trade of cultural products and influences will, in fact, increase cultural diversity within societies, even while it may reduce it across them. Societies will become more alike in offering the same 'rich menu of choices' to their people. They argue, "(the) American culture is accused of swamping world markets and stifling other cultural products. The evidence instead shows that cross-cultural trade provides a varied menu of choice. The larger the global market in culture, the greater the diversity of artists it supports. Wealthy customers buy international art ranging from reggae to hand-woven textiles. And the spread of technology has boosted, for example, Hong Kong cinema, Cuban popular music, and Australian aboriginal painting" (Cowen and Crampton, 2001: 28–29). Globalized culture, Cowen asserts, "far from representing the triumph of consumerism or the debasement of taste, is a gale of 'creative destruction', blowing away the obsolete and the outworn to make room for the robust, the novel, the various, and the re-fashioned" (Cowen, 2002). Reality, however, presents an opposite picture. Not only does globalization fail to offer us the diverse choice as Cowen highlights, the existing cultural choices also seem to fast disappear as a result of it pushing us "into an orbit of shallow consumerist culture" (Saxena, 2003: 87).

Cowen (2002) further tells us that most cultures are in constant change, but critics are commonly opposed to this diversity in time, displaying a preference for stasis. While nobody disputes that the nature of a culture or an identity changes over time like any other phenomena, the issue at stake is the nature of this change. When cultural changes are gradual and the changes retain linkages with their social milieu, people generally accord legitimacy to such cultural changes as it is more or less in tune with their changing social life. Sometimes majority people in a cultural milieu themselves clamour for changes in their cultural practices or institutions which they find oppressive or dated. But when such changes are not only unasked and drastic but also unanchored with the social milieu of a people, they threaten to upset the existing social relationships to the point of confusion and chaos. It is this eventuality which has today beset all people, especially the smaller and marginal ones, of the world. To quote Giddens again,

> (A)s the changes (brought about by globalization) ... gather weight, they are ... shaking up our existing ways of life, no matter where we happen to be. This is not – at least at the moment – a global order driven by collective human will. Instead, it is emerging in an anarchic, haphazard fashion, carried along by a mixture of economic, technological and cultural imperatives. (1999)

This anarchic state is insidiously pervasive in the contemporary world. The root of this anarchy lies at the rise of extreme individualism propagated by the mass media and the simultaneous waning of the concept of community. Giddens, however, attributes such a predicament to the incapacity of our existing institutions and thus calls for their reconstruction as well as creation of new ones "in ways appropriate to the global age" (1999). What Giddens refrains from telling us is the role of the global capitalist forces in weakening these institutions by manoeuvring them to serve their narrow objectives. Without any elucidation on that his call sounds more like a prescription to the common masses to mend their ways in accordance with the conditions created by the contemporary globalizing forces. That he speaks of achieving a "greater control over our runaway world" appears nothing short of an irony.

References

Adorno, T. (1991/2000) "Culture Industry Reconsidered", in *The Culture Industry: Selected Essays on Mass Culture*, London: Routledge.

Adorno, T. and M. Horkheimer (1947/1993) "The Culture Industry: Enlightenment as Mass Deception", in *Dialectic of Enlightenment*, New York: Continuum.

Castells, M. (1994) "European Cities, the Informational Society, and the Global Economy", *New Left Review*, Vol. 204.

Cowen, T. (2002) *Creative Destruction: How Globalization is Changing the World's Cultures*. Princeton, NJ: Princeton University Press.

Cowen, T. and E. Crampton (2001) "Uncommon Culture", *Foreign Policy*, No. 125 (July–August), Carnegie Endowment for International Peace.

Eliot, T.S. (1948) *Notes towards a Definition of Culture*. London: Faber & Faber.

Giddens, A. (1999) 'Globalization', Lecture 1 delivered in London under the BBC's Reith Lectures under the title *Runaway World*.

Gramsci, A. (1978) "Some Aspects on the Southern Question", in *Selections from Political Writings*, London: Lawrence and Wishart.

Panikkar, K.N. (1995) "Culture and Globalization: A Non-Issue at World Summit on Social Development", *Economic and Political Weekly*, Vol. XXX, Nos. 7 and 8.

Petras, J. (1993) "Cultural Imperialism in the Late 20th Century", *Journal of Contemporary Asia*, Vol. 23, No. 2.

Petras, J. and H. Veltmeyer (2001) *Globalization Unmasked: Imperialism in the 21st Century*. Delhi: Madhyam Books.

Robins, K. (1996) "Globalization", in A. Kuper and J. Kuper (eds.), *The Social Science Encyclopedia* (2nd edition), London: Routledge.

Saxena, R. (2003) "Globalization and Culture: Politics and Paradoxes of Transition", in C.K. Sharma (ed.), *Culture Studies: Themes and Perspectives*, NEACTAF: Tezpur University.

Stiegler, B. (2006) "The Disaffected Individual", translated from French by Patrick Crogan and Daniel Ross.

Tylor, E.B. (1871/2010) *Primitive Culture: Researches into the Development of Mythology, Philosophy, Religion, Art, and Custom*. New York: G.P. Putnam's Sons.

Veblen, T. (1899/1994) *The Theory of the Leisure Class: An Economic Study of Institutions*. Mineola, New York: Dover Publications.

Wallerstein, I. (1974/2000) "The World System", in John Beynon and David Dunkerley (eds.), *Globalization: The Reader*, London: The Athlone Press.

13

Globalization and Its Impact on Culture

B.K. Nagla

Globalization is as fascinating a term these days as modernization, development and change have been during the 20th century. To think of the world as a global village was once a daydreamer's delight. Not anymore, instead the end of the 20th century will be remembered for bringing the dream of globalization to reality. On the one side, several outcomes of this transformation are within the reach of a large number of human beings. Availability of fax machine and internet facility are its examples. Who could have thought of its widespread availability in India three decades ago? Globalization as a trend would create its impact on each area of human activity.

On the other side, the process of globalization has generated universal disenchantment. Those who applaud its arrival are few. Disenchantment prevails not only in the developing but also in the developed world. It needs to be analysed as to what lies at the root of such disenchantment.

In this context, the present paper will examine first, historical perspective of globalization. Second, it will examine the notions or concepts of globalization and localization and how this can be conceptualized as well as its relationships between the global and the local. Third, it will look at the theories of globalization. Finally, it will examine the implications of looking at the impact of globalization on culture.

Globalization: Historical Perspective

Globalization is an outcome of the universal logic of modernity. Anthony Giddens (1990) assumes that globalization is the corollary of modernity. The implication of the modernity/globalization view is that the history of globalization begins with the history of West. But it is not precisely the point of globalization as a perspective that globalization begins with world history. However, the time frame of some of the perspectives is as follows:

Author	*Time Period*	*Perspective*
Marx	1500s	Modern capitalism
Wallerstein	1500s	Modern world system
Robertson	1870–1920s	Multidimensional
Giddens	1900s	Modernity
Tomilson	1960s	Cultural pluralization

Source: Nederveen Pieterse, Jan, 'Globalization as Hybridization' in M. Featherstone et al., *Global Modernity* (1995).

Thus, globalization is an objective, all-embracing historical process which began with the breakthrough of capitalism in some countries of Western Europe, notablaly England, in the early decades of the 19th century. From almost its inception, it developed along with colonialism and later in the century, blossomed fully as imperialism.

The globalization process of that period aggravated inequality through exploiting the socio-technical inferiority of the pre-capitalist systems prevalent in the larger part of the world. An important part of that exploitation was the literal ruination of the productive forces of the countries which were its objects, including the direct producers. It was against such backdrop that the national revolutions of the colonial, semi-colonial and 'dependent' countries were directed. Even before the victory of these revolutions, the globalizers had to beat a retreat and effect compromises.

The Myth of Globalization

Allen and Massey (1995: 3) have demonstrated that images of globalization are often compelling and suggestive, emphasizing certain aspects while neglecting or underplaying others; they are, in effect, distorted.

> (T)here appears to be a number of globalization, a number of worlds, taking shape. There is the globalization of telecommunication, the globalization of finance, the globalization of culture ... the globalization of environmental concerns, and that of the struggles of indigenous peoples. Moreover, the networks of connections that each lays down do not map one to the other, some parts of the world are densely highlighted in some accounts, but not in others.

Allen (1995: 110–17) discusses three types of globalization, viz., economic, political and cultural.

The *economic globalization* focuses on the global market where borders are crossed and distances travelled with minimal effort by firms, currencies and commodities.

The rhetoric of *political globalization* is that of the continuing erosion of the nation-state's powers and abilities to control or regulate an increasingly volatile and uncertain global world in the face of many changes; for instance, environmental risks or the rise of transnational organizations on the world stage.

Cultural globalization refers to the homogenization and hybridization of worldwide culture. The basis for this is supposedly the new technologies of communication. These are said to unsettle and loosen more traditional cultural ties, influences and established lifestyle codes, thereby exposing localities to different consumer styles, with the message that to consume is to be a pat of one (western) world. Demand is produced by the global marketing of cultural styles and symbols and is met by global standardization of products. But such a homogenizing view of a global culture is false in two main ways. First, it is presented in a monolithic manner: we do not understand and value consumer products or American entertainment in the same way (Allen, 1995: 117). Second, rather than eroding local differences, global consumerism has to work through them, exploring local differences in order to market them on a wider scale. Additionally, a global culture based on the consumption of western styles and symbols is one that has to be bought into, which for a substantial part of the world's population is not possible. Such a view also underexplores the influence of migration on culture and the creation of multicultural societies.

Globalization: Conceptualization

Globally, globalization, globalism – these are all ambiguous words that have come into common usage since 1980s, but have only been part of the social science vocabulary since the early 1980s. Despite the relative newness of this language, it abounds in the literature on the international relations, sociology and human geography and is creeping into the lexicon of social scientists studying the nature of global environmental change.

Globalization refers to various multidimensional socio-economic and political processes by which the people of the world are incorporated into a single world society, a global village. It tends to homogenize the cultures as well as popularize even unknown cultures of the world. It acts as hetrogenizer with a possibility of pluralism. Globalization strives to make the world as its market where all the people are being brought as buyers and sellers on unequal terms.

Globalization also implies the multiplicity of linkages and interconnectedness that transcend the nation-state and by implications the societies which make up the modern world system. It reflects a process through which events, decisions and activities in one part of the world would have significant consequences for individuals and communities of quite distant parts of the globe. However, for Anthony Giddens, globalization embraces much more than a notion of simple interconnectedness. For him, "globalization concerns the intersection of the presence and absence, the interlocking of social events and social relations at a distance with local contextualties" (1990).

Globalization may also be understood as a dialectical phenomenon in which events at one pole having distance relation often produce divergent or even contrary occurrence at another. While communication and information are increasingly diffused on a global scale, the individuals locally appropriate these inherently in contextual and hermeneutic way. Globalization thus becomes glocalization.

Globalization and Localization

Tim O'Riordan and Chris Church (2001) discuss the perspective of globalization and localization. Globalization and localization unite at all spatial scales.

Globalization and localization are processes of change that impact on economies, cultures and environments in ways that are both global and local. Such changes may take place at any scale and at any level of social organization. Globalism and localism are socially and politically framed interpretations of these changes that have meaning through processes of personal experience, patterns of trust, connectivities of reciprocity, and social networks of interest and bias. These two discourses entwine to form social identity, the basis for self-actualization and the bedrock of any transition to sustainability. Globalism and localism are processes of responsiveness and adaptability that are mediated and defined by various institutional arrangements and swirling patterns of expectations.

Theories of Globalization

Theoretically, there are many precursors to the concept of globalization. Three of the main approaches are: world systems theory; globalization is an outcome of modernity; and globalization as a dual process which centres on culture.

World Systems Theory

Globalization from the perspective of a world system is associated largely with the work of Immanuel Wallerstein. His world systems theory is involved principally with the global capitalist economy and combines a sociological and historical look at its development and maintenance, arguing that it is created by a single 'division of labour' – more complex, extensive, detailed and cohesive than ever before. This body of work posits that the world system consists of three worlds: a centre or core, a semi-periphery and a periphery. There are many criticisms of this approach but the most pertinent is that it represents only a mono-causal explanation of globalization.

Modernization and Globalization

In a general way, the concept of globalization is best understood as expressing fundamental aspects of time-space distinction (namely, the condition under which time and space are organized). Globalization concerns the intersection of presence and absence, the interacting of social events and social relations 'at distance' with local contextualities. We should grasp the global spread of modernity in terms of an ongoing relation between distanciation and the chronic mutability of local circumstances and local engagements: "... globalization has to be understood as a dialectical phenomenon" (Giddens, 1991: 22–23).

Globalization can thus be defined as the intensification of worldwide social relations which link distant localities in such a way that local happenings are shaped by events occurring many miles away and vice versa: "... Local transformation is as much a part of globalization as the lateral extension of social connections across time and space" (Giddens, 1990: 64).

Giddens (ibid.: 7) puts social relations at the centre of his analysis, which comprises four areas:

1. the world capitalist economy,
2. the nation-state system,
3. the world military order, and

4. the international division of labour.

These relate to four institutional dimensions of modernity within which the processes of globalization take place:

1. capitalism,
2. surveillance,
3. military power, and
4. industrialism.

Giddens (ibid.: 55–56) sees capitalism and industrialism as two different dimensions. Capitalism relates owners to capital wage labour; industrialism applies to the link between people and the natural world, including the environment. In this analysis, it is modern institutions, such as money, that are globalizing as they dissembled mechanisms, lifting relations out of local contexts and enabling them to take place across the globe in a manner that was previously regarded as inconceivable.

Criticism of this approach centres on the complexity of this multidimensionality, as well as its failure to provide any specific implications that arise from these globalizing processes, rendering it a "descriptive, nominalistic definition approach to global-level phenomenon" (Yearley, 1966: 16). For Robertson (1992: 145), globalization is not just an outcome of the western project of modernity as Giddens claims. Giddens is also criticized for not taking cultural matters seriously enough.

Culture and Dual Processes

Milton (1996: 215) has examined the theoretical approaches from the perspective of culture, defined as "consisting of everything we know, think and feel about the world". She distinguishes between those who refer to globalization as the way world is seen or imagined, defined as cultural phenomenon, and those who refer to events going on in the world, which although dialectically related to culture are not part of it. The two approaches already discussed come in the latter category, where Robertson treats globalization as occurring both outside and inside culture: "Globalization as a concept refers both to the compression of the world and the intensification of consciousness of the world as a whole" (1992: 8). In this sense, globalization is a dual arrangement, not just events taking place in the world, but also through cultural transformations.

The Global Transformation of Culture

The increased frequency of communications across the globe has been a recurrent theme of the 20th century. Empirically, globalization has broken down cultural boundaries through the wide availability of air travel, the accessibility of telecommunications and the promotion of the mass tourism. The term 'global culture' now implies both the development of a cultural cosmopolitanism spanning the globe and the re-deployment of cultural consciousness for accentuating specific identities in global conflicts.

In the first instance, the worldwide dissemination of modern values and practices has taken its toll on the traditionalisms of many non-western societies.

In the second instance, globalization has reinforced boundaries through the politicization of specific group interests.

In the contemporary West there is a growing sense that culture, as traditionally understood, has lost its anchors. There are at least two senses to this crisis. *The commodity form* that Eagleton speaks of refers in the first place of the global spread of western capitalism and the consequences of its cultural hegemony. An irony of this development is that the relentless drive of western capitalist interest around the world has not only left a trail of territorial conquests and exploitation, but also an indelible imprint of western culture in many foreign lands. For example, English and its cultural expressions are no longer the exclusive property of the British; their variations are found in those parts of the world once under British imperial rule.

In the second sense, imperialist culture becomes an agent of its own levelling. It falls victim to the commodity form that spearheads the marketing of modernity. It is this form that belittles cultural referents, even swallowing them up to the extent that culture can only exist as sign in reference to other signs, a simulacrum without origin (Baudrillard, 1981). We see this in the cultural experiences engendered by the spread of fast food chains and amusement theme parks around the world. Ritzer calls it the McDonaldization of society which "encompasses such disparate phenomena as fast food restaurants, TV dinners, packaged tours, industrial robots, plea bargaining and open heart surgery on an assembly-line basis". This type of consciousness is becoming more widespread with the development of mass tourism.

Global Consciousness

Global consciousness has begun to dawn on the world community. People are getting more and more familiar with others staying in different parts of the globe. In larger countries, not only they now know more about their fellow citizens, and their customs, traditions, cultures, etc., they are also getting familiar with different heritages, trends, practices and also faiths and beliefs. Peoples world over are more becoming conscious of their rights. They are familiar with situations where human rights are respected. They also know where these are being violated and by whom. With more and more getting educated, even those who have suffered for ages on social and economic or cultural fronts would not take these violations lying down. Communications do not keep quite when human rights are violated in different situations. More than preserving one's own rights, one has to ensure that the rights of others are not treaded upon.

Global consciousness would imply respect for others. One has every right to consider one's community, religion and culture as 'neumero uno'. At the same time, one must concede that others also have a familiar right. Each culture and each religion has a basic right to treat itself as the very best. Such an approach should not lead to conflicting situations, if it is reasonable and considerate. We all know that there are difficulties in following such an approach in actual practice. With the gradual internationalization of global consciousness these would hopefully vanish in near future.

Globalization has given rise to apprehension of various types. There are cultures which are trying to remain insulated from the information, super-highways and media explosion. There are instances where TV sets have been thrown out of the windows to prevent the young and impressionable from getting corrupted by the evil influence of alien cultures. How far that would succeed is debatable. It is, however, clear that global consciousness would never favour single culture, one religion or a single way of life. Life would be really pretty dull and colourless if this 'unimaginable' unification actually takes place at any stage. Human beings need to see the full spectrum of all cultures, traditions and religions. Each one of these should have its distinct place and identity. Only that would make this globe a fascinating place.

Globalization and Its Impact on Culture

There are many-levels, theoretically, at which the relationship between the process of globalization and the responses of the local cultures can be analysed. In the postmodern era, the new approach focuses on local, particularistic and reflexive dimensions of culture (see Lyotard, 1987; Dilthey, 1988).

The system of communication has affected or surpassed the boundaries of nation-state; at the same time, they have affected local culture and social forms such as family, neighbourhood and community, and also created forms of social anomie. The system of the folk culture and folk societies due to *marketization of economy* and *commodification of production* in agriculture converts 'peasants' into 'farmers' eroding the traditional cultural patterns.

Globalization: The Indian Perspective

Globalization, competitiveness and liberalization came to India as a booster and through the backdoor of economic reforms. The sanctity of economic reforms had been derived from it. It was argued that the progress is taking place through globalization and economic reforms. Globalization, as a phenomenon, involves access to two different entities:

1. finance capital through MNCs, and
2. new technologies such as computers and telecommunications.

It was viewed that the growth and internationalization of finance capital is good and desirable for projects because it promotes growth of technology. Globalization provides a useful means to develop technologies, which are necessary for the production of goods and services that improve our well-being.

We are becoming 'Netizens' making our friendship with unknown persons across the world neglecting our next-door neighbour. Globalizing panic like AIDS has affected our psychic. A hybridized culture without any root is reshaping us to fit into the globalization process. We want or not, the powerful globalization process has been encircling us.

In political sphere, an international managerial bourgeoisie or transnational capital class, often referred as 'comprador', has been solidifying the power of consumerist culture. They are the cohorts of the MNCs. Coca-Colization or McDonaldization has brought in their world market.

The communication media has fuelled a growing awareness of the interconnectedness and interdependency. It is nourishing a sense of responsibility, however, fragile for a humanity that is commonly shared.

The process of globalization and its impact on culture, both local and national, give it a new urgency. In most studies of cultural change in India, the significance of locality and local culture and its relationship with the nation-state and the national culture has been widely recognized.

When the processes of economic development and social development have been extended, the importance of local culture and the particularistic expression of ideology and sentiments have been taken note of in formulation of the public policies as well as in the analysis of nation-state.

The impact that globalization may bring about in society may be discussed under the following heads:

1. market, trade and finance,
2. communication and media,
3. science and technology, and
4. migration and inter-cultural transactions.

There are also related issues of tourism, migration of professionals and the emergence of diasporic sub-culture.

In structural terms, globalization is a historical process of transition from agrarian to industrial, post-industrial and finally to the stage of information society (Dissananyake, 1988). As stated earlier, it strives to make the world as its market where all the people are being brought as buyers and sellers in unequal terms.

The Impact of Global Trade and Market on Culture

The scope of trade and market, which was accelerated by the process of globalization, poses formidable cultural problems in both developed and developing societies. In India, which traditionally had quite a developed base of trade and market, the impact of the changing role of these institutions has been gradual. The market and trade relations continue to be located in local cultures even today (Ostor, 1980). The economic policy of India up to 1980s has also been that of import substitution and protectionism in trade and market.

In India, the process of globalization gained momentum in the 1990s, but many checks and balances continue to persist. Globalization brought changes which altered the traditional mode of cultural expression, usage of language and communication media at the local, regional and national levels. These have also created new sub-culture in urban areas. The rise of popular culture is a new phenomenon with linkages both in rural and urban centres. Most of these changes have long been in the process of emergence and crystallization. The forces of industrialization and developments in agriculture had impact on the consumption style of people.

The green revolution during the 1970s gave spurt to changes in the consumption style of villagers. The NSS data shows noticeable decline in consumption of cereals both by rich and poor. The shift is towards consumption of milk, poultry and meat products. The electrification in the villages has changed the energy pattern. The use of kerosene oil is widespread. Gobar gas and solar energy are also making dent into villages. The expansion of road networks and means of transport have brought about some homogenization in tastes and consumption patterns, such as increased popularity of tea, coffee, egg, meat and fish.

A remarkable change in the styles and pattern of women's wear has also taken place. It is marked by a shift from *saris* to *salwar-suits*. Culturally speaking, the new changes may not have deeply subversive effect upon the core traditional values or the world view of the people.

Yet, one witnesses periodic incidence of consumer resistance against multinationals promoting new consumer goods or agro-products, e.g., sporadic movements against products like McDonald's hamburger and Kentucky fried chickens. Farmers are resisting the penetration of agro-multinationals in production of seeds, herb's new cereals, etc.

The average number of occupations per community stands at 5.3, of which 1.8 in traditional and 3.5 in the newly acquired occupation (Singh, 1992). Economists have also observed substantial rise in non-agricultural occupations in the countryside.

Globalization is, however, just in a state of beginning in India. Some of its effects upon the local cultures, for example, globalization of markets, have led to conversion of traditional objects or art and aesthetic having mostly ritual use in the local communities into marketable commodities. This has not only rapidly disrupted the autonomy of folk culture, but also destabilized the life of the artisans by creating new networks of competition and price war and a new class of exploitative middle class. In other areas, such as access of local communities to forest resources, land and rivers, hills and lakes, all of which were bounded together in a long enduring cultural ecology of rituals and customs, the penetration of market for profit has started a rapid subversion of ecology.

Globalization has also disrupted the balance in cultural, social and economic life of tribals, artisans, traditional cultural performers, etc. Being in minority and economically vulnerable, these communities suffer loss of their cultural identity, in the process of globalization.

Globalization of Communication, Media and Culture

The electronic media and modes of communication, such as radio, television, computer network via satellites, paging services, telephony, electronic mail and internet web, etc., have revolutionized the banking, trade and management practices, uses of culture and leisure, and most other modes of intercultural and inter-group communicative actions. Most of these media transcend the territorial national cultural boundaries. They may function beyond the sovereignty of the nation-state, and offer individuals enormous amount of choices and freedom in matters of cultural and ideological performances.

The notions of time, space and symbolism of culture undergo new transformation of meanings under the impact of these new telecommunication technologies. Its impact on cultures – local, regional and national – is multifaceted and can be integrative as well as disruptive.

Science and Technology

We are being encircled by some visible and invisible powerful global forces day by day. Its hegemony empowered with hyper-technology and enormous economic resources. From aeroplanes to computer chips, we are using many global products produced by MNCs. In this context, a pervasive global culture as the ideology of consumerism has been knocking every moment on our door. It has occupied a substantial space in our society. A powerful media has been trying to negate our identity to hallow or alter our daily life pattern.

Migration and Intercultural Transactions

Globalization also accelerates the process of migration, tourism and travel. Its cultural and social homogenizing effects progress along with creation of pluralism and cultural diversity. Tourism in India is oriented more to religious pilgrimages combined with sight-seeing and for leisure. Over a period of time, it has strengthened the festive and celebrative activities of various religious groups and communities. And, its diffusion effect has been very strong.

Globalization and Change: Polity, Integration and Identity

The process of globalization has triggered off forces of change which have set people's rethinking about the political institutions such as state, democracy and civil society. In their functioning, the role of cultural pluralism and protection of local cultures is now particularly recognized both in terms of institutional mechanism and as an element of political morality or value system. New thinking is taking place about the changing role of nation-state, its sovereignty and the role of political party, etc., under the growing forces of globalization (Kothari, 1995; Apter, 1941, quoted from Singh, 2000; etc.).

Global Culture

Arjun Appadurai (1990) explains three things for the understanding of global culture: (i) ethnoscope, (ii) technoscope, and (iii) mediascope.

1. *Ethnoscope* is landscope of persons who constitute the shifting world in which we live. For example, tourists, immigrants, refugees, exiles and other moving groups and persons.
2. *Technoscope* is the global configuration of technology that moves at high speed across various kinds of boundaries.
3. *Mediascope* refers to the distribution of the electronic capabilities to produce and disseminate information which are now available throughout the world.

Appadurai says that the combination of ethnoscope, technoscope and mediascope leads to the globalization of culture.

T.K. Oommen (1998) refers to the birth of a 'new world society' by the impact of globalization on culture. He posits that the consequences of globalization could be discerned through four interrelated and interacting processes: homogenization, pluralization, traditionalization and hybridization.

1. *Homogenization:* The more visible aspect of homogenization is that cultural context which manifests in evolving a common lifestyle and consumption pattern, e.g., dress (e.g., Jeans), food (McDonald's), music (Michael Jackson), etc. These are confined to urban population living in metropolitan cities. However, homogenization is more popular in certain other contexts of nuclear family, monogamous marriages, parliamentary democracy, private property and western technology. These institutional arrangements were initiated in colonial era but got momentum in the process of globalization. The homogenization process is characterized by *displacement syndrome,* that is, movement towards homogenization is taking place through the process of displacement. For example, south Indians are wearing *pyjama* instead of *lungi.*
2. *Pluralization:* Pluralization is accompanied by *accretion syndrome.* Pluralization concedes and commends the co-existence of a variety of consumption and institutional patterns. For example, along with McDonald's, other modern variety of junk food and Michael Jackson's music with other recent styles of pop music became too accommodated. This partial change and partial persistence gives rise to pluralization.
3. *Traditionalization:* The *hegemonizing* tendency of globalization gives birth to a loss of meaning and an erosion of identity to the non-West. This leads to the resurrection of roots, a search for identity which reflects a process of traditionalization accompanied by *revivalistic syndrome.* However, this tendency is not confined to the non-West. *Americanization* is resisted even by Europeans, particularly the French. Sometimes, the response for modernity takes the form of cultural revival. This also results in the re-invention of tradition. This emerges not only the religious fundamentalism but also religious freedom.
4. *Hybridization:* The process of hybridization refers to the *mutation syndrome.* The cross-breeding of traditional and modern, the local and the global gives birth to hybridization. Hybridization creates new cultural elements and social patterns which are neither traditional nor global. Hybridization is different from pluralization in which neither co-existence nor elaboration. It is an effort to innovate breakout of cultural and social dead ends. It is simultaneous engagement with both the tradition and modernity, and the local and global. This is the evidence of contemporary institutional arrangements and consumption pattern. The mutation between the local and the global leads to hybridization as is evident in music, art forms and goods items; for example, vegetarian hamburger, Indian rap music, European curry, Japanese pasta, and numerous other examples suggest the relentless march of hybridization. But affluent and powerful polities dominate over the weak and small cultural sections.

Challenges of Globalization

Yogendra Singh (2004) discusses two types of challenges: first, challenges of economic development; and second, challenges of identity.

(i) *Challenges of Economic Development:* The tensions and anxieties on account of globalization are primarily economic which spill over to the anxieties about culture and identity.

Economic development in a balanced manner holds the key to our ability to meet the challenges of globalization and accommodate the upsurge of identities.

(ii) *Challenges of Identity:* Globalization almost everywhere has given rise to a newer and sharper self-consciousness of identity. Such consciousness tends to be pervasive; it is not confined to the cultural minorities, local cultures, ethnic groups, tribes or weaker sections. The identity consciousness and anxiety about preservation of cultural identity extends also in the relationships between nations.

For reasons of history, pluralistic social structure and culture and the democratic path of development that we have adopted, we enjoy tremendous resilience to meet the challenges of globalization.

References

Allen, J. (1995) "Global Worlds", in J. Allen and D. Massey (eds.), *Geographical Worlds*, Oxford: Oxford University Press, pp. 121–43.

Allen, J. and A. Massey (eds.) (1995) *Geographical Worlds*. Oxford: Oxford University Press.

Appadurai, Arjun (1990) "De-juncture and Difference in the Global Cultural Economy", in Mike Featherstone (ed.), *Global Culture: Nationalism, Globalization and Modernity*, London: Sage.

Baudrillard, Jean (1981) *Simulacres et Simulation*. Paris: Galilee.

Day, G. and J. Murdoch (1993). "Locality and Community, Coming to Terms with Place", *The Sociological Review*, Vol. 7, pp. 82–111.

Dilthey, W. (1988) *Introduction to the Human Sciences* (tr. R.J. Bentazps), London: Harvester Wheatsheaf.

Dissananyake, W. (1988) "Communication, Knowledge and a Post-Industrial Society: The Need for Values-centred Approach", in Christian Academy (ed.), *World Community in Post-Industrial Society*, Seoul: Wooseok Publishing Co.

Featherstone, M. (ed.) (1990) *Global Culture: Nationalism, Globalization and Modernity*. London: Sage.

Giddens, A. (1990) *The Consequences of Modernity*. Cambridge: Polity Press.

—— (1991) *Modernity and Self-Identity: Self and Society in the Late Modern Age*. Cambridge: Polity Press.

Kothari, Rajni (1995) "Globalization and Revival of Tradition: Dual Attack on Model of Democratic Nation-Building", *Economic and Political Weekly*, March 25.

Lyotard, J.F. (1987) *The Postmodern Conditions: A Report on Knowledge* (tr. G. Bennigtomn and B. Massumi), Manchester: Manchester University Press.

Milton, K. (1996) "Environmentalism and Cultural Theory: Exploring the Role of Anthropology", in *Environmental Discourse*, London: Routledge.

Oommen, T.K. (1998) "Emerging Diversity: Birth of a New World Society", *Times of India*, October 30.

O'Riordan, Tim (2001) *Globalism, Localism and Identity*. London: Earthscan Publication Ltd.

O'Riordan, Tim and Chris Church (2001) "Synthesis and Context", in O'Riordan, Tim and Chris Church (eds.), *Globalism, Localism and Identity*, London: Earthscan Publication Ltd.

Ostor, Alos (1980) *The Play of the Gods: Locality, Ideology, Structure and Time in the Festivals of a Bengali Town*. Chicago: Chicago University Press.

Robertson, R. (1992) *Globalization: Social Theory and Social Culture*. London: Sage.

Singh, K.S. (1992) *People of India: An Introduction*. Calcutta: Anthropological Survey of India.

Singh, Yogendra (2000) *Culture Change in India*. Jaipur and New Delhi: Rawat Publications.

—— (2004) *Ideology, Theory in Indian Sociology*. Jaipur and New Delhi: Rawat Publications.

Smith, A.D. (1990) "Towards a Global Culture", in M. Featherstone (ed.), *Global Culture: Nationalism, Globalization and Modernity*, London: Sage.

Stacey, M. (1969) "The Myth of Community Studies", *British Journal of Sociology*, Vol. 20, pp. 134–47.

Voisey, Heather and Tim O'Riordan (2001) "Globalization and Localization", in Tim O'Riordan (ed.), *Globalism, Localism and Identity*, London: Earthscan Publication Ltd.

Waters, M. (1995) *Globalization*. London: Routledge.

Yearley, S. (1996) *Sociology, Environmentalism, Globalization*. London: Sage.

14

Globalization and Culture

Solidarity with Social Movements for a Humane Society

S.M. Michael

In the globalized world of today we observe two major trends. On the one hand, some scholars believe that there is only one direction left for the world that is to imitate and incorporate the ideology of the triumphant global free market capitalism and its consequent economic, social, political and cultural paths. This position is articulated by Francis Fukuyama in his celebrated volume *End of History and the Last Man* (1992). Opposing this view, some other scholars are of the opinion that today's world is a diversified world. We cannot trust any of the major ideologies. We need to recognize and further multiculturalism and suspect and oppose the ideologies which try to homogenize cultures, peoples and religions. In today's world, both these ideological trends co-exist with their variations. Thus, we see the dominance of the globalization of the consumerist market capitalistic culture, economy and politics on the one hand, and postmodernism, multiculturalism, nationalism and fundamentalism on the other. People of different countries and regions are sandwiched between these conflicting and contradicting trends of world history.

This paper delineates the present socio-cultural trends of the contemporary world. It is divided into three parts. The first part is a socio-cultural analysis of the present global world. This is followed by an inquiry on the reactions to the above processes in the world scenario. The third part is the conclusion.

Characteristics of Our World

A Globalized World

Whether we like it or not, globalization is the determinant material and social force of our times. Globalization refers to the expansion of global linkages, the organization of social life on a global scale, and the growth of a global consciousness, which leads to the consolidation of a world society. In the context of the end of the Cold War era and the collapse of the Soviet Union, Fukuyama (1992) rhetorically and smugly put forth the thesis of the "End of History", celebrating the triumph of the West-driven free market system, democracy and individualism. Fukuyama felt that globalization is the embodiment of rationalism, efficiency, material abundance and liberal democratic values.

It is supposed that the world has no other choice but to imitate these values in the course of its history. Thus, the process of globalization is said to be the impact of the rapid transformation of cultures currently underway in the world, effecting, churning and bringing about change everywhere. No corner of the world is untouched as globalization carries on its conquest of the world. Globalization is said to lead to cultural homogeneity. Interaction and integration diminish differences; and global norms, ideas or practices overtake local mores and many cultural flows, such as the diffusion of news.

The concept of globalization gained currency from about the mid-1980 at the end of the bipolar world with the collapse of the USSR and the rise of uncontested and unregulated capitalism, which were marked by unprecedented socio-political and cultural changes in the world scenario. The world had to readjust itself to this new phenomenon. Hence, there was the Bretton Woods Conference which set forth the Structural Adjustment Programme (SAP), the introduction of the New Economic Policy (NEP), and liberalization programmes. During this time, the eruption of Information Technology (IT), particularly the Internet, also added the intensity of global contacts. People began to migrate to different geographical regions looking for better prospects. All these brought a new global situation seeking a fundamental restructuring of the economic and political arrangements since the Industrial Revolution, giving rise to a kind of global integration beyond the boundaries of nation-states. Thus, globalization is a complex multidimensional phenomenon that involves simultaneous and complexly related processes at all levels of society – economic, political, social, cultural, technological, environmental, and so forth (Giddens, 1991: 4).

Globalization takes the whole world as a single economic unit and the market as its instrument. The economy in a globalized world is characterized by open, liberal, free market and free trade with less regulatory barriers. It is marked by international investment and instant capital flows. Due to this, multinational companies move into different locations where labour is cheap. People from different national boundaries shift their places of work and residence exposing themselves to different cultural worlds. As a result, the world is becoming a highly interconnected world through economic, social, political and cultural contacts. As a consequence, the world is shrinking in terms of time and space making the world feel smaller and distances shorter. The intensity and the momentum of this process are further enhanced by the sophisticated instant communications and ever-expanding fast travels. Globalization symbolizes a world in motion providing people with resources to new ways of being human in the fast changing world. In other words, globalization means "integrating and connecting cultures and communities in new space-time combinations, and making the world in reality and in experience more interconnected" (Hall, 1996: 619).

In cultural terms, globalization implies an increased cultural interconnectedness across the globe, principally as a result of the mass media, and also because of flows of people in migration, tourism and the global economic and political institutions leading to similar life patterns in different parts of the globe. Globalization opens up the local culture to other ways of living and gives alternatives. As a result of the accelerated pace of life, transience seems to have acquired an edge over permanence and durability. The cultural baggage of globalization is reflected in the worldwide diffusion of American pop culture. Entertainment around the world is dominated by American movie corporations and American-made products.

Thus, globalization also produces new understandings of culture, nationality, environmental relations and many other aspects of social life. All these affect our traditional ways of living and managing world affairs. Globalization excludes a whole lot of unskilled groups of people, giving rise to the impoverishment of a lot of people. Due to privatization, there is a loss of guaranteed employment. Many people are in an uncertain position with regard to their secure and worthwhile future.

A Postmodern and Relativistic World

The globalization project is based on the principles of modernity of the 17th century Enlightenment philosophy. Overall, Enlightenment was characterized by rationalism and skepticism about traditional doctrines and supported the empirical methods of science. The proponents of Enlightenment had supreme confidence in man as a rational being and believed in a rational, scientific approach to religious, social, political and economic issues. They promoted a secular view of the world and a general sense of progress and perfectibility. Such ideas of civilization promoted by globalization dominated the thinking of the intellectual world during the 19th and up to the middle of 20th century. Science and technology were becoming increasingly powerful. Secularization was accepted as the natural and inevitable process in the development of human society.

All the same, a close look at the process of globalization will show that the triumphalism and complacency of globalization is proving to be premature and myopic. The supreme confidence in man and his rationality came to be questioned by the middle of the 20th century. The immeasurable devastation and consequent misery of the two world wars and the increasing depletion of resources and environmental problems of the contemporary world began to question the assumptions of the globalization process. Science and technology have failed to give meaning in both the personal and occupational lives of individuals, and have failed to resolve some of the institutional problems of global society. They have also failed to provide a guide to the human quest for ultimate meaning. In a lecture delivered at Georgetown University in the United States in the late 1990s, the former US national security advisor Zbigniew Brzezinsky wryly remarked: "Democracy has won. The free market system has won. But what in the wake of this great ideological victory is today the substance of our beliefs? What is the human being in the democratic West now truly committed to? Is it to hedonistic relativism? ... I think this emptiness, this potential emptiness, if not yet the reality is dangerous" (quoted in Acham, 2000).

Moreover, the rise of nation-states in Asia and Africa after World War II, and the ever-expanding communication system, with the migration of people from one cultural area to another, have led to multicultural societies. Migrations and population shifts in the wake of wars and natural catastrophes as well as new job opportunities in technologically developed countries have become a common phenomenon. This has added a new dimension to the debate on multiculturalism among western scholars. In USA, England, and the rest of Europe, the population composition is undergoing rapid change in these years. A few years or decades ago, the western world consisted mainly of Whites with a common civilization and Christian by religion. But, today, the situation is fast changing. Immigrants from Asia and Africa are settling down in USA, England and other western countries. The racial and religious composition of the population and the socio-cultural components of these countries are no longer the same. This is a new situation in America and in Europe, which were traditionally mono-cultural. For example, in England today, there are a substantial number of Indians, Bangladeshis, Pakistanis and Afro-Caribbeans. The internal make-up of the country is undergoing transformation. As Bhikhu Parekh points out, "Today you have a landscape with as many mosques as churches. As a result, the Brits are beginning to ask themselves: What are we? Who are we likely to become?" (2001: 5). They are being confronted with the new situation of multiculturalism. The subject of multiculturalism is often in the headlines in the western media these years.

As multiculturalism increases in many parts of the world, each culture and religion claims space and autonomy. They compete with one another as the best culture or religion for the future. As a result, the modernist's quest for a universal culture is under doubt. This has given rise to a postmodern cultural situation.

Postmodernists question the philosophical assumptions of modernism, namely, rationality, positivism and empirical methods in science to know the reality. Postmodern culture sees doubt as a form of health. It often derives meaning or excitement through experiments with sensation, sex and drugs, and if confronted with the teachings promoting traditional values or wisdom of the ages it proudly rejects them as outdated and no more relevant to contemporary humanity.

One of the things that characterizes the times we live in is the breakdown of absolutes. In morals–sexual anarchy; in metaphysics–doubt; in epistemology–confusion and ambiguity. Symptoms of this cultural and intellectual malaise are everywhere discernible. Postmodernism doubts any grand theories and generalizations. A coherent general understanding across cultural boundaries is seen as virtually impossible (Bhargava, 1999). Key analytical categories may not be as universally applicable as in modernism, as we had once imagined. Paul Heelas explains this as follows: "The cultural becomes disorganized; less black and white. The distinction between high and low fades away. The claim that one tradition should be adhered to because it, and it alone, is valid, is rendered invalid. And rather than authority and legitimacy resting with established orders of knowledge, authority comes to rest with the person" (1998: 3–4). In the words of James Beckford, postmodernity consists in a "willingness to abandon the search for over-arching or triumphalist myths, narratives or frameworks of knowledge" (as quoted in Heelas, ibid.). Postmodernism is a revolt and a reaction against modernism. Postmodernism is imbued with the sense of a "collapsed signification and challenged humanism". It is amorphous, eclectic, pluricultural and ideologically and aesthetically not clear-cut.

The implication of the postmodern understanding of 'truth' in a wider cultural perspective has been that all is relative, nothing is sure, not fixed, all is in a flux. Postmodernity goes against certainty and objectivity. It rejects order and certainty. It is skeptical about categories and any idea of a stable meaning. Instead, ambivalence, variation, fragmentation and emotion are celebrated as guidelines for how we should understand the social world. Sometimes, postmodernism stresses instincts and the drive for pleasure as central to how an individual should function. Postmodernism believes that meaning is not universal and fixed, but precarious, fragmented and local.

Postmodern ideas and values are projected in the powerful media. The media has a tremendous impact on the young. In recent years, television has begun to dictate terms in our homes. Children often remain glued to the television and a serial in the evening often replaces the normal conversation in the family.

Today, a large number of world population, more specially the youth, are affected by postmodern culture and its value system. Postmodern liberal ideas hold that what is morally sound and desirable is to be determined by each individual and that one should not judge the actions of other people in terms of one's own moral values. Thus, liberalism inherently entails moral relativism. Karl Acham (2000) points out that the root cause of the cultural crisis in the western world is related to this moral relativism leading to exaggerated individualism.

The phenomenal expansion of cities in the global world, the unprecedented pace of technological and social change and the increasing heterogeneity and diversity of urban population across the world have heightened anonymity, impersonality and alienation. Several social scientists and commentators have pointed out that, by and large, today, human society is faced with fracture, fragmentation and atomization. It is manifested in mindless and compulsive consumerism and hedonism, in the breakdown and disintegration of human relationships, in the growing feelings of insecurity, vulnerability and uncertainty, and in a pervasive existential vacuum.

There is fracture in the heart of families, in which it is becoming increasingly difficult to educate and spend time with one's children given current working patterns. Another problem that affects family life is that of the growing awareness of the issue of gender equality, a subject that leaves many men confused about how to take on a more equal role in the family, and in turn leads to a rise in violent forms of behaviour. The real threat to the stability and cohesiveness of societies according to Acham (ibid.) comes from a growing deterioration in human relationships. Exaggerated individualism has a positive bearing on apathy, indifference and lack of social commitment which, in turn, have contributed to the breakdown and disintegration of the family, erosion of social bonds, loss of faith in public institutions, drug abuse, and the spurt in crime and delinquency in many societies. In Britain, one-third of all marriages end in divorce and nearly 20 per cent of British children witness the divorce of their parents before they reach the age of 16. It is anticipated that this trend will grow and that in a few years only 50 per cent of British children will experience a normal, conventional family life (Bocock and Thompson, 1992; Ahrono and Rodgers, 1987). In recent years, the United States and many European countries have experienced a dramatic increase in the divorce rate. A survey of marriage in more than 30 European countries revealed that living together without the formality of marriage is becoming increasingly common. There is a steady increase in the number of people living alone as well as those who express feelings of loneliness. The high crime statistics that are seen among those living alone in the world points out the rise in stress levels as well as the increasing number of people turning to sects to feel a sense of belonging, acceptance and to be given a clear code of conduct. It is very significant that in the same countries where mainstream religions are on the decline, there has been a marked increase in the number of sects, therapy groups, self-help groups, etc.

So, what is at the axiological root of these various problems of society today? Or, in other words, what are the values that guide our lifestyle, and structure our community that have made these divisions occur? According to several social scientists, the main cause of these multiple fractures appearing in our increasingly globalized world is this so-called social atomism. This atomism, a theory that asserts the importance of the individual in relation to all around him, is encouraged by growing individualism and lack of a sense of community – a situation that is becoming more and more common in the modern world. Symptoms of this atomism could be: feeling like we are islands in the midst of many people, a disintegration of our links with others, no one worrying about what is happening to their neighbour, and the fact that we are becoming less and less involved in what is happening to those around us.

The theory that is at the heart of atomism is that the individual can be fulfilled, and happy (in the sense of having things and enjoying life) without needing others. We could perhaps explain this better if we were to say that the only purpose of other people is always in how they can contribute to one's own personal fulfilment (see Carrera, 2007: 5–7).

Reactions against Globalization and Postmodernism

Cultural Nationalism and Religious Fundamentalism

While globalization as a homogenizing process is active, we also observe cultures and religions asserting their separate identities. Globalization creates a troubled relationship between the native and the international. The claim of the emergence of a global culture is accompanied by cries of alarm that local values and nation-states are suffering a sense of threat to identity (Hall, 1996: 619). This has given rise to ethnic revivals, struggles for indigenous rights and religious fundamentalism as defensive reactions to globalization and relativism. They have risen from a desire to defend and preserve valued ways of life against what are seen to be pernicious effects of foreign and global influences. Fundamentalist religious movements and cultural nationalism emerge in order to strengthen the identity of one's nation and culture. Religious nationalists are not just religious fanatics. For the most part they are political activists who were seriously attempting to reformulate the 'modern' language of politics in order to provide a new basis for the nation-state (Juergensmeyer, 1994: xiii). Religious and nationalist movements often invoke authenticity and 'authentic culture' as a weapon against what was foreign and alien.

Contemporary society has been experiencing both a crisis in religion as well as a global resurgence. This resurgence has taken place, according to social scientists, largely because of an identity crisis and of science and technology failing to give meaning in both personal and occupational lives of individuals and have failed to resolve some of the institutional problems of modern society. They have also failed to provide a guideline to the human quest for ultimate meaning (Wilson, 1966, 1982, 1988; Beckford, 1986; Dawson, 1998; Giri, 1998). Individuals have been realizing the infinite fragmentation that globalization have caused in their lives. As Alvin Toffler points out, "Unless man quickly learns to control the rate of change in his personal affairs as well as in society at large, we are doomed to a massive adaptational breakdown" (1970: 15).

Rise of Global People's Movements

Globalization has both positive and negative potentials as well as dangerous consequences. It is a double-edged sword. It has exciting possibilities and it can usher in unprecedented miseries. Positively, it avails the scientific, medical and other innovations available to all. Unjust laws in some nation-states have been challenged by international law. Local cultures are exposed to ideas such as human rights, notions of social justice and democracy. For example, the dalits challenged the Indian State for violation of human rights in international forums such as World Conference Against Racism, Xenophobia and Discrimination, held in Durban in 2001.

In almost every sphere of activity there are a growing number of transnational organizations, including social movements like Greenpeace, Women's Movements, Concern for Empowerment of Local Communities and Indigenous People, etc. They are becoming even more relevant, linking people in transnational relations (see Cohen and Rai, 2000). The widespread network of international governmental organizations, combined with international non-governmental organizations (NGOs), provides the conditions for global governance. Globalization process also enhances interactions between large humanitarian and charitable operations such as Oxfam, Action Aid, Human Rights Watch, Christian Aid, etc. Similarly, scientific and professional bodies like the International Association of Nutritional Sciences link-up their concerns and ideas globally.

The negative consequences of globalization are growing unemployment due to the inability of smaller industries to compete with international industrial firms, loss of livelihood for traditional artisans and craftsmen, and migration of people from their original environment for livelihood. Since globalization takes the whole world as a single market, labour is losing its voice; national governments are losing their power and there is corporate insecurity and volatility of financial capital. Inequality is rising. Unskilled labour in rich countries has little prospects of employment. Globalization excludes a whole lot of unskilled groups of people giving rise to further impoverishment. Due to privatization, there is loss of guaranteed employment. Many people fail to see how they can have a secure and worthwhile future. Therefore, despair stimulates them to withdraw into their community shells often attracted by anti-social elements. All this has given rise to ethnic strife, religious conflicts, social unrest and wanton violence.

Another important negative consequence of globalization is environmental degradation. Much environmental damage has assumed global dimensions. Acid rain, global warming and deforestation have adversely affected the whole ecosystem of the earth and can only be solved at a global level.

The resources of the world are depleting. But the wants of people are increasing. These wants are artificially created wants. Hence, the competition increases. As nations compete for material progress, the gulf between the rich and the poor keeps on widening. Efficiency is counted as the ability to maximize the resources for oneself. Hence, the ruralites, uneducated, women, tribal, and the like, do not have a place in today's competitive world. The resulting imbalance continues to stir waves of domestic and foreign migrations in search of economic refuge. As a result, serving as their global highways are the megacities that are expanding and interlinking centres of multiculturality.

All this initiates people's movements to bring a new world order which will be more just and humane than that of the contemporary world. Many people in the world look upon institutions of civil society as a means of social renewal and cultural revitalization. Civil society encompasses all the groups, organizations and associations that exist outside the ambit of the state, including NGOs, political parties, interest groups and religious organizations. NGOs constitute the heart and soul of civil society. They argue that the growing fragmentation and emptiness in human society can be filled by voluntary organizations, citizens' groups, human rights organizations, business associations, churches and clubs.

Globalization has more than one face. Global cultural and economic forces, particularly through the dynamics of huge corporations, shapes the picture of the world from above, while a new global consciousness, through the activities of people's movements shapes the world from below (Cohen and Rai, 2000; Jogdand and Michael, 2003).

Conclusion: Solidarity with Social Movements to Build a New Society

The problems of poverty and injustice in the globalized world are so enormous that they require mutual help and understanding between cultures, religions and nations. One culture, one religion and one nation alone cannot tackle this single handedly. In the process of technological and scientific advancement, we need to place the priority of the human over all other considerations. In the globalized world of today, we need to ask ourselves what globalization means for the poor, oppressed and the marginalized. Are they able to experience a sense of common humanity with the rich and the affluent? Or is globalization the luxury of the rich and the powerful?

As citizens of the world we need to be concerned about human dignity and social justice for all people. In the context of globalization, we need to give a direction to globalization in such a way that the poor and the downtrodden receive the attention and care that is due to them. As concerned citizens, we need to ask what globalization means for the poor, the dalits, tribals and other weaker sections. Within the dreams and aspirations of these marginalized groups there lingers the hope of fairness and justice that humanity could offer in the world of globalization.

Such a humanistic globalization has to be pursued with the active collaboration of all people with the emerging people's movements which have similar objectives. All of us should get involved with people's movements in the issues of justice, equality, fraternity and ecological questions. Citizens must be active in the civil society. Intellectuals should collaborate with civil right activists in bringing to light the history and cultural traditions of tribals, dalits and other marginalized people. This would be a constructive move towards a holistic and integral development in the process of globalization and culture today. But, this is not an easy task. It requires a constant struggle.

References

Acham, Karl (2000) "Social and Cultural Problems in Contemporary Europe: On Recent Challenges to Liberal Ideas", in Zdenek Suda and Jiri Musil (eds.), *The Meaning of Liberalism: East and West*, Budapest: Central European University Press, pp. 123–37.

Ahrono, C. and R. Rodgers (1987) *Divorced Families*. London and New York: Routledge.

Beckford, J.A. (ed.) (1986) *New Religious Movements and Rapid Social Change*. UNESCO: Sage.

Bhargava, Rajeev (ed.) (1999) *Multiculturalism, Liberalism and Democracy*. Delhi: Oxford University Press.

Bocock, R. and K. Thompson (eds.) (1992) *Social and Cultural Forms of Modernity*. Cambridge: Polity Press.

Cohen, Robin and Shirin M. Rai (eds.) (2000) *Global Social Movements*. London: Athlone Press.

Carrera, Joan I Carrera (2007) *Identities for the 21st Century*. Barcelona: CJ Booklets No. 127.

Dawson, Christopher (1949, 1998) *Religion and Culture*. London: Sheed & Ward.

Fukuyama, Francis (1992) *End of History and the Last Man*. New York: Free Press.

Giddens, Anthony (1991) *Modernity and Self-Identity*. Stanford, CA: Stanford University Press.

Giri, A.K. (1998) *Global Transformations: Postmodernity and Beyond*. Jaipur and Delhi: Rawat Publications.

Hall, Stuart (1996) "Question of Cultural Identity", in Stuart Hall et al. (eds.), *Modernity: An Introduction to Modern Societies*, Cambridge: Blackwell Publishers.

Heelas, Paul (1998) *Religion, Modernity and Postmodernity*. Oxford: Blackwell Publishers.

Jogdand, P.G. and S.M. Michael (eds.) (2003) *Globalization and Social Movements. Struggle for a Humane Society*. Jaipur and Delhi: Rawat Publications.

Toffler, Alvin (1970) *Future Shock*. London: Pan Books.

Juergensmeyer, M. (1994) *Religious Nationalism Confronts Secular State*. New Delhi: Oxford University Press.

Parekh, Bhikhu (2001) "In Britain Today, the Landscape Holds as Many Mosques as Churches", *The Sunday Times of India*, August 26, p. 5.

Wilson, B. (1966) *Religion in a Secular Society*. England: Penguin Books.

—— (1982) *Religion in Sociological Perspective*. New York: Oxford University Press.

—— (1988) "Secularization on Religion in the Modern World" in S. Sutherland et al. (eds.), *The World's Religions*, London: Routledge, pp. 953–56.

15

Global Society

A New Paradigm in Social Science Research

Maitreyee Bardhan Roy

The challenges of 'multiculturalism' as an expression of disintegrating culture of a nation-state system gave prominence to the present socio-political environment with the development of the concept 'globalization'. With the intermingling of territorial states with globalization the independent entity of 'nation-state' as a distinct socio-political and cultural unit has been in trouble. The increasing influence of globalization also opened up the opportunity for the developed nations to establish their hegemony over the universe. The popular acceptance of the politico-economic domination of globalization thus gave a sense of relief to the international policy makers who have accepted it as the only stable solution against the dominance of nationalism. The growing consensus towards globalization thus suggests that the social scientists of the 21st century need not place attention to the concept of nation-state because it has lost its relevance in the contemporary world and the studies on modern culture need to be veered round the new concept – globalization.

The developments we can discern with the dawn of the 21st century are more complex. Though the dominance of globalization on the nation-state system has created a fresh complication in the international scenario, the strong nationalist feeling in some of the third world countries has brought into existence a regional symbiosis among the states to fight back globalization. The urge for the preservation of independent entity of a nation-state thus enabled the regions to stay united and work for the protection of the state system against the grasp of neo-colonial and neo-imperial domination. The rejection of globalization is so strong among the new-generation nationalists that they encouraged the growing popularity of a new form of multiculturalism as a determinant of their indigenous culture. Their strong attachment towards nationalism leads to terrorism among the new-generation nationalists striving for the protection of nation-state from the grasp of globalization.

The present paper intends to deal with both the positive as well as the negative impacts of globalization witnessed by the people of India – one of the oldest multicultural nation-state of the East.

History of Multiculturalism in India

India under Aryans and Ideological Convergence

India has been the homeland of multicultural races accumulated on the land from different parts of the world since the days of civilization. Interestingly, socio-cultural diversity accompanied by divergent style of living was never considered a serious problem to the survival of the multicultural groups residing in India named 'Bharatvarsha'. The invasion of Aryans in 5000 BC allowed the entry of a new culture group to the country from Central Asia. They invaded the country from the northern part, ruled and domiciled the country with their indigenous customs but never intended to impose their culture over the cultural heritage of the natives. As a result, Indian civilization developed from Dravidian period remained intact even after the settlement of Aryans in the northern part of the country. Though the Aryan invaders drove off the Dravidian from the northern part of the sub-continent, no traces of adversary relation among the groups had been recorded in the history of the country. Once invaded, the spirit of peaceful co-existence continued among them. Thus, the history of multiculturalism bears no trace of cultural competition among the occupier and the occupied during the Aryan rule.

The Medieval India and Convergence

Bharatvarsha witnessed a new group of invaders on its land during 1200 BC. They were famous by the name Mughal dynasty. The Mughal emperors spread their reign over the northern part of the country. Though they were Muslim by religion, history of religious imposition over the other religious groups was unusual. Thus, question of cultural and religious conflict was almost absent during the Mughal reign.

The British India and Convergence

The transfer of civilization towards the West encouraged the European mono-cultural community to concentrate the community culture exclusively within a compact territorial boundary for easy cultural communication. The European community, therefore, came under an unanimous consensus to distribute land mass on cultural or lingual homogeneity. The idea received its expression through the nomenclature 'the State' (a formally defined institution authorized to rule over the people of a definite geographical location with the inherent right to exercise unquestionable authority over them) The concept 'the State' received a formal recognition in Europe through the Treaty of Westphalia signed in 1648. Significantly, the 17th century 'State' concept was made familiar to the European continent only as the leading colonial rulers of the world. The concept was kept away from the colonies of the East with an intention to enable the colonial emperor to dominate them.

Though the invaders travel throughout the country to spread up their hegemony over the people and their resources, they unconsciously carried with them the rich heritage of their culture for the colonies dominated by them and offered them an opportunity to imbibe and enrich them. The British rulers' contribution to India was ran rife through the development of modern system of education in the most sensitive corners of the country. The tribal population of the country, which had been left uninvaded by the Aryans residing in the extreme northeastern part of the sub-continent, was discovered by the Christian missionaries arriving India. They imparted western style of education among the tribal groups and converted them to Christianity. Thus, under the British rule, tribal population received English education and converted themselves into a mixed socio-cultural group developed with a mixture of English with their inherited Mongoloid culture they brought with them from the southeastern part of Asia.

However, the negative impact of British rule was the imposition of 'divide and rule' policy resulting the rise of nationalist movement in India. The involvement of masses in the non-cooperation movement gave an impetus for liberation in the first part of 20th century. To weaken the nationalist movement, the proposal for the partition of Bengal was brought forth by the Britishers. This proposal initiated Hindu–Muslim rift in India leading to the partition of Bengal in 1947. As a result, India was divided into an Islamic Pakistan and secular India. The declaration of partition of Bengal by the British rulers not only marked the beginning of Hindu–Muslim divide in the country, it had also recorded the largest movement of refugee population in the history of the world. Also, it was for the first time in the history of India that the problem of multiculturalism created an adverse impact on the people of India.

Independent India and Convergence with Divergent Ideology: With the end of Second World War and the formation of United Nations in 1942, the nation-state system was decided to be extended unanimously to all countries. Thus, the colonial empires of the West were impelled to surrender their hegemony over the East. As an outcome of the decision of UN, India was declared independent in 1947, but the long three hundred years of British colonial rule over India has left an indelible imprint on the indigenous culture of its original inhabitants. Thus, we observe a noticeable change in the national character. The Indian society has been dominated by different groups like the rich, the educated middle class and the uneducated poor. Though the cultural dilemma of independent India could resist partially the prevalence of western culture throughout the country, it almost failed to overcome the uncanny feeling existing in their environment.

Assimilation of western culture created a new group of anglicized youth unwilling to involve in socio-cultural heritage of the past but their existence on the top level created a cultural disparity among the new generations. The development of this neo-cultural group though enabled the government of the country to maintain unified administrative structure, the religious conflict prevalent in the country continued with the British 'divide and rule' policy.

The constitutional framers of the country though wanted to maintain the plural multicultural setting in the country through the promotion of the vision of secularism, the existence of diversified religious groups in the country led to the development of weak secularism susceptible to the interest of the majority. As a result, neither of the two dominant religious groups could able to dissociate their spiritual problems from the political problems nor the concept of secularism could be defined as tolerance: this expression remains sometime absent in Indian culture resulting the development of religious conflicts in the country. As Dr

Ambedkar observed, "the two major religions in India do not confine themselves to spiritual and other worldly matters rather cover within their fold social behaviour as a whole ..."[1]

Though the Hindu–Muslim riot in Calcutta city on the verge of independence and the partition of Bengal movements in 1905 were considered as the immediate effects of the divide and rule policy of the British empire, the demolition of Babri Masjid in Ayodhya[2], a North Indian city, and the Hindu–Muslim riots in Godhra, Gujarat[3] are not only the examples of anti-secular action of the people of the country, but politics–religion unholy alliance of the people not only challenged the concept of secularism but also gave rise to a group of young Indians, united with an intention not only to maintain religious distance but also they came up as the torch bearer of traditional culture prevalent in the country before the invasion of English rulers. If the socio-religious conflicts among the multicultural groups are looked from the divergent points of view, this divergent culture no doubt vitiated the Indian convergent culture. This can be explained as an outburst of confusing understanding of the country's political hooligans trying to come to the forefront through the uncanny activities but to vitiate the integrity of the country's rich cultural heritage and weaken the social ties existing in the country.

Regional Dissatisfaction and Disarray

Being a multicultural country, India has to face diversified problems which are genuine and need immediate attention of the government for their solution. These are mentioned hereunder:

1. Dissatisfaction among the minority community has become the most sensitive issue in India and demands proper attention from the government. The terrorist movement in Kashmir, for example, has a serious impact on the country. It has severely hampered the GDP of the state thriving on tourism. The revolutionary movement of the tribal populations of Nagaland[4] and Manipur of the northeastern region compelled the government of the country to declare the areas as restricted zone hampering not only its but development also affecting the healthy upbringing of the upcoming generation and, thereby, allowing the large group of 'positive' population (population below 25) to involve in negative activities thus destroying the avenues of their healthy development and vitiating the benefit of convergence under the globalized society.
2. With the aim of preserving the tribal customs, the Sixth Schedule of the Constitution of India allows the administration of the tribal regions in the northeast region to be run under the tribal laws. So far it did not hamper the constitutional laws. The Governor in the northeastern states is entrusted with exclusive supervisory authority over the area and he has been authorized to see that the tribal customs do not contradict the constitutional provisions of the country.
3. Revolutionary upheaval in Darjeeling district for an independent state was partially accepted by the state government. Such are the stray incidences of divergent culture and through the formation of District Council, they have offered an autonomous administration of their own.

4. Demand for a separate state for the tribal population of the plane land opened up a new dimension of problem of multiculturalism in the country. The government of the country took instant step to resolve the same. The states like Uttarkhand in Uttar Pradesh, Chhattisgarh in Madhya Pradesh and Jharkhand in Bihar were formed to meet the demand of the tribes of the areas to satisfy their needs as the citizens of an independent country.
5. The record of lingual conflicts in different parts of country is also an outcome of its multicultural setting. Demand for the state of Upper Assam, the terrorist problem of Boro population on the demand of Biro Land in Assam is the bone of contention to the administration of the country. The country has to survive on this and it has to work out suitable solution of the problems concerning the demand of the people of the country.
6. Extreme effect of multiculturalism in India got its expression through the demand of a separate state Khalistan by the Sikh sect of Punjab (a religious group situated in the northern part of India). Such a demand though temporarily affected the interest of the country as a whole but it could not affect the national integrity of the country in the same manner as experienced by the United Soviet Socialist Republic.
7. Inclusion of the independent state of Sikkim within Indian territory is a positive indication of strength of socio-cultural ties still present in the subcontinent. It is an accepted fact that with its diversified socio-cultural settings, India represents a unique example of the existence of strong homogeneous culture within heterogeneous socio-political groups residing in its territory.
8. With assassination of the then Prime Minister of India, Smt. Indira Gandhi, a strong national heritage of India scuttled down. Break down of the economy of the country opened up the scope of the capitalist world leader (USA) to extend its neo-colonial rule over the country. The US persuasion to Indian development policy not only obstructed the development of an independent economic programme of the country, this neo-colonial leader marshalled a group of widely moved pro-western youths in Indian society to annihilate the rich national heritage of the country and to offer a space to the neo-colonial ruler to establish its hegemony over their conquests through these recalcitrant indigenous communities used to suppress or seduce the homogenous culture of the country.

The postcolonial India not only deserve the credit of preservation of its strong national heritage in the country, it has achieved success in keeping the multicultural community interest under the banner 'multicultural and multilingual state' despite the constant provocation of neo-colonial forces, making attempts to disturb and destabilize the integrity of the people by utilizing the anti-national forces present in the society.

Neo-cultural Group and their Dominance

The post-independent multicultural India gave birth to a neo-cultural group consisting of young educated middle class in India. This group not only has picked up English way of living. They use English language as a means of communication (more than ten million people in India have taken up English as their second language)[5] and prefer to carry out office activities in English. Though the government declared Hindi as the national language of the country, it is not uniformly accepted as the official language by all the states of India.

The medium of instruction at the higher level is English in most of the states. Now one can opt for mother tongue also but it is not uniformly adopted in all the states. Also, the families send their children to the English medium school from the kindergarten level. The children educated in English language develop a strong affinity towards English culture. These English-educated Indian communities constitute a distinct class in the society. They stay at the top layer of the class structure and interfere in important policy decisions of the government and they act as a media to spread up neo-imperial and neo-colonial culture in the society.[6]

The nationalist leaders of colonial countries, while framing a constitution, decided to avoid the influence of the colonial administration designed by the colonial emperor but in actual practice they cannot get out of the influence of colonial policies. While framing the Constitution of India the national leaders of the country faced similar problem. While framing the Constitution of India, the nationalist leaders of the country wanted to take up a model different from British system. In reality, the British way of administration was so intently intermingled with the life of the Indians that the constitutional framers of India proposed for a parliamentary form of government in India with an elected president as the head (British parliamentary system without the king).

However, the greatest contribution of British colonial system was the creation of a uniform culture group that could tie up the multicultural society together under the banner, 'the English culture'. This super cultural group is spread up all over the country and converted the country's multicultural group into a monocultural one under the banner 'India' or 'Indian'. They follow a single language and are not even interested to learn their own mother tongue. Their written and spoken language is English and expression of their thoughts comes out in English too. This new generation Indian, therefore, are the torch bearer of monoculturalism in multicultural India. Thereby literally adopting the concept 'unity in diversity' as is commonly observed in Indian cultural heritage. But who falls under the category of Indian as observed so far? They are no doubt a large part of total population in India and the children of well-to-do families. They are the decision makers, policy makers and the dominant ruler of the society. In a way, they are the deciding factor in their decision-making field and the media also offer them an opportunity to decide the fate of the nations. They are the main initiators of convergence theory as proposed under the globalized era.

Globalization and Multiculturalism in India

Globalization, as a world economic order, gave birth to two distinctly opposite culture group in the country. One group believes that globalization is a positive development force brought for the society. To them, globalization has opened up the opportunities for employment throughout the world. It has opened up the scope for the people to move from one part of the world to the other without abiding by any strict rules imposed by the government of the country (as was adopted by the government under the prime ministership of Smt. Indira Gandhi). The people supporting globalization, however, constitute a separate culture group. Their style of living is totally different from the people believing in the cultural heritage of India. This group constitutes a small fraction of total population of the country availing all the benefits of the society brought forth by globalization.

The group discarding 'globalization' consists of the follower of the traditionalist group. They believe that globalization spoils the traditional national culture of India. They consider globalization a form of neo-imperialism and colonialism. To them saffronization and sanskritization are the two important concept associated with Indian culture and the society should preach for the preservation of this rich culture. However, the activities of this group are politically motivated (the agenda of BJP is sanskritization while RSP preach saffronization). They are eager to politicize their traditionalism to stunt nationalism. This group of nationalists is concerned with the popularization of their political agenda through the propagation of the concepts used by them in the election agenda of the country.

Another extremist group propagating the national culture under globalization is the terrorist group. They profess the reign of terror and has given birth to international terrorist culture which has influenced the people of the whole world, mostly the educated youths trained up by the traditional system of education in the third-world countries. But unfortunately the activities of these terrorist groups are carried out targeting a territorial nation-state, they are, supervised, guided by international gangsters but they work for the preservation of their national as well as regional identity against the concept globalization. Their work plans are determined globally and they believe in terrorizing the globe through their operational activities. The global leaders determine the programme of their activities internationally and the terrorist groups stationed in the respective territorial states are to implement them. The highjacking of a Delhi bound aeroplane flying from Nepal to be hijacked by the terrorist of Afghanistan who killed the male partner of a honeymoon couple, on the demand of the release of terrorists of Kashmir brought under custody of the Government of India[7] is a case in point. The incident of trade centre as happened in September 2003 in USA could be taken up as an ideal example of terrorist activities operating under the era of globalization.

Concluding Remarks

Unity in Diversity

Despite this bewildering diversity, India is a country with unique unity with almost all the races from Central Asia came to India and assimilated with its culture. Besides this, Parsis community, European traders, Dutch, Portuguese traders invaded the country and left a lasting of their culture on it. Thus, the story of its multidimensional development made the country multilingual with Indo-Aryan, Dravidian, Tibeto-Chinese and Austro-Asiatic languages prevalent in India. At present it has 18 official languages. As according to 1961 and 1971 census about 1,652 languages have been listed as the mother tongues in the country.

India is also a country offering shelter to multi-religious group. Of the total population, about 82.64 per cent are Hindu, 11.40 per cent Muslim, 0.48 per cent Jain, 7 per cent Buddhist, 2.5 per cent Christian and 2 per cent Sikh along with some other unrecorded religious groups.[8] Thus, India is a polyethnic society based on race, caste, religion and language territories. Diversities are also present in the modes and means of production but in spite of its multidimensional culture, the country people are beautifully sharing their cultural diversities among themselves. In spite of occasional and scattered incidences the feeling of integrity and unity is maintained among the people of the country. Thus, in spite of the occasional occurrence of conflict and disarray among the different culture group, the people here prefer to stay together and share the peace, happiness, tranquillity and pain among themselves. The researcher feels proud to end up her comment on multiculturalism by quoting the Nobel laureate Dr Amartya Sen. The comment he made in his interview published in *Sunday Statesman* dated 14th May 2006: "I am an Indian citizen. I am a British or American resident. I am a Bengali, the poetry, I like is a Bengali poetry, I am a man, I am an economist. I belong to all these groups, nothing complicated about that". If this realization exists in all then the problem of multiculturalism affects none.

What Unites Indians Together

After a long deliberation on the problems and prospects of multiculturalism, the question that remains unresolved even today is, what force that unites Indians, under the banner 'nation' in the midst of so many odd situations arising in the country from time to time. Even in the era of globalization there are people who have been striving for the protection of motherland from the hands of the so-called foreign power, people of India are still united. How this is possible? It is, in fact, the moral values of the people of the country that reigns supreme. It is the unquestionable respect of the people towards their motherland that unites them together under the banner 'Mother India'. It is the respect towards the community society that still keeps us together. It is our faith towards each other that encourage us to rely on us as a group that tightens up together under the banner 'Ma' (Mother). This concept 'Mother' gives us life, it gives us energy, it gives us the feeling of oneness. Since all these forces are still present in our community, we are united. We do not want to come out of it and separate ourselves from one another, it is natural for a child to make demands to his mother, the state's attitude towards the centre is looked up with a motherly attitude, and it is only these forces that keep us away from the challenges of multi-culturalism. Thus, in spite of religious conflict the community feeling as existing in our country will enable us to stay united as a unified multicultural country under the banner India.

Notes

1. Secularism and Justice: A Review of Indian Supreme Court Judgments by Sanghamitra Padhy, *Economic and Political Weekly*, Vol. XXXIX, Nos. 46 and 47, November 20–26, 2004, p. 5027.

2. 'Never before in the history of the temple movement had the BJP-VHP-Bajrang Dal combine managed to collect such large crowds at Ayodhya on their own. At the final count, an estimated 200,000 persons came from all the states of India barring those in the North-East, a large proportion of them drawn from the RSS cadres. Everyone could not join the *karsevaks;* severe controls and preliminary screening were introduced by the RSS. It was not a purely spontaneous show put up by the faithful, but a tightly organised, fully planned political exercise'. *The Rediff Special*, December 6, 1992, A Memoir.
3. 'Brutality witnessed in Ahmedabad is crime against humanity, and no country, including India can escape from its international obligation of protecting minorities. India in its own interest for salvaging its international image and maintaining internal stability and peace must address the issue of violence against the Muslim community in Gujarat. It must bring to justice all those who are found involved in the massacres. Its record of probing mass violence and punishing the culprits is very poor that gives little confidence that this time around it would be done'. An extract from *The News International*, Saturday, May 4, 2002. India's communal riots or pogroms? The incident occurred on May 3.
4. 'With little over a month left before its ceasefire between the Centre and NSCN (IM) comes up for renewal, the latter has accused the Centre of pursuing a "dual policy". It also warned: "Our tolerance and patience should" not be taken for granted.'

   "The Army and paramilitary forces with some of the state's armed personnel have been deliberately trying to undermine the ceasefire. These acts were aimed at sabotaging the peace process. The government should immediately control and restraint its forces. If this is not done, NSCN will not be responsible for any consequences thereafter," the statement said.

   Talks between the Naga ministerial delegation and the Centre have reached a stalemate after 12 rounds. The Nagas have demanded that integration of Naga-inhabited areas be considered first, but the Centre is unable to do so fearing violence in Manipur and Assam – states that have consistently been opposing the integration of the Naga-inhabited areas. Saturday, June 11, year, 03: 23 AM
5. This data was extracted from the Ethnologue database. Now linked by India WWW Virtual Library. Created on July 16, 1995. Last updated on July 4, 2000.
6. A regional language has its geographical bounds defined within the state (Spolsky 1978: 26). In addition to the designation of Hindi as an official language and fourteen others as national languages, each state can choose its own regional language for use in local government affairs and in education among the languages spoken in its territory. India's constitution guarantees the right of all citizens to communicate in their own language with any governmental agency (Bonvillain 1993: 304). There are over 900 million people and more than one thousand languages in India; the area is thus one of the most diverse linguistic and cultural areas in the world. Thus, it comes as no surprise that there are many problems in classifying and labelling languages in India. One reason is that languages tend to fade into other ones, so that it is difficult to say which are different languages, or which are just dialects of one language (Fasold 1984: 22). In 1971, it was estimated that the rate of bilingualism in India was 13 per cent, 99 per cent of English speakers are second-language speakers, whereas in many other languages there are no non-native speakers at all. (Although there are large numbers of native 65.64 per cent had occasional interaction with native speakers of English; 11.79 per cent had no interaction and 5.12 per cent claimed to have daily interaction with native speakers of

English (ibid.: 110). Downloaded from http://www.languageinindia.com/sep2004/onbegging1.html

English is virtually the first language for many in India. Indian speakers of English are primarily bi- or multi-lingual Indians who use English as in terms of numbers of English speakers, the Indian subcontinent ranks third in the world, after the USA and UK.

An estimated 4 per cent (in 1994) of the Indian population use English; although the number might seem small, out of the total population that is about 35 million people (Crystal 1995: 101). Although the number of speakers of English in India is somewhat limited (as compared to the total population), that small segment of the population controls domains that have professional prestige (Kachru 1986a: 8). English is virtually the first language for many educated Indians, and for many, who speak more than one language, English is a second language in contexts in which English is used among Indians as a "link" or an "official" language. Only a minimal fraction of the English using Indian population has any interaction with native speakers of English according to Kachru's survey (the population of which was graduate faculty of English in the universities and colleges). See Annika Hohenthal, Language in India: Strength for Today and Bright Hope for Tomorrow, Volume 3: 5 May 2003 Multiculturalism in India, English in India: Loyalty and Attitudes; Editor: M.S. Tirumalai. Associate Editor: B. Mallikarjun; et al.

7. KATHMANDU, December 26 – After admitting to the "possibility of a security lapse" at Kathmandu's Tribhuvan International Airport prior to the departure from here on Friday of the Indian Airlines flight IC-814 to Delhi which was later hijacked, authorities here have immediately begun cleaning up their act. THE INDIAN CASE, *Tribune*, Monday, December 27, 1999.
8. N.K. Bose, *Culture and Society in India*, Bombay: Asia Publishing House, 1967, pp. 15–20.

16

Globalization and Social Transformation in India

S.L. Sharma

An overarching trend of our times, globalization signifies a transformative force of enormous significance. It represents a force of reorganization of global economic order based on advocacy of open door economic policy between nations, entailing significant socio-cultural fallouts. While its importance as a catalyst of economic transformation in the developing countries has been widely acknowledged, its role in their socio-cultural transformation has not yet received an intense scholarly attention. It is, therefore, time to undertake systematic studies of socio-cultural impact of globalization in developing countries. A modest attempt in that direction is being made in this paper with a focus on India – one of the major beneficiaries of globalization.

A look at the sociological discourse on globalization in India reveals that it has been concerned more with the cultural consequences of globalization than with its social outcomes, which is evident from the writings of Singh (2000) and Dhanagare (2003) among others. The social fallouts of globalization have received at best a cursory treatment. A question of seminal sociological significance to ask in this regard is: whether globalization has generated a trend of social transformation in India and, if so, what is its direction? This precisely is the question I seek to address in this paper. In order to deal with this question in a systematic manner, I set for myself the following specific tasks: (i) to clarify the concept of globalization; (ii) to problematize the term 'social transformation' and articulate it as a concept; (iii) to delineate the socio-cultural fallouts of globalization in India; and (iv) to apprise their transformational potential. The paper is accordingly organized into four parts, and in that order.

Understanding Globalization

There are many different interpretations of the term 'globalization', almost as many as its interpreters. This is hardly surprising in view of its multifaceted and dynamic character. However, it leaves a reader highly perplexed about the exact meaning of the term. In order to steer clear of the conceptual mess, I would like to unravel the meaning of globalization in a systematic manner. An analytical scrutiny of its various definitions reveals two distinguishable formulations under which these can be subsumed: (a) globalization as a process of unification of the world brought about by extraordinary advances in information and communication technology; and (b) globalization as a process of unification of the world by means of market integration across nations. A number of scholars have defined globalization as a special and temporal compression of the world accelerated by recent advances in information and communication technology. McLuhan was the first to conceive the idea of 'global village' in the context of mounting significance of media in uniting the world. Startling advances in cyber technology that followed have enabled mankind to conquer time and space. Accordingly, Robertson (1992) has defined globalization as a process that "refers both to the compression of the world and intensification of consciousness of the world as a whole". Similarly, Giddens (1990) interprets globalization as 'distanciation' which implies compression of time and space facilitating 'social action at a distance'. More pointedly, Waters defines globalization as "a process in which the constraints of geography on social cultural arrangements recede and people become aware that they are receding" (1995: 3). Viewed in this way, globalization, for all practical purposes, signifies emergence of a 'network world', thanks to the rise of worldwide web and other spectacular advances in information and communication technology (ICT). Turning to the other formulation, i.e., globalization as market integration, the following definition by the International Monetary Fund (IMF) may be cited as a representative one: "Globalization is characterized by increases in flows of trade, capital, information as well as mobility of individuals across borders." Similarly, Friedman and Kaplan (2002) have defined it as "a process of integration of markets, finance and technology ... in a way that shrinks the world". There are such other definitions that project globalization as mobilization of capital, goods and services across borders without much restrictions.

The above delineated two constructs of globalization obviously differ in their points of emphasis – one stressing the communicative aspect while the other highlighting its economic dimension. Their differences of emphasis apart, the two need not be viewed as rival but as complementary constructs. Only that they have to be reconciled in terms of primacy of the one over the other. In my view, globalization is primarily a process of economic reorganization of world aided and accelerated as much by stunning advances in ICT as by sponsored liberalization of domestic economic policies. As a consequence, it also entails informational and cultural flows across borders.

In order to have a proper understanding of globalization, a few clarifications need to be made. First, that globalization in its present import is a new development, and not an age-old process. The earlier moves in the direction of effecting global unification such as those undertaken by world explorers, religious missionaries, and enterprising traders, followed by colonization and modernization, may aptly be viewed as precursors to globalization. While it is true that globalization is cumulative consequence of all these moves, what distinguishes it, however, is the design of late capitalism to launch it as a global project. The idea of globalization actually gathered momentum following three developments of historic significance in 1980s. These events include collapse of Soviet Union, demolition of Berlin Wall and advent of worldwide web. While the collapse of Soviet Union and demolition of Berlin Wall signified triumph of capitalism over socialism, the advent of worldwide web paved the way to a networked world. It is this historic synchronization of the three developments which constructed that specific historical context from which the notion of globalization arose.

Secondly, globalization is not an innocent process of global unification. Instead, it is a transformative project of global capitalism to recast the world in its own mould. The reason in support of my contention are: (a) that a call for globalization came around 1980s from the global development agencies, including World Bank and International Monetary Fund (IMF), to the less developed nations to adopt Structural Adjustment Programme (SAP) and open up their markets for integration with global market; (b) globalization is commended as a new strategy of development for the developing nations, one that is claimed to be more effective than the earlier strategy which laid stress on capital, technology and expertise; and (c) globalization is projected as a progressive policy vis-à-vis, the policy of protective traffic followed earlier. The developing nations are accordingly advised to do away with restrictions on import and export and follow instead an open door economic policy. The creditability of these claims apart, there is more to the idea of globalization than what meets the eye. The fact of the matter is that globalization is a consequence of the development of productive forces of the leading industrialized nations necessitating search for markets in the developing nations to sell off their surplus produce (Castro, 1998). It is essentially their need, that is why, they are powerful advocates of globalization. What is more, their pressure on the developing nations to abandon the policy of protective tariff is in contradiction of their own past policy of protective tariff which they themselves had used as a ladder to reach their present level of development, as documented by Chang (2003).

A third point is that globalization is not a process of free flow of trade, finance, services, etc., across the world, as it is generally projected to be. Instead, it is hegemonically negotiated process of economic and cultural flows across borders. This is evident from the experience of the developing countries which, for most part, have remained largely at the receiving end. Take, for example, the immigration laws of the advanced nations, including USA and Britain, which have become more stringent in recent years restricting the entry of the people from the developing nations. It is the same story with the trade of certain commodities from the developing nations. Most important of all, it is evident from the parleys of the ministerial level meetings of WTO held earlier at Doha and Cancun and more recently at Hongkong where the leaders of the developed nations managed to manipulate reluctant consent of their counterparts from the developing nations, on the question of phased withdrawal of farm subsidies, in spite of the fierce protest by the latter. All this is understandable in view of the absence of level playing field between the developed and developing nations on account of their unequal levels of development.

Finally, globalization is not a fixed but an evolving reality. Its contours have changed significantly in the last few years. Launched as a hegemonic process of unilateral flow of trade and capital from the developed to the underdeveloped nations in the 1980s, globalization has now turned into a multilateral flow of investment and services from the developing to the developed world also. This is evident from the inroads made into Europe and America by the Chinese and Indian multinationals, besides software professionals in recent years. Furthermore, not limited to economic flows, globalization has as well accelerated a stream of cultural flows across the world. It has generated a matrix of growing inter-cultural contact and communication among diverse national cultures which have been brought face-to-face in the market place. It has thus created a scenario of cultural confluence as much as of economic interdependence.

Defining Social Transformation

Few terms have gained as much currency in contemporary sociological parlance as social transformation. This is evident from its frequent use in prevailing sociological discourse as well as in recent writings. Its extant usage is understandable in view of the momentous changes taking place in society. However, the use pattern of the term reveals a tendency of its indiscriminate use. Often than not, it is used in an interchangeable sense of social change. Its referents range from all kinds of passing changes to extraordinary ones. It has thus become a part of sociological vocabulary but not of sociological dictionary. Unlike the other terms such as social evolution, progress, revolution and development, which figure in sociology texts as distinguishable forms of social change, the term 'social transformation' has yet to acquire a technical connotation. There is, therefore, a need to articulate it as a sociological concept and indicate its *differentia specifica*. This is precisely what I seek to do here.

The literal meaning of the term 'transformation' is change from one form to another. It connotes a kind of change that transcends the original form of the object to which it is applied. In this sense, it signifies a systemic change rather than an incidental one. The term 'social' refers to a system of social relationships, institutions, identities and values. Taken together, thus, social transformation literally means systemic change in the frame of social relationship, institutions, identities and values. To illustrate it, it is important to distinguish between two types of changes in society: transitory and transformative. In my view, transformative changes are distinguishable from transitory trends in terms of three parameters, i.e., their profundity, magnitude and power of persistence. Profundity-wise, they are fundamental, magnitude-wise, they are phenomenal and persistence-wise, they are relatively irreversible. To elaborate on the first, transformative change is that which represents a fundamental departure from the root, i.e., from the original form of a social unit/system to which it pertains. Take, for instance, the trend of gay marriages. Given the original and the usual idea of marriage as a union of individuals of opposite sexes, gay marriage represents an instance of social transformation once it gains social acceptability. Moving on to the second distinguishing feature of transformative change, i.e., its phenomenal magnitude, social transformation is not a case of small but of substantial change. Proliferation of civil society groups, such as social action forums, civil rights unions and social resistance movements in a communal society, provides a telling illustration of it in that it is indicative of transformation of a communal society into a civil society. Coming to the third parameter, i.e., irreversibility, a transformative change is that which is not likely to revert to its original point of departure. Rise of a new middle class cutting across caste lines in a caste-ridden society is a graphic example of it.

Radical pace of change may as well be considered as a usual, though not a necessary feature of transformative change. Unlike gradual pace of change, as in the case of social evolution, social transformation is marked by a rapid pace of change. This means too tall a change in too short a time. A good example of it is the change in gender relations from a culture of hierarchy to that of equity. Even as radicalness is a usual feature of transformative change, it cannot be regarded as a parameter of social transformation for two reasons. One, that a systemic change does not necessarily take place as a sudden break with the past. There is generally a cumulative background to it. Two, that radicality is more a distinctive feature of revolution which may or may not result in transformation. In the interest of conceptual precision, therefore, social transformation may better be viewed as a case of fundamental, phenomenal and irreversible change in a given social script.

In order to further clarify the notion of social transformation, it may be reiterated that for all practical purposes, it signifies a case of structural change. Structural change connotes a profound change in social institutions, relational frames, identities and values. To decode it, institutional innovations such as 'live-in' arrangement as an alternative to conventional marriage is a clear instance of profound change. In the domain of relational frames, a trend of change from asymmetrical to symmetrical relations as in the case of inter-caste relations, is certainly an indicator of structural transformation. In respect of identities, similarly, when in-born identities give way to achieved identities, this constitutes a case of transformative change. In the realm of values, a change from communitarian to individualistic value provides a telling illustration of social transformation.

A final point to note about the concept of social transformation is that it is a value-neutral category. This clarification is important in view of the fact that generally the victims of a given system raise a demand for transformation, implying thereby a change for the better. In my view social transformation is a fact, not a value. It is not normative category for two reasons. One, because it stands for all kinds of structural shifts – upward as well as downward. For example, rise of consumerist middle class in a society known for its culture of frugal living as a value is as much an instance of a transformative change as emergence of a civil society in a traditionally communal society. Social transformation is thus about all sorts of structural shifts regardless of their being desirable or otherwise. Two, that treating social transformation as a judgemental construct will render it indistinguishable from such other varieties of social change as progress and development which obviously are value-laden.

Socio-cultural Fallouts of Globalization

The era of globalization started in India in 1991 with the introduction of economic reforms comprising a trinity of liberalization, privatization and globalization, popularly known as LPG. While the three are interrelated, each carries its own specific connotation. Liberalization refers to the policy of liberation of economy from the shackles of state control, marking the end of the era of 'licence-quota-permit raj'. Privatization stands for the policy of allowing entry of private sector in all the fields of economy, including those earlier monopolized by the state such as power, transport, oil, gas, etc., leading to the prevailing trend of disinvestment of public sector undertakings (PSUs). Globalization, as distinct from liberalization and privatization, signifies an open door economic policy for integrating domestic market with the old world market. Among other things, it means allowing foreign multinationals to enter into Indian market as much as Indian multinationals to go global. There are three notable points about the onset of globalization in India. First, unlike many other nations, India opted for it more out of its domestic economic compulsions than of volition. Given its increasing debt burden, fiscal deficit, poor state of balance of payment, high inflation and awful depletion of foreign reserves, the Indian state was left with no other option than accepting the globalization. Secondly, unlike a number of other nations, the Indian state opted for globalization together, with its two other accomplices, that is, liberalization and privatization. Thirdly, unlike several other nations, including China, which settled for selective globalization, the Indian state went for it in a relatively big way.

Whatever be the background, globalization has done a miracle to Indian economy. It has transformed it from a poor, backward and stagnant one to a buoyant, robust and fast allowing one. This is evident from all accounts. Its rate of growth has surged from a low 3.5 per cent in pre-reforms period to a high 9.2 per cent in 2006–07 according to the reports. According to a World Bank report (2005–06), India emerged as the 12th richest nation of the world in 2005 based on its GDP which is growing at 13.4 per cent in dollars. Little wonder that India earned the enviable distinction of being the 'fastest growing free market economy' at the World Economic Forum's annul summit at Davos in 2006. Furthermore, according to a recently released Merril Lynch Capgemini World Wealth Report, the number of dollar millionaires in India grew by 19.3 per cent in 2005, this being the second fastest in the world. The Economic Survey (2006–07) reveals that India's Foreign exchange reserves have reached a record $185.1 billion. This is a far cry from the pre-globalization era when India had to mortgage its gold reserves for getting foreign exchange. Similarly, the total foreign investment inflows into India have risen from almost zero in 1990 to $20 billion in 2005 and foreign remittances to over $24 billion. India is also now the sixth largest service exporter as well as a top destination for off shoring (according to a survey by A.T. Kearney). Above all, India has also become a trillion-dollar economy in April 2007 and thereby joined the elite club of 11 nations with such distinction. In view of these developments, the assessment of India in the Goldman Sachs BRIC Report by Wilson and Purushothaman (2003) as an emerging global economic power along with Brazil, Russia and China sounds so prophetic. By all accounts, Indian economy is on the move on a fast track, thanks to globalization.

When economy is on the move, especially at this incredible pace, society cannot remain unmoved. Globalization has set in motion a stream of changes in India's socio-cultural panorama as much as in Indian economy. These trends are noticeable in the domains of social stratification, institutions, values and identities. In the realm of social stratification, it has sprung up trends such as following: widening disparities in the midst of growing prosperity, rise of a new middle class, marginalization of peasantry, growing caste polarization and dalit assertion. Let us illustrate these before moving on the trends in other domains.

Disparity in the Midst of Prosperity

It is obvious that globalization has generated an overall climate of prosperity in India. One has only to recall the depressing days of pre-globalization phase in order to appreciate the state of relative prosperity today. Globalization has, for sure, opened opportunities galore for people with some measure of competence. Such opportunities were not available to them in the pre-globalization phase. Little wonder that many people of the lower classes have been able to make a grade to the lower-middle classes as claimed by Friedman (2005). Similar sentiment is reflected in Gurcharan Das' book *India Unbound* (2002). It is development such as these coupled with the story of world class enterprise of Infosys in Bangalore that led Thomas Friedman, the *New York Times* columnist, to contend that the world is flattening, the global economic playing field is getting levelled and that many people in India and China have grown out of poverty, thanks to globalization (Friedman, 2005: 9). While the above observation of Friedman is valid, it presents only one side of the coin. Globalization has no doubt enabled a wider population to see the benefits of economic growth, but it has made the rich richer, leaving the poor largely unaffected. For the same reason, it has led to widening and deepening of disparities. This is evident from almost all the available reports. For example, the rounds of National Sample Survey conducted in the mid-90s point to deepening inequalities. Similarly, a recent report of the Department of Economic Affairs, UNO, points to rising economic disparities in India in 1990s. Likewise, India's poverty ratio stands at a disgraceful 28 per cent (Aiyar, 2006). Most important of all, the Gini coefficient, which is a measure of socio-economic disparities, has risen for India from 0.37 to 0.42 in recent years. What is more, according to the 'Wealth Report' published on May 8, 2007 by Knight Frank, India is on the way to becoming a plutonomy – a society sharply stratified by a super wealthy top brand at one end and abject poor at the other, as reported in a leading national daily by Lall (2007).

On top of it, we have abundant observational evidence to see the widening gap between two Indias which I would like to call a *glittering* India and a *littering* India. The glittering India consists of super riches while the littering India consists of the gutter poor. The glittering India belongs to those who are super earners and super consumers, enjoy lavish lifestyle, and patronize mega malls, five stars, multiplexes and night parties. On the other hand, the littering India belongs to pavement dwellers, rag pickers, scavengers and sweepers, richshaw pullers, brick kiln workers and undernourished millions. The story of two Indias may be an old one but what makes it more distressing in the era of globalization is an "almost complete disconnect in between the 300 million, high flying Indians ... and the remaining 750 of their countrymen, many of whom seldom get two square meals a day" (Malhotra, 2006). At any rate, the littering India remains unincorporated in globalized India. Better than the eloquent title of Loretta Schwartz's book *Starving in the Shadow of Plenty*.

Rise of a New Middle Class

One of the most visible consequences of globalization in India is the emergence of a new middle class. It is getting bigger, richer, younger and spender by the day. Its size has grown here to an estimated 300 million, roughly 22 per cent as against 12 per cent elsewhere in the world. The new middle class is different from the traditional middle class in some significant respects, that is, in its composition, age group, income level, lifestyle and social outlook. It is composed of company executives, IT specialists, finance and management consultants, media professionals and neo-riches, including the 'bullock capitalists' from the countryside to use Varma's phrase (1998). In terms of age composition, the new middle class is younger than its traditional counterpart, which is understandable in view of the special value of its professional skills that are in big demand in the fast growing knowledge economy in the era of globalization. Not surprisingly, it is lauded by commentators like Varma (1998) for its buoyancy, energy, entrepreneurship and resilience. Its income levels have risen to an amazing high, thanks to lucrative packages offered by transnational and private corporations, unthinkable in respect of traditional middle class. This has consequently enhanced its purchasing power as well as its spending proclivity. No wonder that the new middle class has emerged as a consumerist class which is willing to pay to live-in-style. More than its mode of living, the new middle class is seen as holding of brief for rethinking conventional morality. Well informed, alert and articulate, the new middle class is getting global in its world view. Progressive on all these counts, it leaves something to be desired in respect of civic sensibility as its glosses over the larger public issues of poverty, inequality, corruption and oppression.

Marginalization of Peasantry

The effects of globalization are not confined to urban India only. They are as well noticeable in the countryside. Globalization has brought the market forces to bear on agriculture in a big way. For the same reason, it has generated trends of corporatization of agriculture, crop diversification, monoculture, genetically modified corps and, above all, creation of Special Economic Zones (SEZs). These trends, coupled with the WTO-induced pressure to reduce farm subsidies, have produced a new dynamics in agrarian structure, different from the one generated earlier by forces of modernization. If the thrust of modernization was on farm mechanization together with use of modern chemical inputs, the stress of globalization is on marketization strategies. In effect, globalization has accelerated a trend of depeasantization of small and marginal farmers as well as immiseration of agricultural labour driving many of them away to cities. It has as well affected middle peasantry and big farmers in some very insidious ways. Sandwiched between rising costs of agricultural inputs and minimum support price fixed by the state, the middle peasantry has come under terrible burden of indebtedness. This has led to alarming trend of increasing incidence of farmers' suicides in several states, such as Andhra Pradesh, Karnataka, Maharashtra and Punjab. A number of studies, including those conducted by (Kumar and Sharma, 1998, 2006), have brought out the pre-eminent role of globalization and accelerating this trend. The latest shot has come in the form of the state policy of setting up

SEZs, a move prompted by globalization, which has intensified farmers' unrest and led to their vigorous protest against the state. Farmer's mobilization in Singur and Nandigram provides solid evidence of it. While land acquisition by the state for the purposes of prompting SEZs has caused widespread consternation among farmers in general, the trend of large-scale buying of rural land close to cities by private estate dealers and builders has as well brought fortunes to some farmers. A number of big estate builders have entered into the fray to buy such land to construct malls and multiplexes and paid huge prices for it. This has come as a boon to some farmers, though their number is very few and far between. By and large, globalization has led to marginalization of rural folk.

Dalit Assertion and Caste Polarization

Dalit mobilization is not a new phenomenon. It dates back to the days of Mahatma Phule and Baba Saheb Ambedkar. Globalization has only intensified it and led to a renewed form of dalit assertion. It has produced this effect on account of its patronage to privatization on the one hand and its stress on disinvestment of PSUs, on the other. The contraction of public sector has led to neutralization of reserved job opportunities made available to Scheduled Castes (SCs) and Scheduled Tribes (STs) in the public sector under the policy of reservations. Irked by this development, the leaders of the Scheduled Castes and Scheduled Tribes Federation as well as the youths of these groups have raised a demand for reservations in private sector. This demand is being stoutly opposed by the leaders of industry and proprietors and managers of corporate sector as well as non-SC students of the professional courses. In effect, it has led to further unionization of dalits, on the one hand, and reaction formation among non-dalits, on the other. The dalit intellectuals have now begun to justify their demand for reservations in private sector on the basis of the systematic data rather than their general apprehensions. The following research-based observation by Sukhadeo Thorat, convincingly illustrates it: "After July 1990, the new measures have led to decline in the employment of SCs in government services and jobs ... Identical trends were observed in employment of SCs in public sector undertakings" (Thorat, 2001: 10). The leaders of private corporations are resisting this move by foregrounding the key importance of professional competence for organizational growth in this age of global competition. If dalit youths are agitated about their shrinking job prospects in the wake of globalization, the non-dalit professional students are militating against the move of reservation in private sector as it sets their careers at stake. Be that as it may, the point to note is that globalization has set the two against each other and thereby intensified the phenomenon of caste polarization.

Impact of Globalization on Basic Social Institutions

Liberalizing Marriage Mores

Turning to the impact of globalization on basic social institutions, it will be apt to focus on marriage, family and gender. Let us take them one by one. Rise in the age at marriage is a notable consequence of globalization. The youth today, particularly those drawn into corporate sector, have begun to accord precedence to career over marriage. This has become a source of anxiety to parents, especially those whose daughters of marriageable age shy away from marriage on account of their preoccupation with the career. Globalization of the culture of dating is another remarkable trend that is catching up with youth in the metropolitan centres. This points to a trend of self-assertion by youth in matters of marriage. Equally important is the trend of commercialization of wedding arrangements which have been taken over by professional agencies leading to change venue from home to hotel and now to a farm house.

Globalization has also set in motion a move towards demerger of sex and marriage. This is evident from the increasing incidence of pre-martial and extra-martial sex, as reported by a number of surveys (Vieira, 1998; Bhandare, 2003; Wadhwa, 2004). This trend is of profound significance in the sense that it runs counter to the domain of marriage, that is, sex in wedlock only. There is now in sight a tendency of ignoring the pre-marital affairs of the mate which earlier used to constitute an important consideration in mate selection. As with pre-marital affairs, so with extra-marital alliance: there seems to be growing a measure of tolerance of it as is evident from the emerging idea of 'office spouse'. There is thus a spouse at home and another at office/organization where one has now to spend a longer time. The office spouse is a colleague of opposite sex with whom one develops intimacy and shares matters which he/she is traditionally supposed to share with his/her life partner. Since the work scenario has changed in a manner that it has substantially cut down one's family time, the couple hardly finds time for sharing and caring together. Office spouse is thus a surrogate partner for fulfilling this need. It signifies more of a romantic relationship than a sexual one. The work organizations are reported to be acquiescent about it in the hope that it retains employees for a longer time at the workplace contributing to organizational growth. This should not be mistaken to mean decline of sexuality in wedlock. On the contrary, globalization has sparked off a 'culture of super sex' in the wedlock. As in the boardroom, so in the bedroom, there is a growing passion for being innovative. Super sex is about getting better, aesthetic, fantastic and creative in sexual pleasure. Yet another development relates to emergence of 'weekend unions' particularly in the case where husband and wife are working for two different organizations located at such a distance that prevents the two to live together at one place. Most important of all is the rise of live-in unions, as an institutional alternative to marriage. The trend of 'live-in unions' first appeared in Sweden from where it has come to India, thanks to the forces of globalization. A side effect of these developments is that marriage is no longer a taken for granted institution. It now takes efforts on the part of spouses to make marriage work. In view of the above, it will not be wrong to observe that conventional marriage is proving inadequate to handle fancies which are being generated by glamourized sex life shown in the media.

Changing Familial Role Relations

The pre-globalization era witnessed a sociological debate on the disintegrative impact of modernization on joint family. In present times, it seems that globalization has led to destabilization of nuclear family as well. The increasing incidence of marital discord, caused by the excessive demand of corporate world over family time of its employees, is proof enough of it. It is a well-known fact that in the era of globalization commitment to career and consumerism has taken precedence over family obligations. This has led to several consequences, including its adverse effects on marital harmony, child care and care of aged parents. Little wonder that it has given rise to trend of childless couples by choice and abandoning of aged parents by grown up sons, resulting in shrinking size of the family. The trend of decline in family size is not altogether new. It has started in the era of modernization itself which paved the way from 'double income single child' (DISC) preference to 'double income no child' (DINC) craze. The rise of globalization with its patronage to private corporate has only served to reinforce the ongoing shift from 'one child' concept to 'no child' preference. What distinguishes it is the new mode of justification. Earlier, it was a consequence of the lure of double income to provide for better parenting; now it is prompted by precedence to professional career over parental role. Though the number of couples opting to stay 'issueless' is quite small, it nevertheless is important to indicate that the thought has germinated and is likely to gain in spread. This is no insignificant development in a society which values parenthood and frowns upon childless couples.

Another remarkable consequence of globalization is the altering conjugal power relations. Globalization has generated opportunities for women to enter high-profile occupations and entrepreneurial positions. This has led to a new kind of power equation between husband and wife, with wife becoming more assertive and husband getting accommodative. The increasing incidence of husband's participation in household chores as well as wife's active say in decision-making is proof enough of it. The role of parents in the socialization of children is another dimension of family change. Father has begun to take on added responsibility in raising children which has made him more of a friendly figure, unlike his earlier image of patriarch. Mother, on the other hand, has begun to assume the role for disciplinarian in her own way. Both the parents seem to be getting concerned more about the career of children than about their character. For the same reason, they are getting the children exposed to additional skill forming courses with a view to sharpening their intellect and making them smarter. This has brought the children under pressure to perform. As such, unlike the popular impression that globalization has led to parental neglect of children, the fact is that it has enhanced parental concern and quality of parenting. It is a different matter though that parental influence in respect of character training is somewhat on decline. Media has emerged as an alternative agency of socialization with greater influence on the young generation. Accordingly, peer culture, which is largely shaped by media, seems to be exerting greater influence over the choices, preferences and value orientation of youth. The mounting influence of media, including television, computer and internet, which is an integral part of globalization, has also impacted parent–child relations. The traditional paradigm of parental authority and child obedience has begun to yield ground to the emerging pattern of child's rights and parental obligations. As a result, what we have is a phenomenon of assertive child and accommodative parents. The parents today are faced with a kind of parental dilemma about their cultural obligation to discipline and restrain the child and the limits set on it by the civil obligation to grant freedom of choice to the youth. This is not just a case of usual generation gap but something more than that. There are two ways to look at it: as a case of generation break and as a case of generation bridge. It signifies a case of generation break in that the young generation today has begun to call into question the rationale of traditional norms in a manner as never before. Given the exposure of the young generation to global information about cultural diversities and more so about the emerging norms of civil society, its interrogation of traditional norms is almost belligerent. Hence, a case of generation break. Viewed from the other perspective, it represents a case of generation bridge in the sense that the old generation is responding to the new situation in a somewhat moderate manner. It is showing a commendable accommodative maturity in putting up with the emerging situation. Both the ways of looking at the changing parent–child relations seem to be valid as they touch on two different but complementary facets of the same reality.

Yet another consequence of globalization for family system is the emerging problem of abandoned aged parents. With their increasing concern for career and demanding corporate obligations, the young adults find it hard to take care even of their children, let alone the ageing parents. Add to it the prevailing ethos of pragmatism and privacy prompted globalization which is taking a heavy toll of bonds of affectivity for which Indian family has been known worldwide. Globalization has thus led to narrowing down of the circle of relations to one's family of procreation with little regard for family of orientation, resulting in many cases in the neglect of aged parents. The enormity of this problem can be gauged from the fact that the Indian State has to come up with the Bill called 'Maintenance and Welfare of Parents and Senior Citizens Bill, 2007' which was introduced in the budget session (2007) of parliament. The purpose of the Bill is to make it obligatory for children to care of their aged parent above 60 years. This only testifies to the fact that globalization has led to improvisation of the graying parents. They have been rendered improvised not only economically but also socially and culturally.

Impact of Globalization on Beliefs and Values

Globalization has impacted not only social institutions but also beliefs and values. This is evident from the outbreak of culture of consumerism, confounding moral ambiguity and appalling state of civility. Let us take them up one by one.

Upsurge of Culture of Consumerism

Celebration of the culture of consumerism is one of the most visible consequences of globalization. This is evident from the proliferation of mega malls, marts, multiplexes and magnificent markets. This is also obvious from the emerging brand-conscious lifestyle, refined tastes, choices and preferences. Above all, this is reflected in the growing mentality of acquisitiveness resulting in processions far in excess of needs.

Culture of consumerism is not just about consuming more. It actually refers to a classy lifestyle. The distinctive traits of such a lifestyle are: concern for brand equity, craze for the latest, and proliferation of wants over needs and a tendency of exhibitionism. Brand equity serves as a measure of status. Accordingly, it is patronized as a status symbol. The connection between brand equity and globalization is clear from the manner in which multinationals and credible domestic companies invest into projection of their brand equity for purposes of marketing. Craze for the latest, another element of culture of consumerism, implies an attitude of discarding the old and adopting the new, i.e., abandoning yesterday's buy in favour of today's fad. This desire for the latest is systematically kept up by the organizations by means of continuously coming up with something 'new and different'. It is also sustained by stimulating a desire to stay ahead of others. The third ingredient of culture of consumerism signifies a crucial distinction between needs and wants. Needs represent necessities, while wants represent desires. One may not need what one wants. This, in fact, is often the case and far more so in the era of globalization. Wants are manufactured desires, generated by advertisements patronized by media. Little wonder that globalization has led to multiplication of wants over needs and a trend of unabashed consumerism. This development is at variance with the values of our culture which puts premium on curtailment of needs. Globalization has thus moved us from a state of 'simple living and high thinking' to that of 'high living and mindless consumerism'. It calls for a revision of Descartes' classic dictum 'I think, therefore, I am' to 'I consume, therefore, I am', as cited in an editorial of a leading national daily (*The Times of India*, February 24, 2007).

Conventional Morality under Interrogation

Morality is a judgmental category. Built upon the notion of human good, it provides a normative framework for judging propriety of conduct pertaining to interpersonal relations including sex norms. Its defining feature is its stern applicability to self as much as to others. Hence, its primary dictum: do unto others what you want others to do to you; don't do unto others what you want other not do to you. Derived from this dictum are certain universal values such as truth, honesty, fidelity, integrity, incorruptibility, non-stealing, selflessness, etc., beyond such universal values which are usually incontrovertible, there are some relative values which are time/space-specific. They vary from community to community. Take, for example, sex-related conduct such as kissing in public, dating and courtship. These are viewed as immoral conduct in India but not in the West. However, even in India, compared to earlier times when they aroused a greater sense of moral indignation, today that is not so. Proud of its glorious tradition of morality, Indian society is abounding in moral ambiguity today. There is ample evidence of deviance from moral norms of truth, public probity, integrity, concern for others, abstinence from kissing in public, pre-marital sex, etc. What is more, there is also emerging a tendency of open defiance of these norms in public. From deviance to open defiance is a notable trend. Conventional morality is increasingly coming under interrogation, and being confronted with 'alternative morality'. Globalization has ushered in a new era of alternative lifestyle (consumerist), alternative sex morality (liberalized) and alternative relational morality (pragmatic). Prompted by market-driven economy, such a morality is now viewed as 'progressive morality' (which is actually permissive morality). Mass media is glamourizing it in a big way. Leisure industry is marketing it vigorously. While the conventional morality has not yet lost its ground, the alternative morality has yet to gain a firm foot. As of now, the custodians of conventional morality view the present situation as a case of value decadence, while the protagonists of alternative morality look upon it as morality in quest of redefinition. Whatever it is it certainly points to a state of moral flux, if not to breakdown of moral order.

Civil Values in Disarray

Civil values are different from moral values in that they pertain to public domain unlike the latter which relate to community domain. Public is a political category while community is a social entity. Accordingly, civil values represent the desirable conditions of public life such as liberty, equality and secularity, etc., while moral values have to do with conceptions of human good. As with moral values, so with civil values; globalization has led to their impairment. This is evident from the disconcerting trend of fundamentalism, recurrent stream of communalism, rampant corruption, criminalization of politics, falling standards of public conduct, callousness towards the downtrodden, and diminishing concern for environment and ecology. Not generated by globalization, for sure, but globalization has certainly led to aggravation of these trends. It has done so by giving upper hand to market over state, profit maximization over concern for ecology and equity, meritocracy over compensatory justice, and 'haves' over 'have-nots'. These unwholesome developments have not gone unresisted. A number of civil and social resistance groups have come up in order to protest against these unwholesome trends. Role of civil rights unions, environment groups, social forums, anti-corruption councils, and, above all, anti-globalization movements are some of the instances in point. Healthy signs, of course, as they point to the rise of civil society, these developments are just unintended consequences of globalization.

Cultural Traditions and Identities under Threat

Globalization is not just economic flows; it is also about cultural flows. As a result, it has generated stirring effects on cultural traditions and identities across the globe, particularly in the non-western parts of the world. Like elsewhere, in India too, there has appeared a debate about the repercussions of globalization on the cultural traditions and identities. Voicing a popular concern in this regard, D.N. Dhanagare has highlighted 'pernicious effects' of globalization on local communities and cultures. In particular, he deplores the role of MNCs and media for exerting shattering impact on ethnic traditions and craftsmen. Without mincing words, he observes: "local economies are being swallowed gradually by the global capitalism and traditional cultures are being displaced by the over-expanding global market and consumer culture" (Dhanagare, 2003: 23). On the other side, there is Yogendra Singh who contended that globalization also accelerates the growth of cultural self-consciousness and cultural identities. Admitting that "the penetration of external market ad capitalist interests may threaten local or regional cultures by new modes of appropriation and capitalist interests may threaten local or regional cultures by new modes of appropriation and erosion of traditional cultural values' he argues that 'improvement and enlargement of the reach of communication may provide means to people to strengthen cultural identities" (Singh, 2000: 96). "In this sense", he adds, "the globalization process, instead of being a threat to such identities, has become a means for their construction" (ibid.: 97).

For a systematic appraisal of the cultural consequences of globalization, I find Fukuyama's conceptual frame of "globalized production of homogenization" (1992) and Appadurai's "globalized production of differences" (1996) quite revealing. I would therefore like to build upon the same for analysing the Indian situation. For sure, globalization has resulted in "globalized production of homogenization". In the cultural field, this is evident from the upsurge of the following: culture of consumerism, commercialization and commodification of cultures, pop culture, and virtual culture. These may be regarded as cultural universals of globalization. As elsewhere, so in India, culture of consumerism has made inroads into all local cultures, its greater visibility in new middle class notwithstanding. The proliferation of malls, marts and multiplexes, the easy availability of finances, the entry of big players in retail and rural marketing – all of this is going to give a further fillip to culture of consumerism. Its disruptive implications for the traditional cultures in a land known for its value of frugal living are too obvious to require any elaboration. Similarly, the trend of commercialization of cultural events and activities as also of commodification of cultural symbols cuts across cultural frontiers, thanks to the rise of global tourism. This has led to trivialization of ethnic cultures as well as distortions in local cultures.

The universal spread of media-patronized pop culture is another force of homogenization. Known for its domination by American themes and concerns, it combines selective elements of British, African and some exotic cultures. McDonaldization, Coca-Colization, Valentinization and Reggae mesmerization are some of its prominent markers among many others. Titillating in its appeal, it is known for luring people, especially youths, away from their cultural roots. More importantly, its contaminating effects on classical as well as folk cultures are much resented in India as in other parts of the world. Emergence of virtual culture is yet another manifestation of homogenization. Virtual culture is a product of the stunning advances in information and communication technology. All productions of electronic media, including films, television programmes and internet communication, are parts of the stream of cultural productions. The stupendous growth of cultural productions constitutes a distinguishing mark of the age of globalization. If the era of modernization was an era of mass-scale material production, the era of globalization is an era of mass-scale cultural productions. These cultural productions have generated virtual culture which consists of animated signs, manufactured images and make-beliefs. Such is the mounting significance of virtual culture in the age of cyber technology that it has acquired autonomy of its own. For all practical purposes, it is independent of existential culture. Its autonomy can be gauged from the quality of its role in the socialization of the young generations. Virtual culture indeed has emerged as a powerful agency of socialization, one that is more powerful in shaping the perceptions, choices and preferences of youth than existential culture and its agencies like the family and the school. Even as virtual culture is largely illusory in its content, it is vital in its impact on the young generation. And, this is so all the world over.

The above outlined forces of globalized production of homogenization have led to erosion of certain aspects of local cultures. This invasion of culture of consumerism has adversely affected traditional lifestyles and tastes, customary practices, sanctity of rituals and even the normative order. Similarly, commercialization and commodification of culture has turned local and ethnic cultures into a marketable commodity and thereby robbed them of their symbolic value. In much the same way, pop culture has not only marginalized classical and folk cultural traditions of art and aesthetics but also led to their obliteration on account of mixings and blending. Above all, the rise of virtual culture has served to erode the very foundations of existential local cultures. For all these reasons, globalization has in some ways created a threatening situation for cultural diversities and distinctions. Little wonder that there is a threat perception in local cultural circle where it is feared that MNCs-led globalization is destroying their traditional cultures and identities.

There is, however, another side of the repercussions of globalization on traditional cultures. This relates to what Appadurai calls "globalized production of differences" (1996). Paradoxical though it may appear, globalization has as well triggered off certain trends which are indicative of upsurge of cultural distinctions and identities. Prominent among them are: enhanced salience of ethnic pride and products, identity assertion by diverse cultural communities, rise of fundamentalism and resurgence of diasporic cultures. Like modernization, globalization has resulted in sharpening of ethnic consciousness as well as craze for ethnic things. The upsurge of ethnic consciousness is a case of ethnic backlash against the homogenizing forces of globalization. But, the craze for ethnic things, including ethnic dishes, crafts and paintings, is generated by globalization in order to cash in on them. Advertently or inadvertently, in both the cases, the net result is the upsurge of ethnic pride. Another fallout of globalization is the trend of identity assertions by diverse cultural groups. Faced with the challenge of hegemonic homogenization thrown up by globalization, local, regional and national cultures have responded by motivated articulation or reinvention of their respective identities. This is evident from the trend of assertive celebration of religious festivals, regional fairs and ceremonial festivals, be it Durga Puja in West Bengal or Ganesh Utsava in Maharashtra, or Guru Parva processions in Punjab (Sharma, 1990). Such celebrations serve as measures of identity re-affirmation by local and regional cultures. In organizing such celebrations, interestingly enough, the local cultural groups enthusiastically use all the new means and resources of globalization to reiterate their respective cultural identity. Thus, there is as much evidence of appropriation of globalization by ethnicity as of ethnic specialties by globalization. Aside from activization of ethnicity, globalization has also precipitated ethnic fundamentalism, especially religious fundamentalism. The spurt of ethno-nationalism as well as of fundamentalism both in India and abroad is a proof enough of it. Academic indictment of Huntington's thesis of clash of civilizations (1996) notwithstanding, the later day incidents of 9/11 and its sequels in Iraq and Iran provide telling illustrations of it. Similarly, the recurrent events of terrorist attack in India bear further testimony of it.

Finally, globalization has led to activization of diasporic cultures. Not a new phenomenon, diasporic cultures have gained salience in the wake of globalization. This is so partly because of enhanced incidence of 'translocation' of cultures on account of accelerated migration of people due to globalization and partly because of emergence of transnational networks between diasporic groups of the same nationality. Globalization has generated a scenario of face to face contact of diverse national cultures in an alien setting. In a situation such as this, every diasporic culture shows a proclivity to retain its identity vis-à-vis, others. As a matter of fact, in such a setting, culture serves as an identity resource for its people to maintain their identity as well as their integrity. This is so much reflected in the diasporic literature. Furthermore, the development of transnational network between diasporic groups of the same 'homeland' has led to further strengthening of their cultural integrity across nations. This fact has been brought out by recent diasporic research (Bhat, 2005).

At this point it will be in order to appraise the above alluded to debate about the cultural fallouts of globalization. Let us take the homogenization thesis first. On the face of it, homogenization thesis seems to be credible in view of near universal spread of culture of consumerism, mass-mediated pop culture and virtual culture. On closer examination, however, these trends neither make for convergence of cultures nor for a uniform global culture, nor neutralization of cultural diversities and distinctions. Therefore, the homogenization thesis is untenable. On the other hand, the thesis of "globalized production of differences", though largely valid, is also not wholly true. Notwithstanding the evidence of backlash of ethnic or local cultures, their identity assertion and the salience of diasporic cultures, the fact remains that they are no longer the same authentic cultures as before, that they represent their reinvented versions, and that they have lost a bit of their integrity under the spell of globalization. Thus, because of globalized production of differences, globalization has made a difference of their authentic forms. In view of the substantial evidence of identity consciousness of local, regional and national cultures, the popular threat perception seems to be a case more of panic reaction than rational contention. All the same, a dispassionate look at the situation suggests that traditional cultures are not going to remain the same any longer.

Theoretical Inferences

Having deciphered the trends of change in the Indian socio-cultural panorama under the impact of globalization, it will be in order to bring out their theoretical implications. To this end, the following three questions are of core sociological significance: (i) Has the structural adjustment of economy led to structural shifts in society? (ii) Has globalization ushered in some new trends of socio-cultural transformation which are different from those unleashed by industrialization and modernization? The theoretical significance of these questions lies in the fact that they address the seminal sociological issue of interrelations among economy, society and culture.

To take up the first question, it is evident from the above analysis that globalization has led to a measure of mobilization in the realm of social institutions and role-relationships. In some ways it has generated some structural shifts as well, such as rise of a new middle class, marginalization of peasantry and proliferation of civil society groups. However, it has not been able to make a dent into, let alone displace, the basic social structure of India which consists of caste system. If anything it has only served to reinforce caste structure as is evident from the vigorous dalit mobilizations from reservation. For sure, the recent caste-based student mobilization, both of the dalits and forward castes, has been precipitated by the impact of globalization on the policy of reservations. However, these mobilizations are indicative of the power of structural diversities to assert themselves in the face of globalization. Similarly, various other primal groups, including ethnic and communal, have been negotiating with the forces of globalization in their own respective ways, thus influencing the course of globalization in India. From all this it is clear that the impact of globalization on Indian diversities is not unilateral. It is indeed dialectical as the socio-cultural diversities have as well been impinging on globalization here and influencing its character.

Turning to the impact of globalization on traditional cultures, it is evident from the preceding section that globalization has introduced some elements of the so-called global culture in India, such as culture of consumerism, pop culture and virtual culture. It has thereby generated a semblance of cultural transformation entailing a threat of annihilation of the identities and distinctions of traditional and local cultures. A deeper probe, however, reveals that the traditional and local cultures have not taken it lying down. There is on record ample evidence of backlash in the form of re-invocation of ethnic pride and reiteration of cultural identities and distinctions. More important than that, there is also noticeable substantial evidence of the traditional cultures usurping the material and communicative resources of globalization for proclaiming their identities and distinctions. On net balance, then, we find considerable evidence of cultural transformation. Stated in theoretical terms, globalization provides a site for the contest of economy and culture. As a form of economic reorganization, globalization has generated some measure of cultural change in India. At the same time, cultural systems have also well shown a great deal of vibrancy and agility to keep their identities intact in spite of bulldozing effect of globalization. The upshot of it all is that like the relationship between globalization and social structure, the relationship between economic globalization and culture is also not unilateral, but dialectical.

Coming to the third question, it may be observed with some measure of theoretic reflection that globalization has generated a few trends of socio-cultural transformation which are distinctive to it. Two of them are particularly notable: one relates to the locus of change and the other to its direction. It is well known that the era of industrialization heralded changes in the forces of production and the relations of production, resulting in the emergence of capitalism and capitalist class structure. Unlike that, the era of globalization is marked by changes in the larger frame of social relations, that is, in the mode of how people relate themselves to one another beyond the frame of class relations. A discerning mind can see it that in the wake of globalization people have begun to relate themselves more in the frame of egalitarian relations than in that of inegalitarian relations of class structure. Globalization has opened up opportunities for all to make a grade and be counted on his/her merit. To recall Friedman's phrase, it has led to the emergence of a 'flat world'. This obviously points to a new direction of change which is from hierarchical to egalitarian, puritanical to liberal, and oppressive to emancipatory. A recall of the trends of change in the wake of globalization, as discussed in the preceding section, clearly indicates this direction. No matter, which sphere of social structure we take, be it gender system, kinship system, caste system or ethnic communities, the trend of change is in the direction of egalitarian, liberal and emancipatory impulse. This renders the impact of globalization distinguishable from that of industrialization which patronized a structure of unequal socio-economic relations in the singular frame of class structure.

Let me hasten to add here lest I am accused of taking contradictory and an untenable stand that I am aware of the fact that globalization in its elemental form represents a project of hegemonic homogenization of the world. Therefore, it is not so much because of its intent that globalization has turned out to be an emancipatory force, but in spite if its intent. Actually, this is due to the emergence of certain ideological developments which coincided with the course of globalization, including the movements for gender justice, compensatory justice to the underprivileged, human rights, and social resistance movements, that globalization has paved the way to libertarian trends. Many of these trends indeed emerged in the era of modernization. Globalization has only served to accelerate them. Thus, globalization has not produced the transformative trends all by itself, or independent of other factors and forces, but in conjunction with them.

References

Aiyar, Swaminathan S. Anklesaria (2006) "End of Poverty?", *Sunday Times of India*, New Delhi, December 17.

Appadurai, Arjun (1996) *Modernity at Large: Cultural Dimensions of Globalization*. Minneapolis: University of Minnesota Press.

Bhandare, Namita (2003) "Classified Information", *Hindustan Times*, December 4.

Bhat, Chandrashekhar (2005) Indian Diaspora and Transnational Networks: The Emergence of Global Networking among the Telugus. Presented at the International Seminar on Indian Diaspora, Sardar Patel University, Vallab Vidya Nagar, January 4–5.

Castro, Fidel (1998) *On Imperialist Globalization*. New Delhi: Leftword Books.

Chang, H.J. (2003) *Kicking Away the Ladder: Development History*. London: Anthem Press.

Das, Gurcharan (2002) *India Unbound: From Independence to the Global Information Age*. London: Profile Books Ltd.

Dhanagare, D.N. (2003) "Globalization: Towards an Alternative View", *Sociological Bulletin*, Vol. 52, No. 1, March.

Friedman, Thomas L. (2005) *World is Flat: A Brief History of the 21st Century*. New York: Farrar, Straus and Giroux.

Friedman, T. and B. Kaplan (2002) "States of Discord", *Foreign Policy*, March–April, pp. 64–70.

Fukuyama, F. (1992) *The End of History and the Last Man*. New York: Free Press.

Giddens, Anthony (1990) *The Consequence of Modernity*. Cambridge: Polity Press.

Huntington, S.P. (1996) *The Clash of Civilizations and the Making of World Order*. New York: Simon Schuster.

Kumar, Pramod and S.L. Sharma (1998) *Suicides in Rural Punjab*. Chandigarh: Institute for Development and Communication.

Lall, Rashmee Roshan (2007) "India's Super Rich are Getting Richer", *Times of India*, Chandigarh, May 10.

Malhotra, Inder (2006) "India's Economic Paradox: High Growth, Growing Disparities", *The Tribune*, October 20.

Robertson, Ronald (1992) *Globalization: Social Theory and Global Culture*. London: Sage.

Sharma, S.L. (2003) "Globalization and its Socio-Cultural Discontents", in Paramjit S. Judge et al. (eds.), *Development, Gender and Diaspora: Context of Globalization*, Jaipur and New Delhi: Rawat Publications.

—— (1990) "Salience of Ethnicity in Modernization: Evidence from India", *Sociological Bulletin*, Vol. 39, Nos. 1 and 2, March–September.

Singh, Y. (2000) *Culture Change in India: Identity and Globalization*. Jaipur and New Delhi: Rawat Publications.

Thorat, Sukhadeo (2001) New Economic Policy and its Impact on Employment and Poverty of the Scheduled Castes. Presented at the National Seminar on Liberalization, Dalits and the State, Chandigarh: Punjab University, Department of Sociology.

Varma, P.K. (1998) *The Great Indian Middle Class*. New Delhi: Viking.

Vieira, Walter E. (1998) "Changing Marriage Mores", *Business World*, July 22.

Wadhwa, Soma (2004) "Sex Survey: Fleshed Out", *Outlook*, December 2.

Waters, Malcolm (1995) *Globalization*. London: Routledge.

Wilson, Dominic and Roopa Purushothaman (2003) Dreaming with BRICs: The Path to 2050. www.goldmansaches.com/insight/research/reports/99.pdf.

17

Globalization and Social Transformation

Yogendra Singh on Culture Change in Contemporary India

Biswajit Ghosh

Globalization is ubiquitous in the contemporary world even though we often criticize or oppose certain processes associated with it. Our economic, social, cultural and political life today is rapidly drawn into much wider and faster networks of 'virtual localities'. As a corollary, individuals, groups and communities, irrespective of cultural or geographical boundaries, are progressively drawn into networks beyond time and space. Hence, distant localities today constitute a continuum and local events are now shaped by developments across the border and vice versa. Hence, beyond the predominant economic and political aspects, the socio-cultural facets of globalization have important ramifications for understanding the changing nature of our time and space. Interestingly, persons opposing globalization constitute a part of it and they do so by being empowered with a technology across space, which is a product of globalization itself. Hence, even in the current context of global market recession, certain aspects of globalization appear to be irreversible for many of us. There is, therefore, uniformity among the social scientists about the far-reaching potential of contemporary globalization to exert deep and qualitative imprint on our economy, society, culture and politics. While economic and political consequences of market globalism today have drawn wide attention of social scientists, we are equally concerned about the socio-cultural impact of such transformation. The questions that have become pertinent for many of us in this context are: Is globalization a threat to local culture? Or, does greater connectivity magnify the differences among societies? If our socio-cultural relationships are not tied to local areas and if such 'globality' also affects our thinking and action processes, does globalization make the people of the 'one world' homogeneous? There are also apprehensions about the resilience of cultural tradition in countries like India. If the economic and political aspects of globalization often produce contradictory results, how are we to apprehend their impact on our society and culture? This essay tries to find answers to these queries by examining Professor Yogendra Singh's views about the sociology of culture change in globalized India. I have particularly selected one important book of Singh, namely, *Culture Change in*

India: Identity and Globalization, published in 2000, for such a review. This book is a collection of essays written by the author during 1992–99. Some other writings of Singh related to social change also were taken into consideration for making a comprehensive appraisal of his views.

The Study of Socio-cultural Changes in India

Yogendra Singh is one of the pioneering Indian sociologists to notice multiple changes in our culture since the introduction of economic reforms. It may be noted that Indian sociologists have utilized the platform of Indian Sociological Association since early 1990s to deliberate on the social dimensions of economic reforms and in the March issue of *Sociological Bulletin* in 1995, four special articles on the issue written by Yogendra Singh, Jaganath Pathy, M.N. Panini and George Mathew were published. The introductory article by Singh spoke about the significance of culture in understanding of social change in India. There he argued that culture is manifested in the technological, mental, moral, social, aesthetic and spiritual achievements of humankind. Hence, it gives meaning to our relationship with the other, as it also forms our subjectivity. Culture enters into the processes of social change in many forms and at various levels. He therefore wrote, "culture defines the quality of social change as its indicator" (Singh, 1995: 1).

It is worth noting here that like many of his predecessors and contemporaries, Singh did not readily accept the paradigms of cultural studies originating in the West. Focusing rather on the historicity of Indian culture and civilization, Singh maintained an acute critical consciousness in arriving at an 'integrated approach' or 'paradigm mixes' for exploring the resilience of culture in the Indian context. According to Singh, the causation of social change is to be sought both from within and without the social system or the tradition. In other words, the heterogenic or exogenous and the orthogenetic or endogenous sources of change are equally important. Singh lamented that the conceptual framework of most studies of social change in India is such that the focus is either on 'social structure' to the exclusion of 'tradition', or on the latter without proper treatment of the former (Singh, 1973: vii). He also reminded us about the need to distinguish between cultural structure and social structure of these two relatively independent substantive domains. Following Redfield, Singh further sub-divided cultural structure into little and great traditions. Similarly, the social structure is divided into micro- and macro-structures. On the whole, Singh stressed on the need to focus upon the contexts through which processes of change could be examined (Nagla, 2008: 251).

Singh had been a persistent and keen observer of social change in India since independence and it would not be out of context to present his views in brief on different phases of social change that the country has witnessed. Thus, to begin with, Singh had studied the process of modernization of tradition in India. We witnessed a brilliant exposition of indigenous concepts and processes in his magnum opus *Modernization of Indian Tradition* (1973). To him, modernization is varied and complex and hence unlike westernization, modernization can be located in the cultural–historic conditions of Indian society. The existence of plural traditions as well as the resurgence of cultural response to modernization represents the challenges and contradictions that India has encountered in the course of its modernization. As the process of modernization is not universalistic, historiographic constructions are necessitated to establish the cognitive–structural attributes of the Indian tradition (Singh, 1973: vii). This is because "a unique feature of modernization in India is that it is being mainly carried forward through adaptive changes in the traditional structures rather than structural dissociation or breakdown. A form of *neo-traditionalization* thus proceeds along with modernization" (ibid.: x). The adaptive capacity of micro-structures like caste, family and village community has attracted the attention of Singh and research on these themes by a host of social scientists proved the unexpected elasticity and latent potential of Indian social institutions. Similarly, Singh brilliantly exposed the structural inconsistencies arising out of the process of modernization in India. Some of these inconsistencies are: (a) democratization without spread of civic culture (education), (b) bureaucratization without commitment to universalistic norms, (c) rise in media participation and aspirations without proportionate increase in resources and distributive justice, (d) verbalization of a welfare ideology without its diffusion in social structure and its implementation as a social policy, (e) over-urbanization without industrialization, and (f) modernization without meaningful changes in the stratification system (ibid.: 210). All these explain the diversity in the pattern of modernization in India and many other societies and hence, "particularistic growth pattern of modernization seems to be more credible than universalistic form of its development" (ibid.: 215).

Interestingly, the whole debate about socio-cultural changes initiated through 'modernization of Indian tradition' was evolved during 1970s and Singh went on discussing the 'crisis and resilience' of social change in India during early 1990s. In another of his book entitled *Social Change in India: Crisis and Resilience* published in 1993, Singh argued that the process of social change in India after 45 years of its independence has taken two specific forms. First, there has taken place a substantial change in the social structure without simultaneously bringing about a structural change in the society. It has resulted into tensions and often social crisis. Secondly, there has taken place a sea-change in the subjective domain or the consciousness of the people in respect of social change. For Singh, therefore, Indian society during early nineties is confronted with a situation of double crisis – one of success and the other of failure. He unmistakably wrote:

> Our investment so far in economic and social development has yielded results which we witness in the ascendancy of a new middle class. It offers dynamics in social and economic change, represent in large measure the resilience of many traditional institutions such as the traditional occupations, joint family system and religious values. It strengthens market, trade and media institutions and provides a massive base of the skilled manpower so indispensable for economic growth. But this success is essentially flawed on account of its self-centred ideological moorings and its narrow social base. This we called the "crisis of our success". The "crisis of our failure" is, however, much pervasive. It is marked by our failures in the field of poverty and social injustice .... Ironically, despite our profession of socialistic pattern of society, our policies in social and economic fields have been most detrimental to the prosperity of the weaker sections of

society, such as the *dalit*, the women, the scheduled castes, scheduled tribes and the minorities .... Our failure in the field of removal of illiteracy, and universalization of education is indeed at the root of the most of our "crisis of failure". (Singh, 1993: 14–15)

Yogendra Singh was not a Marxist, nor did he want to be a theorist of any particular school. Yet like many Marxists of his time he openly acknowledged the growing cleavages across social and cultural lines in 'modern India'. However, to him, the main reason for such cleavages is not merely the extension of the gap between the rich and the poor or between the lower and the middle or upper-middle classes. Along with widened structural hiatus in Indian society, Singh saw reinforcement of such cleavages through counter-ideologies like ethnicity, religious fundamentalism, casteism and regionalism and the like during the decades after independence. He also put the blame on the negative role played by a large section of religious elites in promoting a sense of alienation and despair among the impoverished masses. This analysis led him to conclude that Indian social transformation is not such that can be adequately explained by a linear model of transition from one stage to the other. It is more complex, and cultural changes in India mirror both forces of resilience and transformation.

Globalization and Cultural Change

The foregoing discussion would make it clear that Singh visualized many critical and significant social, economic, political and cultural changes that India has witnessed since independence. But, for him, these changes of pre-globalized India are distinctly different because "globalization constitutes a very special kind of manifestation of inter-cultural encounters and reciprocities". Globalization expands the scope and speed of cultural interactions across societal boundaries; the incidence of migration and emergence of the cultural diaspora bring about intense cultural, social and economic interactions. He, therefore, acknowledged that Indian society has entered a qualitatively new phase since the introduction of economic reforms in early 1990s, and the current phase of global capitalist development is bound to generate several new cultural challenges for us. This is both due to substantial changes in the social structure of the society and also its processes. Singh divided the post-globalized changes occurring in Indian society into two categories: first, those which concerns the substantive structures of culture and its relationship with social institutions; and second, those which refer to the processes of change in culture, especially engendered by the forces of globalization, telecommunication revolution and the emergence of market economy in a qualitative new form. The structural issues of change, for Singh, refer to the (a) impact of globalization upon local culture, (b) the nature of cultural identities at the local, regional and national levels and the extent of their inner resilience to withstand the forces of globalization, and (c) the emerging popular culture in India and its impact of different segments of Indian society. The other substantive issues relate to the processes like nation-building, language as a marker of cultural identity, growth of ethnicity, changes in community structure, changes in leisure activities and the like. Let me now discuss in detail Yogendra Singh's views about the major issues of cultural globalization in contemporary India.

Dimensions of Globalization

The question that crops up in any discussion on globalization is: how does the current phase of globalization represent a break in human history? Certain 'universals of culture' common to all mankind have been a reality ever since the beginning of human history. Singh argued that such sharing of culture should not be confused with globalization. Moreover, processes and dynamics related to globalization are not new to Indians (and many others in the East). For many of the multicultural societies of the East, diffusion of external and mainly western institutions and values through mercantilism, colonialism, westernization and modernization did take place since the early 15th century. Indians were exposed to globalization of ideas, institutions, products, objects and values for many centuries. Notwithstanding the continuity of globalization for several centuries, we should take note of the fact that the earlier varieties of globalization differ from the current one in the sense that different societies globalized differently in the past depending upon their social, economic and political standing. According to Singh, the current phase of globalization is a very special kind of inter-cultural connections. And it is historically and qualitatively different in many ways from related process like westernization which largely in the colonial setting of the past implied cultural encounters between a dominant techno-economic power from abroad and its subject people.

According to Singh, the distinctive historical phenomenon of globalization of culture today or the new challenges that it poses for the humanity can be traced to its unique technological base which has revolutionized the concept and quality of the systems of production, communication, social organization and social interaction. He noted the following five dimensions of contemporary globalization:

(a) revolution in communication technology rendering global circulation of messages and symbols in the shortest possible time and proliferation and diversification of technological means for doing so;

(b) circulation of finance capital on global scale searching for markets and economies of scale through international division of labour and structure of wages with introduction of high technology;

(c) homogenization of consumer products and market processes both in the realms of commodities and cultural symbols, styles and behavioural pattern;

(d) enlargement of the scope of electronic media through telephony, television, fax, e-mail, internet, etc., influencing political values, ideologies and movements; and

(e) an intense degree of circulation of manpower across countries and cultures leading to homogenization of cultures on the one hand and an elevated sense of cultural identity and distinctiveness on the other (Singh, 2000: 71–72).

Such characterization of contemporary globalization led Singh to agree with Arjun Appadurai that modern technologies of communication outcross the boundaries of real time and real space in social interactions. Hence, 'virtual communities' or groups may be possible. But, for Singh, such a community does not overcome the acuteness of crisis of cultural identities. This is because the process of globalization also sets into motion several predictable as well as unanticipated consequences. In most developing countries, this issue assumes very sensitive proportion and Singh noticed articulation of both hopes and fears about globalization among intellectuals particularly from countries like Indonesia, Thailand, Malaysia, Singapore and Vietnam. The most widespread anxiety relates to the possibility of serious damage or loss of cultural identity without commensurate benefits of economic and social developments through globalization of economies. However, Singh noticed that the reactions from South Korea and China to the impact of globalization on cultural identity vary and these countries did not perceive any threat. Hence, it appeared to him that a society with greater ethnic and socio-structural uniformity may be able to cope with the challenges of globalization.

As compared to this, the South Asian countries including India, for Singh, constitute a separate category due to their history, geography, levels of economic development, cultural differentiation and pluralities. A comparative assessment of the situation made Singh realize that the quality and magnitude of the impact of globalization on the culture of a society would depend upon its social, structural and cultural features. To be more precise, the plurality of communities and cultural diversity in India prevented the growth of any sense of threat from globalization for local or regional cultures. There exists a broad-based civilizational unity in India due to several types of linkages articulated both by the elite and folk traditions. Hence, processes of 'universalization' and 'parochialization' have been going on in India for several centuries. Singh, however, did not deny the possibility of 'dislocations' in Indian society due to the entry of new cultural forces despite our cultural resilience in the past. He particularly foresaw the rise of sub-cultures that may directly clash with the general cultural values or practice. Yet, he anticipated that due to the contrary process of intensification of consciousness of identity, selective cultural adaptation will accompany cultural continuity and creativity particularly in the Indian context. I would now review the process of cultural globalization in India based on my own findings (Ghosh, 2011) and match them with what Professor Singh had anticipated at least a decade ago. I need to remind the readers that the broad categories of cultural changes taken up for discussion below do not include many other types of socio-cultural changes Singh had mentioned.

Rise of Consumer Culture

It has been argued that contemporary globalization represents a major break even in the history of capitalism. This is because this globalization now represents an economy that is dominated by services. Consumption rather than production has become the major force of social change today. The growth of 'culture industry' in the contemporary world signifies this. It is interesting to note here that Singh hinted about this process of conversion of 'culture' into 'commodity' due to information–entertainment 'revolution' on the chariot of market capitalism in 1992. Today, there is perceptibly a shift towards a 'buying culture' with more and more stress on commodity consumption in urban and semi-urban areas. Even in rural India, the ethos of consumerism has reached an all-time high and villagers are now more a part of the global market place than ever before. Singh saw a trend towards commercialization of village fairs and festivals. As a corollary, market impulses were fast encroaching upon cultural landscape of rural India. Later on, better roads and improved communication have removed territorial distances among cities, towns and villages. In the pre-liberalized period, a customer has to wait for several months, if not years, to purchase a car or two-wheeler. But now, in the consumer economy, competing private entrepreneurs would push prospective customers to purchase these goods. Travelling is now very fast and cheap and this has allowed expansion of the network of even well-known fast food, leather and jewellery industries to suburbs and semi-urban places. Not only this, the new and expanding areas of our consumption have turned into icons of social status today. This is in spite of the fact that a large segment of our population belong to marginalized and 'backward' sections. The massification and marketization of culture has been influenced particularly by the rise of a strong middle class whose number, for Singh, was around 300 million. Apart from media, Singh had also talked about the role of a class of 'culture entrepreneurs' for undertaking systematic marketing of leisure and culture goods within the country and outside. It is very easy for anyone now to locate such 'experts' in Indian cities and towns who encourage new waves in fashion by organizing 'fashion shows' and emphasizing on ethnic designs, artifacts and instruments of leisure along with a new 'ideology of emancipation'. Travel and tourism have further reinforced this process of cultural change. All these have cumulative impact on the pattern of urbanization and expansion of informal job market in cities and towns.

Media, Internet and Popular Culture

Singh assigned a pivotal role to the mass media for popularizing consumer culture. We all know that there has been tremendous rise in the number of newspapers and periodicals at both national and local levels over the last few years. The survey conducted by the National Council of Applied Economic Research (NCAER, 2009) has noted that newspapers are able to maintain their dominance, with over half (53%) of all literate youth, or 177 million, exposed to them. Again, according to the Indian Readership Survey 2009 (Kohli-Khandekar, 2010), about 68 million people read the 6,000-odd magazines that India has. Similarly, television coverage and cable network along with facilities like telephone connectivity, cooking gas, etc., have extended sharply particularly after private participation in these endeavours in the post-liberalized Indian economy. Nearly half of our population today has direct access to television programmes and in urban India alone such access is much greater. There were just about 50 TV channels in 1996, but the number is more than 500 in 2010. I was surprised to see the presence of dish antenna on the top of many remote households of the tribals in the tea gardens of Jalpaiguri district during a field trip in June 2011.

There is no denying the fact that television, newspaper and computer network have given people greater access to information and allowed them to see an extensive variety of forms of life than previously possible. As a result, global and national issues/events appear to concern us every day over and above the local or regional issues. It is true that modern secular democratic societies rely intensely on the services provided by the mass media and information technology. Multiple media exposure in India today has already proved to be positive for civil society activism and a vibrant democracy. The success of Anna Hazare or Baba Ramdev to exert pressure on the government on corruption issue is linked to media exposure of these issues to a large extent. Mobile phones, computers and internet connectivity today offer wide range of options to their users. Apparently, the use of new technology has positively contributed to quick dissemination of knowledge and information so vital in today's 'information society'. But a deeper analysis would reveal that the impact of new technology on human desires and human relations has also led to what Singh termed as "decontextualization and displacement of meaning and values of cultural objects" (Singh, 2000: 35). It may as well be argued that information technology has also created 'digital divide' between its users and non-users. For many of the Indians living mainly in remote villages, information technology is yet a dream. This is because only 27 per cent of village schools in India have electricity compared to 76 per cent of schools in towns or cities (UNESCO, 2010).

Interestingly, the new means of communication have also augmented and empowered local communities, local cultures and minority sects by extending the reach of their interactions. And Yogendra Singh correctly anticipated such a development two decades ago. For instance, the multichannel viewing in the media might have made Hollywood or foreign films and programmes available at the local cable network; but competition among the local channels has also made community issues or traditional cultural practices, say Horoscopy, being shown or discussed at the global level. The media, which has contributed towards commodification and consumerism, also makes the consumers aware about necessary protection through advertisements. Those who argue for Islamization, Hinduization, indigenization or decolonization today are better equipped to garner support at the international level with the help of latest technology. To quote Singh, "Globalisation, therefore, not only makes people's sense of cultural identity and cultural values more caring of a shared existence within diversity, but it also makes them highly critical and conscious about 'hidden package' of self-serving ideologies in communication" (Singh, 2000: 60).

Similarly, the rise of popular culture in social life today, argued Singh, derives impulse from the urge to manipulate or engineer people's motivations to augment the market forces for profit. Visual media normally reproduces the culture of dominant section of the society in taken-for-granted way and thereby promotes 'cultural hegemony'. Across the nation, the lifestyle and leisure time activities of people have changed dramatically following such changes. Television broadcasts are accepted as models, as simulation of reality, by many of our young boys and girls. In a recent survey of 30 villages in the Malda district of West Bengal (Ghosh, 2010), I have noted many cases of elopement by under-aged school boys and girls. Parents attributed this to the increasing influence of media and cell phone on the children. Examples of school students emulating the crime serials in real life are also pouring in from every corner of the globe. Globalization has therefore intensified the connection between media projection and real-life stories.

Increasing Coverage of Film and Music

Globalization of Indian film and music industry has also attracted the attention of Yogendra Singh. Films have played a very important role in India and it is a popular form of entertainment and recreation. Today, due to technological changes, it has become very easy to export Indian films worldwide. The effect of globalization on Indian cinema can not only be seen in the Bollywood (Mumbai Hindi film industry), but also to the regional film industries of the country. For the public or the investors alike, the entry of the cinema industry into our private space has offered more options. Thus, the frequency and varieties of films shown in different competitive channels have gone up many times. Singh saw films playing a crucial part in promoting educational and reformative values. Additionally, due to technological changes, quick viewing of films now has also made it possible to spread the social message of films rapidly. One must have noticed that of late many Hindi and regional films have been able to provoke public attention at national level on impending social issues like faulty education system, parental pressure on children, bureaucratic approach to rural development, spread of corruption and violence etc. On the whole, therefore, globalization has led to increasing coverage of film industry both socially and economically. At the same time, according to Singh, the need to regulate their content and form in tune with normative standard is a great challenge today.

Simultaneously, there have been revolutionary changes in music transmission following the introduction of new technology and coverage of mass media including FM radio brand. During the last one decade or so, there has been tremendous resurgence of public (and business) interest in music. CDs, DVDs, mobile phones, i-pods, computers, televisions and FM radio have made it possible for us to listen to a wide variety of music as and when required. For many of us today, therefore, leisure time and even working time is a time for music. No doubt, such changes have several positive implications. Interestingly, in spite of a plethora of new varieties of Hindi songs, classic Hindi film songs are all over radio and television, wooing young and the old alike. In certain instances, classic songs are being reissued by the music industry because of their huge demand in the market. This proves, as was argued by Singh, that ethnic and traditional aspects of our culture are also finding sponsors in the media. For instance, there is a spectacular growth of regional music over the last two decades. It should be noted that even some folk songs today punch preludes and interludes on electronic guitar, saxophone, synthesizer and the like. Singh was right to argue that these new forms of creolized art, music and culture have made them global on the one hand, while at the same time generated a renewed 'sense of belonging' at the local level. In this sense, globalization has facilitated our tradition rather than demolishing it.

Food Diversity and Festivals

Indians have always celebrated their food diversities and never before in our social history ready-made, fast or junk food had found so much popularity. It must be noted here that on an average Indians spent a lot of money on food and festivals. Globalization has made it possible for the food-loving Indians to look for myriad quality options from within the country while at the same time opting for cosmopolitan food. Hence, soft drinks, pizza, noodles, burger, roll, pastry, etc., dominate the food choices of our younger generation. Similarly, Singh noticed that the practice of non-vegetarianism and alcoholism has also intensified. In unison, the shift for him is towards consumption of milk, poultry and meat. The rapidly growing fast food and beverage outlets, lounge and bars, resorts, clubs or restaurants have offered such options to urban Indians and particularly young generation. Ever-increasing shopping malls and multiplexes have further contributed to the spread of culture. Changes occurring at the socio-structural level of Indian society have added fuel to the flames. Fascination for food is a new cultural high point due to the intervention of 'television cooking shows' in India in recent times. Frankly speaking, cooking has never been a matter of intense public scrutiny in India cutting across sex and age even a few decades back. This is more so for the urban Indians who are getting addicted to eating outside. Singh agreed that such shifts in choices "are not only a reflection of increased prosperity; rather food preferences have been changing overtime. There is ample evidence about a change in the people's tastes in matters of consumption" (Singh, 2000: 52).

All these have resulted in the opening of a large number of food stalls and restaurants in even towns like Bardhaman or Bolpur in West Bengal. As a corollary, culinary changes and modes of public dining saw rapid changes during the last two decades (Nandy, 2004). Apart from some major players like McDonald's, Nirulas, Pizza Hut and Dominos Pizza, local and regional fast food chain also witnessed dynamic growth during the period. It should also be kept in mind that ethnic food items like *Dosa, Samosa* or *Hydrabadi Biryani* have also become global. Singh, therefore, witnessed both tendencies towards globalization and ethnicization of the consumption pattern in India. He wrote, "within India, the trend to consume and patronize food items of other regions and its culinary practices by members not belonging to that region is now growing fast due to increased inter-regional migration" (Singh, 2000: 101). Consequently, many foreign food manufacturers operating in India today stress on 'indianization' of their food items to suit indigenous tastes. At the same time, it may be argued that notions related to body or sex are profoundly invaded by the influence of science and technology today. Hence, our younger generation is gradually coming under the grip of 'eating disorders' in order to remain slim and this surprisingly coincides with the globalization of food production. Such contrasts connote plurality of our existence to a large extent today.

Similarly, in the fields of many ritual and religious observations too, Singh observed evidences of inter-regional homogenization. For instance, *Durga Pooja* (the worship of the icon goddess Durga), which a few decades ago was confined to West Bengal, Orissa and Assam, has now spread to entire Bihar and Uttar Pradesh, besides being patronized in most cities throughout the country where ethnic groups from these regions have migrated. I have also noticed popularization of North Indian festivals like *Chhatt Pooja* (the worship of Sun god) in Bengal. Again, *Ganesh Pooja* is not merely a prerogative of the people of Mumbai now. Very often, such celebrations go beyond the limited circle of religion and community as in the case of *Id-ul-Fitr* or Christmas and they explain the age-old tradition and mosaic character of Indian civilization. When a cultural style or practice extends its reach, the ethnic or religious group originally attached to it finds satisfaction in such globalization. At the same time, such homogenization leads to celebration of local identity and culture at global level. I would like to argue here that globalization has also contributed to a rise in the influence of religion in public sphere in recent times. An increase in the number of religious institutions and large-scale participation of people in religious festivals like Makar Sankranti, Pongal, Sabarimala, Ganga Sagar Mela, Sangam Mela, etc., are also indications of the greater hold of religion on society. Following Habermas (2008), it may be argued that religion maintains a public influence and relevance in India today.

Fashion, Body Look and Dress

Along with changes in the food habits and consumption style, Singh also noticed significant changes in the pattern and style of women's wear and use of cosmetics. For him, it is marked by a shift from *saris* to *salwar-kameez*. The middle classes are increasingly taking to uses of designer dresses marked by multinationals. The use of modern cosmetics, soaps and detergents, generally of western origin, has reached all sections of the people of India. Yet, as Singh argued, "the ethnic challenges to this industry based on folk and classical Indian medicinal tradition in cosmetics is also growing, and in the usual style of globalization has entered the international market in a big way" (Singh, 2000: 100). The market and media today transcend the territorial, national and cultural boundaries and offer individuals enormous amount of choices and freedom in matters of cultural and ideological preferences. My research into the changing cultural practices of urban tribal girls in Tripura, a tiny state of North-East India, reveals that exclusive preference for western dresses (jeans and shirt/top) now has minimized the influence of traditional dress called '*Riya-Pachra*' in which just two pieces of cloth were used to cover up the upper and lower parts of the body. Even a decade ago, the urbanities were seen using the traditional dress in some modified form by replacing the '*Riya*' with blouse or shirt with a '*Dopatta*' (a piece of cloth to cover the upper part of the body). But, the situation has completely changed today.

While discussing such changes, we should keep in mind two important factors. First, we earlier lived in an era of shortages. But, today, consumers have choices and international competition has brought down prices of goods while increasing the quality of services. Second, the average urban child in nuclear families today is brought up amid luxuries and they are allowed more freedom to take decision at a younger age. Hence, they readily accept a norm that the market popularizes and is being introduced in the peer circle. Both these factors have resulted in changing the choices and mentality of our younger generation very fast. The entry of modern casual dresses however does not mean that *sari, kurta-pyjama* or other traditional dresses have no takers. During special occasions and festivities, Bengalis are still fond of ethnic dresses. And, the demand for ethnic and/or 'glocal' dresses has certainly shot up after globalization and exposure to 'other' culture.

Apart from imported dresses, today's boys and girls from cities and towns also attach importance to body look by becoming a regular customer of a gym or beauty parlour. Everybody seems to be careful now about his or her look. The penetration of media and market into our social life has also compelled the older generation to accept such changes. As a result, the vocation of beauticians and the number of gymnasiums, beauty parlours or health clubs have grown rapidly. Singh's prediction about the extension of these organizations/associations to small towns beyond the metropolises came true in case of West Bengal. In Bardhaman, an agro-based urban centre, for instance, I have witnessed rapid growth of such organizations/associations during the last two decades and one may locate such bodies in all major localities of the town. At the same time, yoga therapy and alternative medicines popularized by Baba Ramdev, or 'art of living' popularized by Sri Ravi Shankar, have gained international popularity today. Such 'globalization of local tradition' is as real as McDonalization or Coca-Colonization.

Occupation, Mobility and Rising Disparity

The early onslaught of economic reforms in India made Singh realize that the country is going to witness a rapid change in the traditional occupational structure of castes and tribes. As these groups have moved to occupy new occupational space, the link between caste or community and the hereditary occupation is severed. At the same time, there is substantial rise in non-agricultural occupations in the countryside mainly due to better linkages with cities/towns and changes in style of life consequent upon increased uses of consumer durables such as bicycle, motorcycle, jeep and electronic devices. Thus, for instance, traditional jobs like tailoring or hair cutting have become less remunerative today while the vocation of beautician, dietician or service provider has become lucrative. I may add that due to the rise of casual and informal sector jobs and services in post-liberalized India, processes like 'informalization', 'casualization' and 'feminization' of workforce in many industries have intensified.

Following Singh's logic, it may further be argued that there are other concomitant changes in the lifestyle and values of our younger generation today. Thus, much of job opportunities in the IT sector do not require higher qualification except some technical skills. Hence, for many city boys and girls today higher education is a low priority. Moreover, the renewed interest in English education and computer training signifies a change in our priorities being dictated by market compulsions. Since jobs are also to be attained by augmenting personal qualities and skills, young boys and girls are keeping safe distance from active politics or unionism. Job in the IT sector or BPO industry also creates a new work culture. They attach importance to success and targets being achieved within a stipulated period. Hence, in post-globalized India, we are confronted with rising numbers of 'mobile family' where the couples live in separate locations due to job requirements. All these are not conducive to the traditional notion of family, caste and social relations, and would call for change in approach or attitudes towards women.

I have argued elsewhere (Ghosh, 2011: 170) that women working in the software or other modern industries are delaying their marriages and accepting a new lifestyle, which goes against their stereotypical roles of wives and mothers. As values regarding sex and family are changing rapidly, it may be presumed that today's boys and girls would gradually seek alternative to marriage and family in order to cope with work stress and lifestyle. It is, for instance, found that divorce rate has risen by an astonishing 30 per cent from 2,493 cases in 2005 to 3,243 in 2008 in Bangalore city. Data from family court reveal that more than 50 per cent of such cases are from the IT/BPO sector (Das, 2008). While financial security is one factor encouraging women to opt out of bad marriages, erratic working hours, work pressure and stress also contribute to marital discord. Increasing stress on consumerism in the age of globalization has also led to expanding dimensions of dowry for fixing marriage. Today, dowry typically represents commercialization and commodification of social relations cutting across caste and class barriers. And, this is in spite of increasing instances of love marriages in all parts of India. Similarly, trafficking of women and children has increased tremendously in India after economic liberalization (Ghosh, 2007).

Changes in the occupational pattern and emerging constrain of our urban and rural countrymen have serious implications for the country as a whole. It is quite clear by now that there is a large 'class of losers' along with a small 'class of winners' in post-liberalized India. There is every reason to believe that economic reforms have widened disparity and distress among people. Stagnant agriculture, higher inflation, market recession, increase in the number of casual, marginal and agricultural workers, and higher rates of malnutrition among children – all refer to increasing stress and exclusion in the life of common man. In this context, NCRB (2009) data reveal that more than 17,000 farmers committed suicide in the country in 2009 alone due to economic hardship.

Global vs Local Culture

Even though Singh postulated the strength of cultural globalization to usher in homogeneity in certain aspects of our life, he was resolute that local and regional social entities have shown capacity for selective adaption to and integration of new cultural values and practices. The strengthening of local and regional cultural identities, for Singh, is an unexpected consequence of globalization. It would be imprudent to undermine the adaptive capacity of our culture and contribute to the growth of self-consciousness and local cultural identities due to the very process of cultural globalization today (Oommen, 2005). Cultural autonomy and ethnic movements of *dalits*, tribals, Muslims and others in India speak about increasing parochialization of culture or its symbiotic form. In case of West Bengal, we have witnessed increasing strength of ethnic identities like Gorkha, Adivasi, Kamtapuri, Matua and Muslim in recent times. Even among the leaders and members of Communist parties in Bengal, today, one can easily identify presence of parochial sentiments based on caste, religion, locality or region which were remote possibilities during 1970s. Increasing incidences of 'honour killing' for caste/family pride in recent times also refer to the challenges of socio-cultural life in contemporary India. It appears to me that if adoption of modern dresses by our young girls is a *manifest* consequence of cultural globalization, the continuation of the tradition of respect to elderly persons is a *latent* aspect of their behaviour. Hence, globalization dose not only mean Coca-colonization or McDonalization as, for instance, *Hydrabadi Biryani* or Indian *yoga* has also become 'global'. The new means of communication also augment and empower these local communities, local cultures and minority sects by extending the reach of their interactions. Sharing of cultural traits by diverse communities and growth of bilingualism are definite expressions of 'creolization' of culture in India. Quite reasonably, contemporary changes do not imply the complete replacement of traditional values or systems by a new one. Rather, they have subsisted upon interdependence among diverse plural social entities. Singh also did not postulate that encounter with global culture and economy is without conflict or resistance. Along with selective acceptance, there is also rejection of values and norms. For instance, Kellogg India has failed to impress upon the Indians to change their breakfast habit from say *parantha* to cornflakes. Similarly, deepening inequalities worldwide has led to spontaneous eruptions of anti-globalization movements in different parts of the world. Wherever globalization has hurt the vital economic interests of farmers, traders, industrial and agricultural workers, its threat perception has remained strong. For instance, the *Karnataka Rajya Raita Sangha* (Karnataka State Peasants Organization or KRRS) led by M.D. Najundaswamy played a prominent role both at the national level and at the global level to oppose globalization of agriculture and free trade in seeds and agricultural products and meat processing. We have witnessed periodic incidences of consumer protest against multinationals like Coca-Cola or Monsanto promoting consumer goods or agro-products. Singh believed that in a country like India where about 65 per cent of population still depend on agriculture, such clash of interests is bound to occur.

Conclusion

It appears from the foregoing discussion that Yogendra Singh's contribution to the exploration and analysis of social change in India in general and cultural changes in the context of globalization in particular is enormous. He is one of the pioneering Indian sociologists to notice multiple changes in our economy, society, culture and politics since the introduction of economic reforms. One may, however, argue that Singh wrote about the impact of cultural globalization in India in the early years of economic reforms and the changes occurring in our society since then were hardly reported and analysed by him. Interestingly, just before finalizing this essay, when I asked my esteemed teacher about any change in his views or perspective about the matter in very recent times, he swiftly replied, "whatever I predicted during late 1990's proved to be true by now. Far from changing my views, I am rather confident about my arguments and views now". In fact, there is enough sociological acumen to support Singh's view about cultural globalization in India today. Singh correctly argued that the quality of resilience and adaptability that Indian culture had shown during westernization is yet being maintained despite certain qualitative changes in recent times. Along with homogenization of certain aspects of Indian culture, globalization has also helped in accelerating the growth of self-consciousness and cultural identities. The growing disparities among different segments of Indian population and the resultant unevenness in the spread of a global culture also proliferate diversity. As a corollary, several aspects of our custom and tradition continue to exist side by side as there is both adoption and rejection. There is enough sociological insight to support Singh's views that tradition and modernity in the Indian context are not dichotomous. Rather, there is continuity between the two. Globalization is clearly at the crossroads of tradition and modernity in India. Hence, the logic of Indians suffering from any 'cultural shock' at the face of exceeding internationalization does not appear to be very appealing. On the contrary, the paradoxical features of globalization due to its positive and negative consequences have given rise to fear and hope. A reading of Singh's essays on globalization has made me realize that the process is much broader, complex and multifaceted. Social and cultural changes today are not unidirectional and there are several contrary trajectories generating processes like homogenization, pluralization, traditionalization and hybridization at the same time. In other words, 'cultural globalization' does not refer to the possibility of a single global culture; it rather signifies the spread of plural cultural elements across the globe (Ghosh, 2011: 172). Hence, instead of being a threat to social-cultural identities, globalization has become a means for construction of new identities and hence it has inadvertently resulted in pluralization. The challenge today for us is to recognize and respect plurality and multiplicity as a better model of globalized social life. Hence, as has been argued by Singh, emphasis on plurality, identity and continuity is essential for a creative balance between continuity and change in Indian society.

References

Das, Dipannita (2008) "Divorce Rates Shoot Up in Techie Land", *The Times of India*, Nation Page, Kolkata edition, December 18.

Ghosh, Biswajit (2007) *Trafficking in Women and Children, Child Marriage and Dowry: A Study for Action Plan in West Bengal*. Kolkata: UNICEF and Govt. of West Bengal.

—— (2010) *Delaying the Age of Marriage in Malda: A Document to Design Interventions for Changing Norms*. Kolkata: UNICEF.

—— (2011) "Cultural Changes and Challenges in the Era of Globalisation: The Case of India", *Journal of Developing Societies*, Vol. 27, No. 2, pp. 153–75.

Habermas, Jurgen (2008) *Between Naturalism and Religion*. Cambridge: Polity Press.

Kohli-Khandekar, Vanita (2010) "It's Dangerous to Think One Country is Like Another", *Business Standard*, New Delhi edition, March 3.

Nagla, B.K. (2008) *Indian Sociological Thought*. Jaipur: Rawat Publications.

Nandy, Ashis (2004) "The Changing Popular Culture of Indian Food: Preliminary Notes", *South Asia Research*, Vol. 24, No. 1, pp. 9–19.

National Council of Applied Economic Research (2009) National Youth Readership Survey 2009. (http://www.ncaer.org/downloads/Media...Readership.pdf).

National Crime Record Bureau (2009) Crime in India 2009. New Delhi: Government of India.

Oommen, T.K. (2005) "Challenges of Modernity in an Age of Globalization", in E. Ben-Rafel and Yitzhak Stemberg (eds.), *Comparing Modernities: Pluralism Versus Homogeneity*, Leiden and Boston: Brill, pp. 149–69.

Singh, Yogendra (1973) *Modernization of Indian Tradition*. Jaipur: Rawat Publications.

—— (1993) *Social Change in India: Crisis and Resilience*. New Delhi: Har-Anand Publications.

—— (1995) "The Significance of Culture in the Understanding of Social Change in Contemporary India", *Sociological Bulletin*, Vol. 44, No. 1, pp. 1–9.

—— (2000) *Culture Change in India: Identity and Globalization*. Jaipur: Rawat Publications.

UNESCO (2010) A View Inside Primary Schools. www.uis.unesco.org/ev.php

18

Globalization of Science and Technology (S&T) in Developing Countries

A Sociological Perspective

Binay Kumar Pattnaik

Globalization is a comprehensive process of socio-economic change that has emerged from Reagonomics and Thatcherism of the early 1980s followed through (Uruguay Round) TRIPS and TRIMS of 1990s via GATT to present-day WTO. Although essentially it is an economic phenomenon but is backed by a long process of political, legal and administrative reforms which otherwise have come to be known as liberalization. If the essence of globalization as an economic phenomenon is optimization of profits through international trade by making the global market as one, the key to this is located in the drive for efficiency and competitiveness. It refers to the ultimate form of market economics so far. But this economic process, backed by a political, legal and administrative reform process, has other repercussions that are social and cultural by nature. The other allied institutions like education, science and technology (S&T), etc., which are linked to the institutions of economy, are not left untouched, rather have consequentially undergone extensive changes. Hence, globalization the process – through two decades, now is a multifaceted reality. The multifacetedness is not confined to various institutional aspects alone, as it has cultural aspects too. It is of course beyond the scope of the present exercise to deal with globalization – the phenomenon – in its entirety. To be more specific to the context we shall be articulating globalization as the institution of S&T from the viewpoint of developing countries only. It is worth being specific here as globalization is not the same for the developed and for the developing countries. Mostly these two refer to the two ends of the same process of globalization, as the two worlds are related by a continuum. Although elsewhere (Pattnaik, 2005). I have spelled out what globalization of S&T regimes means in more general terms, it would be highly pertinent to spell out very concisely what it means for the developed countries. It becomes more essential to do so as subsequently I have to discern it from globalization of S&T regimes in developing countries. Certain primary features of globalization of the S&T regimes in developed countries could be identified as follows:

1. Finding out upcoming and growing large markets (e.g., in China, India, etc.) for their industrial technologies, capital goods and high quality products.
2. Making more profit through international trade and imposition of their IPR regime particularly in that section of the developing countries which was not under the control of international IPR regimes and the countries which did not have developed IPR regimes for themselves.
3. Tapping more resources like cheap technical manpower for their technical/R&D activities and also newer traditional knowledge bases (indigenous) for development of new designs/processes (may be through mergers, acquisitions, collaborations and direct entry through FDI).
4. Making use of the cheap technical manpower in developing countries for services in developed countries, i.e., outsourcing services through BPO/call centres (for e-commerce, banking, data management), etc.
5. Reaching out to the previously inaccessible investment markets (e.g., those in former socialistic countries and in semi-socialistic countries like India where although industrial sector is partly open, but sectors like finance/insurance, higher education, print and electronics media, etc., are still not fully open) through the strategy of international joint ventures/collaborations in the early stage and through the strategy of deep penetration (through subsidiaries or direct merchandise of industrial semi-finished products, intermediary goods, etc.) in a later stage.
6. Making of international scientific and technological consortiums for addressing common research questions/interests (both in the government as well as corporate sectors).
7. Expansion of the university–industry linkages and emergence of entrepreneurial universities (the ultimate goal of course is attaining an information-based society and knowledge-based economy at home countries).

Effects of globalization in developing countries cannot be perceived as an independent phenomenon as globalization entails a qualitatively changed relationship between the centre and the periphery countries although it is inclusive of the (globalization-induced) interactional benefits among the peripheral countries. Of course, globalization of the centre refers predominantly to the interactional benefits among the countries at the centre and significantly the interactional benefits between the countries at the centre and those at the periphery. Hence, the effects of globalization at the periphery/developing countries are greatly reflections of the globalization of the centre and (globalization-induced) interactional benefits among peripheral countries. Needless to say, the centre is always a self-starter and auto-centric because of the inherent dynamism in industrial capitalism. And, the periphery being dependent on the centre mostly experiences growth as a reflection of the dynamism at the centre. This argument unfolds itself in my articulation of globalization effects in the developing countries, as bulk of the features identified in the course of discussion in this essay are in fact consequences of initiatives triggered by the countries at the centre. In their ongoing patron and client relationship, which of course is a matter of reciprocity, countries both at the centre and periphery have gained from each other. But noteworthy is that some countries at the periphery have immensely benefited under this globalized regime and have successfully transformed themselves into what Wallerstein calls the 'semi-periphery' status by displaying some amount of dynamism of their own. The mark of distinction of these greatly globalized semi-peripheral countries is that there too the business driven by scientific and technological innovations is local as well as global. And most notable is that these new global drivers of innovations are non-European, non-American and non-white, notes Friedman (2006: 11).

In the forthcoming pages, I propose to articulate the major features of the 'globalization' of S&T in developing countries under four headings: (a) internationalization of higher education, (b) emergence of entrepreneurial universities, (c) internationalization and globalization of R&D, and (d) globalizing social impacts of the ICT revolution. While doing so the theoretical footing of my analysis remains to be anchored on new-dependence school in general and that of Emanuel Wallerstein's 'world-system perspective' as the analysis entails a qualitatively changed relationship between centre and some selected peripheral countries.

Internationalization of Higher Education

Teaching and learning, research and institution-building have all been influenced by some form of internationalization or the other. Internationalization entails exchanges between domestic and foreign academic institutions interested in these activities. The developed countries, particularly the OECD ones, have an interest and an advantage in exporting educational services. Developing countries, on the contrary, are the recipients of these services. But a few developing countries like China, India, Mexico, etc., are attracting overseas students to their institutions although on a low scale. However, internationalization of higher education is not altogether a new phenomenon even to developing countries.

Owing to globalization, what is new, however, is the much larger scale of such activities and the adoption of new modes of delivery of higher education. Foreign universities/colleges are now opening branch campuses in developing countries and offering joint programmes of study in partnership with local institutions. These are of course examples of new modes of delivery. The use of new technologies that permit students to enrol in foreign educational programmes while sitting at home and learning 'online' is also a novel approach. Government policies that permit foreign investment in higher education and negotiations to treat education as a tradable service under international agreements such as GATS (General Agreements on Trades in Services) are taking the internationalization of higher education to newer heights. The opening up of the economy in many developing countries through the new policies of liberalization (allowing foreign capital flows) has made access to new technologies easier in the field of higher education. This too has created opportunities for education service providers both within and outside the country to invest in institution-building and educational programmes, may be even through joint ventures. This trend has gained currency because of (i) the heavy unmet demands of higher education, and (ii) failure of the state to increase its investment in higher education.

Trends of Internationalization

Internationalization of Teaching Programmes

Chinese and Indian students dominate the world market of higher education today. In the year 2007, more than 3,50,000 Chinese students and nearly 1,30,000 Indian students were studying abroad. As estimated in the *University World News*, by the next 20 years, the number of Chinese and Indian students studying abroad will rise to 6,45,000 and 3,00,000 respectively (Maslen, 2007). Studying abroad by students of developing countries like India, China, etc., is still the most visible mode of internationalization. The recipients are mostly the OECD countries in general and USA in particular. The USA leads the rest in this regard by having 6,00,000 of foreign students in the year 2008. And Indian and Chinese students constitute nearly half of this. China and India today are the biggest exporters of students to the developed countries and have been so for the past two decades (Paul, 2009).

But, the other side of the phenomenon is the home-grown internationalism in higher education in these countries. China has executed an international educational policy since 2000, and India is still debating on it. China seems to be aggressive in this regard as more than 77,000 foreign students were studying in China by the year 2007, of which three quarters were from Asian countries. To be more precise, by the end of 2007, there were nearly 77,715 international students studying in China. Students from Asia still top the list, accounting for 81.93 per cent, while students from Europe and America accounted for 14.36 per cent, those from Africa 2.31 per cent and those from Oceania, accounted for 1.04 per cent of the total international students in China (Ministry of Education, People's Republic of China, website). It offers more than 10,000 scholarships to these students every year although it aims at earning revenues from this population of foreign student. Public-funded Confucious institutions provide Chinese language instruction and cultural programmes to these students. On the contrary, India in spite of its natural advantage of imparting higher education in English, is lagging much behind China in terms of attracting foreign students. In the year 2008, approximately only 20,000 international students studied in India, of which most were from South Asia, Africa, Middle East and India diaspora. In order to attract foreign students, India has to go a long way, in terms of educational infrastructure building and coherent policies. As a regional higher educational power in South-East Asia, India, like China, hosts students from neighbouring countries, such as Sri Lanka, Nepal, Bangladesh and Bhutan. To take advantage of this growing market, foreign education providers are setting up campuses or partnerships with local institutions in many developing countries. Twinning arrangements, cross-border franchise mechanisms, validation, subcontracting and distance learning involving foreign institutions have become more popular in developing countries. Under twinning programmes, students study in their home countries for the most part but go overseas to complete the course and receive degrees from the foreign university (e.g., Indian School of Business, Hyderabad, India).

Making education hubs to attract and serve foreign students is another strategy some countries have adopted. For example, Singapore has attracted 16 foreign universities to offer degree programmes in its city-state. Financial incentives are offered to entice the universities to join this initiative. The project operates in partnership with the local university. The degree programmes are in professional technical fields. Dubai has set up an international academic city with a dedicated tertiary education cluster development.

China, the leading one among the developing countries, has made striking progress in internationalization of higher education as a result of its deliberate strategy. In fact, China leads in the export of students for studying abroad. In the year 1990, China had hardly 7,600 students abroad, whereas today it has more than 3,50,000 students abroad. Surprisingly, it caters to little more than 77,000 foreign students who are enrolled in Chinese institutions. In the year 2004, China had newly started 750 joint programmes in collaboration with foreign institutions of which 165 awarded degrees of foreign or Hong Kong universities (Paul, 2009). But developed countries like US, UK, Canada, Australia and Germany see both China and India as markets for their higher education initiatives. Many western universities (English-speaking) have launched collaborative educational programmes in these two countries. For example, 11,000 students are studying in China for British academic degrees through various collaborative arrangements, and 200 British institutions have programmes in China. American major universities like Johns Hopkins University, University of Michigan and many other small colleges are active in China. As estimated, well over 1,000 foreign academic institutions have some kind of collaborative arrangements in China, including two full-fledged branch campuses of British universities (Fazackerley, 2007). Similarly, currently, at least 150 foreign academic institutions have various kinds of joint degree and all other collaborative arrangements in India, with the largest number (66) from the US and second largest from Britain. Even a legislation allowing foreign universities to operate in India is still pending, but if passed, many leading western universities may enter India. While China had such a legislation in place for regulating foreign collaborations in education in 2003, India is still in the process of making such a legislation. In spite of the fact that 100 per cent FDI in higher education was not permissible under Indian law, in the year 2008, 131 foreign education programmes were offered in India in partnership with foreign educational institutions. Of course, the role of independent branch campuses, ownership institutions, the role of the private and profit-making sectors, quality assurance for franchized overseas degree programmes, etc., in higher education have been controversial in India and are still being debated (Altbach, 2009).

As Paul (2009) notes, the modes of delivery of international higher education in developing countries that help improve quality and access rendering it more equitable are the following:

(i) scaling up the movement of students abroad,

(ii) facilitating the enrolment of students in the distance education of foreign universities (through online learning),

(iii) allowing foreign universities to establish branch campuses,

(iv) encouraging foreign universities to offer joint programmes in collaboration with domestic institutions,

(v) creating world-class universities by awarding contracts to reputed foreign universities to mentor and by making international appointments,

(vi) making of the leading domestic universities as destinations of foreign students and teachers, and

(vii) encouraging leading domestic institutions to have international campuses and build international brand names.

International Collaborations in Academic Research in S&T

The other aspect of internalization of higher education caused by the process of globalization is international collaborations among universities from the developing countries and between universities from developing countries and those from the OECD countries in matters of research. Universities from developed countries seek international collaboration in their research, mostly for two reasons: (i) for filling in the knowledge gap/technical expertise within their laboratories, and (ii) to make use of the cheaper technical manpower available in the universities of the developing countries. On the other hand, universities from the developing countries prefer to collaborate with universities of the developed countries, for obvious reasons like (i) getting (international) exposure to better facilities; (ii) getting better recognition through joint outputs like publications of papers in more prestigious journals (with higher impact factor), publications of books through more prestigious international publishing houses, filing international patents, and the like; (iii) enriching through informal transfer of knowledge and skills; (iv) acquiring better funding and consequently building better infrastructure (laboratories/workshop) and other soft resource bases; and (v) the consequent elevated position within the country and acquiring more competitive edge for funding and attracting better faculty and students compared to other domestic universities.

Research collaborations between universities in different countries are not always smooth, linear and patterned. These are subject to variables like (i) law that apply, (ii) underdeveloped/unenforceable IPR regime, (iii) cultural differences/management style, (iv) export control laws, and (v) awareness of such collaboration opportunities.

In matters of international research collaborations universities in US are more comfortable with and may insist that US laws govern collaborative agreements. And these insist that the USA remain as the exclusive venue of conflict resolution. If the host university is reluctant about agreeing to US litigation, as a compromise, both the governing law and jurisdiction be brought under a third neutral country such as Switzerland which is acceptable to both the conflicting university. Further, if the host university for research is located in a country with unsuitable intellectual property laws or in a country where intellectual property protection is unenforceable, it brings deadlocks to research projects. Similarly, the research with collaboration may face disruption if the employment laws in the host state are inconsistent with the contractual staffing obligations in the collaborative agreement.

The other variable in international research collaboration pertains to cultural differences in management. For example, a principal researcher of the project may be different from the actual decision-maker. Or one party may expect a creative decentralized hierarchy that rewards independent breakthroughs and hands off management style in contradiction to the collective responsibility, collective rewards/punishment management style. Lastly, the other variable for research collaborations involving sharing of sensitive technology with a host university in another country is export compliance and filings. Similar laws may apply for outgoing technology for a host university in another country. In case of US-funded projects, export compliance is triggered even if no goods and services are commercially produced and sold but the finding/technology is simply conveyed under an agreement of confidentiality.

Expansion and Reorganization

These apart, China and India both the Asian higher educational systems have undertaken massive reorganization and expansion inside. Flushed with funds owing to globalization, China has a multifaceted programme to build world-class research universities and well over 20 billion purchasing power parity dollars have been spent to build this elite sector. A series of mergers of more specialized universities were implemented in the 1990s essentially to re-establish the comprehensive universities. The other major efforts refer to two new initiatives funded by the central government such as (i) the 211 higher education project of 1993 that identified 100 universities for converting them into research intensive institutions, and (ii) the 985 project inaugurated in 1998 aimed at creating 40 world-class universities in China (Liu, 2007 and Ma, 2007). This ambitious project has already been implemented with the help of central and provincial governments in China. Ma (2007) has successfully tried to link this phenomenon of expansion in higher education with China's economic reforms.

The 985 project of China emphasized graduate programmes, interdisciplinary centres, teaching in English, publications in highly rated academic journals, hiring faculty with international qualification, etc. This reorganization of higher education with infusion of funds has created islands of excellence in Chinese science and technology and of course a system of stratification among universities in China. Likewise, the Indian higher education system is also experiencing massive expansion. When leading educationists are crying for quality control, the Union Ministry for Human Resources Development is engaged in fund management for this. Under the 11th Five-Year Plan, which is already being implemented, the Government of India has started eight new IITs (Indian Institutes of Technology, the international brand of Indian higher education in science and technology, making it 15 so far), is to start eight new IIMs (Indian Institutes of Management, the international brand of Indian management education) in addition to the existing six, nearly a dozen IIITs (Indian Institutes of Information Technology) (in addition to the existing 4), five IISER/NISER (Indian Institutes of Science Education and Research/National Institute of Science Education and Research), 16 central universities (of which 13 are Greenfield) and 14 world-class universities (*The Indian Express*, 2008).

Emergence of Entrepreneurial Universities

The other notable feature of globalization in developing countries has been the emergence of entrepreneurial universities. As a phenomenon, this trend is found to be emerging steadily among developing countries like India, China, Singapore, Taiwan, Brazil and in a few African countries. The notion of entrepreneurial university is anchored on the triple helix development model which is based on the following assumptions:

(i) The transition from an industrial society to a knowledge-based society necessitates knowledge producing institutions like universities that play central role in innovation and development.

(ii) The transition to a knowledge-based society further necessitates transition of large-scale capital goods-based technologies (that mandate bureaucratic forms of organization) to increasingly flexible smaller scale high technologies developed and utilized by small-scale organizations.

(iii) There has emerged polyvalent knowledge in areas of biotechnology, computer science and nano technology which are both theoretical and practical, patentable and publishable at the same time (meaning that are knowledge intensive technologies).

(iv) The rise of an entrepreneurial university model incorporates the classical Humboldtian elements with a culture of entrepreneurship, innovation and technology transfer.

The triple helix development model comprises of three basic elements: (i) central role for the university in innovation system; (ii) a movement towards collaborative relationship among three major institutional spheres in S&T like industry, university and government; and (iii) in addition to fulfilling their traditional functions, each institutional sphere also takes the role of other. The emergence of university–industry–government relations (tri-model institutions) is the great transformation of late 20th and early 21st centuries. This transformation includes a shift from manufacturing to service occupations, individual firm to strategic alliances, tacit to codified knowledge and technical to organizational innovations. It is also marked by transition from univalent to polyvalent knowledge. The polyvalent knowledge is the outcome of entrepreneurial university where the entrepreneurial scientists combine multiple purposes and multiple sources of funding to support their research enterprises creating further conditions for polyvalent knowledge.

In fact, in recent times, developing countries like China, Singapore and South Korea have abandoned the strategy to create technically trained manpower to support the manufacturing workforce. Because having realized the limits of this strategy they have shifted to a knowledge-based strategy focused on building research institutions and new universities as the basis of future innovation. This is emerging as an academic reform strategy in number of developing countries. Because it is now increasingly realized that continuous flow of scientific and technological knowledge will flow to the economy more rapidly by reorienting universities. This strategy based on triple helix model of development is assumed to be assisting the developing countries to leap-frog stages of industrialization that are now disappearing in their countries of origin like UK and France. Thus, the process of globalization has resulted in bridging a wide gap between scientific research and its utilization.

The 'entrepreneurial university' is a term now being used to refer to universities which possess a wide range of infrastructural support mechanisms for fostering entrepreneurship within the organization as well as packaging entrepreneurship as a product. The entrepreneurial university characterizes its role as a source of future industrial development, both by establishing organizational mechanisms to transfer knowledge/technology by playing a strategic role in regional development. Such a university retains the traditional academic role of social reproduction and extension of certified knowledge but places them in a broader context as part of its new roles in promoting innovation, says Etzkowitz (2003). In an entrepreneurial university, the academic research groups, consisting of faculty, graduate students, post-doctoral fellows, resource associates, technicians, etc., become a quasi-firm, taking on some of the organizational characteristics of an industrial firm. Bringing together research groups across disciplines, often in collaboration with firms and government researchers, takes this process a step further. Hence, the major functions of an entrepreneurial university are: (i) entrepreneurial education (teaching and developing course packages to cater to industrial needs), (ii) consultancy for industry, (iii) technology transfer from university to industry, and (iv) firm formations through spin-offs.

To Etzkowitz et al. (2008) the entrepreneurial university has certain essential characteristics that are found in them as emergent structures and developmental mechanisms. These are:

(i) *Internal transformation:* It implies redefinition of traditional academic tasks and expansions according to requirements of newly emerging functions. The university enlarges its role in innovation, extends its academic mission from dissemination to capitalization of knowledge. Over the time, new rules and roles are defined and legitimized in such a manner that the university reformulates its mission to incorporate the entrepreneurial paradigm.

(ii) *Interface process:* The entrepreneurial university needs an enhanced capability for intelligence monitoring and negotiating with other institutional spheres like the government and the industry. In due course, the interface capabilities emerge as technology transfer offices or spin-off facilitators. Faculty and supporting technical personnel are assigned the responsibilities to assess the commercial viability of research findings and are encouraged to have interactions with external partners.

(iii) *Recursive effects:* The university as an entrepreneur develops capabilities to create new organizations in the form academia spawned firms, or lending leadership for forming regional developmental organizations. The results are the emergence of trilateral organizations where the interface leads to likelihood of collaborations for creating cross-institutional entities. Special centres having personnel from all three institutional spheres and joint ventures involving universities, firms, etc., became possible.

(iv) *Trans-institutional impact (quasi-firms):* The univerity–industry–government relationships explain the current transitions in the research system; the two spheres different from university also increasingly develop similar intermediary capabilities. Gradually, formats for collaboration are institutionalized in legal and customary forms. The implications associated with such characteristics entail the transformation of a research university to an entrepreneurial one.

In a recent empirical study in India, Nimesh Chandra (2008) examined the relevance of triple helix model in the context of Indian Institutes of Technology (IITs). These are the central institutes of technology built in India in the MIT/American model while the traditional university system in India continues to function in the British model. Chandra examined the triple helix model, particularly the notion of entrepreneurial university therein based on the above-mentioned characteristic features spelled out by Etzkowitz (2002). The relevance of entrepreneurial university in the context of IITs could be examined (not directly but) on the basis of development of 'institutional policies to knowledge transfer', the 'rise in sponsored research and industrial consultancy assignments', 'the establishment of technology transfer offices', 'patent cells', 'incubation units', 'spin-offs management' and 'short-term technical programmes offered', etc. Having studied the mode of knowledge generation and transfer in IITs (Kanpur, Bombay, Kharagpur, Madras and Delhi) Chandra found that the orientation of IIT faculty/researchers has remained more towards open science, basic research and on publication of their research results that form the basis for technological advancement. The growth in patenting activities has not hindered the decision of researchers to publish. The knowledge produced at IITs is increasingly seen to be characterized by interdisciplinarity and plurality as collaborations are increasing in research projects, publications, etc. Attributing largely to new forms of linkages arising from industry, government and various cooperative R&D organizations that have proliferated in the past decade, one can say that there is a considerable change in the norms and practices of academic science resulting in an environment much more conducive to industrial application. Although there are evidences of emerging new forms of relations among the three actors of triple helix model in India, Chandra found these linkages however to be more bilateral rather than trilateral. Thus, although the modes of knowledge generation in IITs have been based on the Mode 2 (model), the latest emergent tendencies are a shift towards the entrepreneurial universities because of the growing industrial sponsored and consultancy practices and knowledge transfer through industry–academia linkage institutes like technology transfer offices. Further, there is growing evidence of IITs adopting the spin-off route towards commercialization of research-based knowledge through transfer mechanisms than the mode of licensing and royalty earnings. Even the emergence of strategic coalitions at IITs is to be construed as a notable feature of academic–industry interface. Thus, the recent institutional arrangements like establishment of technology transfer offices, patent cells, incubation units, strategic research coalitions with various industrial clients and several short-term technical programmes offered to industry personnel further lend support to the rising trends of entrepreneurial universities, which is still in its nascent form in India.

But much better today is the case of China where entrepreneurial universities have already come into existence. Of course, bulk of the Chinese universities are in the midst of transition to research and entrepreneurial mode. In the socialistic regime of China where government controls the academia and industry, a transition into triple helix model is highly significant as it makes academia and industry relatively independent. A few of the Chinese universities have created some of the largest and most successful hi-tech enterprises in the country, although the enterprise mode started in 1980 only. But these enterprises, instead of functioning as independent spin-off organizations, remained as part of their originating academic institutions. This created serious legal problems for sponsors, business partners and customers to sue the enterprise as it remained under the university. It is recently that the Chinese government has taken steps to institutionally separate these spin-off firms from their parent universities. However, many spin-offs even today function as university-run-enterprises (UREs) as part of the university administrative structure. These Chinese UREs have three characteristics: (i) university takes up the holding status of its enterprise in asset relationship, (ii) URE operates with the university staff, and (iii) the R&D activities in the URE is completely dependent upon the parent university (Zhou and Etzkowitz, 2006). It has also been found that there exists a kind of hierarchy of UREs which can freely use the lab facilities and resources of the parent universities. It is like an umbilical cord connecting the baby and the mother. This hierarchy is essentially political because most universities in China are public-funded universities. It partly converted the universities to industries and even the process of technology transfer became often difficult because of competition. The UREs although are in the public sector, they do not operate on non-profit basis or on 'social contract philosophy'. These have made enough money for their universities and faculty. Hence, Zhou (2002) notes that "in China poor professors of 1990s have already become one of seven wolves by now". Zhou and Peng (2008) in their empirical study among 34 Chinese universities (in the 985 project) found that the entrepreneurial mode of these universities began as UREs (firms within the university fold). These generally operate in non-hi-tech mode to gain experience, capital and research capacity. Later on these get upgraded to hi-tech entrepreneurship mode. Thus, to the authors, Chinese entrepreneurial university is very much different from MIT and Stanford-type original American entrepreneurial universities. But, they predict that the top few Chinese universities will become truly entrepreneurial universities in the next 10–20 years. Eun et al. (2006) have provided year-wise figures about the UREs in China, particularly the S&T-based UREs which show that although there was an upsurge of UREs in mid-1990s it declined in the early years of this decade. The authors feel that the decline is because of the following reasons:

(i) new government policy to fund higher education/universities heavily,

(ii) development of venture capital guarantees,

(iii) UREs' traditional culture, and

(iv) enhanced absorptive capacities of Chinese firms.

The glaring examples of UREs in the Chinese hi-tech areas are Tongfeng, Wangxin, Dongruan, Gufen and Qingado Tianqiao, Fangzheng Keji, etc. These were established and operated by Tsingua University, Zhejiang University, Dongbei University and Peking University respectively and have become number

3, 12, 15, 18 and 25 respectively among the Chinese top 100 S&T firms in 2002. Large number of these UREs are already enlisted in Chinese stock markets.

Although known as an NIC country, Singapore has responded to the phenomenon of globalization by making a corresponding shift to knowledge-based economy and by converting its major university of research, i.e., National University of Singapore (NUS) into an entrepreneurial university in the mid-1990s. The shift began only in mid-1990s when NUS established its technology licensing office. The major impetus came with the arrival of new VC then with US industry (GE) background who unleashed a series of reforms to begin with. Wong et al. (2007) in their empirical study of NUS have pointed out that corresponding to Singapore moving towards a knowledge-based economy (policy makers' decision to shift from investment-driven economy to an innovation-driven economy, emphasizing the building of intellectual capital and its commercialization for creating values and jobs) the NUS has transferred itself into an entrepreneurial university. The authors have articulated the impact of NUS' shift towards an entrepreneurial university model in terms of (i) manpower development/training, (ii) knowledge creation, and (iii) knowledge commercialization, like (a) incentive disclosures, (b) patenting, (c) licensing, (iv) entrepreneurial spin-offs, and (v) attraction of foreign talents and benchmarking of NUS with universities of Asia-Pacific.

Following the global trend even Brazilian universities have initiated integrating entrepreneurial practices in the recent past. The most striking feature of the practices to link university and industry is the institutional arrangement for technology transfer. Technology transfer offices (TTOs) were created with the objective of stimulating and facilitating the interactions between university and industry – the two agents of innovation. In spite of the diversity that characterized the TTOs in Brazilian universities, the transfer of technology from the university to an enterprise includes the following: (1) interactional activities: (a) technological services–technical analysis, calibrations, measurements, certification of the conformity, tests and verifications, consultancies and others, (b) education services–courses for personnel from industries, similar workshops, seminars and the like, (c) information services–searches in national and international patent data bases, technology information in general, (d) R&D projects–basic research, applied research, experimental and developmental research, (e) projects carried out by companies in incubators, (f) projects of junior companies – consultancy in services, and (2) knowledge transfer through intellectual property licensing: (a) patent and software licensing, and (b) transfer of know-how (non-protected). Ritter dos Santos and Rebolledo (2006) in their paper presented a survey result of 25 Brazilian universities (68% were public ones) on their TTO operation. Of the 25 TTOs of Brazilian universities, the authors found that only three were created in 1980s and rest 22 during the 1990s and later, implying the reflection of globalization (in tune with the international trends). As pointed out in OECD study (2003) most of the TTOs were on average 12 years old in the US and less than 10 years old in other OECD countries. The survey results also pointed out the three major functions of TTOs in Brazilian universities: (i) management of university–enterprise interaction activities, (ii) intellectual property registration, and (iii) technology transfer through licensing of technologies and patent licensing. But, the survey also pointed out that the performances of TTOs are not good, particularly on the transfer of technology. Most of the TTOs function in highly bureaucratized manners. Of course, in order to stimulate the interactions with different productive sectors, these TTOs initiate different institutional arrangements and try to participate in (a) specific networks in intellectual property and technology commercialization, (b) international committees, and (c) industrial forums of various types. Two of the best examples of TTOs in Brazilian universities are: (i) ETT of the State University of Campinas (UNICAMP), and (ii) CECAE of the University of Sao Paulo (USP) (Ritter dos Santos and Rebolledo, 2006). Following the initiatives of these two, several Brazilian universities that have created their TTOs, of course with varying nomenclatures, are the following:

- CT&TT of the Federal University of Minas Gerais
- CRITT of the Federal University of Juiz de Fora
- CERTI Foundation of Federal University of Santa Catarina
- EGT of University of Rio dos Sinos Valley-UNISINOS
- EITT of the Federal University of Rio Grande do Sul

It would be appropriate to refer to the case of African countries in relation to the emergence of entrepreneurial universities. Like many developing countries African countries were reeling under massive debt in the 1990s and the World Bank and IMF responded to these countries by asking them to restructure their economies through structural adjustment programmes. This affected adversely most African universities, particularly the public-funded ones. After this period of retrenchment and decline in funding there followed a period of renewal during which the universities introduced internal reforms (i.e., privatization) by which admissions opened to private fee-paying students, faculty members were allowed to share incomes generated through consultancy, universities accepting donations, opening of private universities, etc. (all through policy measure). Besides, impetus was to give a market orientation of the universities whereby the universities were to relate their acts to their national or regional developments directly, e.g., Makerera University in Uganda's innovation programme in teaching (changing curriculum for teaching civil servants, for 'sandwich training' programmes etc.). The other similar examples could be: (i) the World Bank's financial assistance for the establishment of African Virtual University in 1997 to provide quality education in S&T, and (ii) Rockefeller Foundation supported a noted lecture series through tele-conferencing for African students at University of Natal (Dzisah and Etzkowitz, 2006). Besides these rudimentary forms of reform, there is no other major form of restructuring in African universities in tune with the characteristic features of entrepreneurial universities like organizational restructuring, technology transfer office, patenting, spin-offs, etc. These rudimentary reforms in African universities may be just the first step in the direction of entrepreneurial university. Hence, the African universities have a long way to go in this direction.

Etzkowitz et al. (2008) have argued that transition to the entrepreneurial university is a global phenomenon as part of the broader phenomenon called transition to knowledge-based economy. Drawing on the experiences of countries like US, Sweden, Japan and Brazil, the authors have already argued that a global convergence is currently taking shape towards entrepreneurial universities which are playing a central role in knowledge-based economy. Thus, as mentioned earlier, the rising trends of entrepreneurial university in the peripheral countries is a reflection of trends of globalization at the centre. Conversion into an entrepreneurial university for many leading universities in China, Brazil and India is only a matter of decade or so as the process is already set and some leading universities there are way ahead in integrating entrepreneurial behaviour, the glimpses of which have already been discussed in the earlier pages.

Lastly, having traced the emergence of entrepreneurial universities in developing countries I need to offer an explanation as to why a notion of western developed countries has gained so much of currency among the developing countries and consequently there is a conscious integration of traits of entrepreneurial universities. The explanation that follows is in fact three-fold. First, varying levels of integration of the traits of entrepreneurial university by the universities in developing countries as a phenomenon is emergent of their structural requirements. Because, as indicated earlier, this phenomenon is one of the results of the structural adjustment programmes of these economies, e.g., that of India and some African countries. It hardly needs explication that characteristically the entrepreneurial university is perfectly in tune with the spirit of market economies. Thus, to overcome their dependence on state treasuries the universities were to be self-supportive. And, in order to be self-supportive, universities have to reorient themselves and experience structural reforms as these are prerequisites for commercialization of their knowledge and services. This obviously would stimulate their potentialities and make them more dynamic. Similarly, the phenomenon of URE in China is the result of the conformity to ideological requirements. Because unlike democratic political systems in which academic institutions enjoy the autonomy and freedom of doing research for knowledge sake, under totalitarian and socialistic political system, academic institutions do not enjoy the autonomy and freedom to do research and are to relate the research directly to the need of the economy. Besides under the closed economy of China where inflow of industrial technology from abroad is very limited as the international norms on the intellectual property rights are systemically flouted inside, the universities/research institutes were goaded to meet the technological requirements of the economy by commercializing their knowledge.

Further, policy makers in developing countries have now realized that moving through all the stages of western development model by means of conventional research in S&T and subsequent innovation lead industrialization is not a must and there can be shortcut to development. Because of the emergence of polyvalent knowledge which is suitable for triple helix model, it is argued that developing countries opt for knowledge-based strategy where researchers became source of innovation and incubators of institutional and technological changes. The triple helix visualizes a corporate university that would be the locus of the third industrial revolution to pave a shorter way to knowledge-based economy (that treats knowledge as a commodity).

Lastly, the other conducive reason for the integration of the traits of entrepreneurial university by the universities of the developing countries has been the emergence of new science-based technologies in the fields of drugs and pharmaceuticals, micro-electronics, ICT (software, telematics, etc.), biotechnology and new materials that had a profound impact on manufacturing business in developing countries as it created tremendous business and subsequent employment opportunities. These are knowledge-intensive industries and even can be delinked from production. With this, developing countries like India with a tradition of scientific education but without much industrial experience tried to cultivate and commercialize their knowledge-based capabilities that usually reside in the universities and research institutes. However, except the Indian Institutes of Technology (as discussed before) the university-based research system continues to be conventional and does not show signs of integrating entrepreneurial behaviour. Of course, the Indian Institutes of Management (legally deemed universities) have gone much ahead in the direction of strengthening their industry linkages, particularly in terms of industrial consultancies and training industrial executives.

Multinationalization and Globalization of Industrial R&D

Three concepts – internationalization, multinationalization and globalization – are elusive, particularly in this context of R&D, although these are being used often interchangeably, as if describing the same phenomenon. The globalization of technology and economy is not a new phenomenon, if it refers to the internationalization of flows of technical knowledge, new materials, semi-finished and finished products as well as services within the main industrial sectors. Similarly, multinationalization of national enterprises through gradual extension of MNC activities, the setting-up of direct subsidiaries, and acquisitions or various types of cooperative agreements (e.g., commercial, financial, pure technological, or any combination of the three) has characterized industrial development for nearly a century now. However, globalization is a nascent economic phenomenon that refers to (i) creation, distribution and consumption of goods and services, using structures organized on a global basis for economic exploitation of material and non-material means of production, e.g., by means of patents, databases and highly advanced training of human talents; (ii) the development of world markets or markets that eventually are becoming so to be regulated by universal standards; and (iii) organizations acting on a global basis, whose organizational culture is in conformity with a global strategy. Globalization does not necessarily signify standardized products for homogenous world markets (e.g., even for consumer goods). On the contrary, it signifies adaptation to a variety of local markets. Above all, it is the circulation of products, production methods, organizational structures, decision-making and supervisory processes and entrepreneurial strategies that are global (Petrella, 1992). Being part of the same process of transformation of industrial financial capitalism, internationalization, multinationalization and globalization are obviously interconnected. This overlapped process is further demarcated by the disappearance of a system/systemic features referred to as 'national' (e.g., national bank, national education, national economy, national culture, etc.). Of course, this process of disappearance has already been ushered in by the process of internationalization and multinationalization through the relentless interactions among states, economies and cultures. May be globalization signifies the end of 'national' as a point of strategic relevance, but 'national' continues to be one of the levels of significant relevance in the process of technological innovation. Hence, it would be a mistake to analyse the globalization of R&D activities in isolation from the processes of national R&D strategies and economic development, internationalization and multinationalization of R&D. Internationalization of R&D occurs when two or more industrial firms, research bodies or universities from different countries carry out joint R&D programmes. It can be bilateral or multilateral. Similarly, R&D multinationalization occurs when an industrial firm establishes one or more R&D centres in one or more countries other than its country of origin. Not so differently, globalization of R&D occurs when an industrial firm has developed a global strategy and vision of R&D activities at both internal level (i.e., in-house R&D activities, through internationalization and multinationalization) and external level (i.e., alliances of R&D with other firms, mergers and acquisition, agreements with universities, national research bodies, or governments from different countries, participation in international scientific and technical cooperative programmes or mere outsourcing of support services like database management, etc., from firms of different countries particularly from developing countries with cheap labour) in all the areas of R&D. Thus, globalization has emerged as a more inclusive concept which thematically subsumes the processes of internationalization and multinationalization. Petrella (1992) has mapped out the indicators of globalization process in R&D organizations, like, industrial firms, universities and public research organizations. But, the context of his articulation was that of the developed countries, whereas we are here using the same indicators (may even be adapted) in the context of developing countries, of course, keeping in mind that the same phenomena could be looked at from the vantage of developing countries as well.

With respect to industrial firms in the developing countries, the indicators of globalization could be the following:

(i) increasing investment for R&D activities and facilities located abroad (particularly through subsidiaries/affiliates in developing countries and in former socialistic countries that have liberalized their policies),

(ii) increasing intensity of technological cooperation between the different foreign affiliates of an MNC,

(iii) mergers and acquisition of firms/foreign affiliates with their own R&D centres,

(iv) joint R&D activities with foreign affiliates, and

(v) ad-hoc, short-term contracts with foreign universities and/or public research organizations (both in developed and developing countries).

Likewise, with respect to universities in developing countries, the indicators of globalization could be the following:

(i) being part of multivariant, multinational research networks,

(ii) evolving joint research projects and programmes with foreign universities,

(iii) research contracts with industrial firms both within and outside the country, and

(iv) being part of international/global research activities/programmes/projects.

And lastly, with respect to public research organizations in developing countries, the indicators of globalization could be the following:

(i) liberalizing the normative framework/procedures for facilitating participation of foreign firms/R&D organization in the technical projects/programs within the country and on the contrary facilitating participation of domestic S&T personnel to be part of similar projects/programmes abroad,

(ii) opening-up oversea branches/subsidiaries with technical and financial participation from oversea partners,

(iii) availability of facilities for such research organizations to allow foreign investment as well as technical collaborations (particularly in hi-tech sectors), and

(iv) becoming part of increasing number of inter-governmental scientific and technological agreements.

The major features of globalization of industrial R&D in developing countries could be spelled out as the following: (1) emergence of an international division of labour in S&T research, (2) emerging flatter technological world regime, (3) growing multinationalization of domestic firms from developing countries, (4) globalization of local R&D from developing countries, and (5) growing off-shoring industrial R&D services by firms from developed countries.

Emergence of an International Division of Labour in S&T Research

First Phase of Globalization

The most distinguishing feature of globalization in its initial phase has been the 'scissors phenomenon'. It refers to the tendency among the most developed countries to invest more among themselves, reducing their investment in the developing countries like those from Southeast Asia, Africa and Latin America. The tendency also indicates that inter-firm technological strategic alliances/agreements are very few involving firms from less developed and poorer countries as partners. Even long-term research projects, such as the 5th generational computer, the Human Genome and the Intelligent manufacturing systems projects, which should involve world cooperation, have not envisaged involving a research organization or university outside the developed world (Petrella, 1992). Thus, the 'scissors phenomenon' on the one hand entails increasing integration among the most developed countries in matters of technological/R&D alliances and on the other hand, it also entails the exclusion of the poor and less developed countries which are of course increasingly segmentalized among themselves. Global 'delinking' may not be an outcome of conscious policy against the less developed countries but a phenomenon inherent in the concentration of capital and technology in the triad countries of Western Europe, the USA and Japan. Similar has been the finding of Warrant (1991), involving analysis of geographical distribution of R&D expenditures and personnel that countries of origin remain the preponderant locations of R&D units in Europe, US and Japan (triad countries). This finding has been corroborated by a survey by Pearce and Singh (1990) concluding that (i) very unlikely an industrial group will delocalize its centre of gravity in R&D abroad, and (ii) there was a feedback movement to reconcentrate R&D activities at the group centres. Similarly, Patel (1995) also had observed that the increasing globalization (in the past years) of innovation actually re-enforces the dominance of the technology districts in the triad countries. Chen (2007) also noted that the geographical limits of globalization process (or triadization of innovation) has reinforced the concentration of globalized R&D within the existing technology clusters in the triad countries and MNCs would be hesitant to extend their R&D bases to developing countries due to the latter's weak knowledge-based assets, poor infrastructure and limited market. Having treated the process of re-concentration of investment in R&D as 'triadization', Petrella (1992) states that majority of the developing countries of Africa, Latin America and Asia have no significant roles to play in the global industrial R&D. Their real issue is how to facilitate a successful transfer of knowledge and technology from the triadic world to their own.

Second Phase of Globalization

The latter stage of globalization, unlike the first, witnessed a slow and increasing participation of developing countries in the development of global technologies and R&D, may be through the process of international sub-contracting/outsourcing. Through this participation of developing countries in the global industrial R&D, there has come into existence a new phenomenon to be justifiably called as the 'new international division of labour'. Because it is only the low end, supportive and labour-intensive technical services that are outsourced.

Big MNCs increasingly extend or diversify their field of technological competence through internationally integrated technological networks. These networks in each geographical location try to tap specialized local expertise. Of course, they differentiate their technological capabilities from the geographically separate ones. But they intend to exploit and add it to their own distinct streams of innovative potentials. Hence, Cantwell and his colleagues (1999 and 2000) observed that European MNCs do not only exploit local knowledge assets from developing countries but also contribute to local technological capabilities. These MNCs, by co-developing local technological capabilities together with the local centres of excellence in developing countries, set in motion a cumulative causation process which results in re-enforcement of the hierarchy of global technology districts.

There has been a keen interest among MNCs to establish R&D activities in China. It is now well agreed upon that China is becoming the new magnet for global R&D activities with the number of R&D centres increasing from merely 30 in 1999 to 700 in 2005 (Chen, 2007). Similar would be the case of Indian although in a lesser scale. Ever since India signed the GATT in 1993, more than 60 global firms have set up their R&D centres in technology-intensive sectors for using Indian skilled manpower. Prior to 1991, there were only two such centres. MNCs have internationalized their R&D activities and of late have set up their R&D centres in a number developing countries like India. These centres are either global or regional centres or are technological alliances possibly in joint venture.

R&D centres are all in hi-tech areas of electronics, biotechnology, pharmaceuticals and chemical technologies. Examples of the first type (FDI as global or regional R&D centres) include the following: ASTRA-AB Research Centre India (Bangalore), Texas Instruments India (Bangalore), Asia Pacific Design Centre of SGS-Thompson, Motorola VLSI Design Centre (Hyderabad), GE Research Centre India (Bangalore) and Daimler Benz Research Centre India (Bangalore). Examples of the second type (technological alliances/JVC-R&D centres) are the following: AVL Austria with Mahendra and Mahendra, Affymax with Glaxo India, Wockhardt with Sidemark Labs, Novo Nordisk with Dr Reddy's Lab, Cheminer Drugs Ltd with PRI Inc, Airbus with Hindustan Aeronautics, IDEA with TELCO, Mallinkrodt with NATCO Pharma, Eli Lilly US and Pfizer with Ranbaxy India Labs, Du Pont US, Abbot Labs US, Park Davis US, Smith Klein and Beecham US, all with IITC (Indian Institute of Chemical Technology) Hyderabad and Du Pont US, Akzo Netherlands, GE US, all with NCL (National Chemical Laboratory) Pune, Cadence, IBM with IIT (Indian Institute of Technology), Kanpur and Delhi respectively, Nokia, Nortel, LG Electronics and Rational software with IISc (Indian Institute of Science) Bangalore, and Mobil with Indian Institute of Petroleum (Pattnaik, 2005).

Some of these strategic alliances of R&D between firms are made for purposes such as overseas licensing, global marketing and joint product development. Similarly, the alliances with Indian research institutes have helped them shift their attention to business-led R&D, focusing more on process innovations and product developments in addition to their earlier consultancy works pertaining to troubleshooting, adaptation, testing and problem-solving. That apart, the R&D centres are (i) creating rich employment opportunities for technically qualified manpower in India, (ii) revolutionizing the patenting culture in India and posing to integrate themselves horizontally with Indian Industry in the years to come, (iii) enabling global firms to place more confidence in India's R&D capabilities, and (iv) enhancing skills of those managing R&D and innovation.

Of course, the basic reasons behind this upsurge has been the availability of 'abundant cheap engineers' and the 'large domestic market'. Cantwell and colleagues (1999 and 2000) have pointed out that even if some developing countries, such as India, Singapore and China, did get integrated into MNC global innovations networks, the innovative activities are usually limited to local market product adaptation and adaptation to lower production cost in host developing countries. Hence, R&D in such developing countries will remain at the bottom of the global innovation locational hierarchy, as it has been exemplified by the product life cycle theory. This R&D, although is internationalized/multinationalized, remains limited to low-end jobs (like testing, making components etc.) and are essentially supportive and adaptational by nature (in relation to the parent MNCs), particularly in hi-tech areas of ICT, drugs/pharmaceuticals and biotechnology.

So, as pointed out by Dunning and Narula (1995), the phenomenon of MNC R&D outsourcing from developing countries remained limited primarily to 'asset exploiting' R&D or 'home-base exploiting R&D activities'. This is based on the observation from developing countries like China, India and Singapore that the nature of MNC industrial R&D is limited to home-based exploitation/laboratory type. And 'asset-seeking' or 'home-base augmenting' R&D activities are assumed to be confined to the triad countries only. This new division of labour in industrial R&D has been conclusively demonstrated by Kuemmerle (1999).

Third Phase of Globalization

But, the trends of R&D in countries like China, India, Singapore, etc., appear to have again changed in early 2000–01. There are emerging evidences that some industrial R&D in India and China have become 'asset-seeking' or 'strategic/innovative' essentially because of the high uncertainties inherent in the fast growing large market. Researchers like Dunning and Narula (1995), Florida (1997), Pearce (1999) and Le Bas and Sierra (2002) have found that 'asset-seeking' has become a new tendency in the globalization of R&D. Chen (2007) points out that of late there has been re-integration of 'asset-exploiting' R&D activities (i.e., adaptational, technology transfer, etc., typical to developing countries) and 'asset-seeking' R&D activities (e.g., innovative, technology creating, etc., rare to developing countries) in China. He tries to prove this point with the help of his two empirical observations from China, i.e., Motorola and Microsoft. Both have global innovation networks and are working not only in China but also in other developing countries like Singapore and India. In spite of this, the fact remains that the core R&D of Motorola and Microsoft continues in USA. Nevertheless, Chen (2007) found ample evidences of 'asset-seeking' behaviour in the R&D activities of Motorola and Microsoft in China (i.e, in technology-driven R&D centres and market-driven R&D centres) and their subsequent reintegration with 'asset-exploiting' R&D centres (i.e., production-driven R&D centres and cost-driven R&D centres). Further, Chen (2007) explains this re-integration of 'asset-seeking' and 'asset-exploiting' R&D activities of the two MNCs in China through their two different upgrading models, i.e., (i) bottom-up evolution process (from the vantage of agglomeration of production networks and demanding local customers), and (ii) top-down evolution process (from the vantage of the synergy of Chinese returns and local entrepreneurial culture). To me the current R&D activities of Microsoft and Motorola in India and Singapore would not be much different from that of the counterparts in China.

At the end, the outstanding issue remains, whether China will reap some direct benefits from the plethora of global R&D firms, making China an emerging technological giant or more than just the 'factory to the world'. In his review article, Simon (2007) concluded that China's role in terms of global innovation is slowly growing even if not in a homogenous manner. There is clearly a series of emerging pockets of excellence appearing in Chinese S&T. Similar is the case of India where pockets of excellence with world-class R&D is growing, e.g., in software development, telecommunications, drugs and pharmaceuticals, etc.

Emerging Flatter Technological World Regime

Thus, in the latest phase of globalization, the so-called hierarchical pattern of R&D or international division of labour is mostly giving way to a 'flatter' pattern showing that MNCs are now willing to make some substantial bets on China. Because the MNCs making fast inroads into China and India to build/extend their global networks for R&D or to upgrade their existing R&D activities, are not short-term decisions, knee-jerk responses to new, quick-win opportunities, rather are a new set of imperatives driving the intensely competitive market of globalization. This newly emerging world, technologically flat type, is a fast changing world by virtue of the net addition of five major continental-sized economies like China, India, Russia, Mexico and Brazil to the economic and technological mainstream of global industrial capitalism. Thus, there seems to be slowly emerging a technologically multi-centric world order in place of a technologically uni-centric world order.

Lastly, Simon (2007) offers two perspectives to this unfolding global change in the developing countries, i.e., internal and external perspectives. The internal perspective deals with the questions pertaining to historical and cultural impediments to the building of technologically innovative China. Most crucial in this context is the 'sea of acidic attitudes' towards the 'new and the untried', and 'institutional weaknesses' (e.g., slow moving) deeply en routed to Maoist socialism. So is the case of Russian scientists and engineers who are desperately trying to overcome the then socialistic Soviet mind set/attitudes. The external perspective reflects the view that the 'opening up policy' practised by the Chinese government holds the key to the innovation and growth in China. The liberalization of China's economy has substantially expanded the R&D domain and its scale. The strategic role of Chinese diaspora in USA in encouraging to start MNCs FDI and R&D in China is part of this perspective. Further, the strategic recruitment of western trained Chinese scientists and engineer's by MNCs in China as a substitute to domestic trained personnel (plagued by cultural/attitudinal differences) has miraculously converted a traditionally known disadvantage, i.e., brain drain, into an advantage (called brain circulation). Likewise, in the post-liberalized India, a sizeable section of the Indian technical diaspora has returned home to man the technical positions in the booming ICT industry thriving in the cyber cities of Bangalore and Hyderabad. Later in this paper I would be producing more powerful arguments and evidences in favour of the flatter technological world, particularly in the context of IT/ICT revolution in India and China.

Growing Multinationalization of Firms of Developing Countries

The other striking feature of globalization of R&D in developing countries is the internationalization of their own firms but some industrial firms from the developing countries, like China and India, have become MNCs by themselves. So far we have discussed FDI flow-related R&D growth through MNCs in China but we are to deal with the reverse process of multinationalization of Chinese/Indian firms. Although this is a very recent phenomenon among selected firms, but it is worth noting as to what drives the Chinese companies to set-up R&D overseas. The hypothesis that becomes relevant in this context entails that Chinese firms internationalize their R&D in order to develop alternate channels of technology sourcing from developed countries (Kuemmerle, 1997). For example, Haier, a Chinese firm, has not only industrial parks in US, Jordan and Pakistan, it has also 10 listening posts and design centres in various developing countries and many developed countries. And, the Chinese automobile manufacturer Dongfeng Motors has set up four listening posts in US, UK, France and Germany for the purpose of being close to major competitors (not markets) and their technological bases. It is observed that where Chinese firms operate in large manufacturing sites in developed countries, as local R&D there, it was seen to have emerged in support of product localization and process innovation (e.g., Haier's R&D centre in south Croatia, US and the like). Thus, input-related rationale is the strongest reason for internationalization of R&D by Chinese firms in developed countries. Because of infringements of intellectual property rights at home for using certain western technologies, Chinese companies are debarred from entering into foreign markets. Hence, the local R&D centres of Chinese firms abroad would overcome these difficulties by developing and branding local technologies which in the process would build new technological competencies for Chinese firms. On the contrary, market and output-related determinants are said to be the determinants of R&D expansion in developing countries. For example, Haier's R&D centre at Jordan/Iran developed air-conditioners to cope with particularly adverse desert conditions in the Middle East and designed washing machines that could also handle cleaning vegetables in rural Asia. Apart from Haier, there are other Chinese firms that have internationalized their R&D such as ZTE, 3NOD and HUAWIE (Zedtwitz, 2005). Similarly, Indian firms that have internationalized their R&D in the recent past, because of liberalization of the restrictions in India are Infosys, Wipro, Satyam, HCL and TCS in IT sector, Ranbaxy and Dr Reddy's Lab in pharmaceuticals and Tata Steels in metals.

Like China and India, Brazil also has been a major destination of R&D related FDI. Costa (2005) has reported result of a survey conducted by the Economic Intelligence Unit (EIU) in the year 2004 to show that Brazil is the third major destination among developing countries wherefrom MNCs are planning to offshore R&D, whereas the first and the second major destinations remained to be China and India respectively. I shall be emphasizing the technological developments in later 1990s when some technological upgrading and economic restructuring have taken place in response to competitive market situations. Technological developments in Brazil then were involved in adaptation of newer technologies, both of product and process, including new organizational practices leading to gains in productivity and economic efficiency. The trend even continued further as Costa and Queiroz (2002) reported that by and large Brazilian industrial R&D remains at adaptive level. Hence, the very vital question that emerges is, if the globalization of R&D by MNCs and flow of FDI in R&D to Brazil would facilitate opening of new opportunities for Brazilian industry to move beyond adaptive levels of R&D?

Querioz et al. (2003), assuming a strong relationship between production capacity, technological capabilities and potentiality to attract MNC R&D, note that foreign affiliates with large and long established production capacities are in good position to conduct corporate R&D that results in accumulation of technological competencies and knowledge. Hence, in developing countries, global product development is mostly observed amongst long established foreign affiliates that have accumulated technological capabilities in some product or process technologies. In such cases, knowledge embedded in local R&D team becomes assets for the affiliated MNCs. So Queiroz et al. (2003) noted that MNCs in Brazil are engaged in 'asset exploiting' R&D activities because these capabilities of local affiliates serve to complement the MNCs themselves. This argument has been substantiated by Queiroz et al. (2003) on the basis of empirical evidences from Brazilian automobile industry. Car manufacturing MNC affiliates in Brazil like those of GM, Fiat, Ford and Volkswagen, have accumulated knowledge and also skills in styling, prototype testing, laboratories and proving grounds. These MNC affiliates in Brazil have focused their R&D to adapt to local and regional conditions and also to development of local derivatives. This process of market-oriented R&D by local affiliates of MNCs is known as 'tropicalization'. For instance, in the recent past GM-Brazil proposed to its headquarters the concept of a global derivative (based on new Corsa) called the Meriva model. Similarly, Volkswagen Brazil's TUPI project was a derivative model based on New Polo platform, the Fox model. This enables the local MNC affiliates in Brazil to compete with their sister subsidiaries/affiliates based in other countries for acquiring assignments for R&D. The growing competition among the affiliates around the world for central roles in the MNC global network seems to be a significant feature of globalization of R&D.

Globalization of Local Industrial R&D of Firms from Developing Countries

The other significant observation from the globalized R&D in Brazil has been the globalization of the local R&D (through MNC affiliation) that are of course some niche-based. The interesting case cited by Galina and Plonski (2002) from Brazilian telecom sector is worth looking at. Tetax and Batik – both domestic Brazilian firms with strong R&D capabilities on small switches – were acquired by Lucent – an MNC – in the late 1990s during the privatization process. Since Lucent till then did not have small switches in its product menu, the two Brazilian domestic firms turned into Lucent subsidiaries for their manufacturing and became global centre for technology for small switches. Therefore, it is claimed that high technological competences in some niches can help local MNC subsidiaries to become part of global R&D network. May be these niches are dependent upon particularities of the technologies and the products. This, however, appears to be a 'reverse globalization' process. Pharmaceutical industry in Brazil is of course an interesting case but in the opposite direction. Since drugs and pharmaceutical MNCs have been in Brazil for more than 50 years now, following the earlier argument of Brazilian automobile/telecom industry, one could expect significant R&D activities by local affiliates of the MNCs, may be of 'tropicalization' type (meaning addition of local flavour), or the 'reverse globalization' type. But, on the contrary, any innovative R&D activity worth mentioning in this sector is almost non-existing. These ageing MNC subsidiaries in Brazilian pharmaceutical industry have contributed very little to the local technological developments – be it product or process type.

Costa (2005) concludes that whatever R&D-related FDI may flow into Brazil in the second phase of globalization, i.e., after late 1990s, it seem, R&D facilities are established in order to support productive activities mostly. Cases of innovative stand-alone laboratories/firms are almost non-existent. This is partly because of absence of suitable policy measures in Brazil. Although in this later stage of globalization certain selected sectors of Brazilian industry as pointed out earlier have made some significant innovative type of R&D that have been the 'tropicalization'/'asset-exploiting' type of R&D. This is certainly unlike the Chinese case that has taken a big leap forward.

Perhaps under globalization the most significant and profound change in the behaviour of the MNCs, which is of course strategic by nature, has been the breakdown of an "immutable home country orientation of creative activity (continuously revolutionizing technology for competitive edge) and movement towards globalized programmes in innovation and R&D" (Pearce, 2005). Of course, there has been a stereotype perception that the MNCs' organizational structure is predominantly hierarchical, i.e., home country-based R&D headquarters of MNCs strategically control their subsidiary-based R&D activities in different parts of the world. But this strategic relationship of the controllers with those being controlled has undergone change, as pointed out Pearce (2005). The process of globalization has levelled all of them to be parts of the global strategy of R&D. Hence, the earlier intra-MNCs relationship has been replaced with 'heterarchy' or as dynamic differentiated networks. As a matter of intra-MNC restructuring of relationships, the earlier hierarchical relationship has been replaced with 'heterarchy' on the basis of their current/future potentialities to market. Further, this relationship among an MNC's global network labs/centres is now a dynamic one as their operations in different countries/regions undergo quick change. Of course, this has been possible because of the increasing decentralization of the R&D programmes of MNCs. Their relationship has acquired a dynamic strategic orientation in the MNCs' host countries, particularly those that are at the early stage of competitiveness. Strategically, the MNCs now involve their local affiliates with creative resources may be for the exploitation of local assets or for localization of a global product. Many successful MNCs have benefited from their willingness to respond to local taste differentiations. This has added to the rising significance of their affiliates and subsequently to their heterogeneity.

Offshoring Industrial R&D Services by Firms of Developed Countries

MNCs' FDI and technology transfer are being increasingly interlinked under globalization. Needless to say that MNCs have a very large share in the global R&D activities even today. The largest 700 firms worldwide in the year 2002 had spent $311 billion on R&D (UNCTAD, 2005). Currently, under a globalized regime, marked by rapidly changing technologies and shorter product life cycles, MNCs are offshoring more and more R&D to different parts of the world through both FDI and technological alliances (non-equity mode). This changing pattern of locating R&D differs radically from that of the past and alters the patterned view that R&D activities by MNCs remain confined mostly to their home countries (almost invariably developed countries). Expansion of R&D beyond homeland may not be new but significantly the scale of offshoring is rising and its geographical spread in reaching the developing countries is increasing. The spread of R&D-related FDI to developing countries is part of the broader process of offshoring services which is still rising. With the rising offshoring practices by the MNCs even the very meaning of the term 'offshoring' is broadened. (Offshoring in this context essentially means locating/transferring R&D activities abroad. It is done often internally by moving assets/knowledge-based services from the parent MNC to its foreign affiliates involving FDI or R&D activities outsourced to the third party provider abroad, i.e., could be a local firm in the host country or could be a foreign affiliate of another MNC in the host country). Offshoring is different from outsourcing, which always involves a third party, but not necessarily a transfer abroad. Offshoring and outsourcing overlap only when the activities/services are outsourced to third-party service providers.

The offshoring of R&D activities to locations in developing countries has already become a known phenomenon as well-known MNCs like Erickson, GE, IBM, Intel, Microsoft, Motorola, Nokia, Oracle, Texas Instruments, for example, have moved into developing countries. Between 1989 and 1999, R&D performance by all foreign affiliates of US MNCs in developing countries increased by nine times as compared to three times increase worldwide. In developing Asia, there was an 18-fold rise in MNC-based R&D expenses. During the same period (1989–1999), Japanese MNCs offshoring R&D to developing country-based foreign affiliates grew by ten times compared to their expenditure worldwide (UNCTAD, 2005). Of course offshoring of R&D by European MNCs to developing countries is still in nascent stage.

Indicating the globalization of R&D, foreign affiliates are assuming more important roles in R&D in many host countries. During the period 1993–2002, the R&D expenditure of foreign affiliates worldwide climbed from 10 per cent to 16 per cent of global business R&D (UNCTAD, 2005). Significantly, the expenditures of foreign affiliates in business R&D in the developing world increased from 2 per cent to 18 per cent during 1996–2002 (ibid.). Similar data on green-field R&D projects initiated during August 2002 to July 2004 indicate that of the 1,000 FDI projects in R&D worldwide the majority, i.e., 739, were located in developing countries. Developing countries in Asia and Pacific alone accounted for more than half of the total, i.e., 563, projects. Prominent among these countries were China and India.

Apart from the FDI route, firms also often use non-FDI forms such as technology alliances, R&D joint ventures, R&D consortiums and university–industry linkages to get access to strategic knowledge abroad. These forms of cooperation can be equity or non-equity based (mostly not considered to be outside FDI definition). As part of their alliances, MNCs are outsourcing some technology development activities from firms and research institutes worldwide, including those located in developing countries. However, R&D by MNCs under globalization reached out to only selected developing countries such as China, India, Brazil, Singapore, South Africa and Mexico. But of late other developing countries like Thailand (Toyota project), Malaysia and even African countries like Kenya (MNCs agricultural technology) have slowly acquired global R&D into their folds.

Further noteworthy is that the technological change unleashed by globalization impacted the design and organizational patterns of R&D leading to a proliferation and differentiation of corporate R&D units. As products became modular there took place fragmentation of design and the specialization of knowledge creation in the internal and external networks of MNCs. UNCTAD (2005) has articulated clearly five types of R&D units that have come into existence (of which three at least are of recent origin): (i) technology transfer units (typical to developing country firms) linked to manufacturing units, engaged in technology transfer issues and adaptations of products and processes to local conditions), (ii) local technology units (new to developing countries, set up to develop new/improved products for local market when the MNC affiliate identifies distinctive investment opportunities), (iii) regional technology units (set up to develop new/improved products for regional markets share some common features and need for specialized products), (iv) global technology units (single product for global market, when the MNC allocates parts of its product range to specific affiliates and when the MNC opts for a decentralized but integrated R&D programme, for efficiency drive through offshoring and international outsourcing), and (v) corporate technology units (internationally independent set up to pursue pure/basic research in one area of science and engineering to bring radical product breakthroughs, operating as networks to bring synergetic combination of results, engage in long-term, exploratory research for parent MNC to protect and enhance future competitive edge).

In addition to this, the emergence of new science-based technologies like micro-electronics, ICT, biotechnology and new materials has had a profound impact on business R&D run by MNCs. These new technologies have created opportunities for developing countries, particularly those with a tradition of scientific education, without much industrial experience to catch up with the rest. R&D in micro-electronics, biotechnology, pharmaceuticals, software, etc., could be globalized more easily than in conventional industries, because these industries are more knowledge-intensive and can be presumed even being delinked from production. Further, in these areas of new technologies, R&D activities are so divisible into several modules that certain modules can easily be treated as 'core' and some as 'non-core' activities. Hence, some of the non-core activities can easily be outsourced mostly from developing countries.

The other substantive spillover effects of MNCs' R&D activities in developing countries caused by globalization have been the following: (i) Arrival of commercial culture among research scientists and engineers (different from pure academic culture, i.e., knowledge for knowledge shake). For example, when FDI-related R&D arrived in India, research scientists and engineers from public funded laboratories/academic institutions started focusing on patentable research and some of them became entrepreneurs by themselves. (ii) Emergence of an R&D and innovation culture among local firms, particularly in software, pharmaceuticals and drugs. (iii) Diverting scarce local R&D resources of host countries, particularly human resources, from local firms and research institutions. The best of R&D manpower may be allured to global R&D.

Globalizing Social Impact of IT/ICT Revolution

The rise of IT (including software) industry in countries like China, India, Singapore, South Korea, Taiwan, Hong Kong, Philippines, etc., has become synonymous with globalization because of the timely arrival of digital technology and its inherent capabilities for the faster proliferation. The conducive global economic order has promoted international technological sub-contracting and subsequently international outsourcing and countries like India and China have been the beneficiaries of this. The consequent rise of Chinese and Indian IT industry during the 1990s has been the most spectacular achievement for both Chinese and Indian industries. This industry in India grew at an incredible rate of 50 per cent per annum during the whole of the 1990s. Being export-oriented it has earned 75 per cent of its revenue from exports alone. This industry in 2007 had nearly 1.63 million employees. Subsequently, the ICT revolution in India and in other developing countries (including NICs) has not merely earned enough foreign currencies, but also more significantly, has brought in widespread socio-cultural changes. The impact of ICT revolution on the cultural domain has thrown new challenges to sociologists. Following are some of the socio-cultural areas where the ICT has had major impact:

(i) *Building social capital through the use of internet*: It has been observed to be highly useful for professionals in general and academicians in particular who build up their social capital internationally and realize the benefits in the long run.

(ii) *Ethnocization through internet*: Apart from reinforcing ethnic ties among lose community members and facilitating the resurrection of ethnic beliefs and practices, internet helps ethnic groups to publicize their cultural/religious ideals and reach out to potential new recruits.

(iii) *Internet pushing for a sexual revolution*: Internet contains abundance of pornographic sites/materials, access to which is of course universal and not restricted by any law. Starting from a mere commercialization of human body (sexually) internet is now offering experiences of virtual sex, inter-active sex, through its sites. Hence, as a big source of cultural pollution, it is now posing serious cultural threats to tradition-bound cultures.

(iv) *Emergence of a new class of transnational capitalists:* The first phase of the said revolution in India, known as IT revolution, took place in the last decade of the 20th century, i.e., 1990s and its second phase known as the ICT revolution followed in the early years of the next decade, i.e., 2010s. The IT revolution gave rise to a new class of capitalists who were in fact engineering professionals. This was true of both India and China.

(v) *Emergence of a new class of workers as well as a new sub-culture of theirs in India*: The ICT revolution in India, and in other developing countries (including NICs) more significantly, has created a new class of workers/professionals based on knowledge-based technologies (being fully R&D based), and consequently a sub-culture of their own. In the following paragraphs, we will discuss the impact of the ICT revolution is some details:

Emergent New Class of Transnational Capitalists

It is now well known that a new class of entrepreneurs has emerged out of the IT revolution in India as well as China. As noted by Upadhya (2004), in her study of Indian software industry, most of the founders of software firms in India had middle class origin who had built on their cultural capital of higher education (usually through engineering education) and acquired social capital (knowledge and business networks) through their professional careers. Their social capital enabled them to make use of the trust and cooperation of their professional networks, for making innovative business advancements, because their social capital could reduce the transaction costs, bureaucratic procedures and even corruption. Thus, the combined virtue of cultural and social capital engendered a class technological capitalists in Indian IT sector. This class of capitalists is not only driven by high need achievement orientation but also high level of technological innovations. They could ride innovation-driven business that has flattened the technological world, at least in the IT sector, to a great extent. This class of IT capitalists is also distinguished by its global linkages. Not only that many of them had studied/worked abroad, particularly in the USA, but also their business were (i) greatly dependent upon foreign contracts (particularly US), and (ii) most of them acquired foreign funding either directly or through foreign venture capitals (which were mostly from USA, particularly the Silicon Valley). This class of entrepreneurs is distinct from the traditional Indian capitalist class (Seth Ji's leading family business) and corporate houses like Ambanis, Birlas, Godrej, Bajaj, Kirloskar, JKs, Tatas etc. These are also first generation entrepreneurs. As the offshoot of liberalization of the Indian policies and globalization of the economy, this bourgeoisie is more adaptable to MNCs. Instead of being wary of the presence of the multinationals in the IT sector, this class could find a synergy with MNCs and have learnt to benefit from their presence. Therefore, this class, first being the offshoot and later being part of the transnational IT business, is the strongest votary of globalization. By virtue of creating enormous employment and profit, this industry has influenced Indian economic and industrial policies greatly during the last two decades. Upadhya (2004) calls them the 'icons of the resurgent India'.

Very much like India, there too in China emerged a new class of transnational capitalists which was the vanguard of the ICT revolution. These are harbingers of China's Silicon Valley at Zhongguancun district near Beijing which is in fact overpopulated with thousands of hi-tech firms, including national and transnational firms like NEC, SUN, Siemens, Microsoft, etc. The academic mentors of many of these ICT firms are the Chinese universities leading among them was the Tsingua University which was playing the role the Stanford University was playing in USA which was the birthplace of Silicon Valley as some of the first firms were born in Stanford's industrial park in 1950s. But, the Chinese Silicon Valley Zhongguancun has started with an advantage of 'sea turtles' (like the olive green turtles of the high sea return after years to lay eggs on the beach on which they were born). It is the local nickname for native born Chinese techies who acquired training and work experience in the USA and returned to start business firms in China.

Chinese techies with years of experience in California in particular have turned entrepreneurs and started business firms in Taiwan, Shenzhen and Zhongguancun that were either manufacturing or trading. These too had strong linkages with the Silicon Valley in the USA. Globalization has made it possible. Innovation-driven business in China was being facilitated by informal relations such as those of alumni and professional links of Chinese techies on both sides of the Pacific. Wong (2006), in his study among Silicon Valley Chinese techies, noted that many of them maintained multiple passports and thus be 'flexible citizens' with divided loyalty to the Silicon Valley as well as homeland. Wong furnished evidences of Chinese techies migrating back to their native country but retaining their Silicon Valley homes (by renting out to other Chinese) and propose to return to Silicon Valley either in a few years or after retirement. And, there are many who did not return. Wong further reported that in 1993 an estimated 30 per cent Taiwanese migrant engineers who worked in Silicon Valley had returned to Taiwan and in mid-1990s at least 25 per cent of techies from Hong Kong returned to their land of origin (ibid.: 105) in search of better opportunities. And bulk of these professionals turned entrepreneurs made use of the venture capital funds (e.g., Schoendorf) from the Silicon Valley as their Indian counterparts did. This class too maintained its strong transnational linkages with Australia, North Korea and particularly with US Silicon Valley and among themselves (i.e., those in Taiwan, Hong Kong and mainland China). Wong has also pointed out the existence of strong social capital among these professionals-turned-capitalists who maintain consciously strong professional networks that they make use for business purpose. Again mutual trust and cooperation were keys to social capital. I have already mentioned about the academic entrepreneurs of China in the context of entrepreneurial universities (Chinese UREs). Hence, the academic entrepreneurs and the sea turtle-type entrepreneurs, together, make a sizeable class of new breed capitalists that have revolutionized China's innovation-led business. This class too is an offshoot of China's economic liberalization and subsequently has become part of its globalization.

Emergent New Class of Elite Workforce

This transnational entrepreneurial class has emerged in tandem with a transnational labour regime which has generated a new class of IT workforce in India.

In this context of IT workforce extremely pertinent are the notions of 'techno-coolie' and 'cyber-coolie'. These derogatory terms refer to a new class of elite 'knowledge workers', emerging out of the global outsourcing of services. Emergence of this workforce is not confined to India alone, rather it is spread over several other developing and even developed countries like China, Singapore, Taiwan, Hong Kong, Philippines and Israel. Hence, both the words refer to knowledge workers not merely that of India but to all such workers of countries who have become part of the international outsourcing services. But India has a giant share in this.

Techno-coolie

Software engineers or other IT professionals, otherwise known as techies, of developing countries are seen as a new knowledge workforce that caters to the global informational economy. The workforce is highly flexible and mobile. These IT professionals called as *techno-coolie* are mostly employed in the US, the UK and other European countries like Germany, Belgium, Netherlands, etc., or even many of them who are employed in home countries travel abroad very frequently for 'onsite' delivery of their services. These are essentially immigrants may be Indians, Chinese, Philippinos or Hispanic, engaged in low-end technical jobs. Techno-coolies are also a grossly underpaid lot. The geographically dispersed nature of the software outsourcing business makes physical mobility as one aspect of the migration. The developed form of ICTs even enabled part of the services to be delivered 'virtually'. Software engineers even located in home countries, along with colleagues and mangers spread over distant geographical locations, work as 'virtual teams' to communicate among themselves and deliver to the customer abroad through computer networks. In this connection, they make short foreign visits too. Usually, techno-coolies are hired through a practice called as 'body shopping' from the developing countries because of the international sub-contracting practices followed by large corporations in these developed countries to keep their costs low.

Migration of techies from India to Europe although started in late 1980s, it became significant in late 1990s, particularly due to 'Y2K' crisis. The important routes of this migration from India by the techies were three: (1) through an arrangement called 'body shopping' by which Indian techies were sent on short contracts to work on the customer's site abroad; (2) through outsourcing by American/European firms through Indian software service providers who had a team of techies working both on the project at home and also onsite at the customer's venue abroad. Earlier, TCS, Infosys, HCL, etc., were engaged in body shopping and had offices both in India and US/Europe; and (3) through the Indian subsidiaries of European MNCs like Philips, Rober Bosc, Siemens, etc.

1. *Through body shopping:* This arrangement was not so encouraging for the Indian techies as they were engaged on the customer's site on low-end maintenance jobs with low salaries. Their employment conditions, compensations and nature of contract are determined by consultants (Indian agencies) whereas their works were managed by the customers. The techies were usually on a contract with the consultant company to be paid on hourly rate other than the travel accommodation and maintenance allowances. The duration of the stay abroad is specified in the contract. Usually, the techie cannot break the contract with the consultant for greener pasture abroad as they had to pay back heavily. The Indian consultants were basically sub-contractors suppose to provide mere 'bodies'/engineers with specifications to the MNCs.
2. *Through outsourcing companies:* Those techies travelling abroad by outsourcing arrangements through Indian service providers like TCS, HCL, etc., usually have their base jobs in India but are sent abroad to the client's site for a certain period. They are managed by their Indian service providing agency and not the client; mostly they get the Indian salary, with extra money for Europe/USA stay. The techies could make good money out of this but again carried onerous contracts or bonds with Indian agency not to join the job of the client or anybody in the client's country. Further, on return, they were bound to work with the Indian agency for a few years, and the like. Violation of the bond invites a hefty fine that may drive the techies bankrupt.
3. *Through MNC subsidiaries:* A good number of Indian engineers go abroad to work through their parent subsidiary companies of US/European MNCs like Oracle, Philips, Robert Bosc, etc. These are employees of the MNC subsidiaries in India called software development centres and are in fact better placed compared to the earlier two mechanisms. They go on

short/long-term assignments and are comfortably placed abroad, and as employees of the subsidiaries they are provided with housing, good working conditions, allowances, etc. Even they have to make little or fewer adjustments in terms of work culture, etc. Often they are housed with employees of parent MNCs in block apartments abroad.

The other category of mechanism for the techies was to get employed directly by US/European companies leaving the Indian agencies' contractual arrangements behind. Although most of them had come under 'body shopping' arrangements for onsite delivery, but have shifted away. Their salary and employment conditions are better than in the three arrangements mentioned above.

Apart from predicaments related to mode of recruitments, these Indian techies are marred by prohibitive immigration laws and regulations. It is well known that for Indian techies, obtaining visas, work permits and residence permits for European countries is much harder than for the USA. Upadhya (2006), in her study among Indian techies in Netherlands, Germany and Belgium, has tried to analyse their plight in terms of work culture differences, as victims of European stereotypes about Indian techies, culturally embedded communication patterns, poor time management, inability to adapt to multiculturalism of virtual teams and dim career prospects in Europe. These apart, these techies are to negotiate the quagmire of immigration laws and rules (which are often humiliating) to maintain themselves in Europe and have to chew the common images of immigrant workers, diluted with racism, held by local people. They too struggle for an identity of a professional/knowledge worker as different from unskilled working class immigrants (from other small poor countries). As if these were not enough the Indian techies have to withstand the anti-outsourcing sentiments in Europe and USA and a consequent fear of loss of job. Their isolation and social seclusion add to their owes. Thus, the Indian techie struggles hard not only to acquire the European work culture, multiculturalism, etc., but also engages himself in a reconstruction of his identity and self to relate to a foreign society.

Cyber-coolie

Today, the word *cyber-coolie* refers to that growing workforce which comes under the IT-enabled services (ITES) like call centres, medical transcription and business process outsourcing. This workforce emerged out of the policy of 'offshore outsourcing' of services followed mainly by a few developed countries like the USA, UK and Japan. European powers like France and Germany also do but their scales of outsourcing of services are very limited. And, India being an English-speaking country is favourably placed to be at the receiving end of this international outsourcing of services from USA and UK. Like the techno-coolies, the cyber-coolies are also grossly underpaid. While a 'cyber-coolie' delivers his offshore services through internet being present in his home country, the 'techno-coolie' do so right on the site of the client abroad being present there.

These low-paid technical workers are hired from developing countries to do low-end, low-intensity software jobs. They are employed on a contractual basis only. Even most of the BPO jobs are outsourced from developing countries as part of the policy of international sub-contracting by large MNCs. If in the 1960–70s the large MNCs in the manufacturing sector outsourced their raw materials and sometimes value-added products from the developing countries and in the 1970–80s these again outsourced their components and semi-finished products from developing countries (and sometimes even shifted their manufacturing units to escape rising costs and pollution), in the 1990s and 21st century the large corporations in the manufacturing as well as service sector from those developed countries are outsourcing their technical services from the developing countries. This is the consequence of the growing competition among MNCs in the developed countries and their drastic efforts to reduce costs.

The word 'coolie' (whether techno-coolie or cyber-coolie) has certainly a contemptuous meaning and is used in a derogatory sense. Coolie, *aka,* a poor fellow, dressed in red, scurrying after us and carrying our heavy luggage on his head as we board a train, all for a few pennies. It is indeed difficult to trace the exact origin of the word 'cyber-coolie'/'techno-coolie'. But certainly the word was coined by the Indian left-wing intellectuals who have been against free trade. It is also true that the leftists have been trying to trade unionize this growing workforce which the workforce itself has not entertained. Hence, this contemptuous attribution. The other source of the word 'cyber-coolie' is the British critics of the phenomenon who are yet to free themselves from the 'Raj' hangover. British economy today being more a service economy deals more with financing, banking and insurance than with manufacturing. Hence, it needs 'back up services' in these areas which they outsource from its ex-colony, India, which is also English-speaking. And, this is also true that unionists in Britain do consider these outsourced low-end jobs to Indians as job snatching. Therefore, this envious contempt.

The knowledge workers, emerging as a distinct occupational category in India, is of very recent origin, may be a direct consequence of India's globalization. As a distinct occupational category, it has certain characteristic features and is fast developing a sub-culture for itself. Most of my formulations here are based on information/publications I accessed from the internet. I also borrow the findings of a study, conducted by Babu P. Ramesh (2005) of the V.V. Giri National Institute of Labour, on BPO workers of India. The study was conducted among a sample of 280 customer care agents from six call centres in Noida and 40 managers and team leaders of BPO companies in Delhi, Gurgaon and Noida in 2005. The BPO industry in India alone currently employs little more than 5,00,000 according to NASSCOM.

These knowledge workers are all young, educated and smart Indians who work in call centres and outsourced business processing offices to cater to American and British multinationals. They work through the nights, for good reasons that night in India is daytime for their clients in USA. Since they work through the nights, Harish Trivedi (2004) even calls them a 'Chowkidar' – a derogatory word meaning night guard. They work through phones and webs to deal with their overseas clients. They speak in an American accent which they have painfully cultivated. As their Indian accent is neutralized, their personality, biological clock and identity also have been neutralized. They conceal their real names and country of residence while dealing with the clients. Often they have to introduce themselves as Pete/Greg/Jane from Atlanta/Ohio, etc. Thus, they are faceless workers with pretentious identities (from Hari to Harry or from Shalini to Shelly) who deal with invisible customers/clients located on the other side of the globe.

Many of these BPO workers not only work for very long hours but also at odd hours. Many find that they have little social life left, as they work in nights when their families and friends are at homes. Some develop long-term sleep disorders, some take so much verbal abuse, day after day, from irrate and racist Americans that they actually need psychological help which now some call centres have learnt to provide for. The sources of their heavy stress that characterize the BPO workers have been identified as, (i) absence of job security/seasonal and contractual nature of jobs for vast number of employees, (ii) monotonous nature of their jobs, (iii) odd working hours (nights), (iv) long duration of work without break, (v) continuous surveillance within the office, (vi) racial abuse by overseas customers, (vii) adherence to stiff and strict performance indicators, (viii) little time for family, (ix) sleeping disorder, and (xii) marital discordances emergent of job requirements.

These young people are the scions of middle class urban parents, educated in convents or public schools from where they have acquired a fluency in English and sometimes possess a technical or science degrees but all of them long for an exposure to western popular culture. This workforce, in spite of long hours of work, even in odd hours, also works in the weekends. But this is a grossly underpaid lot. This is why, India is seen as an outsourcing threat. The cost of an Indian BPO employee is seven to ten times lesser than his American counterpart in ITES business. It is true that there exists a large pool of English-speaking low-skilled manpower in India. And, this makes India a western corporate attraction. The key is low wages.

The organizational structure of call centres is basically dualistic, consisting of a core/permanent set of employees and the periphery/temporary workers. All call centre agents are periphery workers, who are substitutable, while team leaders and managers make the core group. The long-term career prospects there now are bleak or virtually non-existent. The dualistic workforce model allows the firm to regulate the workforce and prevent any sign of trade unionism. Trade union is a strange word for this workforce. The labour practices that call centres follow are even much older. Work is monitored on the spot and even after working hours with the help of specially designed software, computer network and closed circuit cameras. All interactions of these employees in office are continuously recorded or taped and randomly checked by the manager. The most of surveillance recorded at work is even comparable with situations of 19th century prisons.

Mistakes at work lead to immediate warnings and those are recorded in 'warning cards' that form part of the daily ratings of workers. If a worker commits three errors in a day, he/she gets a zero rating. Three consecutive zeros lead to counselling or even dismissal. Availing leave without prior notice/consent is considered unauthorized and could be the reason for termination. So, the call centres by and large practise a hire-and-fire policy. As it seems, there is no modicum of labour law in this sector. Thus, the service conditions of this workforce are very poor. But, on the contrary, its working conditions are extremely congenial and much superior to those in the manufacturing sector. Their office premises are very clean and fully air-conditioned. They are provided with free meals, free transport (car pick-up and drop), regular staff entertainment, a concierge service that will book cinema tickets for them, an ambulance waiting at the bottom of the building if they are fallen ill, etc. Apart from less challenging jobs like telesales and customer services, they do render more challenging services by providing value-added 'back office' support in the area of banking and insurance too. Although the work is often monotonous, the monotony is camouflaged by the projection of 'work as fun' – introducing cafes, popcorn booths and ping-pong tables into the offices. In this comforting working environment, spate of calls or e-mails are successfully attended. Besides such a relaxing working environment, a reasonably good salary (₹ 10,000/to 25,000/per month), use of latest technologies, young and educated peers, all make these knowledge workers believe that the job they are doing is of an executive/professional.

Emerging New Sub-culture

That apart, it is a highly disciplined and young workforce. And, because of its education and predominantly middle class origin, it turned out to be a docile workforce with high level of efficiency. But unfortunately this highly productively docile workforce is bereft of labour rights and job security. As stated before, as a distinct and new occupational category, this workforce is fast developing a sub-culture of itself. A recent study by Georgina Thomas (2008) among the call centre employees in the Indian city of Mumbai has referred to the emergence of such a sub-culture among these young elite workers, of course, because of their changing lifestyles. This sub-culture is said to have two aspects: (i) consumerism accompanied by other leisure time activities by both male and female employees like smoking, drinking, frequent partying and movie going, mall shopping, etc. They relish the mall culture. The English they write is of a different variety more of American accent (with abbreviated forms of expressions) like the nature and the types of products they market or products they do value addition. They represent a sub-culture that emphasizes traits like low cost, instant satisfaction, use and throw, take it or forget it, minimum quality assured, go cool, chill out, one night stand, etc. They change their jobs as frequently as they change their boyfriends/girlfriends.

The other vital aspect of the sub-culture refers more gloomy traits like leading a self-centred life, living life in one's own terms and conditions, moving away from community and family life, indulging in frequent pre-marital sex, extra-marital affairs and divorces in the name of what is called as 'one night stand', etc. These traits certainly imply choosing life without commitment/bonds and without certain moral values that augur a free life of primitive type. These are new trends and do make a highly significant component of the sub-culture. This sub-culture emerging among BPO workers is of course anchored on a process of a separate identity formation among them, i.e., (i) different work culture (highly routinized, stressful, odd working hours, etc.), leading to (ii) a different lifestyle, leading to (iii) acquiring new cultural traits, leading to (iv) different perception of their social position and culture by others (including family members), leading to (v) formation of a different self, leading to (vi) a different cultural identity of the employees.

It is precisely because of their perceptions of being professionals that holds back these elite knowledge workers from forming trade unions. Left-wing politics in India has been desperately trying to penetrate its trade unionism into this sector for last several years. Another important reason why these workers are disinterested in trade unionism is that they do not intend to continue in this job for a long time, rather they consider this to be a stepping stone to migrate or shift the job. This kind of job perception by the ambitious young workforce obviously finds the notion of unionism incompatible with itself.

A few internet-based articles on 'cyber-coolie' by Harish Trivedi (2004), Praful Bidwai (2003), Ranabir Ray Choudhury (2003), etc., have provoked strong reactions from amongst this workforce. A frustrated Narayan Ram Hegde of Union Network International (a global alliance of 900 unions), when miserably failed in his effort to induct very few of the knowledge workers into their trade union framework, noted that "these young people have a negative image about unions. But they are more like cyber-coolies. Hopefully, they will be convinced over time". The debate has certainly created some heat in the internet. These young and educated workers claimed themselves to be 'cool professionals' against the attribution of being cyber-coolies. In a website article entitled *'Dancing with Dogs: Interesting Debate'* (August 18, 2004) carrying this debate, one finds some of these cool young professionals loosing their cool. Not only they did heavy left bashing but also literally lead a counter offensive against these left-wing Indian intellectuals for their contemptuous writings.

Thus, there exists a perceptual difference between those of the left-wing intellectuals and those of the elite knowledge workers. Of course, there prevails an ambiguity with regard to the objective conditions of work of these knowledge workers. The objective conditions that are goading an intellectual to perceive the knowledge workers as 'coolies' are countered by another set of objective conditions that go in favour of the agents perception of themselves as 'cool professionals'. May be it is a new class of elite technical workers who by their objective conditions make a class in themselves, but in order to make a class for themselves they need to possess a subjective consciousness of their being. Thus, an objective class is yet to be matched by a subjective consciousness or an objective class is yet to be converted into a subjective class. Therefore, unless and until a class in itself becomes a class for itself, it would be difficult to treat them as cyber-coolies. As in the early stage of industrialization, the sociological problems of industrial workers were inadequate wages, long hours of work (bringing surplus value), poor work environment, job insecurity, etc., and in a later stage the same got changed to alienation (loss of skill and self), technologically deterministic human behaviour, industrial accidents/health hazards, unionization, participatory management, and the like. With the advent of post-industrial society (part of the economy is knowledge-based) the sociological perception of the problems of the knowledge-based workers is bound to be different as the very nature of work has undergone change. This new sub-class of new technical workforce is an off-shoot of the India's recent IT revolution which is still evolving fast. As slowly these new elite workers are coming under the fold of trade unions, their service conditions and salaries are improving. BPO as a phenomenon in India is going to stay, it is not a very transitory phenomenon. Rather it is fast expanding and will be soon stabilized as a feature of Indian economy. The career prospects in BPO industry are going to be brighter like that of their prosperous counterparts in the software sector. It must be kept in mind that this Indian workforce is today envied in the USA and UK as job snatchers.

But, the more enviable job snatchers are another new budding class of highly paid employees engaged in the knowledge-based outsourcing industry of India. These are today known as KPO (knowledge process outsourcing) professionals. These are true professionals like graduate engineers (in areas of CAD, Biotech/Pharma), MBAs, Chartered Accountants, Economists, etc. They are engaged in offshoring knowledge intensive business processes that require specialized domain expertise. Their jobs involve high-end processes like computer-aided simulations, valuation research and analysis, data integration, investment research, patent filing, legal/insurance claims, management consulting, etc. KPO industry may be export-oriented like the BPO. But, unlike the BPO industry that mainly provides the IT-enabled services, the KPO industry provides domain-based processes and business expertise that are more challenging and requires professional as well as technical expertise on the part of employees. The KPO industry in India is slowly growing to reach an export value estimated to be $12 billion by the end of year 2010 (UNI, 2005). This industry is making use of the vast pool of highly qualified but unemployed/underemployed Indian manpower. This too is a new and growing sub-class of Indian professionals emergent of the ICT revolution. Emergence of KPO professionals is in a way going to be a conducive factor for the social positioning of the ITES workforce.

Conclusion

The above discussed trends developments in the globalization of S&T are indicative of the qualitative change in the centre–periphery relations. It may be too sweeping to make a derivation about the qualitatively changed relationship between the centre and the periphery countries as a general phenomenon emergent of globalization. But it would be otherwise safe to conclude on the basis of the evidences produced above that instead of being a general phenomenon this changed relationship between the centre and the peripheral countries is a limited phenomenon confined to the experiences of the handful of developing countries like Singapore, China, India, Brazil, Indonesia, and the like. It is very much possible that of these a few peripheral countries have changed their relations qualitatively with the countries at the centre keeping the general nature of centre–periphery relations unaltered. The qualitative change in the relations of these few peripheral countries with the centre is of course indicative of their new relations as 'semi-peripheral countries'. It would not be inappropriate to perceive the changing relationship of countries like Singapore, China, India and Brazil with the countries at the centre within the 'world system perspective' of Emanuel Wallerstein, as that of 'centre and semi-periphery' countries. Of course, compared to other countries, Singapore had much earlier entered into the semi-periphery club of countries. But, like Singapore, the other peripheral countries have benefited from their relationship with the countries at the centre, may be within the framework of dependence and have successfully transformed their position from that of periphery to semi-periphery. The case of India as a semi-periphery country may be contested, but it is fast moving into the category, if we take evidences of technological developments in areas of IT, biotechnology, pharmaceuticals and drugs and subsequent export of industrial products and services.

References

Altbach, Philip G. (2009) "The Giants Awake: Higher Education Systems in China and India", *Economic and Political Weekly*, Vol. XLIV, No. 23, June 6, pp. 39–51.

Bidwai, Praful (2003) IT Experts or Cyber-Coolies? July 11. Retrieved on 15/12/2006. http://www.rediff.com///news/2003/jul/11praful.html

Cantwell, J. and Janne, O. (1999) "Technological Globalization and Innovative Centers: The Role of Corporate Technological Leadership and Locational Hierarchy", *Research Policy*, Vol. 28, pp. 119–44.

Cantwell, J. and Pocatello, L. (2000) The Location of Technology Activities of MNCs in European Regions: The Role of Spillovers and Local Competencies, Working Paper, Reading University Business School, pp. 1–23.

Chandra, Nimesh (2008) Academia-Industry Interface: Modes of Knowledge Production and Transfer at Indian Institute of Technologies, Centre for Studies in Science Policy, JNU, New Delhi, July, Unpublished Ph.D Thesis, Ch IV and V.

Costa, Ionara (2005) "Technological Learning, R&D and Foreign Affiliates in Brazil", in *Globalization of R&D and Developing Countries*, New York and Geneva: UN, pp. 141–54.

Costa, Ionara and Queiroz, S. (2002) "Foreign Direct Investment and Technological Capabilities in Brazilian Industry", *Research Policy*, Vol. 31, pp. 1431–43.

Chen, Yen-Chung (2007) "The Upgrading of Multinational Regional Innovation Networks in China", *Asia Pacific Business Review*, Vol. 13, No. 3, pp. 373–403.

Dunning, J.H. and Narula, R. (1995) "The R&D Activities of Foreign Firms in USA", *International Studies of Management and Organization*, Vol. 25, pp. 39–74.

Dzisah, J. and Etzkowitz, H. (2006) 'The Renewal of African University: Towards a Triple-Helix Development Model', paper presented in the Ethiopia Triple-Helix conference, Adis Ababa, UN Conference Centre, May 29–31.

Etzkowitz, H. (2002) *MIT and the Rise of Entrepreneurial Science*. London: Routledge Press, pp. 1–19.

—— (2003) 'Learning from Transition: The Triple Helix as an Innovation System', paper presented at the Symposium on Knowledge based Society: A Challenge for EU and Accession Countries, Croatia, October 23.

Etzkowitz, H. and Leydesdorff, L. (2000) "The Dynamics of Innovation: From National Systems and 'Mode 2' to a Triple Helix of University-Industry-Government Relations", *Research Policy*, No. 29, pp. 109–23.

Etzkowitz, H. et al. (2008) "Pathways to Entrepreneurial University: Towards a Global Convergence", *Science and Public Policy*, Vol. 35, No. 9, pp. 681–95.

Eun, Jong-Hak, Lee, Keun and Wu, Guisheng (2006) "Explaining the 'University-run Enterprises' in China: A Theoretical Framework for University-Industry Relationship in Developing Countries and its Application to China", *Research Policy*, Vol. 35, pp. 1329–46.

Friedman, Thomas L. (2006) *The World is Flat: The Globalized World in the Twenty-first Century* (Updated and Expanded), London: Penguin Books, p. 660.

Florida, R. (1997) "The Globalization of R&D: Results of a Survey of Foreign Affiliated R&D Laboratories in USA", *Research Policy*, Vol. 26, pp. 85–103.

Fazackerley, A. (2007) *British Universities in China*. Agora: The Forum for Culture and Education, London.

Galina, S.V.R. and Plonski, G.A. (2002) Global Product Development in the Telecommunication Industry: An Analysis of the Brazilian Subsidiaries Involvement, 9th International Product Development Conference, European Institute for Advanced Studies in Management (EIASM), Sophia-Anipolis, France, May, pp. 12–13. Available at: www.fia.com.br/pgtusp/pesquisas/orq_prorex/subol/SGalina%20%209th%20IPDMC. pdf

Kuemmerle, W. (1999) "Foreign Direct Investment in Industrial Research in the Pharmaceutical and Electronic Industries: Results from a Survey of Multinational Firms", *Research Policy*, Vol. 28, pp. 179–93.

—— (1997) "Building Effective R&D Capabilities Abroad", *Harvard Business Review*, March–April, pp. 61–70.

Liu, N.C. (2007) "Research Universities in China: Differentiation, Classification and Future World-Class Status", in P.G. Altbach and J. Balan (eds.), *World Class Worldwide: Transforming Research Universities in Asia and Latin America*, Baltimore: Johns Hopkins University Press, pp. 54–69.

Le Bas, C. and Sierra, C. (2002) "Location versus Country Advantages in R&D Activities: Some Further Results on Multinational's Locational Strategies", *Research Policy*, Vol. 31, pp. 589–690.

Ma, W. (2007) "The Flagship University and China's Economic Reform", in P.G. Altbach and J. Balan (eds.), *World Class Worldwide: Transforming Research Universities in Asia and Latin America*, Baltimore: Johns Hopkins University Press, pp. 31–53.

Maslen, Geoff (2007) "Chinese Students to Dominate World Market", *University World News*, Issue No. 4, November 4.

Ministry of Education, PR China, http://www.moe.edu.cn/english/international_3.htm

OECD (2003) *Turning Science into Business: Patenting and Licensing at Public Research Organisations*. Paris, France.

Patel, P. (1995) "Localized Production of Technology for Global Markets", *Cambridge Journal of Economics*, Vol. 19, pp. 141–53.

Pattnaik, Binay K. (2005) "Impact of Globalization on the Technological Regime in India: Aspects of Change", *Perspectives in Global Development and Technology*, Vol. 4, No. 1, pp. 63–82.

Paul, Samuel (2009) "Internationalization of Higher Education: Strategic Implications", *Economic and Political Weekly*, Vol. XLIV, No. 9, pp. 37–41.

Pearce, R. (1999) "Decentralized R&D Strategic Competitiveness: Globalized Approaches to Generation and Use of Technology in Multinational Enterprises (MNE)", *Research Policy*, Vol. 28, pp. 157–78.

—— (2005) "The Globalization of R&D: Key Features and the Role of TNCs", in *Globalization of R&D and Developing Countries*, Geneva and New York: UN, pp. 29–42.

Pearce, R. and Singh, S. (1990) 'Internationalization of R&D among the World's Leading Enterprises: Survey Analysis Motivation, Organization and Implications', paper presented at the Conference Technology Management and International Business, Stockholm, June 17–20.

Petrella, Riccardo (1992) "Internationalization, Multinationalization and Globalization of R&D: Toward a New Division of Labour in Science and Technology", *Knowledge and Policy: The International Journal of Knowledge Transfer and Utilization*, Vol. 5, No. 3, Fall, pp. 3–25.

Queiroz, S., Zanatta, M. and Andrade, C. (2003) 'Internationalization of MNCs' Technological Activities: What Role for Brazilian Subsidiaries?', paper presented at SPRU conference in the honor of Keith Pavitt, Brighton, November, pp. 13–15. Available at: www.sussex.ac.uk/units/spru/events/kp_conf_03/documents/Queiroz.pdf

Ray Choudhury, Ranabir (2003) "The 'Cyber Coolie' is Here", *Business Line*, Internet edition, financial daily from THE HINDU Group of Publications, December 8. Retrieved on 15/12/2006. http://www.thehindubusinessline.co/bline/2003/12/08/stories/2003120800360800.htm

Ritter dos Santos, M.E. and Rebolledo, Jose Luis S. (2006) 'Management of Technology Transfer Offices: Lessons for Brazilian Universities', paper presented in Ethiopian Triple Helix Conference, Addis Ababa, UN Conference Centre, May 29–31.

Simon, Denis F. (2007) "Wither Foreign R&D in China: Some Concluding Thoughts on Chinese Innovation", *Asia Pacific Business Review*, Vol. 13, No. 3, pp. 471–80.

The Express News Service (2008) *The Indian Express*, Web edition, online, March 28 and March 29, at 0027 hrs IST.

Thomas, Georgina J.J. (2008) Working in Information and Communication Technology: A Sociological Study of Call Centres in Mumbai, An Unpublished Ph.D Thesis in Sociology (Chapter IV), Institute of Indian Culture, University of Mumbai, Mumbai, pp. 127–70.

Trivedi, Harish (2004) "Cyber Coolies, Call Centre Workers are the New Slave Labourers of 21st Century", *Little India*, October. Retrieved on 18/12/2006. http://www.littleindia.com/october2004/CyberCoolies.htm

UNCTAD Secretariat (2005) "An Overview of the Issues", in *Globalization of R&D and Developing Countries*, Geneva and New York: UN, pp. 1–25.

UNI (2005) 300,000 KPO Jobs Coming to India, rediff.com, December 26, 16: 36 IST. Retrieved on 11/27/2007. http://www.rediff.com/cms/print.jsp?docpath=/money/2005/dec/26bp01.htm

Upadhya, Carol (2004) "A New Transnational Capitalist Class? Capital Flows, Business Networks and Entrepreneurs in the Indian Software Industry", *Economic and Political Weekly*, Vol. 39, No. 48, November 27–December 3, pp. 5141–51.

—— (2006) The Global Indian Software Labour Force, IT Professionals in Europe, Working Paper Series No. 1, National Institute of Advanced Studies Bangalore, IDPAD (2003–2006).

Warrant, F. (1991) Deploiment Mondial da la R&D industriells. FAST Research Paper, Commission of the European Communities, Brussels, April.

Wong, Bernard P. (2006) *The Chinese in Silicon Valley: Globalization, Social Networks and Ethnic Identity*. Lanham, MD: Rowman and Littlefield, p. 267.

Wong, Poh-Kam, Ho, Yuen-Ping and Singh, Annette (2007) "Towards an 'Entrepreneurial University' Model to Support Knowledge-based Economic Development: The Case of the National University of Singapore", *World Development*, Vol. 35, No. 6, pp. 941–58.

Zedtwitz, Maximilian Von (2005) "International R&D Strategies of TNCs from Developing Countries: The Case of China", in *Globalization of R&D and Developing Countries*, New York and Geneva: UN, pp. 117–40.

Zhou, Chunyan and Peng, Yu-Mei (2008) "The Entrepreneurial University in China: Nonlinear Paths", *Science and Public Policy*, Vol. 35, No. 9, November, pp. 637–46.

Zhou, Chunyan and Etzkowitz, H. (2006) 'The Entrepreneurial University and the Future of Higher Education in China', paper presented in Ethiopian Triple Helix Conference, Adis Aaba, UN Conference Centre, May 29–31, p. 12.

19

The Indian Middle Class in the Era of Globalization and Liberalization

Continuity and Change

N. Rajaram

About two decades ago, India shifted gears in its path of development. From being a system where important economic institutions and enterprises were state controlled, India embraced the market and opened its economy in a big way to foreign capital and multinational companies, besides its own private players. The initial steps in this direction were taken around the mid-eighties, but the most important propulsion in this direction came in the year 1991, when India decided to liberalize and throw open its economy. Around this time, changes in information and communication technology – the process of globalization – became more widespread and reshaped human relations around the world. Globalization as this process came to be known also affected the middle class.

The Indian middle class, it seems to be the accepted view amongst intelligentsia, was not responsible for liberalization of the Indian economy,[1] nor was it the one that ushered changes in information and communication technology.[2] However, the changes unleashed by liberalization and globalization affected the Indian middle class in a big way, shaping the direction in which it grew. The Indian middle class embraced the new technology in a big way and made use of the opportunities of privatization and liberalization to grow and enhance. The potentially huge market no doubt attracted foreign capital in a big way. India started to grow rapidly as it used the path of low-wage cost service sector growth. The policy makers hoped that by utilizing these opportunities they could lift people from poverty into the expanding middle stratum of society, called the middle class. Not only did the existing policies and the way economy was run undergo a change, but it also brought about a change in the social relations within India, especially amongst the emerging middle class. This paper examines the continuities and discontinuities in this emerging middle class of India.

The emerging middle class has been referred to as the 'new' middle class,[3] and it has been contrasted with the middle class at the time of independence, which has been called 'old' middle class. This comparison is between the middle class at these two points of time in terms of its attitude to consumerism, to issues of religion, transnational influence and the space given to women during this period. This comparison thus points out to the continuities and discontinuities of the present with that of the past and thus points to the direction that India is being shaped by this emerging middle class.

What is Meant by Middle Class?

Before examining these issues, let me first deal with what is meant by the term 'middle class'. Globally there is no consensus about the concept of what constitutes the middle class. Erik Olin Wright (2007: 8), who has written extensively on the middle class, identifies three approaches to the understanding of middle classes, which he called 'individual attributes approach', 'opportunistic hoarding approach' and 'exploitation–domination approach'. He does not privilege any approach, but his preference is towards the exploitation/domination approach. Thus, he says, "middle class is defined as those positions which are simultaneously in a position of both dominating and dominated, or exploiting and exploited".

In India, André Béteille views the conceptualization of the middle class as being 'composite' because "it had proved impossible to dispense with either the property structure or occupational structure in defining it" (Béteille, 2007: 289). He goes on to say that "any reasonable conception of the middle class must accommodate more than one kind of market situation, work situation, and status situation" (ibid. 296). Thus, it is not surprising that in the various writings on the middle class, this 'composite' approach is very visible. The criteria emphasized are income, education and non-agrarian occupations.

Middle Class in India: 'Old' and 'New'

Misra (1961: 11–13) traces the emergence of the middle class to the onset of British rule, when there was a growth of new occupations in law and bureaucracy. This was also the period of industrialization, and those who took to new occupations became the nucleus of the middle class. As occupations expanded, the middle class also expanded. These new occupations were in administration, law, bureaucracy, academia, engineering, health and medicine, and in other professions. These occupations were non-agrarian and required a certain level of educational skill for a person to get into. During the colonial period, these 'new' knowledge and skills were imparted in English. With time, English became the language which united this newly emerging middle class (Scrase, 2004).[4] Initially, this class consisted mainly of the upper castes from various regions who were the first to take to higher education and consequently enter these new emerging occupations. Slowly persons from lower castes also entered this class. This class played a significant role in the independence movement of India.

Misra also traces the reactions of the middle class to changes in India in the late 19th and in the first half of 20th century. He mentions, "the reformist character or revivalist character" (Misra, 1961: 368) in the reactions of the middle class to changes in late 18th century; and these reactions became more complex with the growth of nationalist movements (ibid.: 390–400). He states that the middle class which led the movement had two components: the 'radicals' who with a socialist viewpoint and the 'conservatives' who had a revivalist fervour. As he says, "India won freedom but was divided. Both freedom and division were the work of the middle classes" (ibid.: 400).

At the time India gained independence in 1947, as Béteille (2007: 952) remarks, "the educated and salaried middle class was a very small fraction of the Indian population when the country became independent". According to one estimate, the middle class comprised about 10 per cent of the then population (Varma, 1998: 26). This was the era where the middle class dominated the administrative bureaucracy.[5] This bureaucracy controlled the economy in the name of taking care of balanced growth in society, as India was under the influence of 'socialistic' ideology advocated by Nehru, the first Prime Minister. Indian democracy, although patterned on the British electoral system, in the early years after independence, was dominated and shaped by the Congress party and Nehru. This feature of the state controlling the leading sectors of the economy continued over the next four decades or so, when in 1991, the Indian economy, as mentioned earlier, changed gears, and threw open its economy to foreign capital and the market was given importance in the distribution of resources and services. This strategic change was influenced by developments both within the country and outside. The collapse of Soviet Union[6] and along with it its model of development, the emergence of new technologies of information and communication and its quick spread the world over – including India (now referred to as the globalization process), compounded by the failure of the then prevailing policies to bring about rapid economic and social development – all led to a paradigm shift by the decision-makers.

Since 1991, the economy has only got more liberalized and globalized in terms of integration to the market of the world economy. A new set of workers and work culture (more popularly known as the BPO – business process outsourcing or better known as the 'call centre' culture)[7] has developed. The developments in software industry, coupled with the cheap labour that India had, have resulted in the development of the service sector in India in what has been called the 'new' economy. The stories of the few young persons who have made 'millions' go round and round, spawning a dream of rags to riches and stories of quick success. Furthermore, the parental generation of these young rich successful persons could not dream of such wealth when they were young. All this has changed the entire scenario in India.

The quick adoption of the new technologies of information and communication by the urban middle class, along with the development of satellite TV channels in news and entertainment, has resulted in newer images being created and marketed in India. This has also resulted in opening up the market to new goods and services, and the Indian middle class embraced it in a big way. This is perhaps captured best by the biggest symbolic shift in the sartorial attire of the Indian male politician. Many an Indian politician who till early nineties would wear *khadi*,[8] now started donning the tie and the suit considered symbols of corporate business managers. This symbolic change captured the shift in the dominant political and social value in India, because till then the emphasis was on simplicity, spartan living, and no ostentatious display of wealth. This symbolic shift was perhaps reinforced by global trends as well; China being a good example of this, where old style Mao suits were replaced by the western managerial attire.

Today, in the second decade of the 21st century, another feature has been added to this scenario. Because of the speed at which newer sectors of the economy are being thrown open to market forces, the notion of 'permanent employment' – which was a euphemism of security of employment – is being replaced without any corresponding social security. Now, this world view is even penetrating in the state sector. This is a radical shift of values and work culture for the Indian middle class. There are numerous cases of persons who have been laid off, or who have taken 'VRS'[9] from various enterprises. But, at the same time, there has not been any concerted and consistent protest to these changes taking place (Fernandes, 2000).[10]

But, Béteille (2007: 948) considers that although privatization and liberalization have "hurt some individuals with secure employment, but they have also created new opportunities for others with drive and initiative but with little prospect for paid employment". Thus, it is not surprising to see that this changing world view has not resulted in a reduction in consumption. In fact, the middle class has started consuming more – be it more of the same things or newer things that have now become easily available than before, as a way to gain social status. Material consumption of goods and services has increased as seen in the consumption of TVs, refrigerators, motor vehicles, computers and the like. Along with the explosion in consumption of material goods, there has also been an increase in the emergence of newer lifestyles. The houses one lives in now have items from various regions of the world. The changes include not only in the way one commutes to work (now by latest models of vehicles, usually cars), or travels to other town (thanks to the growth of cheaper airlines to newer destinations), and how people communicate (thanks to cell phones), but also how one spends one's leisure time. Traditional cinemas have been replaced by multiplexes; the places where one shops are in malls, and of course now more and more Indians go abroad for holidays. The packaged tours are very popular and there is a new breed of the Indian middle class which is doing things completely different from what their parents did. This market-driven consumer culture is no more confined to metros but has spread to smaller cities and towns and even rural areas as seen in the growth of the cell phones, multiplexes and internet to all regions of India.

Further now the middle class approaches matters of nepotism, corruption and ill-gotten wealth (called popularly as 'black money') in an amoral way. Although black money, nepotism and corruption have existed for long, there is no study to suggest that they have reduced or declined in the post-liberalization phase. Further, throughout the post-independent era, the middle class has been a beneficiary of these practices. In spite of regular exposures in the media and other attempts to control them, the attitude of the middle class towards these practices is that of an established practice about which with whom one has to co-exist, rather than attempt to do away with.

Scholars and others in the intelligentsia have noticed these changes and have commented on the distinction between an 'old' middle class – the middle class at the time of independence – with the 'new' emerging middle class in the era of globalization and liberalization.[11] They were quick to point to the differential attitudes to wealth and ethics. While the 'old' middle class was discreet and perhaps reticent in displaying wealth, the 'new' is brash and ostentatious in displaying wealth. The old middle class was more concerned with the role of ethics in social life and probity in public life, while now this is less emphasized.

The Middle Class and the Hype About Its Size

The moment one asks how big this middle class is in the first decade of the 21st century, there is little clarity. Perhaps, it is because the size of the class is related to consumerism (and marketing of goods) there is a lot of hype about its size. The figures that are mentioned vary a lot depending upon which source one is quoting from. All over the world, there is the hype of the 'huge' middle class in India (as it is about China). The middle class is supposed to be fuelling the rapid growth of the economies of India and China.

The answer about the size of the middle class reflects more of speculation than factual data. What is well known is the huge population of 1 billion plus in India (and China as well). This figure gets merged with the hype of the size of the 'growing middle class' to give an image and a picture of very huge market. So perhaps to mention vast figures is in fashion to drive the appetite of the market. Thus, for instance, is the following excerpt from *Business Week*[12] of April 2006, which states, "In industries from telecom to cars, China and India are fast becoming the biggest markets in the world". The same article goes on to state that "these nations are the world's biggest pools of low-cost engineers, scientists, and service workers, (so) multinationals also must be good at hiring, retaining, and managing talent there. They (the multinational companies) must be adept at using these countries as sources of manufacturing, back-office processing, components and new technologies." There are a large number of articles in the print and visual media about the 'huge' market which this 'big middle class' represents in these countries. Perhaps the state in India (and as much in China) has an interest to project and propagate this image so as to attract foreign capital to invest in their respective economies.

So, it is not surprising that the debate about the size of the middle class differs. Thus, for instance, in the case of India, there have been statements that at present the Indian middle class is large than the entire population of USA!

So, what is the basis of such figures? Is there a correct figure out there? It appears that the size is more an estimation; and the figures would keep changing, if the growth rate continues to be high.

In the case of India, the figures for the middle class vary from a low of 62 million (Barnard, 2006) to figures that go up to as high as 400 million.[13] But, the one that is mentioned most is a figure between 250 million (Das, 2006) while some others mention 300 million, a figure repeated by former President of USA, George Bush, in his speeches before and during his trip to India in March 2006.[14] Perhaps the figures mentioned by a committee set up by the Government of India,[15] called popularly as Arjun Sengupta Committee, is about '23 per cent'[16] or 253 millions. However, as a well-known journalist points out, this large figure is valid only if the middle class is defined 'loosely'.[17] Thus, as per this definition, not only the 'slum dwellers' of Mumbai but those living in other smaller cities would constitute part of the Indian middle class, even though many of them may lack some of the basic civic amenities.

Whatever be the actual figures, there seems to be a general consensus that the size of the middle class is growing and increasing in India[18] (and China). However, what impact the economic downturn in global economy which began in late 2008 has had on the growth of the middle class is difficult to gauge at this moment.[19] But, at the same time, it is interesting to note that there is a lot of expectation that the middle class of India (along with that of China) would help the world economy to reverse this economic downturn! As far as India is concerned, although the economic downturn has resulted in jobs being lost, with fears of more being lost in the near future, there is no noticeable change in attitude to consumerism.

Increasing Consumerism and the Ambivalent Attitude

How has the middle class reacted to this increasing consumerism? An ambivalent attitude has emerged to the embracing of the consumerist lifestyle by the emerging middle class. The ambivalence noticed by scholars to this emerging consumerism is not of the state but that expressed by the members of the middle class itself.

Today, Indian democracy is not characterized by dominance of one party nor is it ruled by one dominant ideology. Ideological views and opinions differ as do the interpretation about the middle class itself. The Indian middle class is heterogeneous because it comprises persons of different castes,[20] religious, linguistic and ethnic groups. What is common to them may be their consumption of material goods and the importance given to this consumption as a social marker of status and class, and which may be termed as the middle class lifestyle. Today, English language is a significant, although not the only marker for this class; and it is this language which unites them across their divergent caste, religious, linguistic and ethnic backgrounds. The role of English amongst the middle class is very well discussed by Timothy Scrase (2004). Scrase argues that English was the language of the middle class and it is by the usage of English they maintain their hegemony. Now, with globalization, the middle class considers English as an important cultural resource to negotiate globalization.[21]

Although the middle class emerged with those who were involved in non-agrarian occupations, today it would also include those who have one foot in agriculture and another in non-agrarian source of income. Such persons would include the farmer-businessmen and those who earn from investments in shares, bonds and the like, or by combining blue or white collar work with agriculture.[22] For them, English has become an important cultural capital to negotiate the globalizing world.[23] With the growth of modern technology, including information and communication technology, it has become easier to lead urban middle class lifestyle in rural areas.[24]

In this kind of globalized situation, the middle class is influenced about different lifestyles by media and also partly because of migration. Arjun Appadurai (1997) says, more and more people consider a wider set of lifestyles than what they could think of before. These new forms of consumption by the Indian middle class have not gone unnoticed by scholars. Broadly, there are three kinds of reactions to this trend.

First, there are a few scholars like Gurcharan Das (2001) who welcome this trend. He points out to the emergence of a confident new middle class and at the same time how uninhibited and amoral it is in its approach to matters of displaying wealth. Das thinks the new middle class is a sign of success of the country and its policies; for him, the future of India is bright as he expects the numbers of middle class to increase. Unlike the old middle class – whose principle virtue was education and merit – the emerging new middle class is more concerned with self, and is street smart. It is driven by desire to achieve success monetarily and get things done; and its politics is driven by this goal.

Then, there are the critics. Pavan Varma (1998) was the first to point out that the emerging middle class was self-centred and was abdicating its responsibility to the poor and the nation as a whole. He says, "Keeping up with the Jones' was somehow a less compulsive pursuit than keeping up with the image of refinement associated with a restraint on materialistic exhibitionism in a poor country – an ideal directly imbibed from Gandhi, Nehru and the freedom movement". Over the years, the commitment to democracy and electoral process has declined. Further, he makes a case for middle class intellectual dishonesty. Hindi was not made the official language as the middle class was comfortable with English; it favoured industrialism over agriculture as it was professionally more qualified to benefit from it. This is a new ideological-discursive projection than in a shift in the base of the middle class. Finally, he states, if the middle class is insensitive to the need of the poor, it does so at considerable risk of political instability which will go against the very prosperity it so desires.

At the same time, there are critiques who express their apprehension about the new middle class being concerned only with the self. Leela Fernandes (2000) is one person who explains how the middle class, while accepting new consumerism, is actually insecure and is facing a situation parallel to that of the working class. But this has not led to political opposition to this growing consumerism and the changes in work relations and work culture.

Fernandes argues on the basis of her study of Mumbai city that the actual experience is contradictory. Their actual experiences are parallel to the restructuring faced by the industrial labouring class.

Margit Van Wessel (2004), a Dutch scholar, analyses the specific interaction of the consuming public with the images that are produced for them. According to her, the nation is a non-entity in the imagining of the emerging middle class. For them they do not see themselves as individuals or as a class to work for the poor or for the greater good of the nation. For them, there is a crisis; but it is a moral crisis and not based on doing 'good' to the nation or the poor. The discourse around the emergence of a consumerist middle class culture centres on ideas of self-restraint and proper social living through community, family loyalty, and abstinence from material pleasures. She bases her findings on an empirical study of Baroda in Gujarat to state that the discourse people use is of local repertoire and is perceived as morally sound. According to her, this construction provides for people to dissociate themselves from consumer practice, in that it allows speakers to construct and present themselves as being "*in* the world but not *of* it", and this imparts agency to the individual who can use it for self-affirmation.

Van Wessel's argument brings a different dimension to the debate. But what she says about the ambivalence in moral terms is perhaps now seen in the middle class as a whole in the country. There is weight in her argument that the middle class do not consider it necessary to work for the poor an argument which gets reinforced with the kind of inadequate response to the earthquake in Kashmir (October 2005). In contrast to this was the response which the middle class displayed to the earthquake in Kutch (Gujarat) in January 2001. Some consider the 2001 earthquake and the response to it as a 'middle class earthquake', owing to the overwhelming response and outpouring of aid by the middle class. This is attributed to the first images of destruction of middle class localities and elite areas of Ahmedabad and Surat (two big cities of Gujarat) that were broadcast by TV and other media, perhaps making them wonder, "what if it happened to us". It touched a chord in a class which was and is known for being self-centred!

In India, this emerging middle class is increasingly insecure. There is the new culture of 'hire and fire'. Further, whatever social security that was offered by the state is getting eroded. Indeed some have pointed out to this aspect of persistent insecurities. T.N. Ninan (2005) writes, "It is a shock to discover, for instance, that despite the evident emergence of a strong middle class, barely 10 per cent of all households has life insurance cover – traditionally the first form of savings for anyone with a reliable income flow and with dependents. And medical insurance is available for barely 1 per cent of all households."

Middle Class and Visible Religiosity

The Indian middle class has perhaps always had an ambivalent attitude to matters of religion. During the independence movement, in the late 19th and early 20th century, religion was the backbone for many of the leaders of nationalist movement – be it Bal Gangadhar Tilak, Lala Lajpat Rai or Bipin Chandra Pal (Misra, 1961). There was similarly a religious revivalism amongst Muslims then. But, the success of Russian Revolution of 1917 had its impact on India and its middle classes, leading to the emergence of reformist/radical and secular leaders like Jawaharlal Nehru and others. So, in the early years of independence and thereafter, perhaps owing to the dominating influence of radical left ideas, the middle class in India did not display it religious proclivities publicly in spheres and arenas considered secular, like institutions of learning. But, with the collapse of communism in Eastern Europe in late-80s and the decline of Soviet Union itself in 1991, and with China itself embracing capitalist market in a big way, leftist ideology, especially Marxism, has had a setback. Along with it the practice of secular lifestyle took a beating in general. The ideological vacuum thus created, it appears, has been filled by religion. The revival of religions in the countries of Eastern Europe has led to religious leaders coming to positions of influence once again. This has coincided with forces of globalization. All these changes have had an impact on the Indian middle class as well.

Perhaps because of the changes mentioned above, the visible display of religion has increased. This display by the middle class is increasingly visible in areas which were considered taboo.[25] It is this assertion of religiosity, especially by the Hindu middle class community, which is something new. This assertion is now seen more and more amongst the salaried section of the middle class. The self-employed sections perhaps did display their religiosity in the past as well just as they tend to do now. In certain states like Gujarat, where business ethos and values dominate, the business communities follow the Hindu religious calendar. The day after the Hindu festival of 'Deepavali' is the beginning of the new year, when accounts books used to be opened with a 'puja' (ceremony of worship) to Goddess Lakshmi (the goddess of wealth) for a fruitful and profitable year to come.

But now, what is seen is that in institutions considered secular and patronized by the middle class, like colleges and universities, buildings and institutions would be named after some religious head of a Hindu sect. Another feature seen more frequently, the person nominated to a high office performs (Hindu) rituals in the chamber before assuming office.

Parallel to this assertion of religiosity is the usage of modern technology and means of communication – be it internet, computer or mobile phone – by religious organizations to reach out to their followers worldwide, including those belonging to the middle class. Thus, it is not surprising to see the usage of a modern assembly line approach in the production of CDs, DVDs, and sending them to various destinations just like that of a marketing network of multinational companies.[26] Religion and marketing of religious material has adapted to changes in technology fast, facilitating the Indian Hindu diaspora to their religious leaders back home.

Further, this modern technology has helped in establishing a transnational religious market – linking middle class clients in villages (like seen in rural Gujarat) to their patrons in USA or UK.[27]

The expanding middle class now comprises of persons belonging to diverse caste, ethnic and linguistic backgrounds. Those belonging to lower castes undergo a process of sanskritization (Srinivas, 1966). This is seen in various upper caste rituals being practised by those castes which hitherto did not practise them.[28] But this middle class has in the process also redefined the very process itself, as it has imbued this process with what may be called western influence and values. Amongst some of the religious sects of Hindus, women now do *havans*[29] which they previously were not allowed to do. At the same time, there are certain practices and festivals[30] of lower castes which are now celebrated with gusto by middle class persons belonging to lower castes. These two instances illustrate a new way of accommodating religious practices (of lower castes) and at the same time reinventing Hinduism so as to give more space to women. This reflects the cultural contradictions in the process of modernization, mentioned Yogendra Singh (1978), wherein in the religious sphere, we see the co-existence of elements of tradition and modern.

Middle Class, Globalization and Changing Lifestyle

The Indian middle class has increasingly become transnational in taste and lifestyle in the post-liberalization era. This is a contrast to the situation in the first decade after independence, when nationalist feelings and tastes seemed to be widespread.

The Indian middle class perhaps was western and global, owing to the process of westernization (Srinivas, 1966). Certain regions of India, like Gujarat and Punjab, had a long tradition – dating back to the 19th century – of persons going abroad for study or for work.[31] This continued throughout the 20th century. When opportunities opened up in Europe and America in the latter half of 20th century, migration to these areas became the most preferred choice. However, the migration to the developed countries of West got more pronounced with liberalization of the economy, as many of the former restrictions on foreign travel got relaxed. The period of liberalization of Indian economy coincided with the onset of growth and expansion of changes in information and communication technology. And, with the growth of the Indian economy, conspicuous consumption by the middle class increased and its lifestyle increasingly reflected global tastes and touch. To add to this, they are subject to transnational influence because of NRI (non-resident Indian) relatives. The Indian middle class at the end of the first decade of the 21st century has an established network of kin and family relations across the globe. In many a case, these NRIs are wooed by the Indian political leadership[32] not only for investments but also for votes!

Thus, in the last two decades, one not only sees the middle class travelling abroad for holidays, but also consuming items which were previously only available in the developed world. This transnational dimension is also seen in the way the middle class send their members to developed countries for studies and/or to work.[33] This migration is seen amongst both the salaried and self-employed sections of the middle class.

Middle Class and Women: Increasing Visibility and Vanishing Girl Child

One of the interesting features of the emerging middle class in India, especially since the last two decades of 20th century and the first decade of 21st century, is the visibility of women in spheres which hitherto were dominated by men. One of India's pro-business weeklies *India Today*, brought out a special issue on women, where they write in a lauding manner how the urban Indian women is 'doing it all' – be it the kind of work she does and the choices she is making[34] regarding her own lifestyle. Whether this visibility has made a difference to bring about a change in the patriarchal norms and usher in gender-just lives, or does it reflect an increased presence in the organized sector, could be a matter of debate. But this visibility of women in India amongst the middle class has increased or paralleled with the growth of the women's movement since the 1980s.

Women, especially from the middle class, took the initiative and have provided leadership to the women's movement. Today, the women's movement is diverse and has different ideological strands. Women's activists have started focusing on separate areas of interest. Thus, there are those who work on health concerns of women, others on developmental issues, while others on political aspects, and so on. All this has resulted in a robust NGO sector of women's organizations, a movement well spread and effective and which has been in the forefront of a variety of issues concerning women. This has had its impact in a number of spheres – be it business, bureaucracy, media, sports, armed forces, professions like law, medicine, management, and so on. In the newly emerging service sector of BPOs, women have been recruited in large numbers. But they had to work in night shifts, as the working time in USA happens to be nighttime in India. This has led to redefining the family norms (of women having to work out late in the night). At the same time, during this period, cases of discrimination against women have come out more in the open. This has resulted in defining the boundaries of decent behaviour in the workplace, and attempting to make life for women better in general and especially for working women belonging to the middle class in particular.

However, along with these developments, there has been one very disturbing development. There appears to be no change in its conservative attitude regarding preference for sons. This strong preference for son, reflecting the continuance of patriarchy, has resulted in using modern technology to determine the sex of the child they wish to have. This has led to a decline in sex ratio of the girl child in an alarming manner. This was brought into relief by activists of women's movement during the last decade and half. This issue of declining sex ratio concerns more the newly emerging middle class than the poorer sections of society.

In India, the more developed states like Punjab, Haryana, Gujarat and Maharashtra have a declining sex ratio. The ratio has declined sharply in the age group 0–6 during the last two decades! These are the states which have developed economically[35] and are held out as models for others!

Further, in these states, the developed urban regions have a much lower sex ratio as compared to the rural areas. The sex ratio amongst the upper social strata is lower (Edlund, 1999) than those lower in the social hierarchy. Further, "discrimination against girls has found to increase with prosperity and education level of mothers in India".[36] The abuse of modern medical technology has affected the middle class sections most.

The medical fraternity, especially doctors, who are considered the icon of the middle class, has been hand in glove in this nefarious activity of sex-selective abortion well known now as female foeticide. It is often justified by those in the medical fraternity: "If the people want it, why should we not give it. Do they not have a right to decide the sex of the child they want?" The greed for money seems to be distorting the values of some doctors; and the extent to which these doctors violate medical ethics, rules and regulations, is now coming out in the open. Women's organizations were the first to take the initiative to point to this issue. Now, the media has also started exposing the role of doctors and their nefarious activities.[37] The attempt by such exposures is to bring about a change in attitudes in society to the issue of female foeticide and also force the authorities to take action against the doctors who connive in this practice and violate the law.

Women's organizations have also pointed out that in the Indian context the shortage of women would have shocking and disastrous consequences. In Haryana, this has already led to cases of kidnapping of women and forcing such women into marriage. In some cases, a woman has been married to a group of brothers! In some villages, no '*barat*'[38] has been seen for a long time. In states like Gujarat, there are reports of tribal women being brought as brides amongst certain communities. The shortage of women does not follow the rules of market. Instead of raising her status (as women are in short supply), it has only resulted in making her life more miserable!

Conclusions

In the above analysis, I have tried to trace the social transformation of the Indian middle class by showing the continuities and changes that have taken place in the last two decades. The 'old' middle class exhibited probity in public and showed concern for others, whereas the 'new' middle class is brash in lifestyle exhibiting self-centred consumerism as indicators of being 'modern'. This increasing consumerism has accompanied increasing insecurity in the conditions of employment and insecurity. This ambivalence in attitude is visible to the increasing consumerism.

Another feature is the increasing religiosity of the middle class, and this is visible especially among the Hindu component. While religiosity has increased, there is also attempt to reinvent it, where women have been given more roles in rituals and practices.

The middle class has become global in taste, lifestyle and consumption. Women belonging to the middle class have got more and more opportunities to take to new occupations emerging in the new economy – like BPO sector. However, in some regions of India, especially in the north and western states, there is also a worrying trend; the sex ratio of females has been declining amongst the middle classes, indicating a strong son preference in spite of increase in wealth and education. All this portends to a future for the middle class which is contentious and worrying. It also reflects that in spite of increasing consumerism (as indicator of being modern) there is still the continuance of traditional norms of hierarchy and son preference.

Notes

1. There is a widespread view that liberalization of Indian economy in 1991 took place because of the pressures of IMF and World Bank. The structural adjustment policies advocated by 'Washington Consensus' put forward by economist John Williamson (2004) for countries of Latin America, were those to which countries like India accepted in 1991, when faced with an economic crisis in balance of payments.
2. Changes in information and communication technology took place in the western world, specifically USA first before coming to India.
3. The terms 'new' and 'old' are used heuristically; Singh (1985) uses this distinction as well.
4. Another argument is that English got entrenched because of the bureaucracy. See Stevenson (2005).
5. Béteille (2007: 952) says that this middle class "had a very great influence in creating and sustaining the open and secular institutions which carried forward the modernization of India. The middle class was not only small in size, it was also socially exclusive. Hindus belonging to a handful of upper castes predominated in it and the backward castes and religious minorities were disproportionately few in number, particularly in superior professional, managerial and administrative positions."
6. Béteille (2007: 948) says "the polarization thesis, or the thesis of increasing antagonism between the bourgeoisie and the proletariat, which was the fulcrum of the Marxian approach to class, appeared to be increasingly at odds with the reality of industrial societies as they moved from the 19th to the 20th century."

7. Some persons consider this work as the equivalent work of physical labourers, as they are at the lowest end of the social prestige spectrum.
8. *Khadi* is the Hindi word for homespun cotton. Khadi was popularized by Mahatma Gandhi.
9. VRS refers to 'voluntary retirement scheme' introduced by some companies. It is a way to lay of employees by offering them a lump sum financial amount as compensation for retrenching them. Although called 'voluntary', there is an element of coercion as the employee has very little choice. He is cornered to accept this 'lump sum' compensation package or work on terms which are difficult, like lower wages, usually at a different place, and the like. Even for those who have accepted the compensation package, there are stories of persons who have been paid only a part of what they have been promised! In some cases, the amount promised is released in installments and usually after pressure is brought upon the management. This involves expenditure, and very often the person fighting the legal battle loses a good chunk of the compensation amount in the process.
10. Fernandes makes this point effectively. She points out how there is acceptance of the change without much protest (Fernandes, 2000).
11. See Singh (1985), Rajaram (2007) and Bose (2007).
12. "What firms need to succeed in India, China?", *Business Week*, April 7, 2006. Retrieved on April 7, 2006 from http://in.rediff.com/money/2006/apr/07bspec.htm
13. The figures vary according to the criteria employed. The figure of 400 million is from *Himalayan Trade Travel Journal*. Retrieved on February 21, 2006 from http://www.httj.com.np/feb_2005/pata.htm. On the other hand, Margit Van Wessel (2004) mentions that the middle class is usually estimated at 100 to 350 million people, depending on the criteria employed.
14. This figure is also high. The NCAER study took household annual income of 1800 dollars as the minimum for middle income families; at this income level, Indian families can purchase motorbikes, televisions and refrigerators.
15. This report is titled *Report on the Conditions of Work and Promotion of Livelihoods in the Unorganized Sector* and was set up by the National Commission for Enterprises in the Unorganized Sector, New Delhi, the chairman was Dr Arjun Sengupta. The report was submitted in August 2007 (source: www.nceus.nic.in: Report on the Conditions of Work and Promotion of Livelihoods in the Unorganized Sector).
16. See *Report on the Conditions of Work and Promotion of Livelihoods in the Unorganized Sector*, Table 1.2 and p. 6.
17. T.N. Ninan, editor of a business standard, quotes this figure of 300 million. See Ninan (2005). Business Standard along with the National Council of Applied Economic Research collaborated in a market survey in India of 300,000 households. The Arjun Sengupta Committee Report considers those who earn an amount as low as ₹ 20 per capita per day in 2004–05, as belonging to middle income group!
18. The Arjun Sengupta Committee found that the middle income category grew from 18 to 23 per cent! (See *Report on the Conditions of Work and Promotion of Livelihoods in the Unorganized Sector*, Paragraph 1.30, p. 7).
19. Media reports tend to be contradictory and conflicting. Thus when President Obama decided not to give tax breaks to companies which outsourced jobs, one Gujarati newspaper (*The Gujarat Samachar*, Vadodara, May 6, 2009) on its front page in an eight column headline – 10 lakh Indian professionals struck by Obama! On the same

day, *The Times of India* (Ahmedabad edition, May 6, 2009, p. 8) carried a news item that nearly 50,000 employees in India could be handed pink slips (i.e., euphemism for job loss).

20. For the emergence amongst the dalits, see Nandu Ram (1988).
21. For an interesting discussion of the changing role of English in India and how different sections have been reacting to it, see G.J.V. Prasad (2006).
22. This kind of situation is seen in various regions of India like Gujarat, Punjab, Haryana, Maharashtra, Tamil Nadu, Andhra Pradesh, Karnataka, and Kerala.
23. There is mushrooming of schools called 'English' medium schools in big villages and towns. Many of them tend to have names which appear Christian, owing to the association of missionaries with imparting of education in English. Thus there would be a name like "St. Kabir"! Some ignoramus would pronounce it as "Sant Kabir" school! A recent media report mentions that English as a medium of instruction in primary schools occupies second position by 2007; and the growth has been remarkable in most states, increasing in some by three-fold in some states (Source: http://epaper.timesofindia.com/Default/Scripting/ArticleWin.asp?From=Archive&Source=Page&Skin=TOINEW&BaseHref=TOIA/2009/12/05&PageLabel=1&EntityId=Ar00102&ViewMode=HTML&GZ=T (December 5, 2009).
24. Income from agriculture is not taxable; and thus there are a number of middle class entrepreneurs who are using modern technology in agriculture to do business across the world.
25. The minority religious communities like Muslims, Christians, Sikhs and others did enjoy certain benefits under the constitution to run institutions to serve and preserve their community identity. Now they have started carrying their religious identity by emphasizing on markers to distinguish them from others. It may be wearing the burqa to the college; and I have found that burqa-wearing girls mixing with opposite sex in ways no different from non-burqa wearing girls. But it is the assertion by the majority Hindu community – which is new; so now middle class Hindu men come with tilak on their forehead to the class; or the officials in universities performing Hindu puja before beginning their duties. On one occasion, while taking a viva voce exam in a room in a university in Maharashtra, the person concerned in whose room we were made to take the exam, came and disrupted the examination as the puja had to be performed. The examiner was asked to vacate the chair, as the person sat and completed the puja.
26. Thus in a study on how Swadhyaya, Swaminarayan sects, in which I was associated during 2000 to 2003, I saw the way these sects produce and send their literature and other material to various corners of the world.
27. During a fieldwork in rural areas of Kheda and Anand district, I have come across instances where internet was used to get orders to print religious material, calendars and so on from clients in USA/UK.
28. This includes upper caste ceremonies like 'seemanth', performed in the seventh month of pregnancy of first child. In addition, the middle case and lower caste wear the cross thread while performing *havans*.
29. *Havan* is the ritual prayer in which offerings are made to sacred fire. 'Gayatri Parivaar', a Hindu sect, now allows Hindu women to do the offerings along with their husbands.
30. One example of this is the celebration of '*dasha maata*' (literally meaning goddess of condition) celebrated by the lower castes who at one time were poor, continue to do so with gusto. Usually this festival involves the immersion of goddess in a pond late in the night.

31. Gandhi and Sardar Patel are two names from Gujarat who went to UK to study. Migration to East Africa, Southern Africa and countries like Fiji had persons from Gujarat going in late 19th century.

32. NRI being wooed for investment is not uncommon; and there are regular conclaves held for this purpose in various states. But in the 2009 elections to the Lok Sabha, the Chief Minister of Gujarat who is a leading light of BJP was seen in a video release addressing specifically NRIs and asking these NRIs to tell their relatives in India to vote for BJP. Many groups working and promoting Hinduism in other countries exist in various countries of the world. The largest number of websites on Hinduism exists outside India.

33. Many middle class students take loans – either from private sources or from institutional sources – to go and study and/or work abroad.

34. *India Today*, April 24, 2006. Women's Special Issue. One article even mentions that India has 15 million working women across 25 cities. This work force has increased by 10 per cent between 1993 and 2003, which the study claims is based on a survey of 10,150 women, across 28 locations ("She Buys to Conquer", pp. 34–35).

    Traditionally there has been asymmetrical structural relationship between male and female workers. Women's participation in organized employment is low; it was as low as '22 per cent'; but in unorganized sector occupations, majority of them are women (See Venkata Ratnam, C.S. and Jain, Harish C. (2002).

35. See (a) *Census of India 2001, Provisional Population Totals*, Chapter 6 Sex Composition of the Population (source: www.censusindia.net/data/chapter6);

    (b) Patel, Vibhuti (2003).

    (c) Retherford, Robert and Roy, T.K. (2003).

36. Edlund (1999: 1280) quotes from other studies to substantiate this claim. This is supported by NFHS data as well (see end note 23).

37. The first case was in the state of Haryana in March 2006. This made headlines. Now on April 7, 2006, another news channel, Sahara Samay, has been exposing the role of doctors (including lady doctors) in Rajasthan (Chittaurgarh, Jaipur, Hanumangarh, Ajmer and Dhaulpur districts), Madhya Pradesh (Gwalior), Uttar Pradesh (Agra), and Gujarat (Palanpur). These sting operations will perhaps compel the medical fraternity to give up this practice of abetting in this crime. The news channel claims that they have caught 100 doctors involved in this crime!

38. *Barat* is the wedding procession of the groom; the groom comes to the bride's place for wedding. The expenditure of the wedding is borne by the bride's family.

References

Appadurai, Arjun (1997) *Modernity at Large: Cultural Dimensions of Globalization*. Delhi: Oxford University Press.

Barnard, Patrick (2006) When it Comes to China and India, Technology Companies must be Patient. Retrieved on March 11, 2006 from http://news.tmcnet.com/news/2006/jan/1278146.htm

Béteille, André (2007) *Marxism and Class Analysis*. Delhi: Oxford University Press.

Bose, Pradip (2007) "Emerging Middle Class in India and China", in Chumling Li (ed.), *International Forum Middle Class Research with Comparative Perspective:*

Conference Papers, Beijing: Sociology Institute, Chinese Academy of Social Sciences, pp. 154–60.

Census of India (2001) Provisional Population Totals, and Chapter 6 Sex Composition of the Population (Retrieved on ??? from: 6). ???

Das, Gurcharan (2001) *India Unbound*. New York: Knopf.

—— (2006) "The India Model", *Foreign Affairs,* July/August. Retrieved on June 1, 2007 from ???

Fernandes, Leela (2000) "Restructuring the New Middle Class in Liberalizing India", *Comparative Studies of South Asia, Africa and Middle East*, Vol. XX, Nos. 1 and 2, pp. 1–25.

Edlund, Lena (1999) "Son Preference, Sex Ratios, and Marriage Patterns", *Journal of Political Economy*, Vol. 107, No. 6, Part 1, December, pp. 1275–1304. Retrieved on April 8, 2006 from ???

Government of India, National Commission for Enterprises in the Unorganized Sector (Chairman Arjun Sengupta) (2007) *Report on the Conditions of Work and Promotion of Livelihoods in the Unorganized Sector*, New Delhi.

Misra, B.B. (1961) *The Indian Middle Class*. London: Oxford University Press.

Ninan, T.N. (2005) "Middle Class has Arrived", *Business Standard*, July 2.

Patel, Vibhuti (2003) 'Political Economy of Missing Girls', paper presented in seminar on *Missing Girls in India: Science, Gender Relations, and the Political Economy of Emotions*, Delhi: Department of Sociology, University of Delhi, October. Retrieved on April 7, 2006 from ???

Prasad, G.J.V. (2006) "A Minute Stretching into Centuries: Macaulay, English, and India", *Nineteenth Century Prose*, Vol. 33, No. 2 (Fall), pp. 175–96.

Rajagopal, Arvind (2001) *Politics after Television*. Cambridge: Cambridge University Press.

Rajaram, N. (2007) "The Emerging Middle Class in India and China: Issues and Concerns", in Chumling Li (ed.), *International Forum Middle Class Research with Comparative Perspective: Conference Papers*, Beijing: Sociology Institute, Chinese Academy of Social Sciences, pp. 161–77.

Ram, Nandu (1988) *The Mobile Scheduled Castes: Rise of a New Middle Class*. Delhi: Hindustan Publishing Corporation.

Retherford, Robert and Roy, T.K. (2003) "Factors Affecting Sex-Selective Abortion in India and 17 Major States", *National Family Health Survey Reports*, No. 21, New Delhi. Retrieved on December 1, 2009 from http://pdf.dec.org/pdf_docs/PNACR987.pdf#search=%27declining%20sex%20ratio%20in%20India

Scrase, Timothy J. (2004) 'The Hegemony of English in India', paper presented in 15th Biennial Conference of Asian Studies Association of Australia in Canberra, 29 June–2 July. Retrieved on April 20, 2006 from http://coombs.anu.edu.au/SpecialProj/ASAA/biennial-conference/2004/Scrase-T1-ASAA2004.pdf

Singh, Gurcharan (1985) *The New Middle Class in India*. Jaipur: Rawat Publications.

Singh, Yogendra (1978) "Traditional Cultural Values and Contemporary Challenges", in *Essays on Modernization in India*, Delhi: Manohar Publications, pp. 176–89.

Srinivas, M.N. (1966) *Social Change in Modern India/*. Bombay: Allied Publishers.

Stevenson, Jane (2005) 'Take My Word for It', Review of *Empires of the World: Language History of the World* by Nicholas Ostler, *The Observer*, March 13. Retrieved on November 1, 2009 from ???

Varma, Pavan K. (1998) *The Great Indian Middle Class*. New Delhi: Viking.

Van Wessel, Margit (2004) "How an Indian Middle Class Dissociates from Middle-Class Life", *Cultural Dynamics*, Vol. 16, No. 1, pp. 93–116.

Venkata Ratnam, C.S. and Jain, Harish C. (2002) "Women in Trade Unions in India", *International Journal of Manpower*, Vol. 23, No. 3, pp. 277–92.

Williamson, John (2004) The Washington Consensus as Policy Prescription for Development, a lecture in the series *Practitioners of Development*, delivered at World Bank, January 13. Retrieved on December 26, 2009 from ???

Wright, Erik Olin (2007) "Three Logics of Class Analysis", in Chumling Li (ed.), *International Forum Middle Class Research with Comparative Perspective: Conference Papers*, Beijing: Sociology Institute, Chinese Academy of Social Sciences, pp. 1–9.

20

Shifting Identities

Consumer Culture and the Middle Class in a Globalized World

Antony Palackal

Maya received quality education in her schooling and is a post-graduate in Social Work. At present, she is working as a counsellor in a reputed organization in Thiruvananthapuram, the capital of Kerala state. She is thirty-five plus and her husband is an engineer and son, a middle school student. She originally hailed from a rural setting in Mavelikkara, not very far from Thiruvananthapuram, in the northern direction. She moved to Thiruvananthapuram after her marriage in 1996. One day, Maya talked to me about the new shopping culture and the manner in which the changed nature of market creates an atmosphere in which people tend to be caught up by the tentacles of the new market culture unaware:

> Our buying habit has changed a lot these days. Earlier, we used to prepare the list of necessary items in advance, and made it a point to purchase only those items in the list. But now the situation is quite different, especially with the advent of Super Markets, Big Bazars, Oberon/Reliance Malls are so common. When we walk into the department store with a basket and are free to pick and choose any item that we want, the tendency is to simply pick whatever items that capture our attention. Sometimes we would not have even thought of getting those items, but still we just want to try them. And the interesting part of it is that some of them are really useless and go as sheer waste. Then we regret saying 'oh ... we have simply wasted money'. I have particularly experienced this with stuffs meant to make soft drinks.

Maya points to the contemporary market situation in which aspirations of the people are whetted by the increasing exposure to the kind of life that tends to replicate the consumer propensities of the West. The advent of globalization in the Indian sub-continent has brought the ever-widening middle class into new prominence in terms of its ability to consume. The middle class, as the predominant social group in the Indian polity, has been engaged in forms of consumption that resembled the cosmopolitan cultural forms in other parts of the world. Consumer culture, the pervasive by-product of globalization, forms the specific canvas of the article.

The objective of this paper is to explore the manner in which consumer culture constructs the identity of the middle class people. That is to examine whether possession of objects and display of signs of affluence affect the subjective view of the middle class. Hence, it seeks to address the problematic whether consumption characterizes the mode of being, a way of gaining identity, meaning and prestige in contemporary society, with special reference to the middle class? Hence, an attempt is made here to look closely into the practices of everyday life of the middle class and discover how subjects mediate the processes constructing identities in the emerging context ushered in by globalization. In other words, the cardinal question that this paper addresses is: how does consumer culture constitute middle class in a globalized society? Based on qualitative data, it argues that cultural, underpinnings of globalization, spearheaded by the permeating consumer culture are very likely to impinge on the formation of the self and, therefore, consumer culture, more than any other category, is the privileged stage where the contestations and negotiations of identities occur in contemporary society.

The experience of globalization becomes tangible when its effect is perceived locally, namely, at the microlevel. The continued reorganization of market conditions and market networks affects the livelihood of people and their life trajectories. This becomes clearer when one begins to look at the shifting patterns of consumption and the manner in which they link persons and communities to the global market. At the local level, it is difficult to understand the subtle ramifications of the global market and its dynamics as it is being played out in the everyday destiny of an ordinary person in relation to his/her locality. Therefore, the paper intends to open up a line of enquiry on the local consequences of this global interconnectedness. The constituent component of this enquiry involves the analysis of the global spread of market culture with its commodities both material and non-material.

Contemporary phenomenon of globalization constitutes the larger context of the paper. The objective social process of globalization (macro), driven primarily by the global economy and communication and information technology, inheres simultaneously a subjective component (micro) that is reflected in the small and concrete, the spatially particular, the self and the cultural symbols, all of which bear the signature of the global. Founded on this proposition, the paper broadly seeks to deal with the sociological debate regarding the dialectics between the macro and the micro aspects of globalization, which is reflected in the paradoxical relation between *global* and *local*. In the first section of the paper, I elaborate on consumption, identity and middle class, the triple variables the paper is centred around, and next I discuss the theoretical approach. The approach focuses on Baudrillard's theoretical constructs of 'sign value' and 'hyper-reality' by which he tries to link consumption with the dynamics of identity formation. In the second section, I describe the unique contextual background of the area wherein I have conducted the empirical study, followed by the presentation of the methodology of the study and the final section contains the analysis and discussion of the empirical findings.

Consumption Craze

'Consumption' has become a fundamental modality in a globalized world (Kemper, 1993; Appadurai, 1996). The force of the market and of the rules of the status battle of life is inescapable in today's consumer world. Consumption has come to be associated with the present so much that members of a society often see modern goods as necessities indispensable for life today. Goods that were out of the reach of local people earlier have come to be seen as essential requirements for fulfilment in life. In recent years, Indians are engaged in forms of consumption that resemble the cosmopolitan cultural forms in other parts of the world. The ever-growing proliferation of consumer goods and commodities of all kinds in myriad forms are flowing into the local markets in India. The most vibrant and dynamic marketing and delivery systems in abundance, the dynamism of the food and restaurant industries, the growing national frenzy over sports such as cricket, the palpable growth in domestic tourism, the rapid inroads made by television and video cassettes, CDs and DVDs into the domain of cinema, the penetration of the countryside by voracious media and advertising forces, and the general commodification of cultural objects are all part of this process, which has many other expressions as well (Sarup, 1996).

Since the eighties, the Government of India gradually abandoned the earlier state perspective that was led by an ideal of self-reliance. When the state opted for a liberalized policy entailing free imports, less restrictions and encouragement to foreign investors, the lifting of controls on production resulted in a considerable increase in the availability of consumer goods in the Indian market. As Dreze and Sen (2002) rightly pointed out, "the reforms that were introduced by the end of 1991 have concentrated mainly on removing the 'license raj' and the 'ever-proliferating bureaucracy". As a result of this globalized market, there developed radically new forms and ways of life in India centred on consumption. This cultural scenario is referred to as 'consumer culture'. Consumer culture essentially characterizes and manifests the contemporary wave of globalization. It is an all-embracing mode of consumption and lifestyle along with the accompanied codes of values, attitudes and ethics. Hence, consumer culture broadly refers to the pervading atmosphere that encompasses the entire gamut of material as well as symbolic goods and items available to the public for consumption.

Improved modes of communication and information, together with rationalizations in methods of distribution (e.g., inventory control, packaging and market feedback), have made it possible for commodities to move around through the market system at a faster pace; twenty-four-hour-a-day financial services and markets have increased the mobility of capital; and the mobilization of fashion in niche markets has facilitated a speed-up in the pace of consumption in clothing, ornaments, and across a wide range of recreational activities and lifestyles such as pop music styles, leisure and sporting habits, and video and children's games (Inda and Rosaldo, 2002).

Resultantly, radical changes have occurred in the consumption behaviour of Indians in general. More or less, simultaneously, there has been a fast spread of exposure to commercial television. Numerous television channels now bring to Indian homes images of luxurious lifestyles that encourage unscrupulous consumption. Wessel (2001), in her ethnographic study on the Indian community in Baroda, has observed that consumption has come to be associated so much with the present that members of the middle class often see modern goods as necessities indispensable for their lives today. Prior to the advent of 'the consumption era', life was 'simple'. The range of goods present in the lives of earlier generations was limited, and desires were in tune with that reality. Now, the presence of wealth and a much wider array of goods have paved the way for a new standard in consumptive aspirations.

Rising Middle Class

In India, discourses on nationalism from the outset have been closely linked to the categories of class and nation. Anti-colonial nationalism is characterized as a fundamentally middle class phenomenon. Postcolonial nationalism has also been embedded in the discourse of the middle class. Hence, it is not surprising that the dominant vision of the future of the Indian nation is fundamentally middle class in its orientation. Even less surprising is the fact that the Doordarshan officials, policy makers, serial producers and advertisers have conceptualized the expanding middle class as their 'target audience'. No wonder that the middle class phenomenon in India has been a subject of domestic debate and international attention since the mid-1980s. The international attention followed the sudden recognition that the rising Indian middle class would be a major market in the 1990s.

In 1991, when India embarked on a process of economic reform, opening up its economy and inviting foreign investment, the Indian middle class assumed new status. *Business India* reported: "when liberalization began in 1991, the Indian middle class acquired a new prominence as one of the world's largest markets, as a different breed of entrepreneurs and consumers" (August 18, 2002, pp. 52–58). When state controls on production were lifted and India opened the door to foreign investors, it resulted in a considerable increase in the availability of consumer goods in the Indian market. The availability of the new consumer goods, combined with the exposure to satellite television, has contributed to changes in the lifestyle among all classes of society. Historically, this constituted the momentous period, which marked the emergence of middle class as an outstanding section; so was the emergence of this class as a significant group in the Indian polity.

Delineating the sociological boundaries of middle class has been not an easy task (Tanter and Young, 1990) although they are composed of a heterogeneous historical bloc with differential access to relations of production, status and political power. What constituted them as middle class was their aspirations to upward mobility and modernity through consumerism. It has been rightly noted that the new economic policies enabled the middle class to consume goods that had till recently been luxury items but were now perceived as crucial indices of upward mobility: household appliances, toiletries, packaged foods and other consumer goods (Mankekar, 1999). In this way, the demographic expansion of the middle class was reinforced by its cultural constitution.

This class has grown in size over the last 100 years to such a proportion that many have come to doubt the wisdom of calling it a single class and prefer to designate it in plural terms as 'middle classes' (Nair, 1974; Singh, 1985; Bhatia, 1994). That has made the task of defining the class in concrete terms all the more an exasperating affair for the sociologists. This is so because the middle class has now come to represent so great a diversity in terms of income, status, vocations, skills and educational qualifications among groups and individual constituents that it becomes difficult to group them together and designate them as a single social class. The wide spectrum of middle class ranges from 'dominant proprietary classes', namely, the industrial capitalists, the rich farmer and the professionals both civilian and military including white-collar workers to blue-collar workers in the organized industrial sector, managerial cadre employees of both private and public sector enterprises, opinion makers and middle peasants in the rural areas (Bardhan, 1984; Varma, 1998). So, the middle class as a social group, denotes a not too homogeneous section of population. According to Varma (1998), the creation of a native elite in India in its own image was the most spectacular and enduring achievement of British colonialism in India.

Since the early nineties, when liberalization policies became more pronounced, the middle class has been the focus of considerable media attention. The middle class, an elastic group ranging from 100 to 350 million, suddenly became an entity worthy of observation and debate that focused on their ability to consume. The middle class has been targeted as the prime consumers of the new goods that liberalization policies had made available in the Indian market. Hence, the 'liberalization' package, tailored to make India a player in the 'globalized' economy, suddenly directed the spotlight on the middle class for an entirely new reason: If India was to open up to the world markets, it was essential to know how much it could buy. It became evident that the middle class contained the largest concentration of purchasing power in India today. Varma rightly observed that the logic of economic reform dictated that the middle class now be analysed not for its lack of ideological moorings, or its lack of commitment to anything but its own material well-being, or for its utter insensitivity to social and moral causes, *but for its craving for and ability to buy what the developed countries could sell to it* (emphasis added) (ibid.: 170–73).

Identity: A Contested Ground

In the contemporary social scenario, the problem of identity consisted in how an individual constitutes, perceives, interprets and presents oneself to others and to the self. Identity is a discovery and affirmation of an innate essence, which determines what I am. Against all collective identities, individuals are attempting to construct their own personal identities, though often highly mediated by collective forces. The quest for individuality and particularity in one's look, image, style and life continues apace, both at the individual and collective levels. In reflexive modernization thesis, Giddens (1991) postulated a sharp decline in the power and legitimacy of authoritative norms of the yesterdays. In the place of the normative fabric of the recent past, there occurred a corresponding rise in exploring new forms of identity and a subsequent decline in the capacity of social institutions, such as religion, family, education, etc., to dictate people's biographies. While these changes represent a kind of 'freeing' of individuals from the constraints of institutions and normative standards, they also make people much more susceptible to the risks of their life decisions, notably in the market.

Interestingly, as a result of the commercial lifestyle, trans-national and trans-cultural aspirations tend to define people's existence much more than what they really are. This defining identitykit has come to stay as more 'real' to people today than the surviving vestiges of class solidarity. Indeed, the two great traditional markers of collective identity – nation and class – are seen to be disintegrating under the onslaught of global media. Media market now has the power to move people not just to buy the products of the culture industries, but to buy into networks that offer forms of community/collective identities that can transcend the confines of class, gender, regional and national alliances.

In the backdrop of consumer culture, the issue of 'identity' has come to surface as more pressing and contested than ever before. If we track the global flow of commodities and concentrate on the consumption of goods, we find that the goods often mediate the 'encounter' between peoples and cultures around the world. Friedman (2002) explores how consumption becomes an aspect of broader cultural strategies of self-definition and self-maintenance. Strategies of consumption can only be truly grasped when we understand the specific way in which desire is constituted. Friedman writes: "Consumption within the bounds of the world systems is always a consumption of identity, canalized by a negotiation between self-definition and the array of possibilities offered by the capitalist market" (ibid.: 235). When goods are regarded as the building blocks of life-worlds, they can be further understood as constituents of selfhood and social identity. In this sense, the formation of identity encompasses the practice of consumption.

Consumption and Identity

Consumer culture marks a shift from considering consumption as a mere reflex of production to conceiving consumption as central to social reproduction. It points not only to the increasing production and salience of cultural goods as commodities but also to the way in which the majority of cultural activities and signifying practices become mediated through consumption (Baudrillard, 1983; Jameson, 1984). Influenced by the structural linguistics of Saussure, Baudrillard (1981) argues that commodities are structures made into a system of sign values governed by rules, codes and a social logic. What are sign values? Marx analysed the commodity in terms of 'use value' and 'exchange value'. Use value was defined by the use and enjoyment of a commodity in everyday life, whereas exchange value was defined by its worth in the marketplace. To Marx's concepts of use and exchange values, Baudrillard added the concept 'sign value'. Sign values are socially constructed prestige values, which are appropriated and displayed in consumption. Commodities are not the locus of the satisfaction of needs, as classical political economy claims, but they confer social meaning and prestige, which serve as indices of social standing in the consumer society.

Baudrillard (1981, 1983) argues that we live in a 'hyper-reality' of simulations in which images, spectacles and the play of signs have replaced the logic of production and class conflict . Using McLuhan's cybernetic concept of implosion, he claims that in the contemporary world, the boundary between representation and reality implodes, and that, as a result, the experience and the ground of 'the real' disappear. In this new social order, it is signs and codes that constitute 'the real'. The individuals are so caught up in a world of commodity signs, media spectacles, representations and simulations that there is no longer any access to a sense of the 'real' which is itself presented as an effect of the code or system. In such a world, everything becomes undecidable. It becomes increasingly difficult to distinguish true from false, or good from bad, for in the society of simulations it is impossible to gain access to a 'real', or to perceive what is determining or constituting various events and processes.

Baudrillard views that consumption is seen to play the critical role in defining people's identities and consciousness, so that styles of consumption are held to have superseded the old class consciousness. In his early work, Baudrillard was much influenced by Thorstein Veblen's *Theory of the Leisure Class* (1899). Whereas in Veblen's book display is confined to the upper classes, Baudrillard sees the entire society as organized around consumption and display of commodities, through which individuals gain identity and prestige. Consumption progressively involves the consumption of signs and images. Consumer culture, in this sense, points to the ways in which consumption ceases to be a simple appropriation of utilities, or use values to become a consumption of signs and images in which the emphasis upon the capacity to endlessly reshape the cultural or symbolic aspect of the commodity makes it more appropriate to speak of commodity signs.

The culture of the consumer society is, therefore, held to be a vast floating complex of fragmentary signs and images, which produce an endless sign-play that destabilizes long-held symbolic meanings and cultural order. This implies that certain objects or brands are chosen over others because of their sign value – that is, their relative prestige over other brands or types of commodities. Hierarchies of sign values constitute consumer societies in which one's social standing and prestige are determined by where one stands within the semiological system of consumption and sign values. In this sense, it may be submitted that the plethora of consumer culture is the privileged stage where the contestations and negotiations of identities occur in the present-day society. Given this frame of reference, the task is to examine the dynamics of the formation of middle class subjectivity on account of global economy entering into the local culture.

Area of Study

Kerala, the southernmost state of India, constitutes the specific context of this study. The state of Kerala is widely acclaimed for its unique pattern of development. The 'Kerala model' of development is a much-debated topic all over the world and it has been regarded as a model for many other developing societies. The state, with its distinctive socio-economic and demographic characteristics, has been compared with developed nations (Ramachandran, 1996; Oommen, 1992, 1999, Vols. 1 and 2). The enviable progress and unique features notwithstanding, Kerala remains to be one of the poorer regions among the states in India. The bleak economic scenario of the state contradicts its well-publicized achievements in recent years. The per capita income, for instance, is notably below the national average and that of many other states (George, 1993). Paradoxical, as it were, a high level of consumption marks the living standard of the people. Kerala has been referred to as a consumerist society. Not surprisingly, the middle class forms a significant and outstanding group in Kerala. In recent years, the middle class people of Kerala have been engaged in forms of consumption that resemble the cosmopolitan cultural forms of the more developed regions of the world.

Methodology

The study is conceived as an ethnographic narrative on the cultural effects of globalization at the local level. In view of constructing this ethnography, as a non-participant observer, I moved with a group of respondents totalling about hundred, falling within the selected category of middle class for one academic year, developing friendly acquaintance with all of them and closely associating with them as a colleague, teacher or co-worker. Maximum number of respondents belonged to the category of youth in the age-group of 18–30. Females had a slight edge over their counterparts in terms of the gender composition. An individual belonging to a middle class household was treated as the unit of the sample. Conceptually, the middle class was classified into lower-middle class, middle-middle class and upper-middle class within the limits of a monthly income ranging from ₹ 8,000–15,000, ₹ 15,000–25,000 and ₹ 25,000–50,000 respectively. These amounts were fixed on the basis of the monthly salary of the various categories (classes) of employees in the state government service, before the recent pay revision. On the basis of occupation respondents were classified as (1) those working, and (2) studying. The majority belonged to 'studying' category as most of the participants of the ethnographic project being students. At another level, the subjects were further categorized into 'salaried', 'business' and 'foreign' in order to understand the basis of their family income. The majority contingent comprised of 'salaried' category followed by 'business'.

I have subjected their consumer behaviour and lifestyle to an ordered and systematic observation engaging several conversations with several of them using a semi-structured interview guide. The purpose of this ethnographic query was to understand how participants perceive the world around them and consequently how their world views got shaped and conditioned as they encountered global economy with its new market culture. This ethnographic endeavour has enabled me to gather data on the everyday perceptions, aspirations, attitudes and value systems of the participants who were identified as middle class men and women. This data of the qualitative nature has been presented in the form of narratives and case stories so as to form ethnography. The phenomenological preoccupation with this ethnographic gaze was to render primacy to gathering insights from probing and understanding the 'insiders'. All the participants in this ethnographic project belonged to Thiruvananthapuram district because the pilot study that I had administered prior to this ethnographic project, revealed to me the fact that Thiruvananthapuram, being the capital of the state of Kerala, contained a cross-section of the middle class from all parts of the state.

Analysis and Discussion

Buying Culture

Bobby, a post-graduate student, was elected college chairman in the year I was conducting my field study. He was very much liked and appreciated by other students and proved himself as possessing certain convictions and opinions. He made a general observation on the changed buying habit of the times:

> Now, there is marked change in our buying habit. For instance, food items: we buy them in huge quantity. Lots of food items are available in the market, which are more attractive, and with better ads (...) this creates a craving in us to experiment with newer items, models and brands. In my case, I have a special liking for clothes. I buy more clothes of late; may be because I am a student.

It is obvious that the middle class purchase things in higher quantity and frequency, compared to their buying behaviour about two decades ago. Samir, another post-graduate student, affirmatively pointed to the perceived changes in the market scenario and the buying habit, thus: "We are struck by newer items everyday that we are tempted to possess them, or the attitude is that if I don't buy those items my neighbours or friends buy, it is bad for me. I have noticed this tendency in our group; if somebody buys a shirt, I too should have that." In the order of their priority, the list of some of those items which the middle class buy more include the following: fashionable clothes, cosmetics, vehicles, essential and nutritional food articles, and footwear. It is revealing that clothes, cosmetics and vehicles top the list of items that middle class desire is centred around.

Santhosh, possessing an MPhil in Business Management, works as a faculty member in the PG Department of Personnel Management. He took up this lecturer's post on contract basis, leaving a lucrative job as Industrial Sales Promotion Officer of LML Motors. He recalled: "Promote sale and enjoy was the slogan there; hefty marketing ... 100 kilometres speed ... celebrations ... drinks ... Symbolizing the 'LML Freedom' that the company advertises with pride ..." But later it occurred to him that though this work was very profitable, it was not ethically satisfying. Hence, he left that and took up this monetarily less attractive job. Santhosh recalled his experience of the market and a case of being trapped by the market recently:

> Market has definitely changed from what it was ten years ago. It was then need-based. Now we are induced. We fall into the trap at times. Market gives the impression that certain items are essential for living. The other day we had an experience at home. The representative from Eureka Forbes Vacuum Cleaner came home and demonstrated that bed and so on contain lots of dust that we inhale. We then thought that a machine of that kind is very essential for us and ultimately we opted to buy it.

The 'must buy' tendency of the contemporary middle class seems to spread like wildfire. "We want more because we see more" appears to be the kind of slogan that governs middle class consumers today. Maya has told me this with a tint of guilt: "We sometimes go for outings and tours as a family. Then I make it a point to do some extra shopping. Of late, this appears to be a more frequent affair with us. Apparently, I look forward to such trips. Definitely these are times of extravagance". Winston, hailing from a rural setting and working as a senior officer in a collaborative project meant for children in distress, initiated by the Government of India, once spoke about a new tendency that is noticed in the food habits of his neighbours. "Ours is a village, but Noodles, Macaroni, etc., have become very common in our place. One reason for this is the permeating presence of ads. When people, especially children watch those ads, they are enticed." Maya further explored the ramifications and dynamics of these emerging shifts in the food habits and tastes when I posed this issue before her:

> We get plenty of Macaroni, Noodles and such food items. (...) I find that the use of Maggie Noodles has become so common, and even lower middle class people buy them as frequently as the upper middle class or rich people. When I was working in General Hospital, I have seen that even the last grade staff who lived on loans and borrowings used to get these special items. When I heard about their food pattern and style I was astonished. They say that our children like them and they are very convenient and so on. I must tell you that they have even transformed our old taste. I doubt if these new tastes go with our traditional and indigenous tastes.

The fact that the lower-middle class is the major group among the middle class that fall within the accommodative framework assumes great significance. The posture of the lower-middle class vis-à-vis consumer culture appears to be somewhat similar to the practice undertaken in the process of 'sanskritization' wherein lower *jatis* try to achieve social mobility and higher status by adopting the religious and social customs of the higher *jatis*. This pervasive tendency of the lower-middle class, which cut across other pertinent categories of sex, age, caste, religion, education, occupation and political party in a globalized context, may be termed as *middle-classisation*. It denotes the perilous efforts undertaken by a section in India which by virtue of their income and assets fall just above those identified as poor, and treated as lower middle class, in order to rise to the levels of status and prestige hitherto monopolized by the middle class sections well above them. The crucial feature of the post-capitalistic era seems to be that the lower rungs of middle class, irrespective of religious, caste and political affiliations, as insistent agents and advocates of consumer culture, are trying to seek social mobility and status elevation.

Accommodation or Resistance

The consumption of soft drinks also has increased in Kerala compared to ten years ago. Samir spoke about its pervasive nature: High-income group students who come from rural locality buy lots of soft drinks. They are simply taken up by ads and the attractions of the ambassadors who are heroes and heroines. Winston has told me that even in their pucca village *pettikkada* (street vending shop) Coca-Cola and such other soft drinks are available and there are many takers for it. The widespread use of beverages is an instance par excellence that confirms the perception of Cvetkovich and Kellner (1997) that the resultant 'electronic reach' of Hollywood, McDonald's, Coca-Cola, Nike, Adidas, etc., is a distinguishing trend of the contemporary world resulting in the spread of a 'new world culture'. Cvetkovich and Kellner observe: "The consumer society, with its panorama of goods and services; trans-national forms of architecture and design; and a wide range of products and social forms is traversing national boundaries and becoming part of a new world culture" (1997: 7).

On the other hand, we must also say that even if the general consumption of these products, which are considered typical commodities that proclaim the pervasive nature of consumer culture and symbolize it, a high proportion of the middle class in a way maintains due discretion in the use of it. However, is this perceived discretion something related to any value or ideology, or merely utilitarian and functional? On this question, Bobby had the following to say:

> If available, I like to drink bottled drinks. But I have a feeling that they are not good for health; hence my interest in them has declined of late. But there is a general tendency today that it is preferable and prestigious to drink these beverages. I have a feeling that we have to resist this tendency; I liked the idea of tender coconut revolution. In Changanacherry, where I come from, it clicked.

In this context, the pertinent question is whether thirst-refreshment is merely a physiological effect, or, is it psychological because of the knowledge that a particular product is quality-approved by a laboratory and clinically tested. Knowledge, especially produced in laboratory, is treated as powerful. Dipankar Gupta (2000) is of the opinion that mass extraction and synthesis of plant compounds occur in reaction to consumer demand. He submits that social, economic and political power is etched into lab technologies and tests. Coming to those participants who choose not to use beverages, as Bobby stated, primarily on health grounds because they have learnt that soft drinks are unhealthy compared to water and other ordinary local drinks. So, the attitude and behaviour of the middle class regarding the use of beverages seem to be not necessarily motivated by a principle or ideology. Nevertheless, there is a minority who resist it partly on account of their articulated ideology too. Samir, for instance, belongs to this group.

> Somehow I was not fascinated by these multinational beverages like Coca-Cola. And from the time I came to know more about such beverages, I decided not to take it. Not because they are *Videshi* (foreign) products, or I am a person who likes to lead a *Swadhesi* (of local, indigenous) life. But I have come to know about the ill-effects, and heard lots of talks about them. They bring cultural, economic and even environmental problems with them.

Respondents, who belonged to the genre of Samir, shared some reasons for their apparent objection to beverages that are closely linked to the prevailing consumer culture in the age of globalization. The reasons included the following: "to resist the undue influence of ads and other propaganda spectacles", "not to yield to the multinational strategies of commercial operations", "to be aware of the danger of imbibing western values and tastes", and "the need to promote local markets". However, only a very thin percentage of respondents remarked such plausible propositions; for the larger proportion, health concern still remained the main reason that factored in avoiding the consumption of beverages. Hence, the disposition of the respondents in general seems to suggest that utility and function, rather than value or ideology, mostly determine the attitude of the middle class to consumer culture. In other words, the middle class, by and large, seem to operate in an accommodative and integrationist framework to the consumerist changes facilitated by the phenomenon of globalization. Winston was more vocal about the ill-effects of beverages when he says:

> I think multinational companies who manufacture these beverages in our land have to be packed off. They make us stupid and exploit us; their production cost is so cheap, but they take exorbitant price from us cheating us with all kinds of

> ads and publicity. Our traditional products and items are rated as third rate and their market is reduced so much. If we use tender coconut and fresh juice, that will benefit our farmers and good for our health too.

In the final analysis, the middle class in general submit to the lifestyle promoted by consumer culture from an accommodative framework and their rhetoric on the compatibility of consumer culture with the indigenous cultural tradition, they seem to operate in a resistance mode. Hence, the behaviour and outlook of the middle class in Kerala towards consumer culture at the microlevel exhibit a paradoxical tendency of accommodation and resistance, integration and conflict, and negotiation and ambiguity.

Commenting on this aspect of contradiction in the lives of the middle class, social scientists have observed that if the middle class seemed eager to adopt modern lifestyles through the acquisition of consumer goods, they also became the self-appointed protectors of 'tradition' (Nandy, 1990; Van der Veer, 1994; Mankekar, 1999). This is especially striking in the case of the Hindu middle class, many of whom appeared to have formulated their aspirations in the form of a strident, often exclusionary, nationalism. The 1980s generally witnessed the resurgence of religious identities in the political arena. The communalization of nationalism seeped into Doordarshan's construction of 'the Indian past' and its representation of national culture in terms of monolithic and normative Hindu identity.

Beauty on Sale

Annie works as the chief of a well-established centre of Voluntary Coordinating Agency for Adoption. Annie has three children. The eldest boy is in the high school and younger in the primary. The only daughter is just three years old. Annie with the sentiments of a mother shared with me the 'beauty preoccupations' of her children which in fact add to her 'motherly worries':

> My children tell me that we as parents need to be beautiful and should have good appearance. Even my little girl who is seven years old is very much conscious of beauty. She wants to use lipstick. (...) Girls want to imitate heroines in the movies because they consider them as their models. There are fashion show competitions for the beauty queens and the best model. It is only to promote cosmetics and the cosmetic industry is flourishing.
>
> What worries me now is that they make it a point to go to beauty parlour even for a hair cut. They want to visit these centres especially when we have to go for some special functions. My son enjoys going there and getting face wash, etc. In my younger days there were no such things. *'Look'* has become very-very important today.

Bobby admitted that he definitely spends more money on cosmetics than ten years ago. He thinks, "Beauty consciousness has increased and *'appearance syndrome'* is undoubtedly on the high. Correspondingly, the use of cosmetics too has increased. And everywhere we find ads on cosmetics". Prakash, a college lecturer in the Department of Personnel Management and Industrial Relations, comes from a rural setting, about 25 kilometres from Cochin, the business and commercial city in Kerala. Prakash makes a penetrating introspection as he commented on this:

> I am conscious of my *Look* to a certain extent. I know that varieties of cosmetics and their ads in the media do influence me in shaping my notions of beauty and appearance, because they generate newer aspirations. For instance, there is the ad of Sachin Tendulkar appearing as the brand ambassador for TVS Victor and making an impact in the sale of it. And we feel like possessing things that he advocates. In general the *look* has become very important, even to the extent of the sole criterion for getting the attraction of the opposite sex.

Seema added her case, complementing Prakash:

> My aunty is a beautician and she has lots of customers and her beauty parlor is located in the vicinity of a college. It is a good business for her. Mostly I find ordinary people coming to her beauty parlor. Students, teachers, housewives all come there. She conducted a fashion show recently and I too joined. It was held in Pathanamthitta near her centre. The show was part of the function of a women's group and my aunty has taken the initiative to organize it because she wanted to attract more customers to her centre.

These testimonies ascertain that the middle class section in Kerala seems to have succumbed to the 'business of beauty' along with its portend 'look good syndrome' that is a characteristic feature of consumer culture. It is also evident that middle class youth as a category is the most influenced by the present-day cult of look and appearance propagated by the advocates and agents of consumer culture as part of the spread of globalization. Making a reference to her niece's 'beauty craze', Maya narrated her experience of visiting beauty parlours:

> My niece who is a graduate student goes to beauty parlours very frequently. For her, it is part of her timetable that periodically she makes it a point to go to beauty parlour. By the way, I too have visited beauty parlours, but not as frequently as my niece; may be for some special functions. But I tell you it is a nice experience to go there. We feel good and feel like a different person once we come out of it. The cost depends on what are the items we want to do there. I normally do facial, bleaching and eyebrow shaping and this would cost a maximum of 200 rupees.

This also points to the fact that it is this group of young middle class girls who appears to be the most accommodative of the consumer market. "Feeling good is looking good" seems to be an important slogan that influences young girls in the ambience of consumer culture. Along with girls, boys too seem to be so much preoccupied with this business of 'look' and 'beauty'. Here is an indicative remark on this new trend. Sejal Shah, in a characteristically journalistic style, observes:

> That beauty salons, once the exclusive preserve of women, are bursting with men, their faces well 'masked' and feet and hands stretched out for the beautician's attention. Hair on the head is styled to suit the face and that on the chest and legs is ripped off with hot wax. Appearances do matter in these dog-eat-dog days of global competition (...) Men are becoming conscious about their looks. (*The Week*, March 30, 1997: 34)

The article further says that in India, the concept of the well-groomed male came in with liberalization. "All of a sudden even the common people became aware of designer brands like Reebok, Armani, Rolex and Piaget and the awareness came through television and other media" (ibid.: 36). It attributes to the arrival of foreign companies and the media exposure to the global outlook. Another reason for this consciousness is the manifold increase in the Indian consumer market for men. In this context, Prakash observed that men rather than women visited beauty parlours more:

> We can find any number of gent's beauty parlours and massaging centres in every nook and corner. Even my village, which is typically a rural area, has got beauty parlours. Although I don't go myself, I know personally that there are some very ordinary, middle class customers who regularly go for massaging and facial; some of them are my own friends. One is a vehicle broker, about twenty-five years old. It comes to 300 to 350 rupees each time.

Young men seem to believe that confidence comes with good grooming, which is very important for their job and social standing. With more and more middle class males putting their best foot forward to look good, the cosmetic industry thrives, so much so that male cosmetics are the fastest growing market internationally. With the policies of globalization and liberalization there has been an unprecedented growth in the beauty industry. One day, I had a chance to talk to Santhosh about this burgeoning business:

> Gent's beauty parlours shoot up like anything; now there are even mobile parlours (...) I too went for a facial in connection with a marriage function. I spent about 375 rupees. I feel that it is okay going to a beauty parlour when there are special functions. We feel good and confident with flashy cheeks and so on ....

The market has grown because men have realized that it is high time they looked and smelt good. The foreign companies have seen the potential among the middle classes and are brainwashing them. "Cosmetics maketh the man" seems to be the new dictum. And so the average Malayali as a middle class person seems to believe that beauty care is the key to feel nice, to look good and to climb the social ladder.

An explosion of the beauty industry has given rise to widespread proliferation of favourable attitudes towards the 'glamour' industries such as modelling. In this connection, Santhosh recollected his experience of taking part in a fashion show which he relates to this culture of the business of beauty which has crept in, recently in the lives of the middle class:

> Beauty consciousness has definitely increased. You know why? The models that appear in ads are invariably beautiful. Seeing them everybody wants to be beautiful (...) Modelling too is like that. I too had the fortune to be a model in a function at my college. I felt great; as though I got elevated to a celestial state. At that time people like film star Madhavan and so on were present for the programme. Feeling so great yaar ....

During a conversation on the 'cosmetic industry' and 'the business of beauty' Maya made a poignant comment:

> (...) the reason for such a widespread interest in cosmetics is because there are lots of ads on fashion and models, etc. Lots of students have gone into such fields to become models and anchors which brought them big glamour and fame. So students must be thinking that if they also move according to the current trend,

> they also become great and glamorous. But I don't like myself or others whom I like, going into that field. It may affect our family bonding and we will also be forced to exhibit us.

Maya's remark that "(...) I don't like myself or others whom I like going into that field. It may affect our family bonding and we will also be forced to exhibit us", is a pertinent point that requires further reflection. In the backdrop of the flourishing 'cosmetic industry' that thrives on the created 'look good syndrome' in the domain of consumer culture, there is an argument that the emphasis on physical appearance means to be preoccupied with sensuality and externals. Prem Kumar touched upon this aspect of 'look good syndrome' that consumer culture consciously cultivates with the thriving cosmetic industry:

> I watch F channel. But I don't want my kith and kin to go for modelling and fashion shows. I know that people will look at us with contempt. Modelling and Fashion shows have now turned out to be NOT (emphasis added) an exhibition of new dresses and patterns, but they have actually become shows without any dress. F channel type of things and shows has already come in Kerala. Many in our society are going for modelling. But you know that they are going astray and are exploited. Even if they do not want they will later be forced to. But in between they amass lot of money and have a jolly good life. Business people want to promote these nasty ideas on body and sex.

The point that Prem Kumar is trying to strike here is that cosmetic marketing sets a new standard in people's relationship with their bodies. Men and women are now obliged to maintain a certain image, as an attribute of their masculinity and femininity. The efforts involved in cultivating the appearance today necessitate the continuous acquisition of a growing number of commodities. In the changed culture of the market, "happiness amounts to beauty and being sexy". In this process of gaining a new face and body, one simultaneously confronts the fate of losing one's own. This way consumer culture is likely to build on fears and unsatisfied longings, defining the body in a new fashion, both its look and its smell, as well as its tactile sense and self-perception. In this sense, a new cult of the body seem to have taken its roots in society wherein the middle class young men and women seem to have risen as the ardent 'beauty ritual performers and devotees'. Beauty parlours are likely to be the 'temples' par excellence initiating the potential devotees and performing the 'cult of the body'. In the final analysis, these are some of the ways in which commodity aesthetics take possession of the middle class.

Sign Value

It is evident that the influence of consumer culture not only operates on a large scale, but also penetrates the significant, the routine and the most intimate aspects of life so much so that *Homo sapiens* are now transformed into *Homo consumers*. However, there are marked differences in the added values imputed to the commodities in the country of origin and management and in other satellite consuming countries. This is the reason why the term 'consumer culture' points to the ways in which consumption ceases to be a simple appropriation of utilities, or use values, and is transferred to a realm of consumption of signs and images which continuously reshape the cultural or symbolic aspect of the commodity. As a result, the culture of the consumer society transforms itself to be a vast floating complex of fragmentary signs and images, which produce an endless sign-play that destabilizes long-held symbolic meanings and cultural order. Winston's perception directly points to this vital dimension in the making of the contemporary middle class identity in Kerala:

> Certain items have become status symbols in our society today. For instance, we bought a washing machine recently, not because we really needed it, but because it was a status symbol. Some two years back shoes were a compulsory thing for me, thinking that to be glamorous and stylish shoes are essential. But now I don't feel like that since I am aware of the danger involved in such thinking.

In one of my conversations, Annie touched upon this important dimension of the widespread buying habit of the people today. She said: "People buy too much these days (...), actually it is a status affair. If certain items are missing in our home it will affect our image. That is the reason why people even go to the extent of availing loans in order to get those prestigious items."

Franklin was more forthright in disclosing the question of status and prestige which the middle class attach to consumer durables:

> In my house we borrow money and get all the items we want. Mother is more interested than me in acquiring luxurious goods; because she feels that when neighbors have certain items, which we don't have, we are below them. Hence we get furniture, round table and other appliances on loan. We are also planning to change our flooring, and renovate it with latest marble chips. Certain items we get for installment scheme; items like bed, mattress, fans, etc. All the conveniences are available to us these days. We have to avail all that. Now I got my two-wheeler on loan. We also plan to buy a car by taking loan. These days we get special loan for car. Without these we cannot enjoy life now. Everybody enjoys it. Then why don't we too?

As Franklin states, "we should not be lower than our neighbours" seems to the cherished slogan that governs the life of middle class in general, especially those who belong to lower-middle class. The middle class as a category characterized by their consumer habit could be described as a section of the population with vast differences within itself in values, aspirations, earning capacity, taste and style, but united as a consuming class. Capitalistic values come to dominate their world view that is oriented to seeking personal gains, security, status, prestige and respectability by individualistic rather than collective means, which in other words may be termed as typically middle class values. In this sense, middle classness is to be regarded as a structure of mentality, the habitation of a safe space that distinguishes one from the less fortunate others. They are the people caught between the thin crust of the aristocracy above, and the mass of workers below. Referring to this aspect of consumer culture, Maya made a pertinent comment:

> This has also something to do with status symbol. I think now we have special fascination for the West that we want to imitate western styles in our basic life-situations like food, dress, etc. In my case when I was younger, the West was something like what I could only dream about, especially when we read about the progress they make and when we see the lifestyle of our own people who come

from there. It was certainly a big dream for us, that I thought we can lead an affluent life there (...) 'must be a very beautiful place to live in' such kind of feelings. But later these whims and fancies got reduced and now I don't entertain these thoughts. Perhaps now, whatever we desire is available within our reach; all those attractions, which haunted my youthful dreams, can be realized here and now; anything and everything is available to us now in our own place.

Maya seems to be pointing to the debate on the issue of unidirectional cultural flow that is built into the globalization project. It entails more than just the simple spread of American or western cultural goods, more than the development of a global taste for McDonald's, Levis, Coca-Cola and the like. At a deeper level, it involves the worldwide installation of a western version of basic social-cultural reality, namely, the West's epistemological and ontological theories, its values, ethical systems, approaches to rationality, technical-scientific world view, politics, culture, and so on. In other words, consumer culture entails the dissemination of all facets of the West's way of being.

In this sense, Maya seems to be referring to the 'westoxication' tendency about which Gupta (2000) speaks. According to Gupta, westoxication "is about superficial consumerist display of commodities and fads produced in the West" and it is usually mistaken for westernization (2000: 11). The trajectory of westoxication in fact constitutes the 'localization' de tour of consumer culture, wherein the two-way process of 'universalization of particularism' as well as 'particularization of universalism' occurs. It is marked by the development of what King (1990) aptly termed, 'global cities' as local sites of global interaction, a huge increase in the flows of commodities and cultural products, and finally the worldwide spread of western-style consumerism. All this, in a way, points to the overarching "social process in which the constraints of geography on social and cultural arrangements recede and people become increasingly aware that they are receding" (Waters, 1995: 3). We learn that people are virtually influenced by the global, but this is interpreted locally and local transformations are as much a part of consumer culture as the lateral extension of social connections across time and space.

The empirical exploration brings us close to the fact that consumer culture is basically geared to radically pull culture apart from places, and dislodge it from particular locales. The signs of this disembedding are the ubiquitous presence and demand for the cultural objects – food, drinks, appliances and so forth, and their circulation through ever-expanding networks. At the same time, images too are drifting easily across the globe, allowing an increase in the number of middle class to participate in the imagined realities of other cultures. Hence, the consumption tendencies, practices and the lifestyle of the middle class point to the fact that our society has become a world of culture in motion. Culture in contemporary environment has to be understood as a product of a continuous interplay between its universalistic aspects and its particularistic reproduction. As Appadurai (1999: 231) argues, much of the work on globalization has been framed in terms of the dialectic between 'the global' and 'the local'. The cultural landscapes in the 1990s saw a complex of initiatives centred on new narratives of consumption and desire, wherein the new cultural space is criss-crossed by a fluidity of national/regional and global cultural styles mediated by the recognition of a new agent 'the consumer-subject'.

One way of approaching global culture is in terms of Schiller's (1985) influential macro-economic domination theory, which holds that cultural imperialism, as well as the anticipated cultural homogenization arising from it, results from multinational capitalism and its insatiable drive for new markets and maximum profits. It is undeniable that new communicational technologies are shrinking the world and, as Cvetkovich and Kellner (1997: 3) put it, there is a "dramatic perpetration of global forces into every realm of life in every region of the world". Beck talks of cultural 'de-location' and 're-location' and concludes that "(...) local cultures can no longer be justified, shaped and renewed in seclusion from the rest of the world (...) there is a compulsion to re-locate de-traditionalized traditions within a global context of exchange dialogue and conflict" (2000: 47). This situation would naturally result in two things: first, it would prompt the border categories of lower-middle and middle-middle groups to yield to the pervading buying sentiments of the emerging market; and secondly, the seductive value elevation of the commodities in the context of globalization may compel them to find ways and means to possess those prestigious items and services and thus to satisfy the created urge for conspicuous consumption.

If consumption represents the psychological competition for status, then middle class society is the institutionalization of envy. As a result, a large majority of the people constitutes a homogeneous bloc in terms of consumer practices and behaviour and is being knit together by assimilating an individualistic outlook and identification with the objectives of the post-capitalist enterprise. They subsequently discard the traditional loyalties of workmates, trade union and class. Instead, the apparent growth of a typically middle class concern with status and social image makes them more family-minded and home-centred and lesser and lesser socially sensitive and collectively conscious. Invested with meaning, commodities 'speak' to consumers. The symbolic meanings of commodities and consumption have been analysed by scholars such as Arjun Appadurai (1996) and Dick Hebdige (1979), who focus on the 'social life of things' and of the communicative aspects of consumption, respectively. Since it is embedded in larger significatory chains, consumption necessarily involves the production of meanings. In a consumer cultural environment, the middle class becomes easily identifiable not by their income level, but by the desires, buying habits, possessions of goods and services, or in other words, of status and values. That means what they tend to buy and possess would render them status and prestige which ultimately constitute their identity.

Conclusion

The cultural purview of globalization has opened up the whole gamut of consumption as constituent of the normative behaviour that primarily signifies one as a member of society. In a globalized market culture, the consumer cannot avoid the obligation to consume. Consumption has emerged as the principal mode of social integration and hence the purview of key ethical arena of behaviour within a society. In other words, individuals, all over the globe today, are primarily socialized into consumer culture. While the excitement and brashness of consumer culture has an undoubted appeal, it erodes a public space based on the ideal of rationality. While consumers may be critical decoders of advertisements, multinationals who are not subjected to any kind of democratic control and whose prime concern is profit, shape the terrain.

The study sought to examine the dynamics of identity formation of the middle class within the purview of consumer culture that is characteristic of contemporary society in the age of globalization. The study has brought to surface that the middle class as a social group appears to be highly prone to the impact of consumer culture. There seems to be more elements of accommodation of the global consumer culture than elements of resistance in the everyday lives of the middle class. Youth as a category is likely to be highly vulnerable to the influence of contemporary consumer culture and the notions of middle class men and women on their physical appearance and body are primarily defined by the prevailing consumer culture. It is submitted that consumer behaviour is likely the privileged entry point to gauge the influence of contemporary globalization in its everyday effect. Consumer culture in a way influences the identity construction of the middle class.

It is likely that the contestations and negotiations of social mobility and status occur at the intersection of diverse income groups from within the middle class in the ambience of consumer culture. Therefore, it is more likely that the domain of consumer culture carves out the sociological boundaries of the middle class, transcending all other boundary-constructing categories such as religion, community, region and politics. This is how the middle class, which is otherwise, regarded as a heterogeneous historical bloc with differing access to relations of production, status and political power, is brought under a homogeneous umbrella. In this sense, the middle class is not a pure economic construct; rather it constitutes a cultural reality tending to generate middle class materiality as well as mentality, imbibing like-mindedness in certain values, tastes, ideology and demands.

References

Appadurai, A. (1996) *Modernity at Large: Cultural Dimensions of Globalisation*. Minneapolis: University of Minnesota Press.

—— (1999) "Globalisation and the Research Imagination", *International Social Science Journal*, Vol. 160, pp. 231–38.

Bardhan, P. (1984) *The Political Economy of Development in India*. Delhi: OUP.

Baudrillard, J. (1981) *For a Critique of the Political Economy of the Sign*. St Louis: Telos Press.

—— (1983) *Simulations*. New York: Semiotext(e).

Beck, U. (2000) *What is Globalization*. Cambridge: Polity Press.

Bhatia, B.M. (1994) *India's Middle Class*. Delhi: Konark Publishers.

Cvetkovich, Ann and Kellner, Douglas (eds.) (1997) *Articulating the Global and the Local*. Boulder, Colorado, US: Westview Press.

Dreze, J. and Sen, A. (2002). *India: Development and Participation*. New Delhi: Oxford University Press.

Friedman, J. (2002) "Globalisation and Localization", in Jonathan Xavier and Renato Rosaldo (eds.), *The Anthropology of Globalisation*, Massachusetts, Oxford: Blackwell.

George, K.K. (1993) *Limits to Kerala Model of Development: An Analysis of Fiscal Crisis and its Implications*. Thiruvananthapuram: Centre for Development Studies.

Giddens, A. (1991) *Modernity and Self-Identity: Self and Society in the Late Modern Age*. Cambridge: Polity Press.

Gupta, D. (2000) *Mistaken Identity: India between Worlds*. New Delhi: HarperCollins.

Hebdige, D. (1979) *Subculture: The Meaning of Style*. New York: Methuen.

Inda, Jonathan X. and Rosaldo, Renato (2002) "Introduction: A World in Motion", in Jonathan Xavier and Renato Rosaldo (eds.), *The Anthropology of Globalisation*, Massachusetts, Oxford: Blackwell, pp. 1–35.

Jameson, F. (1984) "Postmodernism, or the Cultural Logic of Late Capitalism", *New Left Review*, Vol. 146.

Kemper, S. (1993) "The Nation Consumed: Buying and Believing in Sri Lanka", *Public Culture*, Vol. 5, No. 3, pp. 377–93.

King, A.D. (1990) *Global Cities*. London: Routledge.

Mankekar, P. (1999) *Screening Culture, Viewing Politics: An Ethnography of Television, Womanhood, and Nation in Postcolonial India*. Durham and London: Duke University Press.

Nair, R. (1974) *Middle Class in Kerala*. Trivandrum: The Kerala Academy of Political Science.

Nandy, A. (1990) "The Politics of Secularism and the Rediscovery of Religious Tolerance", in V. Das, *Mirrors of Violence: Communities, Riots and Survivors in South Asia*, Delhi: Oxford University Press.

Oommen, M.A. (1992) *The Kerala Economy*. New Delhi: Oxford and IBH.

Oommen, M.A. (ed.) (1999) *Kerala's Development Experience*, Vol. 1 and 11, New Delhi: Concept Publishing.

Ramachandran, V.K. (1996) "On Kerala's Development Achievements", in J. Dreze and A. Sen (eds.), *Indian Development: Selected Regional Perspectives*, Delhi: Oxford University Press, pp. 205–356.

Sarup, M. (1996). *Identity, Culture and the Postmodern World*. Edinburgh, Edinburgh University Press.

Schiller, H. (1985) "Electronic Information Flows: New Basis for Global Domination?", in P. Drummond and R. Paterson (eds.), *Television in Transition*, London: BFI.

Singh, G. (1985) *The New Middle Class in India*. Jaipur: Rawat Publications.

Tanter, R. and Young, K. (eds.) (1990) *The Politics of Middle Class Indonesia, Clayton, Victoria*. Australia: Centre of Southeast Asian Studies, Monash University.

Van der Veer, P. (1994) *Religious Nationalism: Hindus and Muslims in India*. Berkeley: University of California Press.

Varma, P.K. (1998) *The Great Indian Middle Class*. New Delhi: Viking, Penguin Books.

Veblen, T. (1899) *The Theory of the Leisure Class*. New York: New American Library of World Literature Inc.

Waters, M. (1995) *Globalization*. London and New York: Routledge.

Wessel, M.V. (2001) *Modernity and Identity: An Ethnography of Moral Ambiguity and Negotiations in an Indian Middle Class*. Amsterdam: University of Amsterdam.

21

Modern Society and Risk

Towards a Cultural Understanding of the Risk Society

Sherry Sabbarwal

Humanity has been subjected to a number of calamitous events since a long time. However, in the past years, their frequency and intensity has increased multifold. In fact, in the past decade itself, we have witnessed various catastrophes in the form of terrorism, climate change, migration, hurricanes, earthquakes and the tsunami. Countless people around the world have been affected on different scales and in different ways by these occurrences. Two perceptions emerged out of these events – the first one, a sense of a global imagined community and the second, the inevitability of risk. Whether it is droughts or floods, industrial or air travel safety, water, air or food pollution, we find that 'risk analysis' has become an important part of the public perception and government policy agenda in many countries. Issues such as mad cow disease, avian flu, genetically modified food, dengue and even cloning are fostering an anxiety-ridden atmosphere all over the world. A major concern is regarding the course that our technology is taking and its management in the future. Ironically, despite living longer and healthier lives than ever before, we have come into an age of 'risk society' where economic prosperity, technological advancements and individual freedom go hand in hand with practices that produce hazardous environments. Processes such as globalization, large-scale production and unpredictable technological outcomes have resulted in creation of apprehensions about the future.

Risk and Risk Society

As is wont with all conceptions, the conception of risk has changed over time. So much so that even our present understanding of risk, whether factual or not, will continue to change in future too. The word 'risk' is based on the Latin word *riscum* that was frequently used till the middle ages, to connote the chance of hazard to ventures, in maritime shipping insurance, and other business. An important attribute of this conception of risk was that it clearly ruled out the idea of human fault and responsibility in engendering or fostering risks which, depending on the level of development in a society, were viewed as being caused by some incomprehensible natural or mysterious, even divine force or occurrence.

Since then, the concept of risk has come a long way. As John Adams (1995) puts it, at one time risk was something that you participated in for the sake of thrill. Placing bets on horses or other sport events, for instance, brought some excitement to one's otherwise neat, mundane existence. In its new version, however, risk is an inevitable part of our lives. Each of us consistently confronts unfamiliar risks. Even worse, most of them are inestimable in nature; no more are they 'calculated'. In fact, in today's world, risk is a synonym for 'nobody knows'. Most importantly, risks are no longer taken voluntarily, but are forced upon us. As a result, what used to be the job for experts in risk analysis, has become the main concern of the modern individual and we all try and manage our real or imagined risks using a variety of means ranging from using a computer or calculator to a visiting an astrologer. Adams holds that we are living in a random risk society rife with random risks, from which there is no escape.

The concept of risk society has been in popular use since 1986 when German sociologist Ulrich Beck used it in his famous book *Risk Society: Towards a New Modernity*, which was then published in its English version in 1992 by Sage. Since then, of course, there have been umpteen efforts focusing on this concept and a fair amount of literature has emerged on the subject. This paper, however, will focus on three eminent scholars who have written on risk society, namely, Beck himself, Anthony Giddens and Mary Douglas with the hope that by contrasting their theories one may get a better understanding of the cultural reality of risk perception.

Relating Risk to Modernity: Ulrich Beck

The term 'risk society' was introduced into sociology by Ulrich Beck (1986, 1992). Beck's book is divided into three parts each discussing three different ideas. The first part provides a discourse on the theory of industrial society as well as the concept of 'modernity,' delineating their journey from the times of Marx and Weber to their arrival at critical theory. The second part evaluates the accountability of science and instrumental rationality in modern society. The third part contains a treatise on a singular type of society that presents a special perspective on the way in which we are subjected to risks, especially those pertaining to health and the environment. Beck gives it the name of the 'risk society'. Let us look at the main assertions of Beck's notion of risk society.

Risk society is a concept signifying a condition in the postmodern world, where occurrences in all aspects of life involve a heightened awareness or sense of danger and risk (Lawson and Garrod, 2006). The contention is that the earlier modern society offered a great deal of steadfastness to its members. For instance, in social relations, class and caste systems provided a sense of certainty, as each individual was sure of one's well-defined position in life. Postmodern world, however, witnesses the dissolution of these certainties, thereby making life more risky.

For Beck, modern society has changed fundamentally from a society characterized primarily by inequalities of wealth and income to a society where, along with the already existing inequities, other problems have taken centre stage, such as environmental hazards, which cut across traditional inequalities. Or take the example of risks such as nuclear and chemical pollution, which while not affecting everyone equally, nevertheless exhibit a pattern that leaves no one untouched by them.

In a later book (Beck et al., 1994), it is further clarified that 'risk society' stands for a type of thought and action not perceived by 19th century sociologists. In that era both government and industry were able to calculate risks, devise solutions and ensure definite outcomes. They were able to do so because the bases of social order in the society of that time were relatively unambiguous. A century or so later a quite different situation has emerged. Risk is omnipresent and is no longer calculable in the same way. Risk is an inevitable outcome of production of goods and the set of material conditions necessary to bring them into production. The most noticeable risks emerge from nuclear or chemical mega-technology, and most recently from genetic research. Other aspects of risk include arms sales and increased carbon emissions from industrial production and use of automobiles. Risks no longer take traditional or natural forms; instead, they derive from decisions deliberately made by humans, often for the sake of technology and advancement.

In Beck's view, today, one cannot choose or reject risk and exposure to risk is an outcome of industrial and political processes that are oblivious to their own effects and threats. "Risks accumulate because they are automatic side effects of the whole industrial process and are infinitely reproducible. Industrialism in its advanced stage, from the second half of the 20th century, has increasingly produced effects that can no longer be encompassed or covered by the calculus of risk and insurance" (ibid.: 181). As risks increase, the mechanisms of rational control in industrial society – more technology, more government and more market opportunities – no longer seem to be able to cope. Social, political and economic hazards escape the institutional monitoring of risk in industrial society, and threats far exceed the social ideas of safety.

Since it is increasingly tough to calculate risk, the institutional monitors of risk seem to be blind to this new trend in the pattern of risk. But, according to Beck, such blindness is no mere accident. The business firms, policy makers and experts, who analyse and formulate policies about risk in contemporary society, have actually built up this discourse on risks as a means for disowning their responsibilities. As a consequence, everyday life in world risk society is characterized by a new variant of individualization. The individual must cope with the uncertainty of the global world by himself or herself. Here, individualization is an automatic outcome of a *failure* of expert systems to manage risks. Neither science, nor the politics in power, nor the mass media, nor business, nor the law or even the military, are in a position to define or control risks rationally. Consequently, the individual is forced to mistrust the promises of rationality of these key institutions and people are thrown back onto themselves, they are alienated from expert systems but have no other substitute. Thus, modernization entails not only structural change but also changed relationship between social structure and the individual. The individual may seem to be less controlled by the structure, but becomes a prisoner of one's own personal doubts. With independence come anxieties, neuroses, guilt and sickness. Social crisis becomes individual crisis. In other words, despite the outward appearance of liberation, people are actually becoming more constrained by external forces since they may either rely on the advice of the experts or make their own decisions, a task, for which they feel utterly inadequate.

Nevertheless, the dangers of the present situation have led to a new form of politics – 'life politics'. The idea is that reducing environmental hazards is the only way to restore a general feeling of security in the society. Beck states that 'life politics' takes the form of a number of new social movements. In an earlier era, namely, the modern or industrial society, the sources that gave meaning to life were faith in technical progress and class consciousness. These have lost their charm for the people in the postmodern era and now it is the social movements, which strive to provide new sources of meaning to life itself.

To summarize, Beck feels that risk is the defining characteristic of our times. Outlining a transition from the pre-industrial to risk society via the industrial society, he adds that though all three stages faced hazards, yet, as mentioned earlier, these risks are induced by humans themselves. Further, these risks are abstract and, consequently, less easy to resolve. The world is no longer a safe predictable place. Instead, it is marked by uncertainty that give birth to risks both at the global and the individual levels. In the industrial modern society the profit maximization was the driving force, which was indicative of growth and progress. But, in the risk society, people's main concern is survival, with somewhat bleak expectations from the future. Since everyone is prone to risk, it is no more a class society as it was in the industrial phase, but is now a risk society.

Anthony Giddens' Views on Risk

Although Ulrich Beck authored the term 'risk society', the analysis of 'risk' is related more clearly to the concept of 'security' in the work of Anthony Giddens (1990, 1991). Giddens sees modernity as double-edged, since it has created vastly greater opportunities for human beings to enjoy a secure and rewarding existence than any pre-modern system, but it also has a 'somber side'. Giddens (1990) feels that science and technology offers, on the one hand, advantageous options to humanity and, on the other hand, creates new risks for them – be they emergence of a totalitarian society, 'total wars' leading to complete annihilation (e.g., nuclear strike), arbitrary economic changes and environmental calamities.

Preoccupation with risk in modern social life has nothing to do with the actual prevalence of life-threatening dangers. On the level of the individual lifespan, in terms of life expectation and degree of freedom from serious disease, people in the developed societies are in a much more secure position than were most in previous ages. However, although one can come up with an impressive list of the ways in which the physical security of human beings has been enhanced in industrial societies but it is balanced by a list of new risks: war, motor accidents, drugs, environmental pollution, etc. Both can be seen as results of the operation of the abstract systems of modernity.

Like Beck, Giddens' discussion of risk and security is also embedded in a discourse of modernity and globality. But, unlike Beck, Giddens sees no fundamental rupture between 'modernity' and 'postmodernity'. For him, the continuities of modern society are more important than the discontinuities. However, despite his denial of any radical historical rupture, his analysis of risk does refer to certain features of 'late' modernity. High modernity in Giddens' view is doubly problematic as it creates a situation where firstly, the individual has to face a new risk at every step and secondly, taking a decision becomes additionally difficult since in this age of uncertainty, there are no right answers.

Giddens makes it plain that 'risk' is not just a matter of individual action. There are also "environments of risk that collectively affect large masses of individuals" (ibid.: 35). He distinguishes pre-modern (traditional) and modern environments of risk. The risk environment of traditional cultures was dominated by hazards of the physical world and the threats emerged from nature. The modern risk environment is "structured mainly by humanly-created risks" (ibid.: 106, 111). Giddens stresses the importance of the environment, war and personal relationships in modern experiences and constructions of risk.

Giddens also argues that the nature of risk has changed. Firstly, there is a 'globalization of risk in the sense of *intensity*', e.g., a nuclear war having greater impact than anything has had till now. Secondly, risk has also changed in terms of its *spread* with the increasing number of events 'which affect everyone or at least very large numbers of people on the planet'. Thirdly, new risks arise from the nature of modern social organization: there is *risk 'stemming from the created environment*, or socialized nature': the infusion of human knowledge into the material environment, and the development of 'institutionalized risk environments affecting the life-chances of millions' (e.g., investment markets). In addition, and very importantly, there is greater '*awareness* of risk as risk', well distributed throughout society.

While humans have always been subjected to a level of risk, modern society is exposed to a particular type of risk that is the result of the modernization process itself, altering social organization. Risks can be of two types. There are risks such as natural disasters that have always had negative effects on human populations, but these are seen to be produced by non-human forces and are beyond human control. Giddens calls them *external risks* (Giddens, 1999). Good examples of external risks are natural disasters such as earthquakes and volcanoes. Modern risks, on the other hand, are the product of human activity and, thus, can be referred to as *manufactured risks*. Manufactured risks are risks that are produced by the modernization process, particularly by innovative developments in science and technology. They are unexpected but happen regularly. They create risk environments that have little historical reference and are, therefore, largely unpredictable. It is manufactured risks that produce a risk society. Giddens also distinguishes between 'low-consequence' and 'high-consequence' risks. The former are *within the control of the individual agent* (e.g., peculiarities of diet which may have certain medical consequences), the latter are *remote from the individual agent*, although affecting every individual's life chances. Examples of high-consequence risks range from mercury in tuna fish to the nuclear accident at Chernobyl.

For Giddens, the 'institutionalization of risk' is an essential feature of the new role of risk in modern society. As Shaw (1995) puts it, "a significant part of expert thinking and public discourse today is made up of risk profiling – analysing what, in the current state of knowledge and in current conditions, is the distribution of risks in given milieus of action." Like Beck, Giddens also feels that the greater occurrence of risk is not because life has become more risky but because in the modern society, thoughts on risk and risk assessment have become a universal chore for the common person as well as for the experts.

The increased critique of modern industrial practices has resulted in a state of reflexive modernization. Reflexivity is a process of monitoring behaviour and its contexts. In traditional societies reflexivity took the form of re-interpretation and clarification of tradition. Reflexive modernization is a process of modernization that is characteristic of risk society whereby progress is achieved through reorganization and reform. The social practices are constantly examined and reformed in the light of incoming information about these practices. This process is less concerned with expanding the resource base, but rather with re-evaluating that which is already being used by society. There is a constant flow of information between science and industry, and progress is achieved through the resulting reforms and adaptations. Examples of reflexive modernization that have recently gained political momentum are sustainability and the precautionary principle.

Regarding the future prospects, Giddens is of the view that social movements will provide guidelines for future transformation. For instance, the labour movement gave the necessary impetus to social change in an era epitomized by capitalism and industrialization. Similar roles will be played by peace movement, ecological movement, or democratic or nationalist movements.

Critique of Risk Theory

The theory of risk society has undoubtedly fired the imagination of social thinkers and has gone on to become one of the most discussed approaches. However, its main propositions have also met with a lot of skepticism and criticism.

The first problem is regarding the dichotomy of natural and technological or artificial risks, implying the shift from natural to artificial risks. Although one cannot deny that the nature of risk has changed to an extent from natural to man-made, yet in the age of tsunamis and AIDS, how can one deny or overlook that we are still subject to the vagaries of nature.

Second, the conceptualization of risk in this approach is limited to the technical and environmental risks as being the unforeseen consequences of industrialization, leaving out the emotional and aesthetic (Lash, 2000) or socio-cultural (Tulloch and Lupton, 2003) perceptions and responses to risk.

A third problem is that the risk theory makes sweeping generalizations without providing balanced illustrations. The works of both Beck and Giddens operate at the level of grand theory with less interest in empirical information regarding how people in reality conceptualize and experience risk. For instance, there are questions like to what extent people *actually* perceive risk, how reflexive are they, how the 'at risk' people respond to their labelling by experts and government, what and how much information of experts is trusted, how do risks interact with ethnic, gender, age, class categories, or at different sites of workplace, leisure, home, and the role of mass media – and these issues are not tackled seriously by either of these authors.

Yet another problem with the word 'risk' is that it refers to the future, and the future does not exist except in our imaginations. Moreover, future is viewed through the filters constructed out of all previous experience. The point being made is that such virtual risks are unresolved, and perhaps even unresolvable, by science.

Fifth, it is also pointed out that although uncertainty has to be accepted as a fundamental modern experience, the approach to coping with uncertainty needs to be changed. It is not a problem of how to produce order and certainty. This perspective implies that it is already decided that the transformation of uncertainty into certainty, disorder to order, and ambiguity into clearness would be the optimal and only solution that should be strived for. This is clearly a utopian perspective. A more practical approach would be to focus on how uncertainties can be *managed* or how they could be managed best. The focus should be on coming up with a process of managing unpreventable uncertainties and not on a final transformation of uncertainty into certainty.

Sixth, risk theory suffers from absolutism, that is, risks are deemed as being global and not open to any contestations. Alternative approaches like the 'socio-cultural' approach propounded by Tulloch and Lupton (2003) and 'risk culture' by Scott Lash (2000) portray risk as a more dynamic process, indicating that the risk knowledge has a historical and local context, and it needs to be frequently questioned regarding the nature of risks, their control and who is to blame for their creation.

Finally, there is still a tendency in risk theory to distinguish between objective statistical or technical risks as the *real* risks and social or subjective risks as biased perceptions of *objective* risks. But it must be remembered that it was the acknowledgement that risk problems are deeply embedded in the society we live in and that they cannot be coped with by objective and technical risk assessment, which was the initial trigger for risk sociology. In this context, especially, the failures of governmental risk management have shown that there is such a thing as society, which needs to be taken into account.

From Modernist to a Cultural Approach to Risk: Mary Douglas

Mary Douglas (1966, 1992) is another leading writer on risk (see also Douglas and Wildavsky, 1982). She defined risk simply as the probability of an event occurring and the degree of loss it would cause. According to her, the origin of risk theory lies in the gambling theory and the mathematics of probabilities.

Douglas offers a cultural and social constructionist view of risk implying that risks are culturally perceived. She attempts to explain why people identify some hazards as risks and some not. She points out that identifying and classifying hazards is a selective process and relative to social groups and organizations. Each group tends to create norms against what they define as deviance and violation and through this, each group attempts to create a social order.

Douglas related risk to her idea of purity/pollution, saying what is seen as polluted is risky and dangerous for society and for the social order. Her approach is culturally specific and focuses on the difference between self and the other. Risk is a site for blame in which risky groups and institutions are singled out as dangerous. A 'risky other' is supposed to pose threat to the integrity of one's own self or physical body or to the symbolic body of the community/society. Thus, for

Douglas, the notions of risk are expressed through cultural beliefs, and thus, are shared standards and expectations rather than individualistic judgments of the individual decision-maker. Risk provides explanations for things gone wrong or are foreseen to go wrong. In old societies it was sin and taboo that acted as the source of explanations. Their new avatar in modern society is risk, which is supposedly more scientifically established and characterized by neutrality.

Focusing on the idea of *blame*, Douglas describes how certain individuals are blamed for failure to conform to the norms. However, she adds that this is a political move as risks are transferred from a social to an individual focus. The important thing is that those blamed tend to be members of particular groups: minorities, blue-collar workers, the barely literate, children, and so forth. Simon Carter (in Adams, 1995: 142) has also noted elsewhere that a range of social practices exist, connected with risk assessment, which historically have often targeted specific groups.

Despite this politicization of risk, for Douglas, risk and danger are actually functional for the society. In the older times people were controlled by the local community but with globalization the authority of the local community declines and with it the concept of what is right and wrong, risky or safe. To compensate the absence of the local justice system, the world community creates new parameters and political priorities to ensure justice and welfare. The earlier societies used definite moralistic yardsticks to condemn or absolve the deviant and in doing so, provided protection to the member of the society. Risk discourse does the same, as it is usually centred on the rights of the individual. Douglas holds that in a society focused on risk, individual autonomy becomes the key political priority, which provides a glimmer of hope to each person.

In the same vein, Douglas says that the two common strategies used in assessing risk are blaming the victim and blaming the other. Thus, in the first instance, an automobile or tire manufacturer could protect its mechanically failed product and blame the accident or the injured driver and, in the second instance, environmental groups could blame petroleum or timber companies for aspects of environmental change which the activists view as degradation. Both forms of blaming serve a purpose for the society and the individual. Blaming the victim facilitates social control of persons, whereas blaming the other engenders group loyalty and solidarity vis-à-vis, other groups. Both strategies serve to prevent the divide and dissensions (Douglas, 1985) in a group. Douglas, thus, works within a Durkheimian framework of social solidarity.

Critiquing the modern society, Douglas says that liberation from the small local communities may lead to an escape from the absolute control of the community but it leave the individual exposed to the larger world. To be modern we give up our old protections, thus rendering ourselves vulnerable. At the local level, the traditional norms were our protection. At the global level, this role is played by risk because we need new concepts and new protection mechanisms. Risk is universal, supposedly neutral and scientific and open to objective analysis. In the traditional societies, we had other sources to blame – magic, supernatural events or natural phenomena. Now, we have new people or groups to blame.

Finally, Douglas criticizes the individualization aspect of the risk theory. She holds that if risk is all about taking decisions, as Beck has pointed out, then risk decisions are not taken individually but always in consultation with others. She highlights the processes of inter-subjectivity, consensus building and social influences while discussing decision-making. For a psychologist, risk is a human factor impacting an individual. For an anthropologist, it denotes the general structure of authority in an institution or group.

Douglas' is a structural-functional analysis of the cultural response to risk in communities and organizations. How risk is perceived and tackled is based on the collective ethos of the group, i.e., the group and other constraints and expectations shape social relations in the form of a grid. Groups with high collective orientation and high grid are hierarchical and cope with risk in terms of group norms, i.e., placing their faith in institution. Opposite to these are those who are individualistic and prefer self-regulatory approach to risk. Thus, Douglas works in a Durkheimian tradition claiming that throughout history when social solidarity is weakened or threatened, people react by evoking shared beliefs about impending catastrophe. The cultural value of the impending disaster helps in denouncing the threat to group disunity. In an effort to protect themselves against a perceived danger, people identify 'others' as the cause of the threat. In this way, they are provided a shared outlet for their anxieties through the casting of blame on those identified as threatening to disrupt a preferred way of life. So, this collective representation of risk performs an integrative function in the mainstream of social solidarity. Douglas' cultural theory, although a rigid model, goes beyond focus on the individual and his/her cognitive/psychological response. Instead, a socio-cultural context is applied where individual is situated and through which he makes judgements about risk.

Some Final Thoughts

The first thing all these theories highlight is that in the contemporary times *risk is internalized*. In the earlier societies, there was social externalization of the risk since it was attributed to some external, natural or even supernatural agency or cause. Now humans are acknowledging the responsibility of causing the risk. Also, since risks are believed to lie in the future, they depend on the decisions taken by us today. Secondly, the focus in on the aspect of *non-knowledge or limited information* regarding everything available to the experts, as well as, to the layperson, which implies that while the experts present only speculations and conjectures while assessing risk, the layperson rejects the former's estimates and thus constructs the idea of 'dread risk'. Thirdly, risk society does not imply an increase of risk in society, but rather emergence of a society that is organized in *response to risks*. It is a society increasingly preoccupied with the future (and also with safety), which generates the notion of risk.

Fourthly, risk is *social construction* in more sense than one. Each society may define risk differently and may perceive it differently based on its own experiences. For example, the dominant risk belief and risk tendencies of Europe and the US government are quite different since the Europeans and Americans live in different worlds. For Europeans, issues like climate change, xenophobia and mad cow disease are much more important than the threat of terrorism, while, for Americans, the threat of terrorism is paramount. So, Americans may feel that the Europeans are suffering from an environmental hysteria, while many Europeans may see the Americans as struck by terrorism hysteria.

Fifthly, for scholars like Steven Miles (2001), the idea of risk society is an exaggeration. Do we really spend our whole life focusing on the risks faced by us?, he asks. Quite, on the contrary, is his view. So, what mark the present society are not actual risks but an alarmist *perception* of risk. The world may not be as riskier than before but there is simply a heightened awareness of potential risks due to more effective communication. Our perception of risk may simply be our unconfirmed anxieties caused by a fast changing world. Wildavsky (1988) goes so far as to say that the fears attached to technology have become instruments of enslavement. One can witness how the panics created on account of environmental risks, mostly exaggerated by the media, have created a market for items that may not otherwise attract buyers.

The question then is what is the usefulness of risk discourse? Douglas points out that by creating and heightening risk perceptions, the risk discourse may perform a positive role for the society as it persuades society to look inward and assess in a critical manner the way in which life is constructed in it. So risk society is also an opportunity society, not as out of control as is declared. Similarly, both Beck's and Giddens' accounts prove that risk analysis not only describes but may also offer a way to change the world. By using the concept of 'life politics' Beck's analysis no longer remains simply academic talk. Rather he points towards the new meanings of risk as being rooted in localism and in the political thrust of civil society in order to reshape society from below. Similarly, Giddens pays tribute to the various types of social movements that would play a crucial role in social transformation in a risk society. Thus, the risk society debate can be viewed as a major attempt to understand new social movements and emergent social problems.

And finally, as Douglas points out, this discourse can be used to cope with the uncertainties by making us feel that at least we can assess the dangers ahead and once forewarned, may be deal with them to some extent. Today, may not be hopeful, but one can hope for a better tomorrow. More importantly, it is clear that risk controversies are no longer solely about 'risk'. Risk unites scientific doubt with values and beliefs in such a way that they go on to impact politics, lifestyles and the character of democracy. It is pertinent to remember that the notions of exclusionary discourse and secret strategizing by politicians, technocrats and business lobbies are obsolete practices in these times of mass media and transparency and, therefore, risk analysis and assessment can no longer remain the monopoly of the so-called experts and it is time to encourage more and more civil society participation in this respect.

References

Adams, John (1995) *Risk*. London: UCL Press.

Beck, Ulrich (1992) *Risk Society: Towards a New Modernity*. New Delhi: Sage (originally publ. 1986).

— (1992b) "From Industrial Society to the Risk Society: Questions of Survival, Social Structure and Ecological Enlightenment", *Theory, Culture and Society*, Vol. 9, No. 1.

Beck, Ulrich, Anthony Giddens and Scott Lash (1994) *Reflexive Modernization: Politics, Tradition and Aesthetics in the Modern Social Order*. Cambridge: Polity Press.

Douglas, Mary (1966) *Purity and Danger: An Analysis of Concepts of Pollution and Taboo*. New York: Praeger.

— (1992) *Risk and Blame: Essays in Cultural Theory*. London, New York: Routledge.

— (1985) *Risk Acceptability According to the Social Sciences*. New York: Russell Sage Foundation.

Douglas, Mary and Aron B. Wildavsky (1982) *Risk and Culture: An Essay on the Selection of Technical and Environmental Dangers*. Berkeley: University of California Press.

Giddens, A. (1990) *The Consequences of Modernity*. Stanford, CA: Stanford University Press.

— (1991) *Modernity and Self-Identity: Self and Society in the Late Modern Age*. Cambridge: Polity Press.

Lash, Scott (2000) *The Risk Society and Beyond*. London: Sage.

Lawson, Tony and Joan Garrod (2006) *Complete A-Z Sociology Handbook*. London: Hodder and Stoughton.

Miles, Steven (2001) *Social Theory in the Real World*. London: Sage.

Shaw, Martin (1995) 'The Development of 'Common Risk' Society: A Theoretical Overview', paper delivered at a seminar at Garmisch-Partenkirchen, Germany on 'Common Risk Society' available on http://www.sussex.ac.uk/Users/hafa3/crisksocs.htm

Tulloch, John and Deborah Lupton (2003) *Risk and Everyday Life*. London: Sage.

Wildavsky, Aron B. (1988) *Searching for Safety*. New Brunswick: Transaction Books.

An Academic Profile of Professor Yogendra Singh

Born on November 1, 1932 in Basti district of Uttar Pradesh and educated in Economics and Sociology from Lucknow University, Prof. Yogendra Singh started his academic career from the Institute of Social Sciences, Agra. His passion for teaching took him to the University of Rajasthan (Jaipur), Jai Narayan Vyas University (Jodhpur), McGill University (Montreal, Canada) and Stanford University (Stanford, USA) between 1959 and 1971. Then he was invited by Jawaharlal Nehru University to take up the responsibility of the founder chairpersonship of the Centre for the Study of Social Systems in 1971 where he continues to be associated as Professor Emeritus.

The intellectual contribution of Prof. Yogendra Singh includes sixteen books and nearly one hundred papers published in major professional journals in India and abroad. His works on modernization, sociology of culture, social stratification and social change, sociology of non-violence and peace, sociology of knowledge and ideology, and globalization have inspired three generations of social scientists in India. He has been honoured for his academic work by Swami Pranavanand Award, National Nehru Award in Social Sciences and national lecturership as well as visiting professorships in the universities of USA, France and Holland. Prof. Yogendra Singh has addressed conferences and seminars in Mexico, Moscow, Montreal, Leningrad, Beijing, Tokyo, Boston, Honolulu, Manila, Paris, Berlin, Freiburg, Barcelona and Rome.

Prof. Yogendra Singh has been one of the leaders of the sociological community of India and has served as President and Secretary of the Indian Sociological Society, President, Indian Academy of Social Sciences and Convener, National Panel on Teaching of Sociology. He has also served as an intellectual guide in a number of research institutes including National Institute of Science, Technology and Development, National Labour Institute, Institute of Economic Growth, V.V. Giri Institute of Social Sciences, National Institute of Family Welfare and Public Health and A.N. Sinha Institute of Social Sciences.

Prof. Singh has made significant contribution as a sociologist in the context of policy making of our country in the last several decades. He has served as Member of Working Group on Doordarshan (Ministry of Information and Broadcasting), Backward Classes Commission, Planning Commission and Indian Council of Social Science Research.

There is so much to write about the personality of Prof. Yogendra Singh as well as his professional achievements and positions which he had occupied not only during the course of his teaching career but even now. Since the admirable traits of his personality and contributions have also been outlined by various authors of this Festschrift, it would now be pertinent to chronologically place some of his major professional positions and awards which he has received so far.

Professional Positions

1. President, Indian Sociological Society (ISS).
2. Member, Research Advisory Committee, Planning Commission.
3. Member, Research Advisory Committee, ICSSR.
4. President, Indian Academy of Social Sciences.
5. President, Indian Leisure Studies Association.
6. Member, Planning Committee of the International Sociological Association (ISA).
7. Expert Member, Mandal Commission, Government of India.
8. Member, Working Group on Doordarshan, Ministry of Information & Broadcasting, Government of India.
9. Convenor, National Panel on Teaching of Sociology, University Grants Commission.
10. Editorial Fellow, Social Sciences: Communication, Anthropology and Sociology, Centre for Studies in Civilizations, Calcutta.
11. Chief Editor, Trend Reports in Sociology and Social Anthropology, ICSSR, New Delhi.

Membership of the Governing Boards and Councils

1. National Institute of Science, Technology and Development, Delhi.
2. National Labour Institute, New Delhi.
3. National Institute of Family Welfare & Public Health, New Delhi.
4. A.N. Sinha Institute of Social Sciences, Patna.
5. V.V. Giri Institute of Social Sciences, Lucknow.
6. Institute of Economic Growth, Delhi University, Delhi.
7. India International Institute of Social Sciences, Jaipur.

Awards

1. National Lecturer, University Grants Commission, 1974.

2. Swami Pranavanand Award, 1991 for work in Sociology & Social Anthropology, University Grants Commission.
3. National Nehru Award in Social Sciences, 1991 for contribution to Social Sciences, Government of Madhya Pradesh.
4. Title of Professor Emeritus, Jawaharlal Nehru University, 1997.
5. D. Lit. (Honoris Causa) at the 84th Convocation of Benaras Hindu University, 2003.
6. Lifetime Achievement Award of the Rajasthan Sociological Association, 2005.
7. Lifetime Achievement Award of the Indian Sociological Society, 2007.

Visiting Scholar/Professor

1. *Research Associate and Visiting Associate Professor*, Department of Sociology & Anthropology, McGill University, Montreal, Canada, 1966–67.
2. *Visiting Fullbright Scholar*, Department of Sociology, Stanford University, U.S.A., 1967–68.
3. *Visiting Professor of Sociology*, MSH, Paris, France, 1991.
4. *Visiting Professor of Sociology*, jointly sponsored by ICSSR and CASA, Amsterdam, The Netherlands, 1992.

Publications

Articles

1. 1958, 'Land Reform and Social Tensions in Villages', *Journal of Social Sciences*, Vol. I, No. 2, Institute of Social Sciences, Agra University, Agra.
2. 1959, 'Group Status of Factions in Rural Community', *Journal of Social Sciences*, Vol. II, No. 1, Institute of Social Sciences, Agra University, Agra.
3. 1959, 'Institutional Factors in Land Reform Policy', paper presented at 42nd Annual Conference of Indian Economic Association, and published in Conference Number of the *Journal of Indian Economic Association*.
4. 1959, 'Role of Sociology in Planning', paper presented at the Social Planning Seminar, organized by the Institute of Social Sciences, Agra University, Agra, and published in *Journal of Social Sciences Supplement*, Institute of Social Sciences, Agra University, Agra.
5. 1960, 'Social Change and Social Problems: A Study of Crime in Six Villages of UP', *Journal of Social Sciences*, Vol. II, No. 2, Institute of Social Sciences, Agra University, Agra.
6. 1960, 'Youth Problem and Welfare: A Sociological Approach', *The Economic Weekly*, Vol. XII, No. 45.
7. 1960, 'Development of Caste Consciousness in Indian Children from 4 to 10' (with S.D. Singh and K. Singh), *Journal of Research (Letters)*, Vol. VIII, Part 1, Agra University, Agra.

8. 1960, 'Role of Sociology in Planning', *Journal of Social Sciences Supplement,* Institute of Social Sciences, Agra University, Agra.
9. 1961, 'Changing Caste Stratification and Problem of Integration of Indian Society', *Journal of Social Sciences,* Supplement Volume.
10. 1964, 'Cultural Integration and Changing Values', *Sociological Bulletin,* Vol. XIII, No. 2.
11. 1965, 'Disciplinary Growth of Sociology and Its Teaching in India', Sociology in India, *Seminar,* Vol. 109.
12. 1965, "Traditional Culture Pattern of India and Industrial Change", in A.B. Shah and C.R.M. Rao (eds.), *Tradition and Modernity in India,* Bombay: P.C. Manaktala & Sons, Pvt. Ltd.
13. 1967, "The Scope and Method of Sociology in India", in T.K.N. Unnithan et al. (eds.), *Sociology for India,* New Delhi: Prentice Hall of India.
14. 1968, 'Caste and Class: Some Aspects of Continuity and Change', *Sociological Bulletin,* Vol. XVII, No. 2.
15. 1968, 'Academic Colonialism: Sociological Issues', *Seminar,* 112.
16. 1968, "The Class Structure and Political Processes in Village India", in M.V. Mathur and Iqbal Narain (eds.), *Panchayati Raj, Planning and Democracy,* New Delhi: Asia Publishing House.
17. 1969, "The Changing Power Structure of Village Community: A Case Study of Six Villages in Eastern U.P.", in A.R. Desai (ed.), *Rural Sociology in India* (4th revised edition), Bombay: Popular Prakashan, pp. 711–23.
18. 1970, 'Modernisation: Political Aspects', *Seminar,* April.
19. 1970, 'Indian Council of Social Science Research: Its Promise and Dilemmas', *Economic and Political Weekly,* Vol. V, No. 16.
20. 1970, 'For a Sociology of India', *Contributions to Indian Sociology,* No. 4.
21. 1970, "Chanukhera: Cultural Change in Eastern Uttar Pradesh", in K. Ishwaran (ed.), *Change and Continuity in India's Villages,* New York: Columbia University Press, pp. 241–70.
22. 1972, "Academic Role Structure and Modernisation", in Satish Saberwal (ed.), *Beyond Village,* Simla: Indian Institute of Advanced Study.
23. 1973, 'The Role of Social Sciences in India: A Sociology of Knowledge', *Sociological Bulletin,* Vol. 22, No. 1.
24. 1974, "Sociology of Social Stratification", in *A Survey of Research in Sociology and Social Anthropology,* Vol. I (ICSSR), Bombay: Popular Prakashan, pp. 311–82.
25. 1974, "Concepts and Theories of Social Change", in *Research in Sociology and Social Anthropology,* Vol. I (ICSSR), Bombay: Popular Prakashan, pp. 383–431.
26. 1975, "Process of Socialisation and Education", in I.P. Desai and M.S. Gore (eds.), *Sociology of Education in India* (reprint), New Delhi: NCERT.

27. 1977, "Ideology, Theory and Method in Indian Sociology", in Stien Rokken (ed.), *Quarter of a Century of Social Sciences, 1952–77*, New Delhi: Concept.
28. 1979, 'Constraints, Contradictions and Interdisciplinary Orientations: The Indian Context', *International Social Science Journal*, Vol. XXXI, No. 1.
29. 1984, 'Relevant Sociology (I): Conceptual Issues', *Relevant Sociology*, Vol. 1, No. 1.
30. 1984, 'Relevant Sociology (II): Conceptual Issues', *Relevant Sociology*, Vol. 1, No. 2.
31. 1985, "Sociology of Social Stratification", in *Survey of Research in Sociology and Social Anthropology*, 1969–1979, (ICSSR), New Delhi: Satvahan Publications, pp. 37–79.
32. 1986, "Some Emerging Issues in the Indian Sociology of Social Stratification", in K.L. Sharma (ed.), *Social Stratification in India*, Delhi: Manohar.
33. 1986, 'Law and Social Change in India: A Sociological Perspective', *Relevant Sociology*, Vol. III, Nos. 1–2, April-October.
34. 1988, 'Quest for Relevance: Teaching and Research in Sociology', *Indian Journal of Social Sciences*, Vol. I, No. 1.
35. 1988, 'Literature and Social Change: A Sociological Perspective', *New Horizon*, ICCR, New Delhi.
36. 1988, 'Social Process and Dimensions of Indian Nationalism' (I.P. Desai Memorial Lecture), Surat: Centre for Social Studies.
37. 1989, "Relevance of Max Weber for the Understanding of Indian Reality", in Krishna Bhardwaj and Sudipto Kaviraj (eds.), New Delhi: Sage.
38. 1990, "Country-Town Nexus: Social Transformation in Contemporary Indian Society", in K.L. Sharma and Dipankar Gupta (eds.), *Country-Town Nexus*, Jaipur: Rawat Publications.
39. 2007, "Composite Culture, Community and Identity: Interface with Social Change in India", in Bipan Chandra and Sucheta Mahajan (eds.), *Composite Culture in a Multicultural Society*, New Delhi: Pearson/Longman, pp. 195–218.
40. 2009, 'Social Praxis, Conceptual Categories and Social Change: Observations from a Village Study', *Sociological Bulletin*, Vol. 58, No. 2, pp. 178–95.
41. 2010, "Cultural Discourse in India: Identity and Development", in Yogendra Singh (ed.), *Social Sciences: Communication, Anthropology and Sociology*, Vol. XIV, Part 2, Delhi: Pearson/Longman, pp. 451–62.

Books

1. 1965. *Towards a Sociology of Culture in India* (ed. with Unnithan and Deva). New Delhi: Prentice Hall.
2. 1967. *For a Sociology of India* (ed. and contributed with Unnithan et al.). New Delhi: Prentice Hall.

3. 1969. *Towards a Sociology of Non-violence and Peace* (with Unnithan). New Delhi: Council for Social Development.
4. 1972. *Traditions of Non-Violence in the East and West* (with Unnithan). New Delhi: Heinemann.
5. 1973. *Modernization of Indian Tradition*. New Delhi: Thompson Press.
6. 1978. *Essays on Modernization*. New Delhi: Manohar Publishers.
7. 1978. *Social Stratification and Social Change*. New Delhi: Manohar Publishers.
8. 1978. *Social Aspects of Scientific and Technological Revolution* (with Ralph Dahrendorf et al.). London: Sage Publications.
9. 1984. *Image of Man: Ideology and Theory in Indian Sociology*. New Delhi: Chanakya Publishers.
10. 1986. *Indian Sociology: Social Conditioning and Emerging Concerns*. New Delhi: Vistar Publications.
11. 1991. *Sociology of Culture* (with Boris Erasov). Moscow: Progress Publishers.
12. 1993. *Social Change in India: Crisis and Resilience*. New Delhi: Har-Anand Publications.
13. 2000. *Culture Change in India: Identity and Globalization*. Jaipur and New Delhi: Rawat Publications.
14. 2004. *Ideology and Theory in Indian Sociology*. Jaipur and New Delhi: Rawat Publications.
15. 2006. *The Sociology of Culture* (with Boris Erasov). Jaipur: Rawat Publications (Indian Reprint).
16. 2010. *Ed. Social Sciences: Communication, Anthropology and Sociology: History of Science, Philosophy and Culture in Indian Civilization*. Delhi: Pearson.
17. *Ed. ICSSR Research Survey and Exploration in Sociology and Social Anthropology: 2003–2009*, New Delhi: ICSSR (forthcoming).

Reports

1966. *Jaipur City: A Study of Selected Sociological and Economic Aspects, Vol. 1, Ajmer City, Vol. 11,* and Kota *City, Vol. III,* reports of a survey directed jointly with Prof. T.K.N. Unnithan for Government of Rajasthan.

1977. *Modernisation of Syllabi in Sociology and Social Anthropology*, report based on core regional workshops organized by the UGC Panel on Sociology and Social Anthropology, UGC, New Delhi.

1978. *Traditional Socio-Cultural Systems and Economic Growth in Developing Countries in Asia and the Pacific Region: The Case of India*, prepared for the Asian Development Bank, Manila, Philippines.

Contributors

K.L. Sharma, formerly Professor and Chairperson, Centre for the Study of Social Systems, School of Social Sciences, and Rector (Pro-Vice-Chancellor), Jawaharlal Nehru University, New Delhi, and Vice-Chancellor, University of Rajasthan, Jaipur. He is presently Vice-Chancellor, Jaipur National University, Jaipur.

Devorah Kalekin-Fishman, Faculty of Education, University of Haifa, Israel, and formerly Vice-President (Publications), International Sociological Association (ISA), and Editor, International Sociology Review of Books and Associate Editor, *Sociopedia.ISA*.

Paramjit S. Judge, Professor of Sociology and Dean, Faculty of Arts and Social Sciences, Guru Nanak Dev University, Amritsar.

Volker H. Schmidt, Associate Professor, Department of Sociology, National University of Singapore, Singapore and President, Research Committee on Conceptual and Terminological Analysis (COCTA), International Sociological Association.

Lech W. Zacher, Professor of Sociology and Director, Centre for Impact Assessment, Studies and Forecasting, Leon Kozminski Academy of Entrepreneurship and Management, Warsaw, Poland. He is also Editor-in-Chief of the interdisciplinary journal "Transformations".

Anand Kumar, Professor of Sociology and Coordinator, Global Studies Programme, Centre for the Study of Social Systems, School of Social Sciences, Jawaharlal Nehru University, New Delhi. He is also a former Secretary of the Indian Sociological Society.

P.N. Pandey, Professor of Sociology and formerly Dean, Faculty of Social Sciences, Banaras Hindu University, Varanasi.

Partha Nath Mukherji, Ford Professor, S.K. Dey Chair at the Institute of Social Sciences, New Delhi. He is also a former Director, Tata Institute of Social Sciences, Mumbai and President of the Indian Sociological Society.

Jaikant Tiwary, Professor and Head, Department of Sociology (Sociology and Social Work), Banaras Hindu University, Varanasi.

Manish Tiwari, Lecturer, Department of Humanities and Social Sciences, U.N.S. Institute of Engineering & Technology, V.B.S. Purvanchal University, Jaunpur.

Ishwar Modi, Director, India International Institute of Social Sciences, Jaipur, and a Member of the Executive Committee and President of the Research Committee on Sociology of Leisure of the International Sociological Association.

Yogesh Atal, retired as Principal Director for Social and Human Sciences, UNESCO, Paris.

Chandan Kumar Sharma, Professor, Department of Sociology, Tezpur University, Assam.

B.K. Nagla, retired as Professor of Sociology, M.D. University, Rohtak.

S.M. Michael, Professor, Department of Sociology, Mumbai University, Mumbai and Director, Institute of Indian Culture, Mumbai.

Maitreyee Bardhan Roy, Principal, Basanti Devi College, Kolkata.

S.L. Sharma, formerly Professor and Head, Department of Sociology, Panjab University, Chandigarh.

Biswajit Ghosh, Professor of Sociology, University of Burdwan, Bardhaman.

B.K. Pattnaik, Professor of Sociology, Department of Humanities and Social Sciences, Indian Institute of Technology, Kanpur and Vice-President, Research Committee on Sociology of Science and Technology, International Sociological Association.

N. Rajaram, Professor of Sociology, School of Social Sciences, Central University of Gujarat, Gandhinagar.

Antony Palackal, Assistant Professor and ICSSR Senior Fellow, Loyola College of Social Sciences, Thiruvananthapuram.

Sherry Sabbarwal, Professor and Head, Department of Sociology, Panjab University, Chandigarh.

Index